ADVANCED FICTION

Bloomsbury Writer's Guides and Anthologies

Bloomsbury Writer's Guides and Anthologies offers established and aspiring creative writers an introduction to the art and craft of writing in a variety of forms, from poetry to environmental and nature writing. Each book is part craft-guide with writing prompts and exercises, and part anthology, with relevant works by major authors.

Series Editors:

Sean Prentiss, Vermont College of Fine Arts, USA
Joe Wilkins, Linfield College, USA

Titles in the Series:

Environmental and Nature Writing, Sean Prentiss and Joe Wilkins
Poetry, Amorak Huey and W. Todd Kaneko
Short-Form Creative Writing, H. K. Hummel and Stephanie Lennox
Creating Comics, Chris Gavaler and Leigh Ann Beavers
Advanced Creative Nonfiction, Sean Prentiss and Jessica Hendry Nelson
The Art and Craft of Asian Stories, Xu Xi and Robin Hemley

Forthcoming Titles:

Fantasy Fiction, Jennifer Pullen
Experimental Writing, William Cordeiro and Lawrence Lenhart
Poetry 2nd ed, Amorak Huey and W. Todd Kaneko
Environmental and Nature Writing 2nd ed, Sean Prentiss and Joe Wilkins

ADVANCED FICTION

A WRITER'S GUIDE AND ANTHOLOGY

Amy E. Weldon

BLOOMSBURY ACADEMIC
LONDON • NEW YORK • OXFORD • NEW DELHI • SYDNEY

BLOOMSBURY ACADEMIC
Bloomsbury Publishing Plc
50 Bedford Square, London, WC1B 3DP, UK
1385 Broadway, New York, NY 10018, USA
29 Earlsfort Terrace, Dublin 2, Ireland

BLOOMSBURY, BLOOMSBURY ACADEMIC and the Diana logo are trademarks of
Bloomsbury Publishing Plc

First published in Great Britain 2023

A catalogue record for this book is available from the British Library.

Library of Congress Cataloging-in-Publication Data
Names: Weldon, Amy E., author.
Title: Advanced fiction: a writer's guide and anthology / Amy E. Weldon.
Description: London; New York: Bloomsbury Academic, 2023. | Series: Bloomsbury writer's
guides and anthologies | Includes bibliographical references and index.
Identifiers: LCCN 2022055777 (print) | LCCN 2022055778 (ebook) | ISBN 9781350180109
(hardback) | ISBN 9781350180093 (paperback) | ISBN 9781350180116 (pdf) |
ISBN 9781350180123 (epub)
Subjects: LCSH: Fiction–Technique. | Fiction–Authorship. | Fiction–Collections. | LCGFT: Fiction.
Classification: LCC PN3355 .W374 2023 (print) | LCC PN3355 (ebook) |
DDC 808.3–dc23/eng/20230222
LC record available at https://lccn.loc.gov/2022055777
LC ebook record available at https://lccn.loc.gov/2022055778

ISBN: HB: 978-1-3501-8010-9
PB: 978-1-3501-8009-3
ePDF: 978-1-3501-8011-6
eBook: 978-1-3501-8012-3

Series: Bloomsbury Writer's Guides and Anthologies

Typeset by Deanta Global Publishing Services, Chennai, India
Printed and bound in Great Britain

To find out more about our authors and books visit www.bloomsbury.com and
sign up for our newsletters.

Dedication: For my students.

CONTENTS

Contents

Contents

ACKNOWLEDGMENTS

Students and former students who've helped shape this book:

Craft Studios: Shannon Baker, Levi Bird, Ian Wreisner, Andrew Tiede, Joel Murillo, and Kari Myers.

Text and feedback: Matt Benson, Kyla Billington, Kira Dobberman, Katie Fetting, Grace James, Ethan Kober, Siyabonga Mabuza, Romaney MuGoodwin, Arthur Mortell, James Nysse, Sea Orme, Gideon Perez, Canon Reece, and Carter Wittrig.

Career Studio: Andrew Chan, Derek Lin, Reed Johnson, and Annika Dome.

Keith Lesmeister for his interview and featured story in the MFA Studio.

Annika Dome, Student Production Assistant (funded by Luther College Provost's Office).

Michael Bartels, who translated my diagrams to illustrations.

Colleagues and professionals, at Luther and elsewhere: Nicole Aragi, Jennifer Acker, Tim Barringer, Richard Curtis, Adam Eaglin, Alfredo Alonso Estenoz, Rosemarie Garland-Thomson, Andy Hageman, Lise Kildegaard, Jim Lance, Lindsey Row-Heyveld, Rob Spillman, Matt Weiland, Colson Whitehead, and Novian Whitsitt. Special thanks to Vikki Barness, Jane Fosaaen, and Jeff Naatz of the Luther College Document Center.

Thanks to Joe Wilkins and Sean Prentiss, series editors; Lucy Brown and Aanchal Vij, editorial team at Bloomsbury Academic; and Sophie Beardsworth and Vishnu Prasad, production team at Bloomsbury Academic.

To all the authors whose work I've read with delight over the years—particularly those included here.

CREDITS LIST

CHAPTER 1
WHAT MAKES ADVANCED FICTION WRITING "ADVANCED?"

To say things! To know how to say things! To know how to exist through the written voice and the intellectual image! That's what life is about: The rest is just men and women, imagined loves and fictitious vanities, excuses born of poor digestion and forgetting, people squirming beneath the great abstract boulder of a meaningless blue sky, the way insects do when you lift a stone.

—Fernando Pessoa (1888–1935)[1]

What makes "advanced" fiction writing different from what you've been doing already? Over twenty-plus years of teaching and thirty-plus years of writing, I've thought a *lot* about an answer. Here's my current one:

> *As an advanced writer and reader,*
> *you have—and are always looking for more—experience*
> *with the partnership of technique and risk*
> *in order to serve your reader's experience of your fictional world.*
> *And you're committed to playing the long game:*
> *building and sustaining a writing and reading life*
> *to make art that matters*
> *to you and to your readers over time.*

Every word here is keyed to some aspect of an advanced creative writer's journey. Yet when students and I talk about "what makes advanced *advanced*," we always seem to start in the same place: *the mind*. We may be filled with the same purpose that animates Portuguese writer Fernando Pessoa, above (even if we don't share *all* his emotions), but we may also face challenges that spring from our habits, our histories, our assumptions, our fears, our motivations, and what we know or don't (yet).

Accordingly, let's accept that personal change and self-examination are part of every aspect of the writing process itself—especially the more "advanced" you get. Novelist Sonya Chung writes that "the difference between a writer and someone who 'wants to be a writer' is a high tolerance for uncertainty," because a writer's own development is so uncertain: "There are many paths to a writing life; those paths twist and turn and are haunted by the cruelties of subjectivity, along with the inevitably erratic application of our gifts." Yet, Chung concludes, "As when you learn to drive a stick shift, there is a kind of 'friction zone,' where your inner imperative to write and your tolerance for uncertainty cross each other, and the energy balance of that intersection either sets you off into motion, or you stall."[2] Moving into life at the "next level" asks you to build an appetite for *more*: a big reading habit (because there *is* no writing without reading), a desire to revise and grow, and a curious, active relationship to the writing world. Writing challenges and changes you in unpredictable—and marvelous—ways.

Therefore, I'm going to start this book with some questions to take you to the next level.

What is this really about? Why am I really doing this?

Break these two adaptable questions apart or treat them as aspects of the same one—they help you discern a story's engine, as well as your own motivation for writing, and to ask, "what releases me toward, or into, the best version of myself? Toward my most intimate, truthful contact with the images that are moving me to write right *now*?" What's in the tank that fuels your desire to write—what kind of emotions, images, energies? What activates you? *Freedom* and *pleasure* can be important compass points, as novelist Saul Bellow advised: "You should of course find the kind of writing in which your pliancy is greatest and your imagination freest." So can *challenge*—which can ultimately help you grow.

Advanced students often find themselves at a transition point between "being a good student," driven by external praise and obligation, and "becoming a writer," fueled by desire for the process itself (see Chapter 7). My teacher Barry Hannah (1942–2010) used to tell us (echoing the words of his beloved Bob Dylan), "But I'll say now, having been close or on the deathbed briefly, THAT WE'RE ALL BUSY DYING. Cut the crap, get to work. But not unless you love writing deeply, feel the angst of vacuum without it." *The angst of vacuum*: that's what I personally would feel now without writing, a creeping suspicion that a necessary source of purpose in my life is gone. For me, that's an answer to these questions and fuel in my tank. "Why am I really doing this?" Working through your answer takes you, and your writing, somewhere new.

Am I reading a range of writing—across genres, places, cultures, forms, and times—as part of becoming a mature artist and engaged literary citizen?

Reading shows you how other writers approach the same craft challenges you face, and it expands your sense of what's possible on the page. Wide reading as research is necessary to build knowledge for immersive worlds like those described in Chapter 6. And, as we'll read in Chapters 4 and 8, your reading patterns have real consequences for you and other writers too—when readers ask for a range of stories in their bookshops, libraries, and syllabi, the industry responds, the conversation widens, and everybody wins. Start with this book's selections and works listed in the notes at the back.

How/am I imagining my reader?

When your imaginary world is vivid in your own mind, it's easy to forget that your readers know *nothing about it except what you give us*, sentence by sentence, on the page. So in revision, you can reverse-engineer: What information, what details, what patterns of sentences might ease your reader's passage into your fictional world from her *own* mind? The anticolonial theorist Frantz Fanon writes, "You can explain anything to the people provided you really want them to understand."[3] Adam Mars-Jones reminds us of "the reader's experience—without which a book doesn't exist except as an object."[4] Matthew Salesses promotes "writing toward the audience whose expectations matter to you."[5] It's a fine balance that can easily tip from "considering your reader's needs" (good) to "paralyzing yourself with worry about how readers will react" (not so good). Nevertheless, advanced writers think about their readers, and how their words might land in readers' minds to create a desired experience, a *lot*.

How does my language-craft serve my readers' experience of my fictional world?

As novice writers, we may fall prey to a beloved myth: that "good writing" is always "fancy." Not necessarily. To be sure, as we'll see in Chapter 3, experimental structures and prose can be wonderful. So can sharpening lazy or habitual language to create something marvelous. Yet simple thesaurus-hunting or falling back on favorite tricks (which is flashbacks, for me!) can also be *evasion*. "Writing fiction is my work," writes Jennine Capó Crucet (anthology), "my form of artful avoidance that always inevitably leads me right back to the heart of the thing I am avoiding."[6] Look how sensory and direct the prose becomes at key moments of James Joyce's "Araby" (Craft Studio 1) and Rick Bass's "Fish Story" (anthology), because it's asking us to look closer, too. When do you need to lean in, slow down, focus? Where does your writing get vague or precise? How's this connected to your knowledge of your fictional world (Chapter 6)? Your overall voice and style (Chapter 7)? Good thing we have revision (Chapter 7) to help us get there.

How/am I inhabiting "reality as my character understands it?"

Eudora Welty's story "A Worn Path" (1941) traces the journey of a very old woman named Phoenix Jackson from her home deep in the Mississippi Delta to the town where she intends to pick up medicine for her grandson—prompting letters from readers who asked whether the child was actually alive. In her essay, "Is Phoenix Jackson's Grandson Really Dead?" (1974), Welty wrote that "The story is told through Phoenix's mind as she undertakes her errand. As an author at one with the character as I tell it, I must assume the boy is alive."[7] Over time, I've expanded this in my own mind to the concept of *inhabiting reality as your character understands it*. As we'll see in Chapters 4 and 5, becoming "at one with the character" can mean imaginatively inhabiting that character, seeing through that person's eyes, pretending to be them as an actor does—whether being there feels entirely comfortable for you and your reader, or not.

So what builds a character's reality? Here are some factors:

- Plot is shaped by the interrelated *pressures* of events (internal or external) to which a character responds, what they want, and the obstacles in their path, and by the friction generated among them, their surroundings, and other characters. Pressure is both *ongoing* (from something that's been happening since before we enter the story) and *immediate* (from something that happens within the story, as we watch).

Where the story's taking place adds to both. In "Araby" (this chapter's Craft Studio), the young narrator's adoration of Mangan's sister forms an *ongoing* layer of pressure, while the opportunity to buy her a gift at the bazaar adds an *immediate* layer—both of which move the narrator to act. The writer Paul Yoon has called these two layers of pressure "chronic and acute tension." Over multiple drafts, writers weave these two layers with one another, with the story's place and time, and with other aspects of the character's own personality or life (more on this in Chapter 6).

 — Crafting the layers of pressure will help answer another important question: *Why will my reader care about this situation?* Do we feel that urgent tug of motivation, conviction, obsession, and emotion that impels a character, and will compel us to keep turning pages? Return to the earlier question: *Why am I really doing this?* Why does it matter to *me*? Can readers feel that purpose and energy?

 — Closely connected to this are the linked questions: *What does my character want? What happens if they don't get it? What are the obstacles in their way?* Can your readers detect at least some answers to these questions?

- What's being staged *in scene* in your story—as a situation or interaction we watch play out in a physical space in front of our eyes? Charles Baxter, in *The Art of Subtext*, refers to a scene as the "staging of a desire." Do we need more *scenes* of physical bodies acting in physical places to increase the weight and pressure of a story's world and show us what characters want and are willing to do to get it? And that world matters—*place* (Chapter 6) vitally builds sensory texture and pressure.

- Is your story too indebted to a familiar narrative or trope—the romance, the action-hero, trauma and recovery,[8] violence (Chapter 6), stereotype (Chapter 4)?

- *Point of view* and *psychic distance* (Chapter 5) will dictate how you shape each sentence around your character's viewpoint. With these tools, you "play your character's role," kind of like an actor, in such a way the reader feels immersed in *the character's* subjectivity, not intruded upon by *you* as the author.

- These elements help to build *subtext*, which I think of as the kind of subtle, atmospheric knowledge a reader gains from dwelling in the character's world and seeing through her eyes. Shannon Baker's story "Habits" (in the Student Craft Studio) shows how one student built up her subtext through detail and research.

- These elements also build a sense of *authority*: you, the writer, are at home in your fictional world and setting out knowable terms on which the reader can accept the experience your story is offering. "This is how my fictional world will work, okay? Stick with me, and I won't let you down." This implicit *contract with the reader* is renewed on every page.

Student Craft Studio: Shannon Baker, "Habits"

Shannon, a precise and skillful writer, found her imagination taking flight when she did a favorite exercise: literalizing a figure of speech. "The elephant in the room" (something that's obvious to everyone but that no one wants to discuss) yielded a funny, poignant story about a fading relationship watched over by an actual elephant, invisible to everyone but Sadie, the main character. Emotional significance (and pressure) are heightened by Sadie's baking hobby; the desserts get more elaborate as she gets lonelier and her bond with the imaginary elephant gets stronger. This sensory detail heightens the subtext of the story: Sadie's desire for more nourishment and pleasure than she's getting. Overall, "Habits" beautifully shows how imagery, subtext, characterization, and emotional significance can reinforce one another. And I'm not the only one who thinks so—written in my advanced creative writing course during the Fall of 2019 and published in the undergraduate journal *Catfish Creek*, "Habits" was selected for inclusion in *Plain China: A National Anthology of the Best Undergraduate Writing*.

Excerpt from "Habits"

On the weekends, when Dex was supervising an open house or running with his cardio group in the Esplanade, Sadie would try out a new recipe from her favorite cookbook, *Sweet: Desserts from London's Ottolenghi*. Back when she and Dex had started dating, they'd baked together at least twice a week. Little by little, Sadie would teach Dex the simpler techniques: how to cream butter and sugar for cream cheese sugar cookies, or when to treat cake pans with butter and flour before pouring in the batter. She'd let him measure the flour or make the frosting while she folded egg whites into bowls to make a light, foamy meringue. Sometimes, Dex would come up behind her where she worked and dance his flour-coated fingertips over her cheekbones, and she would yelp in surprise before he spun her around and pressed his forehead to hers in laughter. He was a quick learner and always eager to help. Sadie often dreamed of mornings spent beating cream into soft peaks to make rolled pavlova with peaches and blackberries or combining halva and tahini to make Middle Eastern millionaire's shortbread—Dex and her, baking all day, just because they felt like it.

But that had been then. After those first couple of years, Sadie's pans and spatulas grew to recognize just one set of hands. For the past year or so, while Dex clocked miles in the park, Sadie had kept her baking adventures alive with the help of the elephant. The elephant would hand her the whisk or the spatula when she needed it, sometimes holding onto it a second longer than necessary, forcing her to play tug-of-war with its trunk. When the peanut butter molten bundt cake or the honey-and-orange amaretti was done, she'd let the elephant lick the spoon, watching it maneuver the too-small silverware to its mouth and fit it in, its pink tongue pushing the batter to the back of its throat with large, circular movements. The elephant even helped her with the dishes, plunging its trunk eagerly into the soap suds, splashing Sadie where she stood by the sink, towel in hand and ready to dry. She laughed and threw the towel over its eyes, watching it bob its head, its trunk curled up in the air in a sideways S.

Later, in the evening, when Dex was reading on the couch, she would sit outside the sliding glass door on the balcony with *Sweet* propped in her lap. The elephant never came outside, but it would stand at the door, its massive frame filling up the glass. It became commonplace, when Sadie went out to the balcony, for her to sit in the plastic Adirondack chair, her feet tucked under her with a mug of oolong tea steaming on the armrest. Not a minute after she was settled in, she would hear a faint tapping of ivory-on-glass as the elephant tried to press its nose to the door. It couldn't have been easy, given the curvature of its tusks. To accommodate it, Sadie would hold her book a little higher so the elephant could read over her right shoulder if it wanted. For hours, she and the elephant would fantasize about the next time they might be alone in the kitchen, baking a chocolate tart with hazelnut, rosemary and orange, or maybe an almond ricotta cheesecake coated in a decadent chocolate ganache. Eventually, Dex would knock sharply on the glass two times, give her a little wave, and motion that he was turning in for the night. Disrupted, Sadie would take one last look at the creamy raspberry swirls of the knickerbocker glory, dog-ear the page, whisper goodnight to the elephant—wherever it was—and follow her boyfriend to bed.

Shannon says: "One of the challenges I encountered in writing 'Habits' was understanding how to use Sadie's baking hobby to add to the reader's understanding of Sadie's dormancy and discontentment in her relationship and not distract from it. In early drafts, the incorporation of food was sporadic—it wasn't woven throughout the entire story. I wasn't sure how to involve food more minutely, as in the little moments, in the midst of other actions, etc. Dr. Weldon recommended that I involve myself in the act, that I put myself in Sadie's baking shoes so as to better understand those tiny details—the smell of the dishes, their tastes, the effort required to make them. I selected recipes from the same book Sadie uses, *Sweet: Desserts from London's Ottolenghi*. After struggling through a couple hours of blanching hazelnuts and melting chocolate to create a ganache, I was better able to appreciate Sadie's efforts, her emotions, her fascination with this food. I was able to see how dialogue might intermix with specific baking actions. Through my 'research,' I not only was able to more seamlessly weave in Sadie's hobby throughout the story, but I was also able to understand how it might be used to say things without saying them. To create subtext in my story, I had to submerge myself in the concrete/visible actions my character experienced."

Writing-Mind, Ethics, and Curiosity

Writers are often uncomfortable with "morals" or "preaching," and rightly so. "[O]ne thing I feel very certain about is that writers are under no obligation of any sort in their writing," says Deborah Eisenberg. "Writers aren't obliged to be compassionate or insightful or intelligent or decent human beings in their writing in any way; writers are perfectly free, in their writing, to be scum. That's one of the great powers of the medium—its unfettered latitude, its unruliness."[9] Yet in myriad ways, fiction *can* prompt experiences in readers that color their moral or ethical understanding; Eisenberg's own story "Window," for instance, has forever deepened my understanding of domestic violence. Therefore, I suggest that you can often see some moral and ethical realities operating in fiction, as in adult life:

- Actions have consequences—even delayed or invisible ones. "No man is an island," in the words of John Donne (1572–1631): a person's actions don't only affect that person. How characters respond to these facts will show you who they are *and* will make their choices and changes feel significant.

- Trouble and sorrow enter every life. Bad things happen. Clarity can be hard to find. Art is a way we examine and live with these realities. Philosopher Simone Weil writes of the *Iliad*, "what does that epic give us: a negative field against which we can find the beautiful, lovely, affirmative in life."[10] Trouble creates a "negative field" against which your characters will reveal themselves—even when, as in Jane McClure's "The Green Heart" (see Anthology), that revelation can break the reader's heart.

- Fiction's setting and characters may not be "real," but its *emotions* are. (See "The Tiger's Bride" in Chapter 6 Craft Studio.)

- Your view of the world and your capacities as a writer often grow together as they're fed by life experiences, relationships, and engagement with social reality, history, science, and art of all kinds. "Inevitably," says Eisenberg, "as one gets older and sees more and learns more, the world beyond oneself occupies a greater proportion of one's mental space."[11] Your mental aperture widens, and so does your sense of what's possible—including narrative shapes and stories beyond the expected ones. "This is why there are no great eleven-year-old novelists," writes C. J. Hribal. "[W]hat does one gain through distance? Clarity, objectivity, wideness of vision (that is, perspective), which lead to proportion (life is not all one thing or all another), which leads to inclusion and therefore generosity."[12]

- As people and writers, we make choices and judgments: what's life-giving or destructive, what's worthwhile or not. Yet even then, few situations can be quickly reduced to clear-cut either-ors, and few emotions are unmixed. What "should" happen (in a perfect world) is not always what *does* happen. Fiction is curious about how, and why, that is.

- People are always more complex than they appear. Their actions make sense, at some level, to them, or they wouldn't do those things, even if they might not be able to articulate why. So illuminating them believably as characters means showing readers the places from which their motivations arise—places the reader (and writer) may recognize, sometimes in spite of ourselves.

- As William Faulkner said, the real subject of fiction is "the human heart in conflict with itself." Therefore, successful fiction usually contains the possibility of *change* at some level, for the character and/or the reader; whether that change is accepted or refused, we need to feel its presence. Randall Kenan invoked this in a craft talk at the Sewanee Writers Conference in 2019, before his too-early death: "Redemption is a powerful force in fiction, and you can't have redemption without sin."

- Conflict is one word for what sparks change and development in a story—*friction* is another. "The standard advice in a fiction workshop is that stories are made from conflict," says writer Anne Elliott. "The word *conflict* conjures Western-style showdowns and Shakespearean sword fights. But do all stories need to involve battle? Maybe the word is wrong, but the idea is right—and what stories really need is *friction*, the coming together of opposites to generate electricity and heat."[13]

- Curiosity—toward the world and toward other people, on and off the page—is a life-giving impulse that lights up your life and your work. What if you try to understand your character as *she* is—not as *you* are—and forget what you think you know?

- Increasing the range of things you feel *and* can *admit* to yourself that you feel expands you as a person and a writer—including "I don't know."

- The practice of writing can teach postures of attention and commitment that can shape other practices in our lives, helping us discern what matters and live with purpose, thoughtfulness, and joy.

- Ambition and heart are essential. Take a risk. Take yourself and your work seriously. Give a damn. And move forward in passionate humility, eager for what you'll discover next. As the angel in Allan Gurganus's great story "It Had Wings" advises: "Don't count on the next [world.] Notice things here."

Craft Studio: James Joyce (1882–1941), "Araby" (from *Dubliners*, 1914)

Before James Joyce ascended to Modernist-Writer Olympus alongside his friend Ernest Hemingway and his contemporary Virginia Woolf, before his landmark novel *Ulysses* (1922) was banned in England and the United States on obscenity charges, before he turned the English language inside out in *Finnegans Wake* (1939), he was a Catholic boy from Dublin, Ireland, enmeshed in family and church and elders and traces of the past all around him as he yearned for a future, reaching for books and dreaming of *more*. As a rural Alabama kid, I knew that feeling, especially after Professor Judy Troy—who'd published stories in *The New Yorker!*—led a discussion of "Araby" in my first college fiction-writing class. Professor Troy asked us: "If there is a central opposition which structures this story, what might it be?" After we wrestled with it, Professor Troy offered an answer: "The sacred, and the profane." Almost thirty years later, I'm still grateful for the way those words cracked the story open for me while respecting its mystery.

But "Araby" keeps changing shape as you look closer. To be sure, it's a great template for short fiction. Start with an initial image (like Mangan's sister on her doorstep) or a richly charged place (villagey Dublin with rows of little houses and the nineteenth century still lurking in horse-harness, the back-alley stables, and the priest's yellowing books, the "blind" [dead-end] street into which the boys, unlike the girls, are "set free" when school ends). And then ask that image, in my student Ethan's words, to "tell me more." How did we get here? Who's doing the looking and the telling? What do they want, fear, hate, love, and what happens if they don't get what they want? What are their obstacles? What do they know and not know? What are the oppositions in the story, and how might these frictions arise *organically* out of *this* place and situation with *these* people?

The somber, ecstatic spirit of "Araby"—utterly serious about beauty and about (inevitable?) disappointment in our searches for it—is less easy to name. In Joyce's Dublin, beauty begins in the church, where the Virgin Mary is a serene, backlit figure, distant and adored as Mangan's sister on her stoop. The silence of the bazaar is like that which "pervades a church after a service"; the moneychangers are in the temple, counting the evening's profits and flirting (with the English, no less). Aged somewhere between eleven and thirteen (like an altar boy), the narrator bears the "chalice" of his love through a "throng of foes" that include the adults he must beg from and tolerate. His emotions are so large, so confused. But we can't mock this little knight, who insists, wordlessly, that there's more to life than the teacups and hatbrushes with which grownups have become content. His mission to Araby fails. But he does become a man who can tell us this story—a man who, we hope, will never give up his pursuit of that thing that sends him through the "high, cold, empty, gloomy rooms . . . singing."

"For myself," Joyce once wrote, "I always write about Dublin, because if I can get to the heart of Dublin I can get to the heart of all the cities of the world. In the particular is contained the universal." Look how precise and honest the writing in "Araby" is, and how the retrospective narration lets Joyce access both the feelings of the boy and the controlled, gorgeous language of the man ("her very name was like a summons to all my foolish blood"). When he finally speaks to Mangan's sister, the boy's "confused adoration" heightens each glimpse ("the white curve of her neck," the edge of a petticoat just visible as she stood at ease") just as intense real-life emotions heighten scraps of sound and image we remember. But the girl turning her bracelet on her wrist is imprisoned on that stoop and in her convent school in a way the boy is not ("it's well for you," she says—is that an emphasis on *you?*). The story knows this. The boy's blurted promise of a gift, and the man's clear memory of that moment, suggests he knows this too. And sentence by sentence, we journey into the radiant, painful event in which the boy, and we, are changed for good.

James Joyce, "Araby"

North Richmond Street, being blind, was a quiet street except at the hour when the Christian Brothers' School set the boys free. An uninhabited house of two storeys stood at the blind end, detached from its neighbours in a square ground. The other houses of the street, conscious of decent lives within them, gazed at one another with brown imperturbable faces.

The former tenant of our house, a priest, had died in the back drawing-room. Air, musty from having been long enclosed, hung in all the rooms, and the waste room behind the kitchen was littered with old useless papers. Among these I found a few paper-covered books, the pages of which were curled and damp: *The Abbot*, by Walter Scott, *The Devout Communicant*, and *The Memoirs of Vidocq*. I liked the last best because its leaves were yellow. The wild garden behind the house contained a central apple-tree and a few straggling bushes, under one of which I found the late tenant's rusty bicycle-pump. He had been a very charitable priest; in his will he had left all his money to institutions and the furniture of his house to his sister.

When the short days of winter came, dusk fell before we had well eaten our dinners. When we met in the street the houses had grown sombre. The space of sky above us was the colour of ever-changing violet and towards it the lamps of the street lifted their feeble lanterns. The cold air stung us and we played till our bodies glowed. Our shouts echoed in the silent street. The career of our play brought us through the dark muddy lanes behind the houses, where we ran the gauntlet of the rough tribes from the cottages, to the back doors of the dark dripping gardens where odours arose from the ashpits, to the dark odorous stables where a coachman smoothed and combed the horse or shook music from the buckled harness. When we returned to the street, light from the kitchen windows had filled the areas. If my uncle was seen turning the corner, we hid in the shadow until we had seen him safely housed. Or if Mangan's sister came out on the doorstep to call her brother in to his tea, we watched her from our shadow peer up and down the street. We waited to see whether she would remain or go in and, if she remained, we left our shadow and walked up to Mangan's steps resignedly. She was waiting for us, her figure defined by the light from the half-opened door. Her brother always teased her before he obeyed, and I stood by the railings looking at her. Her dress swung as she moved her body, and the soft rope of her hair tossed from side to side.

Every morning I lay on the floor in the front parlour watching her door. The blind was pulled down to within an inch of the sash so that I could not be seen. When she came out on the doorstep my heart leaped. I ran to the hall, seized my books and followed her. I kept her brown figure always in my eye and, when we came near the point at which our ways diverged, I quickened my pace and passed her. This happened morning after morning. I had never spoken to her, except for a few casual words, and yet her name was like a summons to all my foolish blood.

Her image accompanied me even in places the most hostile to romance. On Saturday evenings when my aunt went marketing I had to go to carry some of the parcels. We walked through the flaring streets, jostled by drunken men and bargaining women, amid the curses of labourers, the shrill litanies of shop-boys who stood on guard by the barrels of pigs' cheeks, the nasal chanting of street-singers, who sang a *come-all-you* about O'Donovan Rossa, or a ballad about the troubles in our native land. These noises converged in a single sensation of life for me: I imagined that I bore my chalice safely through a throng of foes. Her name sprang to my lips at moments in strange prayers and praises which I myself did not understand. My eyes were often full of tears (I could not tell why) and at times a flood from my heart seemed to pour itself out into my bosom. I thought little of the future. I did not know whether I would ever speak to her or not or, if I spoke to her, how I could tell her of my confused adoration. But my body was like a harp and her words and gestures were like fingers running upon the wires.

One evening I went into the back drawing-room in which the priest had died. It was a dark rainy evening and there was no sound in the house. Through one of the broken panes I heard the rain impinge upon the earth, the fine incessant needles of water playing in the sodden beds. Some distant lamp or lighted window gleamed below me. I was thankful that I could see so little. All my senses seemed to desire to veil themselves and, feeling that I was about to slip from them, I pressed the palms of my hands together until they trembled, murmuring: *O love! O love!* many times.

At last she spoke to me. When she addressed the first words to me I was so confused that I did not know what to answer. She asked me was I going to *Araby*. I forgot whether I answered yes or no. It would be a splendid bazaar; she said she would love to go.

—And why can't you? I asked.

While she spoke she turned a silver bracelet round and round her wrist. She could not go, she said, because there would be a retreat that week in her convent. Her brother and two other boys were fighting for their caps, and I was alone at the railings. She held one of the spikes, bowing her head towards me. The light from the lamp opposite our door caught the white curve of her neck, lit up her hair that rested there and, falling, lit up the hand upon the railing. It fell over one side of her dress and caught the white border of a petticoat, just visible as she stood at ease.

—It's well for you, she said.

— If I go, I said, I will bring you something.

What innumerable follies laid waste my waking and sleeping thoughts after that evening! I wished to annihilate the tedious intervening days. I chafed against the work of school. At night in my bedroom and by day in the classroom her image came between me and the page I strove to read. The syllables of the word Araby were called to me through the silence in which my soul luxuriated and cast an Eastern enchantment over me. I asked for leave to go to the bazaar on Saturday night. My aunt was surprised, and hoped it was not some Freemason affair. I answered few questions in class. I watched my master's face pass from amiability to sternness; he hoped I was not beginning to idle. I could not call my wandering thoughts together. I had hardly any patience with the serious work of life which, now that it stood between me and my desire, seemed to me child's play, ugly monotonous child's play.

On Saturday morning I reminded my uncle that I wished to go to the bazaar in the evening. He was fussing at the hallstand, looking for the hat-brush, and answered me curtly:

—Yes, boy, I know.

As he was in the hall I could not go into the front parlour and lie at the window. I felt the house in bad humour and walked slowly towards the school. The air was pitilessly raw and already my heart misgave me.

When I came home to dinner my uncle had not yet been home. Still it was early. I sat staring at the clock for some time and, when its ticking began to irritate me, I left the room. I mounted the staircase and gained the upper part of the house. The high, cold, empty, gloomy rooms liberated me and I went from room to room singing. From the front window I saw my companions playing below in the street. Their cries reached me weakened and indistinct and, leaning my forehead against the cool glass, I looked over at the dark house where she lived. I may have stood there for an hour, seeing nothing but the brown-clad figure cast by my imagination, touched discreetly by the lamplight at the curved neck, at the hand upon the railings and at the border below the dress.

When I came downstairs again I found Mrs Mercer sitting at the fire. She was an old, garrulous woman, a pawnbroker's widow, who collected used stamps for some pious purpose. I had to endure the gossip of the tea-table. The meal was prolonged beyond an hour and still my uncle did not come. Mrs Mercer stood up to go: she was sorry she couldn't wait any longer, but it was after eight o'clock and she did not like to be out late, as the night air was bad for her. When she had gone I began to walk up and down the room, clenching my fists. My aunt said:

—I'm afraid you may put off your bazaar for this night of Our Lord.

At nine o'clock I heard my uncle's latchkey in the hall door. I heard him talking to himself and heard the hallstand rocking when it had received the weight of his overcoat. I could interpret these signs. When he was midway through his dinner I asked him to give me the money to go to the bazaar. He had forgotten.

—The people are in bed and after their first sleep now, he said.

I did not smile. My aunt said to him energetically:

—Can't you give him the money and let him go? You've kept him late enough as it is.

My uncle said he was very sorry he had forgotten. He said he believed in the old saying: *All work and no play makes Jack a dull boy*. He asked me where I was going and, when I told him a second time, he asked me did I know *The Arab's Farewell to his Steed*. When I left the kitchen he was about to recite the opening lines of the piece to my aunt.

I held a florin tightly in my hand as I strode down Buckingham Street towards the station. The sight of the streets thronged with buyers and glaring with gas recalled to me the purpose of my journey. I took my seat in a third-class carriage of a deserted train. After an intolerable delay the train moved out of the station slowly. It crept onward among ruinous houses and over the twinkling river. At Westland Row Station a crowd of people pressed to the carriage doors; but the porters moved them back, saying that it was a special train for the bazaar. I remained alone in the bare carriage. In a few minutes the train drew up beside an improvised wooden platform. I passed out on to the road and saw by the lighted dial of a clock that it was ten minutes to ten. In front of me was a large building which displayed the magical name.

I could not find any sixpenny entrance and, fearing that the bazaar would be closed, I passed in quickly through a turnstile, handing a shilling to a weary-looking man. I found myself in a big hall girded at half its height by a gallery. Nearly all the stalls were closed and the greater part of the hall was in darkness. I recognized a silence like that which pervades a church after a service. I walked into the centre of the bazaar timidly. A few people were gathered about the stalls which were still open. Before a curtain, over which the words *Café Chantant* were written in coloured lamps, two men were counting money on a salver. I listened to the fall of the coins.

Remembering with difficulty why I had come, I went over to one of the stalls and examined porcelain vases and flowered tea-sets. At the door of the stall a young lady was talking and laughing with two young gentlemen. I remarked their English accents and listened vaguely to their conversation.

—O, I never said such a thing!

—O, but you did!

—O, but I didn't!

—Didn't she say that?

—Yes. I heard her.

—O, there's a . . . fib!

Observing me, the young lady came over and asked me did I wish to buy anything. The tone of her voice was not encouraging; she seemed to have spoken to me out of a sense of duty. I looked humbly at the great jars that stood like eastern guards at either side of the dark entrance to the stall and murmured:

—No, thank you.

The young lady changed the position of one of the vases and went back to the two young men. They began to talk of the same subject. Once or twice the young lady glanced at me over her shoulder.

I lingered before her stall, though I knew my stay was useless, to make my interest in her wares seem the more real. Then I turned away slowly and walked down the middle of the bazaar. I allowed the two pennies to fall against the sixpence in my pocket. I heard a voice call from one end of the gallery that the light was out. The upper part of the hall was now completely dark.

Gazing up into the darkness I saw myself as a creature driven and derided by vanity; and my eyes burned with anguish and anger.

Divining the Source: Why Do You Write?

In many traditional rural cultures are people called water diviners, or dowsers. Holding two ends of a forked stick lightly in their hands, they walk and pay attention and wait for the third end of the stick, pointing downward at the ground, to start quivering. That subtle motion indicates the presence of water, that wordlike thing: fluid, quick, life-giving, buried, and waiting to be raised to the surface of the visible world.

Similarly, many writers have crafted and published essays on why they write (Terry Tempest Williams, George Orwell, Joan Didion, and Barry Hannah are just a few). Like the dowser's rod, asking this question points you to hidden sources of energy that can re/activate your own writing life. We started this chapter by asking, "why am I really doing this?" Novelist Claire Messud answers:

Because naming is magic. Spells are essentially a private language; and the magic that they work is very particular. [. . .] [I]f I say "Marjorie Riches" to my sister, I am performing an act of magic: I am conjuring a person. Marjorie Riches was our maternal grandmother, and simply in saying her name I am recalling an entire life, in my childhood, in Toronto.[14]

The details—of Marjorie Riches and her house—unspool in a dreamy, fascinating flood:

I am conjuring, too, our child's delights in her house, with its laundry chute and the hatch next to the side door for the milkman, where foil-topped bottles and pounds of butter would appear before breakfast; the oxblood-colored concrete floor in the basement with a drain in the middle, around which we rode a tricycle in circles, at speed, even when we were too big really to do so and our knees were pulled up to our chins. I'm bringing back the bowl of pastel-coloured nonpareils on the side table in the living room, our lunches of tinned ravioli in wintertime, eaten on a creaky stool in the sunroom overlooking the snowy garden. I am conjuring, simultaneously, the apartment of her old age, and the high firm ship of her long-widowed marriage bed, and her glossy crimson Underwood typewriter, that she kept on a little table near the window. There is her jewel box full of sparkly clip-on earrings, and the powder-puff music box with its filigree silverwork. Here, now, we picture the particularity of her handwriting, the slight downward slope of her signature—whether she wrote "Marjorie Riches" or, on all our cards, "Grandma." And here, too, the warm, flowery smell of her neck, which lived in her scarves long after she died, and which, having taken a few of them home to my apartment (I was an adult by then) I would inhale greedily every so often just to bring her back, until one day the scent was finally gone.

And then Messud concludes:

I realized that in *making up* stories, as in reading stories, I could create a contained world in which an experience is shared in its entirety. I could invent characters, name them, evoke them, and around them a society, or a landscape, born of my experiences but as free as my imagination. Weaving together the known and the unknown, the public and the private, I could cast a spell.

Exercises:

- Why do *you* write?
- *Claire Messud Spellcasting Exercise:* Start with the sentence, "I hereby conjure [Name of a beloved person or place]." Then let the details unspool, like Messud does earlier. Try it first with a person or place who/that is gone. Go fast and get the details and feelings down. Circle a detail or two that feels particularly "alive," emotionally rich, close to the bone. And reflect: What might be a connection between the quality of language on your page and sensory texture and emotion— or energy—there? Might this be your inner wellspring, your dowsing rod, the "fuel in your tank" as a writer?

CHAPTER 2
GETTING IT DOWN
SELF-ORGANIZING, FROM MIND TO PAGE

So long as I remain alive and well I shall continue to feel strongly about prose style, to love the surface of the earth, and to take pleasure in solid objects and scraps of useless information.

—George Orwell

The room hummed with excitement as we gathered around a table of prints and engravings in the Yale Center for British Art. On the table was a small red leather notebook, about four inches high and eight inches long, that once belonged to the British painter Joseph Mallard William Turner (1775–1851). Turner filled giant canvases with light and water: he loved ships and skies and stormy seas. Yet those tremendous scenes began in this little book. Each page glowed with a miniature watercolor sky, a quick horizon line against washes of color that must have taken three minutes, or fewer, to make. *Wow*, I thought, *Turner did the same thing I do*: grab a notebook to catch that quick line, that initial gestural impulse within which the whole work of art is curled, waiting for the light of attention to lift it into bloom.

We may wonder about the purpose of notebooks and handwriting (so analog!) in our digital age. Mike Leigh's 2014 film *Mr. Turner* depicts the old painter in a photography studio, wary of this new medium that could make painting—even seeing and remembering—obsolete. Yet even alongside the ever-more-visual torrent of social media, notebooks survive. Maybe that's because notebooks offer artists and writers something screens don't: the kind of "friction" Sonya Chung and Anne Elliott mentioned back in Chapter 1. Energy and life are sparked by a human being recording an impulse that has sprung to life in some mysterious, marvelous "friction" between the eye and the world. That kind of motion and energy need a private place in which to grow. Writers nurture habits of notebooking, journaling, and image-capturing for just that reason, "taking pleasure" in the "scraps" life throws at us just as George Orwell describes in the foregoing quote.

Yet friction and privacy—which artists, and humans, need—are the very things screens are designed to reduce. To be sure, screens are tools to help a variety of embodied writers and readers see, hear, and save their words. But even as writers digest the internet in fictional form (see Chapter 3), we can't afford to lose a basic skepticism about what its corporate imperatives and addiction-based engineering ask us for, and the kind of selves we become as a result.[1]

Screens and the Artist's Self

First, let's start with devices. "It's more efficient," students say, "to take notes on my phone/tablet/laptop than on paper." Well, let's think about what *efficiency* actually means. Neuroscientists know that a little friction and challenge literally activate the brain. Yet as screen-devices take over the daily work of remembering, wayfinding, and choosing, it's getting harder to engage with life in the world and words on the page. *Efficiency* is a good goal for engineers, who must design functional, profitable, predictable machines. But art jumps up from what *isn't* predictable: what stands out, what makes us pause, what sparks delight.[2]

Artists have another reason to be skeptical of screenish "efficiency": in smoothing your private self into that engineered shape, screens also tilt it toward the public gaze, which can kill a work of art at birth. "Rather murder an infant in its cradle," says the great poet and engraver William Blake (1757–1827), "than nurse unacted desires." Yet social media (in particular) can breed a weird, stealthy habit of self-surveillance-in-advance, a low anxious hum that can "murder" any "unacted desires" before they've ever had a chance to seek the light. *What will they think?* can become *better not post it*, then *better not write it*, then—as George Orwell dismally forecast in *Nineteen Eighty-four*—*better not think it at all*.[3] It can also become *let me perform for "likes"*—a dangerous drug to get hooked on in writing world, where "likes" can be scarce (Chapter 8).

To be sure, a writer can mindfully deploy any form or tool—including a smartphone. Lauren Elkin's *No. 91/92: A Diary of a Year on the Bus* (2021) is composed of short meditations typed on her phone as she travels through Paris each day, a style of direct observation pioneered by the French surrealist Georges Perec (1936–82).[4] Yet stay with that word "mindful": for many people in 2023 and beyond, it's a notebook, not a smartphone, that will shake up perceptions enough (see Chapter 3) to be of best creative use, because the form of the smartphone *itself* comes pre-loaded with so many habits and tools that are designed to profit its makers—not us.[5]

Weirdly, your electronic tool may actually block your writing by locking you into a perfectionist mode through *its very physical nature* and *the social assumptions it fosters for its own profit*. Sounds strange, but I see this blockage in students a *lot* (especially after Covid-19 locked us all onto screens during 2020 and 2021). Tony (not his real name), a smart first-year student writing about a topic he loved, found himself frozen before the screen, with a deadline looming. The word he kept using was "overwhelmed." And the device itself became the locus of his anxiety.

"Everything is *here*," Tony said, holding up his phone. Yet the more we talked—and the more he wrote by hand on a piece of paper, with a pencil—the more open and relaxed his voice and posture became. His phone slipped through the cushions of the chair, and—caught up in writing and conversation—he let it fall. When he looked down at the papers in his lap (the small scraps I discuss later), he looked pleasantly amazed to see how many ideas he actually had. Eventually, he said that "smart kids" grow up learning that being "smart" means "being constantly on call to your phone," as if you were an organ transplant surgeon. Writing on paper seems regressive, inefficient, and, for many, literally painful, so they avoid it.

Yet how did Tony *literally* get his writing done? With a pencil, on scraps of paper, by hand. What was *literally* making him feel blocked and overwhelmed? That electronic device on which "everything is *here*," that thing at the end of our arms like a knotted muscle that we must unknot to restore our body's flow of energy and health. This goes for laptops too. What if that flat glowing screen *is the block* because of all the other assumptions that come with it and "murder" your early draft? What if you are stuck in a story of "successful = phone-addicted" that's just not true? What if you put the screen away and restore your physical relationship with your work: scribbling, making a mess, grabbing a pen? Especially in early stages?

Indeed, the early stages of a work *are* particularly delicate, for artists in many fields. Exposing your work too early to social media, for instance, can sap it of some energy it needs to grow in private. Virginia Woolf, in her journals, worried about "talking the book out," diffusing the energy of the images coming together in her mind by telling other people about them too soon. My favorite director, Federico Fellini (1920–93), felt a similar horror: "I think talking about the film before you do it weakens it, destroys it," he said. "The energy goes into the talking. Also, I have to be free to change."[6] Others (including me) feel the same. "I believe that creative people need to keep a certain area of their brain completely private," writes Fiona Pitt-Kethley, poet and travel writer. "I think of the psyche or inner daemon as something like the air in a rubber ball. Dissect too much and all the bounce might go."[7] Writer Kristen Roupenian describes this feeling: "By preserving a private space inside me, one that was safe from other people's observations and judgment, [reading] preserved the part of me that knew I existed even without other people around," she writes.

> Eventually, like a caver navigating through a single, narrow tunnel, I was able to move from that one small opening into other, larger caverns: *this is what makes me feel good, this is what makes me happy, this is what matters to me, these are my values, this is who I am.* By building a self that I knew could exist apart from other people, that was safe from them, whether they approved of me or not—and by allowing them, too, to preserve parts of themselves that I was not allowed to judge—I became capable of creating something of value that could be shared between us: a space where art, and love, could live (emphasis in original).[8]

Iowa Writers Workshop director Lan Samantha Chang advises writers, beautifully, to "hold onto that part of you that first compelled you to start writing":

> Hold onto that self through the vicissitudes of "career." A writing life and a writing career are two separate things, and it's crucial to keep the first. The single essential survival skill for anybody interested in creating art is to learn to defend this inner life from the world. Cherish yourself and wall off an interior room where you're allowed to forget your published life as a writer. Breathe deeply. Inside this walled-

off room, time is different—it is flexible, malleable. We're allowed to bend it, to speed it up, slow it down, to jump forwards and backwards, as our minds do. We can circle back to our thoughts and memories, picking and choosing the most meaningful to us. There's a hushed, glowing sound, like the sound coming from the inside of a shell.[9]

If we are always performing ourselves for social media, how much energy are we reserving for our inner lives—as artists and people? Who *are* we when nobody's looking?

One last thing: being a writer and keeping your notebook is about *noticing*, experiencing the world freely and curiously with your mortal, sensory body, yet online life desensitizes and diverts your energies and desires into addiction. (Yes, social media is literally engineered to activate the same neurological anxiety-and-pleasure centers as addiction does.[10]) Poet Kaveh Akbar asks, "Were you ever a kid who would hold your shirt out . . . and fill it with stones or shells or whatever? I feel like I'm just moving through the world with my shirt out in front of me, filling it with language and images."[11] Yet how many of us phone-focused folks have such outward-looking, roving, playful senses anymore? How many of us find our minds occupied with checking the feed, waiting for our next hit—and, therefore, unfree for our art? What are we using our screen-addictions to avoid? How might we live with greater purpose and joy in the only life on earth we'll ever have?

Evaluating how screens shape your writing can start with knowing yourself as the artist and person you have the right to be—not just a monetizable "content creator," social-media addict, or unpaid provider of algorithmic advertising fodder.[12] Around 2015, my creative writing students (including Reed Johnson, MD, in Chapter 8's Student Career Studio) had a lively in-class debate about whether then-new Instagram could serve as a notebook. They decided not—precisely because of the public nature of the medium.

Student mindfulness about the internet gives me hope, because increasingly I'm convinced that this thing can't just be fixed. Someone under thirty—maybe someone not yet born—will have to invent a whole new way of doing internet for the next generations, *and* the legal structures and personal safeguards to go with it. Because the internet can and must be better for humans, nonhumans, and the world we share than what we have. And it will start with individual changes and choices in our twenty-first-century economy, where, to paraphrase futurist Jaron Lanier, data—and attention—are the new oil.[13]

Until that brave new internet arrives, I think we writers will need to cultivate mindful, conscious internet consumption if we're committed to a certain idea of artistic process, self-determination, and privacy in our work. Of course, we can use computers or smartphones as tools, but let's "think what we are doing," in philosopher Hannah Arendt's words. Let's think about what it means to be a person, in charge of your own energy and presence in the world. Let's think about what it means, as I said in *The Writer's Eye*, to "*take yourself seriously*." This can start with designing a philosophy of artistic process and resource- and idea-storage that works for you. Everyone's may be different, as needs, bodies, and minds change over time. But for me, now, everything comes down to the desire to

save my best energy for writing,
reduce or eliminate avoidable attention drains,
support an economy that prizes a livable world for humans and nonhumans
over algorithms, addictions, and profit,
and *capture words and images before life's inevitable busyness whisks them away,*
because
I don't want to look back with regret at what I haven't done now,
and *I've learned the hard way that without mindful habits,*
I don't write work I can be proud of over time
or live life in general with purpose and joy.

My current systems have evolved into a mix of paper- and computer-based systems (and no social media) that help me fulfill these goals, because I've learned the hard way that *disorganization means missed opportunities.* I ask myself a lot, "*A year from now, what will I wish I had done now?*" Here are a few suggestions to get you thinking about how you might build your own systems. Trust your instincts—you know yourself better than anyone.

Notebooks and Journals

When I was about twelve, I saw a photograph of Anais Nin (1903–77) with a massive stack of her famous diaries, which, eventually, totaled more than 35,000 pages. Someday, I hoped, I'd have a stack like that, and then I'd be a real writer. Now, at age forty-eight plus, having published four books and gotten into volume #111+ of my journal, I've got a pile of journals too—am I a "real writer" yet? The journals' role shifts, but they do have an overall recording-the-shape-of-my-life purpose, and they usually stay at home. Notebooks, though, travel with me every day to receive notes, lists, images, or in-class exercises (written alongside students). My current journals are Pentalic softcover 8 × 10 sketchbooks, and my notebooks are flexible Moleskines; both have unlined pages. Importantly, both are places I don't have to perform—for anyone.

"Do you go back and read them?" people ask. (Not much; the value lies in *doing* them.) "How do you find what you've written?" (I can only say that having written it makes it more likely to rise to my memory when needed.) "Do you write every day?" (Depends on what's going on, although seldom less than twice a week.) Of course, I let both journals and notebooks be messy, sticking pictures, emails, fallen leaves, or flowers to the page sometimes. Once, I pressed my journal page against the surface of a disappearing glacier, wordlessly hoping for a message *writ in water*, as John Keats would say. When I find a visual image that helps me sharpen a written one—like the wonderful 1606 portrait of two-year-old Lettice Newdigate that helped me envision a real seventeenth-century English child—I print it out (preferably in color) and stick it to my notebook page. Therefore, journals and notebooks are always hands-on seedbeds that I can dive into and work with anytime, without a screen.

Interestingly, I'm finding a freedom in handwriting that gets deeper and wilder all the time. (Novelist Lauren Groff writes her first two or three drafts of her novels completely by hand, on legal pads, for this reason.[14]) Seeds of novels or stories now often ask me to be written down by hand rather than typed. Some images whisper *give me a notebook of my own—I want to be a novel.* My task is to arrange my life and brain so I can say *yes.*

Typing, Scribbling, Editing, and Cutting

Even if you're used to composing start to finish directly on an electronic document, you may find that facing a screen—laptop or even smartphone—locks you prematurely into a sense of formality that can make improvising or revising seem difficult. Therefore, try writing by hand in the homely, messy privacy of your notebook, especially if you're trying to capture a fresh idea. (Andrew Chan does this in Chapter 8's Student Career Studio.) Recopy something you've already typed. Draw something you're struggling to describe. Start writing on little scraps of paper you can rearrange on your desk or the floor—one sentence or image per scrap. Circle the most interesting thing on a page, write it at the top of a fresh page, and keep writing. Put aside your old draft completely and start writing on a fresh piece of paper, from the image that's uppermost in your brain, as the person you are right *now.* Susan Bell's *The Artful Edit* says that printing out a draft too many times before it's complete can make the piece feel more "finished" than it is; wait until you complete a full draft before printing it out and writing on it by hand. Cut your manuscript printout apart with scissors to move paragraphs or sentences around and reassemble them in a new order with tape. Physical manipulation of physical materials helps punch some air-holes in the mental stasis of staring at words on a screen. So does talking with a friend (or a voice memo). So does changing your physical location, or stepping away from the screen and getting outside.

Clotheslines, Envelopes, Files for Bits and Pieces

When working on a book project, I find it really helpful to string a "clothesline" across a corner of my room and clip scraps, images, or pages to it in any order I like. This helps preserve a kind of spontaneity that feels important early on. Bulletin boards or whiteboards are two-dimensional versions of this tool. Novelist Claire Lombardo covered a wall with masses of post-it notes she rearranged as she wrote her novel *The Most Fun We Ever Had* (2019). My students love to tape their cut-apart-and-retaped work to closet doors or hang it in long vertical strips from doorjambs, like those 1970s bead curtains. A physical file or envelope into which you can stuff those scraps helps you keep track of them, too.

Computers: My Basic System

The big challenge of life with computers is to use them, not let them use you. Here's how I manage information to reduce mental noise.

- Paper calendar/planner: For thirty plus years, this has given me a visual memory of appointments and deadlines—and offered a non-screen-based clarity about what must be done and what's happening next. (I use the At-a-Glance Weekly Appointment Book, with fifteen-minute slots and a column for each day.)

- Non-smart wristwatch: I know the time without distraction (or surveillance).

- Email: I work in a Google suite (mail, docs, appointment calendar), so I use labels in Gmail to archive email, in addition to "unsubscribe" and "delete." Inbox zero is my goal; if it's still in my inbox, I need to do something with it.

- Into an electronic folder for each project on my laptop, I drop screenshots, PDFs, or JPEGs of articles or images I find online that spark connections or build research. (Ctrl+P—"Adobe PDF" will make a PDF to save to a computer file.) This alleviates a lot of anxiety: even if there isn't a place for this cool bit of information in my current project, I have it if I ever want it again. Once my notes and notebook scrawls reach a critical mass, I type them into MS Word and start a somewhat-orderly manuscript, even if it is a single giant document with lots of disconnected bits (I call these "bucket drafts").

- Webpage and social media: While I maintain an author webpage, http:// amyeweldon.com, I quit Facebook in January 2020 and have never had a Twitter or Instagram account.[15] I have no intention of ever using social media again. Students say, accurately, that this is professionally more possible for someone of my generation than theirs (see Chapter 8). But you can still make choices about social media use.

- The digital detox: Writer Cal Newport, in his book *Digital Minimalism: Choosing a Focused Life in a Noisy World* (2019), suggests a "digital detox," which works like a food-based one: remove all electronic devices and social-media processes except those you need to function in your job or life (answering work emails, taking that call from your mom). Then you can make mindful decisions about what to add back in by asking, "What value am I really using this to add to my life?" "Is this technology really the best way to add that value?" and "If I *do* decide to keep this technology, because of a value I can define, how can I limit its presence in my life, by time and place?" For instance, you may decide that Twitter helps you keep up with a political or professional conversation (see Chapter 8 on how I use it in publishing-world). That's fine, but define times to scroll through and get up to speed. At work, set aside particular times (at the top of the hour, for instance) to check email. The point is that you are *choosing*, according to your own values, to focus your attention rather than allow it passively, or habitually, to be eroded in bits and pieces throughout the day, building that scattered-yet-overwhelmed feeling that blocks writers. Digital-detox users report a noticeable result: greater mental freedom, and literally more available time.[16] That time will let you invest in your answer to the essential question, *"A year from now, what will I wish I had done now?"*

All this organizing, of course, can't be allowed to take the place of *writing*. And you may have your own habits and methods. Nevertheless, I hope this discussion has helped you "think what you are doing" as an artist and build a system that will help you create your own words.

Exercises:

- Commit to carrying a notebook and pen to capture sparks by hand in the moment.
- Use your phone to record a voice memo and/or "thirty seconds of sound" in a place. Capture that sound in words on a page.
- Try something in your notebook you haven't tried before, including a literal mess (coffee stain, pressed flower, words crossed out). Does that shift your relationship or level of comfort with your notebook?
- Draw something in front of you instead of taking a picture of it.
- Draw something you are also trying to describe in writing.
- *Circle the most interesting thing:* Look through an old notebook or previous pages in your current one, circle the most interesting thing (without thinking too hard about what that is, or reading too carefully what's around it), then bring that most interesting thing to the top of a blank page in your current notebook and write for ten minutes without stopping. Circle the most interesting thing there, put it at the top of a new page, and keep going. (Repeat as desired—especially to push a first draft to a second draft.)
- An endlessly adaptable exercise, for academic and creative writing, is to write individual sentences, ideas, lines, images, little stick-figure sketches, whatever on small individual scraps of paper (like post-its or sheets from a memo pad), then arrange and rearrange them on a table or the floor or the wall, adding more as needed. Grab words and images and fling them down on paper to get past the mental vapor-lock of the blinking cursor.
- Try to interrupt the cycle of screen-checking: at a time when you'd normally look at your phone, do something else that does not involve your phone. Go in an opposite direction. Be less predictable. What do you notice?
- To build a passage that needs work: Cut out that passage from your typed manuscript page, then cut the passage itself apart, sentence by sentence. Tape the sentences to a blank page with spaces in between them, then fill those spaces with handwriting.

CHAPTER 3
MYSTERY, CONVICTION, FORM, AND RISK

He went to sea
in a thimble of poetry
without sail or oars
or anchor. What chance
do I have, he thought?
Hundreds of thousands
of moons have drowned out here
and there are no gravestones.

—"Poet Warning" by Jim Harrison

This poem invokes perfectly, I think, how writing can prompt a particular mix of excitement and fear: *I want to do this thing. I love it. I just do. But—where do I even start? What if I get it wrong? What if they read it and they laugh at me? Who am I to write about this?*

"Well, here's some good and some bad news," fiction writer Jim Shepard responds.

Where do you get off writing about anything? Where do you get off writing about someone of a different gender? Of a different race? Where do you get off writing about something that never happened to you? Writers shouldn't lose sight of the essential chutzpah involved in trying to imagine another sensibility, and they should take heart in that chutzpah. The whole project of literature is about the exercise of the empathetic imagination. Why were we given something as amazing as imagination if we're not going to use it?[1]

Poet Frank Bidart adds, "I don't think one really gets permission to do things. You do them because you have to do them, and nothing else will do."[2]

We'll talk in Chapter 4 about ways to avoid causing hurt. But for now, let's stay in the larger mental and emotional space of *artistic risk* and of the rewards that can come from it. Because as scary as it is to take a risk, without it you get nowhere—on the page or in life. Writing can create what Claire Messud (Chapter 1) calls *magic*—a spell, an alchemy, a voyage into blank space to make something that didn't exist before. "I see fiction not as the construction of an alternate world," the critic Hilton Als has said, "but as what your imagination gives you from the real world."[3] What your imagination gives you asks, in turn, to be given space on the page. "[Writing] is such a mysterious thing," Als continues, "but we don't get a lot of credit for bringing mystery to the table, or trying to understand

and explicate something in front of other people." Luckily, writers can reflect among ourselves about the mysteries and risks of what we do.

The Terrain of Risk, Part One: The Page

"Thrill Me": Doing a New Thing

Consider this: every time you put words on the page, you're making something—a new thing in the world—that wasn't here before. Isn't that thrilling? Perhaps this is why my own former teacher, Barry Hannah, used to instruct us students, "Thrill me!"[4] Literary form, language, and an experience or image you want to write about can shape one another in unpredictable—even thrilling—ways. Namwali Serpell, author of *The Old Drift* (2019) and "Account" (anthology), has said, "Constraint is the mother of originality, so the delight I take in writing often comes from figuring out which form resonates with the experiences that intrigue me at any one time. These are often quite distinct."[5] As you grow and get more experienced, you may also find that your initial impulse may suggest its own form earlier, in the process.

Weird Shapes and Monsters[6]

What if your story literally *looks* weird—in a good way? How might the constraints of a form shape what you write? (Constraints can be a great prompt to creativity, as theatrical improv artists know: "say *yes, and* to what your partner says.") Looking at short forms in particular, you see that what a story may lack in length it has to make up for in some other kind of energy and dynamism: it has to "sparkle harder"—in language, leaps, voice, whatever—to make a big impact in its small space. Here are some interesting forms:

Square stories: Danish writer Louis Jensen (1943–2021) invented "square stories"—literally square-shaped, super-short tales, the size of the palm of your hand—and he completed 1,001 of them before his death. A delightful man with bright blue eyes and silver hair in a Tintin quiff, he radiated a thoughtful curiosity about the world, which I was lucky to witness when his English translator, my colleague Lise Kildegaard, brought him and his square stories to Luther College. Like the work of his fellow Dane Hans Christian Andersen, "square-story world," says Kildegaard, "has its own highly particular rules," in which alphabet letters can talk, baked goods march themselves off to be eaten, and lemons have a secret they never dare speak aloud. Each begins with the Danish equivalent of "once upon a time" that also marks the story's place in its sequence: "a nine hundred and forty-first time," for instance.[7] Marketed to children, they're beloved by readers of all ages. (See p. 225).

Graphic flash fiction: Sofia Samatar (b. 1971), an American writer of Somali and Swiss-German descent, writes rich, distinctive work that crosses the borders of countries and genres, into and out of the realms of fairy tale and fantasy. Her collection *Monster Portraits* (2017) contains short prose sketches that travel among fiction, memoir, and scholarship, each illustrated with a drawing by her brother, graphic novelist Del Samatar. Samatar inspires students and me to connect fairy tales, graphic novels, and ekphrasis (writing about art) in new ways, just like *Monster Portraits* does. (See p. 229). Graphics and storytelling are obvious kin—just ask graphic memoirists like Marjane Satrapi (*Persepolis,* 2000), Alison Bechdel (*Fun Home,* 2006), and Thi Bui (*The Best We Could Do,* 2017), to name a few. (So are graphics and politics—try Timothy Snyder's *On Tyranny,* reissued in 2021 with illustrations by Nora Krug.) What if you couple your story with— or tell your story as—an illustration?

Twenty-minute stories: American writer Aimee Bender (b. 1969) is known for her bittersweet, surreal fiction that beautifully exemplifies a principle we'll talk more about in Chapter 6: even the most fantastical fictional concept is lit by human emotion. "The Woman Was Born With Snakes for Hair" (p. 230) appeared in Issue 12 (2003) of the literary journal *McSweeney's,* for which editor Dave Eggers asked writers to craft a story in twenty minutes. The time and place of the story's completion were listed at the bottom. I still can't believe Bender wrote this gorgeous little story in twenty minutes— but I love it. And I am thrilled to be the first person to publish it in book form, right here, with gratitude. Generate a strong first line or image (maybe with a mythic twist, as in Chapter 6), then write for twenty minutes: what happens?

Ghost stories: In each of his novels and stories, American writer Kevin Brockmeier (b. 1972) creates a delicate, melancholy fictional world with a philosophical spine. His collection *The Ghost Variations* (2021) includes one hundred stories loosely definable as "ghost stories." Each one is two pages long, and each offers an original twist on the idea of a "ghost story" (like "The Sandbox Initiative," p. 233) while still being true to some idea of a ghost, a haunting, an afterlife, a lingering presence. Put a ghost in your story, or write a ghost story, loosely defined: What do you discover? Especially if you limit yourself to two pages?

Object as story: Harvard professor Namwali Serpell (b. 1980 in Zambia) is author of the novel *The Old Drift* (2019), mentioned earlier, a 563-page epic she calls "the Great Zambian Novel you didn't know you were waiting for." With wit and poignancy, "Account" (2016, p. 234) recasts the story of Artemisia Gentilschi (1593–1653) as a twenty-first-century bank statement. "I was recovering from surgery when I wrote this story," says Serpell.

> I spent an inordinate amount of time in bed working on the design layout. I wanted it to look exactly like a real bank statement. I was pleased to learn that I succeeded with at least one reader. When I emailed it to my agent, he thought I had been on such strong pain medication that I had deliriously sent him my own bank statement by mistake![8]

Novelist Jennifer Egan crafted another dark revenge tale in the form of a to-do list, written in twenty minutes as part of the same McSweeney's challenge that Aimee Bender undertook. The famous advertising campaign for Burma-Shave shaving cream (1927– 63)[9] featured a sequence of four to six signs staked on the right side of a highway, to be read in sequence as you drive past, for example "Angels / Who Guard You / When You Drive / Usually / Retire At Sixty-Five / Burma-Shave." (They *did* have a Flannery-O'Connor-ish morbid streak—but I think that's part of their charm.)[10] What object—menu, prescription, label, memo, billboard—can you use to tell a story, deploying that object's own form?

Single-sentence or single-paragraph story: Irish writer Nuala O'Connor (b. 1970), who's also written as Nuala Ni Chonchuir, works in a variety of forms, including novels, poetry, and marvelous short fiction like "Menagerie" (from *Birdie*, her collection of historical flash fiction). Consisting of a single long sentence and two shorter ones—and totaling one paragraph in length—"Menagerie" (p. 241) traces a not-quite-realistic, not-quite-explained path with a dreamy yet urgent atmosphere that keeps me reading and rereading.

What the . . .?!: Defamiliarization and Speculative Forms

Cynan Jones, "Sound" from Stillicide (2019) (p. 236)

If the subject of your story is strange—and I use that term with appreciative generosity—then how might the form of your story help readers experience that strangeness? Writer Jeff VanderMeer has christened such forms "The New Weird," because they use a blend of science fiction, dystopia, and fantasy to represent a reality that's getting weirder every day—especially regarding climate and the internet. Samuel Beckett anticipated this in a 1961 interview: "To find a form that accommodates the mess" of the life around us, he said, "that is the task of the artist now."[11] But mixed in the mess is also beauty, as Megan Mayhew Bergman writes: "Even damaged," she says, "even fraying at the seams, the world remains stunning and full of stubborn wonder."[12]

Defamiliarization is, basically, the experience of being unsettled by art: pausing, readjusting your assumptions, and re-thinking the world *and* the art in front of you. According to the Russian aesthetic philosopher Victor Shklovsky (1893–1984), defamiliarization is the point of any artistic experience. Since our brains so easily become habituated to familiar things, the artist must "defamiliarize" language and form to help us encounter them afresh. "Habitualization devours works, clothes, furniture, one's wife, and the fear of war," Shklovsky memorably declared in his essay "Art as Technique" (1917).

> Art exists that one may recover the sensation of life; it exists to make one feel things, to make the stone *stony*. The purpose of art is to impart the sensation of things as they are perceived and not as they are known. The technique of art is to make objects 'unfamiliar,' to make forms difficult, to increase the difficulty and length of perception because the process of perception is an aesthetic end in itself and must be prolonged.[13]

Speculative fiction (including science fiction, climate fiction, fantasy, dystopias, and more) accepts Shklovsky's challenge by immersing readers in a carefully created alternate world, steadily teasing and testing our concepts of the "familiar" by asking us to compare our own realities with the page. In the process, it asks us to question the way we form ideas about "reality" itself. Therefore, it offers readers a fresh perspective on technology, politics and economics, gender and bodies, climate change, urban infrastructure, and racial injustice, to name only a few concerns of writers from N. K. Jemisin, Samuel Delaney, and Kim Stanley Robinson to Ray Bradbury, Hao Jingfang, and Octavia Butler, Margaret Atwood, George Orwell, and the godmother of them all: Mary Shelley's *Frankenstein* (1818). When reality clashes with our assumptions, art can help us reframe and understand both.

As the internet reshapes perceptions and reality, it's reshaping fiction too, as seen in books like Gary Shteyngart's *Super Sad True Love Story* (2010), John Lanchester's *Reality and Other Stories* (2020), Lauren Oyler's *Fake Accounts* (2020), Dave Eggers' *The Circle* (2013) and *The Every* (2021), Benjamin Percy's *The Dark Net* (2017), and Jennifer Egan's *The Candy House* (2022). (Mark McGurl's 2021 *Everything and Less: The Novel in the Age of Amazon* suggests that the commercial, everything-on-demand nature of the Amazon .com juggernaut has not just reshaped the way writers sell their novels but the form of the novel itself.[14]) Namwali Serpell's story "The Work of Art" (see Chapter 3 Exercises) includes text messages within a standard narrative form, including subtle references to recent Twitter-heavy art-world controversies. Patricia Lockwood's novel *No One Is Talking About This* (2021) tries to replicate in sentence form how it feels to be on Twitter. "What about the stream-of-a-consciousness that is not entirely your own?" she asks. "One that you participate in, but that also acts upon you?"[15] Veering across psychic distances, self-interrupting, yet (for me at least) brilliantly, horribly recognizable, Lockwood's narrative mimics the leaps and swerves of the internet itself:

> Every day their attention must turn, like the shine on a school of fish, all at once, toward a new person to hate. Sometimes the subject was a war criminal, but other times it was someone who made a heinous substitution in guacamole. It was not so much the hatred she was interested in as the swift attenuation, as if their collective blood had made a decision. As if they were a species that released puffs of poison, or black ink in a cloud on the ocean floor. I mean, have you read that article about octopus intelligence? Have you read how octopuses are marching out of the sea and onto dry land, in slick and obedient armies?

Especially considering climate, what can match the shapes of our new weird world? In *The Great Derangement: Climate Change and the Unthinkable* (2017), novelist Amitav Ghosh argues that to represent the kind of ruptures, strangeness, and previously unseen events that climate change presents worldwide each day, writers must reinvent the form of the novel: although fiction will still need to proceed with narrative logic, it may not be exactly the kind of logic we've previously known. And "logic" can be usefully disrupted by artistic form: "As a species with relatively short lives and even shorter attention spans, humans struggle to grasp the long-term scope of an evolving emergency they will not live to experience in full," writes Zoe Lescaze about visual art in *The New York Times*:

The most effective protest art, then, does not confront us with evidence we've already proven perfectly willing to ignore. Instead, it broadens the narrow ways in which we tend to conceive of time and our position within larger ecologies, without necessarily mentioning climate change by name. The resulting works are not demands for immediate action but ones that expand our psychological capacity to act.[16]

For writers, this is a thought-provoking way to understand and build literary forms that "expand our psychological capacit[ies]" in multiple ways. Jenny Offil's novel *Weather* (2020) proceeds in fragmentary short chapters, echoing its protagonist's struggle to get her mind around climate change. The environmentalist and writer Paul Kingsnorth (b. 1972), who currently lives off the grid with his family in the West of Ireland, scripts his novel *The Wake* (2014) in a partly invented version of Old English to illustrate how struggles with land and dispossession recur throughout time. (Russell Hoban's *Riddley Walker* [1980], Anthony Burgess's *A Clockwork Orange* [1962], Ishmael Reed's *Mumbo Jumbo* [1972], and Percival Everett's *Erasure* [2001] also mash up invented languages and multiple styles to invoke out-of-kilter worlds.[17]) Three great stories about floods—Karen Russell's "The Gondoliers," Kevin Barry's "Fjord of Killary,"[18] and Genesis 6–9—deploy particular kinds of exaggeration in sometimes hilarious, sometimes harrowing ways to summon the too-much-ness and terror of rising water. As I've said in *The Writer's Eye*, representing reality may also rewire some of our previous notions of aesthetics, requiring a confrontation with what is deliberately "unpretty" or "awkward." (Levi Bird's story "On Stable Ground" in the Student Craft Studio does the same.) And in taking those risks, a successful story can teach us how to read it, initiating us into its own logic as we go.

Welsh author Cynan Jones's *Stillicide* (2019, p. 236), which is marketed by its US publisher as a novel and its UK publisher as a collection of linked short stories (see Chapter 8), examines climate change and water shortage. "Sound" begins in a place we think we know: "The calf gave a confused hiss, and lowing, then dipped slightly as if it would bury into the water." With "harpoon" in the second sentence, readers begin, dismally, to shoulder the burden of whaling's ecological grief. Maybe we think of Herman Melville. Yet—wait a second—this is the twenty-first century ("Hypalon-coated polyester"). And a lot depends on the double meaning of the word "calf" (*sound* has triple meanings). By the end of the story, our initial assumptions have been inverted: these men *are* hunters, but for an object that has a dire new use in a parched world. Jones prolongs our encounter with a dystopian (yet recognizable) future by extending the time it takes for us to realize what's actually happening, then blending familiar mechanical terms ("davits," "outboards") with a lingering sadness. Defamiliarized, we finish "Sound" with fresh unease: Is this our future? Maybe.

The Terrain of Risk, Part Two: The Political World

In his essay "The Creative Process" (1962), James Baldwin writes that the artist accepts the daily risk and challenge of telling himself and the people around him the truth as he also strives to conquer "the great wilderness of himself": "The precise role of the artist, then," Baldwin writes, "is to illuminate that darkness, blaze roads through that vast forest, so that we will not, in all our doing, lose sight of its purpose, which is, after all, to make the world a more human dwelling place."[19]

But, indisputably, the world is full of risks for writers who undertake this task. As I write the final draft of this book in spring 2022, the world is reeling from Russian president Vladimir Putin's brutal invasion of Ukraine; under a law signed on March 4, writes *The New York Times*, Russian journalists who call the war a war rather than a "special military operation"—Putin's preferred term—or accurately describe Russian bombing of Ukrainian cities and civilian deaths may face up to fifteen years in jail.[20] And Russian journalists are not alone in being threatened by the people they would expose. Ahmet Altan (b. 1950) is a Turkish journalist, novelist, and essayist who was imprisoned by his government for five years, an experience he describes in his memoir *I Will Never See the World Again* (2019).[21] Roberto Saviano (b. 1979) is an Italian novelist and anti-Mafia journalist who travels with police protection against death threats. Novelist and filmmaker Tsitsi Dangarembga (b. 1959), the first Black Zimbabwean woman to publish a novel in English, has been arrested for peaceful anti-government-corruption protests. Famously, Sir Salman Rushdie (b. 1947) is technically still living under a *fatwa* after the publication of his novel *The Satanic Verses* (1988).[22] Elif Shafak (b. 1971) has lived in exile from her native Turkey since 2013 after drawing the government's ire for "immorality" in her many books. Xu Zhiyong (b. 1973), according to the international free-speech and writers' advocacy organization PEN America, "was detained in February 2020 after writing an essay that critiqued the leadership of China's president Xi Jinping, including his handling of the Covid-19 outbreak, and called on Xi to resign." The fictional journalist in Chimamanda Ngozi Adichie's "The American Embassy" (see Chapter 5 Craft Studio) brings government wrath on himself and his family. To international outrage, Saudi Arabian journalist Jamal Khashoggi (1958–2018) was brutally assassinated at what the CIA has now concluded was the direction of Saudi Crown Prince Mohammed bin Sulman.[23] The fall of Kabul, Afghanistan, to the Taliban on August 16, 2021, left observers worldwide in doubt about the fate of journalists, feminists, anti-Taliban dissidents, and so many others.

What do all these writers—and many more, known and unknown, worldwide—have in common? For them, the risks of artistic, journalistic, and political expression are not just imaginative but literal. Alas, America's not immune: the FBI kept extensive dossiers on a number of civil rights activists, artists, and writers, including James Baldwin. Finally published in 2017, Baldwin's dossier was 1,884 pages long, covering the years from 1958 to 1974—"the longest yet extracted on an African American author active during [J. Edgar] Hoover's five decades as a Bureau executive," writes its editor, William J. Maxwell. Homophobic and racist paranoia pervades the file: "Isn't Baldwin a well known pervert?" scribbled Hoover on a July 17, 1964, memo, despite what Maxwell calls Hoover's own "participation in the worst-hidden gay marriage in official Washington."[24]

As George Orwell demonstrated in his classic novel *Nineteen Eighty-four* (1949; see Chapter 5), state harassment or surveillance can create an atmosphere of intimidation and stress that can kill ideas, thoughts, and freedoms, even when it does not literally kill people. The notorious "red scare" of the 1950s, fueled by an "anti-Communism" that bled into an all-purpose anti-intellectual mania, saw Hollywood screenwriters—just to name one group—blacklisted and banned from working under their own names, or at all. And throughout the history of the United States and other countries, those viewed by the government as "suspicious" or "marginal" (artists, activists, minorities, and all three) have been monitored, surveilled, and harassed. Who's defined as "dangerous," by whom, is always shifting in response to pressures that, to say the least, bear scrutiny.

In the twenty-first century, the internet makes this landscape, and the questions of *surveillance* and *censorship*, even rockier. Even as activists and artists circumvent firewalls and dodge government surveillance,[25] online harassment, hate, and abuse are at all-time high levels. Indisputably, social media galvanizes bad actors, from junior-high bullies to Capitol insurrectionists. Disinformation—the deliberate creation and dissemination of false images and words—is used to manipulate people. As ever, technology outpaces law and ethics, which labor to define and prosecute hate speech, harassment, and the creation of hostile environments online.

A full discussion of all these factors is beyond the scope of this book. Yet I raise them here—in deliberately vague terms, to accommodate their inevitable proliferation and mutation over time—because writers must always be mindful of them. You're a writer in the globalized, climate-threatened, digitally connected twenty-first century, which means you have great opportunities to effect positive change and balance rights and responsibilities, even as the internet will shape your life in ways we can't predict. Read widely (including George Orwell's *Nineteen Eighty-four* and Timothy Snyder's *On Tyranny*), keep up with PEN America and *The New York Times*, stay curious and stay informed, develop your own perspectives about the world beyond your page, and use your freedoms for good. Resist standard narratives, cliché, easy answers, and what Chimamanda Ngozi Adichie (Chapter 5) has called "the danger of a single story." There—that should accommodate the internet and politics for the next few years, at least. (I'd settle for fifteen minutes.)

For some inspiration, ponder Nathan Englander's story "The Twenty-seventh Man" from his collection *For the Relief of Unbearable Urges* (1999), which reimagines the real-life "Night of the Murdered Poets" under Stalin. Its complex artistry pairs beauty and political tragedy as facets of the human story that includes all of us, right now.

The Terrain of Risk, Part Three: Your Own World

How can we deal with the fact that our work, even though it's fiction, is nevertheless rooted in our real lives and emotions, at least a little? What if our friends recognize themselves? What if people identify our characters too easily with *us*? What if our writing makes us feel vulnerable? How can we stabilize ourselves and keep going?

First, let's admit that vulnerability exists, and writing is going to expose it, even if no one else reads our work, and even if our characters are not "really us." Irish writer Kevin Barry, when asked "what's most difficult to write about," replied, "Sentimentality, nostalgia, love . . . it's always the stuff that's close-in to your own personality, and I'm a man quick to tears at the best of times."[26] Sometimes, the riskier thing is the more interesting one, for you and your readers. Even though writing about something may rouse difficult emotions and fears of all kinds, you may also feel drawn to invoking them on the page: as critic Hilton Als has said, "I think writing takes you where you need to go."[27]

Risk and difficulty and shifting attitudes to your work are part of your life as a writer too, and even successful writers seldom feel free of them. My own way to address that anxiety has grown, over time, into something like this: (1) admit I feel that anxiety, (2) recognize that it's not going to kill me, even if it doesn't feel great, (3) take a break from the work if I need to, and (4) get back to work, even if it feels shitty, because, really, what are my other options? This also gets easier as I get older. (Kind of.)

Writers know how much our own lives and feelings seep into their fiction, even if we're not consciously deciding what from "real life" to "base a story on" or writing an experimental blend of fiction and nonfiction like Elizabeth Hardwick's novel *Sleepless Nights* (1979). "Here is what it is," writes Patricia Lockwood, "no force on earth will keep a writer's preoccupations out of their fiction. You are not necessarily looking for them, but you find them every time."[28]

Alongside this truth, in his book *Turning Life into Fiction*, Robin Hemley points out that "sources" for fiction are not always so directly traceable to reality as readers (or writers) might think. Our priority as writers should be adapting reality to the *story* in order to make the story work on the terms it's setting out for itself, not being true to "what really happened." That said, Hemley writes, "It's nearly impossible to stop our real lives from intruding into our fiction, even when the story is clearly not about ourselves." He notes that "We can even see real life bleeding into the fictional world of a writer as absurdist as Samuel Beckett":

> In a letter to a friend, he wrote of watching old men in the park flying kites "immense distances" and "right out of sight," and how transfixed he was by the sight. "My next old man or old young man [meaning his next character in a fictional work] must be a kite flier," he wrote. At the time, Beckett was working on his novel *Murphy*, and true to his word, he included the following scene in which an old man is lying in bed, imagining himself flying a kite. Note the similarities between the wording in the letter and that of the scene:
>
> "Before you go," said Mr. Kelly, "you might hand me the tail of my kite. Some tassels have come adrift."
>
> Celia went to the cupboard where he kept his kite, took out the tail and loose tassels and brought them over to the bed.
>
> "As you say," said Mr. Kelly, "hark to the wind. I shall fly her out of sight tomorrow."
>
> He fumbled vaguely at the coils of the tail. Already he was in position, straining his eyes for the speck that was he, digging in his heels against the immense pull skyward. Celia kissed him and left him.
>
> "God willing," said Mr. Kelly, "right out of sight."[29]

As Hemley aptly notes, this is a "marvelous scene." You can see here, too, the power of the image, as in Chapter 2—observed in the world and brought to the page, transformed, as imagination can always do.

When you bring a real event into your story, consider not only whether you might want to disguise it (see later) but whether you can make of it an artistically satisfying shape. "But it really happened" might not always be an effective defense against doubtful classmates reading your story—even though it might sometimes represent a reality that those classmates might not see as you do.[30] A good question to ask about "reality" in fiction, therefore, might be Vivian Gornick's point about memoir from *The Situation and the Story:* "What happened to the writer is not what matters; what matters is the large sense the writer is able to *make* of what happened."[31]

The Nobel-prize-winning Polish poet Wisława Szymborska (1923–2012) wrote an anonymous advice column for a literary journal for twenty years; recently collected in *How To Start Writing (And When to Stop),* her responses are both funny and wise. To "M.S. from Koszalin," she writes:

> "I've been criticized for making my stories up and not taking them from experience. Is this correct?" No, it is not. Such doctrinaire assumptions would exclude three quarters of world literature. No writer draws on his life alone. He borrows others' experience when it suits him, and fuses it with his own—or uses his imagination. But a true artist imagines events with all the force of reality: they become personal experience. Flaubert declared he was Emma Bovary for precisely this reason. If naysayers had persuaded him that imagination was off-limits, he'd have dropped the novel in hopes that some real Madame Bovary would come along to finish it.[32]

But what if a friend or family member reads your work, recognizes themselves, and gets upset?[33] This is a common concern among students, and here are some responses:

- *Many people don't read as closely or as much as writers do, so they won't associate themselves with the character, if they even read your work at all.* Sounds harsh, but it's often true. A disguise—like a change of hair color, gender, or place—can help.

- *Even if people do recognize themselves, they might not react the way you fear, especially if you write with fairness and nuance.* Memoirist and novelist Patricia Foster, a fellow Alabamian, once told me that when people object to written depictions of themselves, it's usually because that character is one-dimensional; people want to see themselves represented as fully human, even if the character has negative as well as positive dimensions.

- *See that disclaimer in the front of a novel?* Pick up just about any work of fiction and you'll find, early in the front matter, something like this: "This is a work of fiction. Names, characters, places, and incidents either are the products of the author's imagination or are used fictitiously. Any resemblance to actual persons, living or dead, events, or locales is entirely coincidental." That's designed as legal protection for the publisher and the writer.

- *You* do *have the right to write, especially since "writing" does not* inevitably *mean "going public" or "telling the whole story for everyone."* No one will know about your writing if you don't show it to them. Pseudonyms are possible. But publishing or sharing with readers doesn't *inevitably* follow writing, for all kinds of reasons. If other people want to write their own stories, they're welcome to do so. The only story you can (or perhaps should) take responsibility for is the one *you* want to tell at this time.

Of course, none of this is simple. Critic Greg Tate has written, "To read the tribe astutely you sometimes have to leave the tribe ambitiously, and should you come home again, it's not always to sing hosannas or a song the tribe necessarily has any desire to hear."[34] Irish journalist and memoirist Nuala O'Faolain has written,

> [M]any families do have one person who breaks a silence, or speaks out in some way, or in some way describes and defines a family which up to then had no agreed-upon identity. But a family hangs together by remaining undescribed, so that each member can see it and themselves in relation to it in whatever way suits them best. The member who disturbs this comfort is asking for trouble.[35]

Yet what kinds of "comfort" are worth protecting? What stories are worth the risk to tell? And why is it worth it to you to press ahead and tell your story, as you *do* have the right to do?

Only you can answer these questions. Carry with you the words of Zora Neale Hurston from her 1942 autobiography *Dust Tracks on a Road*:

> If writers were too wise, perhaps no books would be written at all. It might be better to ask yourself "Why?" afterwards than before. Anyway, the force from somewhere in Space which commands you to write in the first place, gives you no choice. You take up the pen when you are told, and write what is commanded. There is no agony like bearing an untold story inside you.

Student Craft Studio: Levi Bird, "On Stable Ground"

"On Stable Ground" is narrated by a young, mysteriously ill narrator, Tracy, a former track standout whose wit, candor, and love for a sweet boy named Brody completely engaged Levi's classmates. When they reached the story's last lines—retrospectively reframing our entire understanding of the story—they gasped. Yet this wasn't only sympathy for Tracy: it was empathy, a well-earned anger at what Tracy has undergone, and artistic respect. For Levi, a self-described gay first-generation college student from rural Wisconsin, the experience of writing "On Stable Ground" was risky—would his classmates identify him too closely with Tracy and Tracy's traumatic experience? Had he gone "too far?" What would his parents think? But as class ended, students approached Levi to say not only *good work* but *thank you*; his artistry defamiliarized our perceptions and lingered with all of us.

The Last Third of "On Stable Ground"

By the time that spring came, I was finally able to walk around the house normally. No shaking. No tripping. All of the snow had melted since it was a warm and early spring. Outside, yellow-green sprouts popped against the brown grass left from the winter, the leaves were beginning to grow on trees, geese honked outside as they flew up toward the lakes—everything was finally beginning to come alive and be free. Except for me. I was still stuck in the house.

Toward the end of March, I decided to try to convince Mom and Dad to let me finally go outside for a walk. After all the physical therapy appointments and visits to the psychologist, I just wanted to go outside by myself. We were all sitting in the living room on the long couch, my parents on one end and myself on the other. Dad was engrossed in watching the March Madness finals. His bracket had been broken during the first week of it, but he still seemed determined about seeing who the winner was. This was the first time he was actually able to convince me to sit down and watch a game with him. He lounged with his arm around Mom's shoulders, leaning back into the burgundy upholstery.

The reds and greens of the players' uniforms on the screen scrambled like Christmas tree tinsel every time Dad yelled. My focus wasn't really on the TV, though; I was looking out the living room window. Outside, the Saturday's afternoon sunbeams danced against the fresh green. The light cast shadows of leaves on the carpet, beckoning me to come outside, if only for a little while. Halftime was too long of a wait. When the next timeout finally came around, I took my chance.

"Hey, can I go for a walk outside?" I wrung my fingers a little in my lap.

"I don't know if that's a good idea." Mom furrowed her eyes at me with a hard, but gentle look.

"It'd just be down the block." I sat up and stuck my hands by my sides. "Not too far. I promise."

"Brad, what do you think?" She turned her head toward Dad.

"I think it'd be good to let Tracy go outside for a walk." He looked over at me. "It ain't good for a kid to be locked up in a house for so long."

Mom's eyes misted a little when she turned back toward me and saw my face. Silence hung in the air for a few moments and my eyes darted down at the floor.

"All right," she gave in. "But you need to be back in half an hour."

"Thanks, Mom," I stood up from the couch and walked over to them. I hugged her tight and felt a sniffle before pulling away and walking past Dad. "Thanks, Dad." He smiled and winked at me.

I walked to the front door at a smooth, normal pace, then slipped outside barefoot, hoping my parents wouldn't notice that I had forgotten my shoes. I jogged across our yard, under the new leaves of the elm tree, through the damp grass, and stood on the blacktop, letting the golden rays bounce off my body. The ground beneath my feet was warm. I started running down the street, running for the first time in a long time. Down Michigan Street and around the corner down Park Street, I ran and felt the familiar pulse in my body again. The breeze pushed back a little and my legs ached for the first time in a while. I ran and ran and ran and felt the wind blow around me again and breathed the fresh air again.

God, if Brody could see me—I stopped in the middle of the street when I saw the park's beech tree up ahead. The old, withered bark was still tattooed by romantic Michelangelos with pocket knives. As I smiled and traced the one he had etched our initials into with my fingers, the sun dipped behind a large cloud and the wind picked up a little. My legs began to shake.

No, no, no, I began to panic. *Not again.*

My breath seeped out of my lungs and the shadows behind the tree grew darker and longer. They reached their winding wrists toward me and shaped into the figures from that night, the night before the shaking started. My legs locked up at the sound of the deep cackling, the kind I heard in the hallways of my high school all the time. The group of shadowy figures surrounded me and I tried to look for him among them, praying that somehow merciful angels really did exist, hoping that Brody would be there tonight to make sure nothing bad happened. But he wasn't.

On that Friday night, I couldn't sleep well so I sought company in the cool, fall air. I didn't think I would run into them. I knew why they were after me and I tried to find a way out but they tackled me to the ground and two of them pinned my arms while a third pinned my legs. I struggled against them, but they were football players so what could I do? They stretched and ripped my clothes and took turns at me while the other two held me down. I felt my insides become torn up by them and I tried to scream and call for help, but they gagged me and threatened to kill me if I wasn't quiet. I struggled against them until I couldn't anymore. I laid there beneath the tree, staring at the heart surrounding "TB & BS" as tears clouded my vision until the last one stood up and buckled his belt.

"No one will believe you if you tell them," he chuckled. "So don't even bother." They walked away laughing.

As the episode unfolded before me for the thousandth time, my knees buckled under my weight and I crumbled to the ground. Tears dropped down onto the dirt beneath me as the fog and laughter slipped slowly away from my mind.

I don't remember how I got home that night or when I threw those stupid skinny jeans and ripped shirt away. I haven't told my parents or my psychologist or my doctors what happened, I haven't even told Brody, the guy I love, the guy who loves me and cares about me. And I don't know if I can.

As more tears rolled down my cheeks and my knuckles turned white on my knees, I remembered something Dad had told me when I was little. So, shakily, I got to my feet, wiped the tears away, and turned to walk slowly back down the street toward my house, repeating the mantra. Men don't cry.

Men don't cry.

Men don't cry.

Levi says: "For me, the most notable thing about this story is not what you'd expect. It's not the scene where Tracy is raped nor the sudden reveal at the end.

Rather, I'd say the most notable aspect of the story is the author's mindset at the time: a nervous, hand-wringing sophomore who hadn't been out for longer than six months, who has no personal experience with sexual assault, and who decided to leap into a twisting, gender-defying story that would leave himself still questioning two years later whether or not he should have taken this risk in putting it to paper.

At the time he wrote this story, then-Levi had been coming to terms with the idea of letting go and allowing himself to like and even love more "feminine" styles of clothing, scents, even colors. He wondered about what the universe had looked like where he had accepted being gay much earlier on and could've let his gender expression lie in those "feminine" styles. So, it's safe to say that for then-Levi, giving Tracy—a feminine, cheesy-romance-loving, gay kid in the Midwest—a voice on a page felt perhaps just as risky as writing about sexual assault, an experience he was privileged by his gender to never experience. If I'm being honest about then-Levi, he had been that stereotypical man who would think about (though rarely bring up) the experiences of men with sexual assault when talking about the #MeToo movement. And I think I can speak for then-Levi when I say that I wanted to tell this story in a way that didn't invalidate the experiences of trauma and sexual assault of women, and instead lifted up the perspective of gender through a man-on-man perspective of abuse.

I remember the way the story began to shift after I had written the sexual assault scene and started developing Tracy as a character beyond a male victim of rape. The lavender and floral colors in Tracy's room, his collection of Twilight books and other romance novels, and even the comparison of his size to that of the other track athletes—every other part of Tracy became a sort of idolized image of what I wished my life could have been during high school. So, you can imagine the amount of anxiousness I felt at sharing this story in my class as a very young writer. But, I shared it nonetheless, and my classmates supported me in my writing endeavor.

Two years down the line, although I may never let this story move past the pages of this book, it served me well in helping me move beyond the prepubescent, writerly voice cracks and wrestling more with the internalized homophobia I had been feeling. Today, the risk of writing beyond the boundaries of gender feels within my wheelhouse as a writer, and the heavier risk that remains was the risk I took in writing about sexual assault. I still don't know if I made the right choices or succeeded in writing both honestly and respectfully.

I share all of this background with you so that you know that there will be times that your writing feels risky, perhaps immoral, or even ill-intended. What I invite you to do is write, reflect, revise, and repeat. What I want you to know is that venturing into risk is good because it's an opportunity to truly sit and wrestle with your perspective and biases as an individual. It's a chance to ensure that you do the characters of your story and the people who reflect those lived experiences justice. Today, I know that there are more biases I hold beyond the homophobia I had been untangling at the time, and I know that some parts of my writing today may not feel as risky in perhaps another two or twenty years. The most important part of this writing was not just leaping into a risky topic and staring with wide eyes or a furrowed brow through the window at Tracy's life; it was seeing my reflection through the window pane, questioning my own intention and identity as a writer, and deciding to take a risk."

Why Do We Write? Because Life Is Short

Man is a mystery. This mystery must be solved, and even if you pass your whole life solving it, do not say that you have wasted your time. I occupy myself with this mystery because I want to be a man.

—Fyodor Dostoevsky (1821–81), age eighteen, in his diary

We die. That may be the meaning of life. But we do language. That may be the measure of our lives.

—Toni Morrison in her 1993 Nobel Lecture[36]

So why accept writing's risks and rewards? Because we want to make the most of our lives: to "be a man," as Dostoevsky says earlier, and to take the full "measure of our lives," as Morrison says earlier. My life in the present moment is the green, forward-questing tip of a long bloodline vine of ancestors, strivers, and dreamers—known and unknown—rooted deep in the past and growing into the future. Once, they were as alive as me. Yet this fact inspirits me with purpose as well as sadness. Can I keep chasing that intangible sense of fulfillment and wonder and beauty I've been using words to chase since I was thirteen, even if the process seems—to say the least—unrewarding? Can I turn away from that awful feeling of regret for what I *didn't* do and turn toward action and meaning? Can I keep trying to give order and voice to what's asking to be said and seen? Can I bear witness?

Writers often feel a sense of purpose in the face of time. Consider the poet and ex-doctor John Keats (1795–1821), who died of tuberculosis at age twenty-five. When Keats was your age, I tell my students, he knew three big things: that he was a gifted poet, that he was in love with the girl next door, and that he was terminally ill, with the same disease that killed his mother and younger brother. So much life pulsed in him, yet it wouldn't last: How does a 23-year-old man handle *that*? He writes what are still some of the loveliest poems in English, sorrowing at the beauty of the world he's bound to leave yet feeling all his senses heightened by that fact, lingering in that space of sharp uncertainty to see what he can make of it. "Heard melodies are sweet," he writes in "Ode on a Grecian Urn" (1819), "but those unheard / Are sweeter." More than a hundred years later, Saul Bellow echoes Keats in his novel *Humboldt's Gift* (1975): "Death is the dark backing that a mirror needs if we are to see anything."[37]

Perhaps mortality shapes fiction's deep engagement with reality, and the shapes of stories themselves—since without limitation, we have no reason to make choices, experience consequences, or feel sorrow or joy. An immortal life could be plotless and tedious, and, therefore, in classical myth, is often a curse. Quoting Bellow, the novelist Andrew O'Hagan discussed this: "[Novels] are about lives, and exuberance, and you pack a novel, if you can, at whatever level and in whatever way, with life. [. . .] And even in a book that was full of joy and jokes and music and belief," like O'Hagan's marvelous novel *Mayflies* (2020), "there's no escaping what fate might bring. The novel tries to conjure with those problems. It's a Bellovian problem to me. How do you have a full life in the midst of a certainty that death is coming? The novel dramatizes that."[38]

Life juxtaposed with death—this is one of the reasons juxtapositions of many kinds can carry a strange sort of clarity, even wisdom. Two things apparently opposed can exist side by side, and often do. The ability to hold those two things in mind without seeking false resolutions—even in times of personal, historical, and ecological difficulty—is a kind of artistic (and personal) maturity John Keats famously described as *negative capability*. So, given the risks and rewards of the writing life, and the wild, mingled realities of this world, ask yourself why you write, why it matters, and why you want to keep going. Making art that lasts—it's a risky, joyful, life-giving thing to pursue.

Craft Studio: Charlotte Perkins Gilman (1860–1935), "The Yellow Wallpaper" (*New England Magazine*, 1892)

Now more than one hundred years old, "The Yellow Wallpaper" still shocks readers, lit by an electric connection to its author's life. Suffering from depression after the birth of her daughter Katherine in 1885, Gilman wrote directly to seek treatment in 1887 from the leading "nerve specialist" of her day: Silas Weir Mitchell (1829–1914), who prescribed a "rest cure." Mitchell "sent me home," Gilman later wrote, "with solemn advice to 'live as domestic a life as far as possible,' to 'have but two hours' intellectual life a day,' and 'never to touch pen, brush, or pencil again as long as I lived.'" According to nineteenth-century medical understanding of women's bodies and minds, this sensory and intellectual deprivation would avoid "exciting" and overheating what was believed to be the inherently unstable substance of a woman's sanity, tied to her reproductive system and her "natural" role as wife and mother.[39] Everyone involved surely believed that the well-respected Dr. Mitchell was merely fulfilling the first tenet of the Hippocratic Oath: first, do no harm. But the opposite proved true.

"I went home and obeyed those directions," Gilman later wrote, "for some three months, and came so near the border line of utter mental ruin that I could see over."

> Then, using the remnants of intelligence that remained [she continues], and helped by a wise friend, I cast the noted specialist's advice to the winds and went to work again—work, the normal life of every human being; work, in which is joy and growth and service, without which one is a pauper and a parasite; ultimately recovering some measure of power.
>
> Being naturally moved to rejoicing by this narrow escape, I wrote *The Yellow Wallpaper*, with its embellishments and additions to carry out the ideal (I never

had hallucinations or objections to my mural decorations) and sent a copy to the physician who nearly drove me mad. He never acknowledged it.[40]

"The Yellow Wallpaper," Gilman continues, found a ready audience among nineteenth-century psychiatrists (or "alienists," in the language of the day)—one of whom "admitted to friends that he had altered his treatment of neurasthenia since reading" it—and patients, one of whom was released "into normal activity" and "recovered" after the story "terrif[ied] her family."[41] One Kansas physician "wrote to say that it was the best description of incipient insanity he had ever seen, and—begging my pardon—had I been there?"[42]

Gilman was to become used to such questions as she lived out the twentieth-century feminist maxim that *the personal is political.* For nineteenth-century women, speaking openly about sexuality, reproduction, and illness was taboo, although writers, public intellectuals, and doctors and public health specialists like Elizabeth Cady Stanton, Susan B. Anthony, Elizabeth Blackwell, and S. Josephine Baker belied the notion that women's "limited" bodies limit their minds. Gilman went on to write, among other books, the novel *Herland* (1915), in which three men stumble upon the all-female utopia of the title.

But no amount of historical background can account for the eerie power of this story. Its suffocatingly close first-person psychic distance (see Chapter 5) and diary-like telegraphic pulses from an ever-receding frontier of sanity bring readers into the consciousness of a woman suffering from others' assumptions about what's best for her. Its social purpose doesn't diffuse its crackling atmosphere of mystery, its indefinable ending, or its risk to Gilman's own reputation. One Boston physician wrote to Gilman that "such a story ought not to be written . . . it was enough to drive anyone mad to read it." Undaunted, Gilman retained her purpose. "It was not intended to drive people crazy," Gilman wrote, "but to save people from being driven crazy, and it worked."

Charlotte Perkins Gilman, "The Yellow Wallpaper"

It is very seldom that mere ordinary people like John and myself secure ancestral halls for the summer.

A colonial mansion, a hereditary estate, I would say a haunted house, and reach the height of romantic felicity—but that would be asking too much of fate!

Still I will proudly declare that there is something queer about it.

Else, why should it be let so cheaply? And why have stood so long untenanted?

John laughs at me, of course, but one expects that in marriage.

John is practical in the extreme. He has no patience with faith, an intense horror of superstition, and he scoffs openly at any talk of things not to be felt and seen and put down in figures.

John is a physician, and *perhaps*—(I would not say it to a living soul, of course, but this is dead paper and a great relief to my mind)—*perhaps* that is one reason I do not get well faster.

You see, he does not believe I am sick!

And what can one do?

If a physician of high standing, and one's own husband, assures friends and relatives that there is really nothing the matter with one but temporary nervous depression—a slight hysterical tendency—what is one to do?

My brother is also a physician, and also of high standing, and he says the same thing.

So I take phosphates or phosphites—whichever it is, and tonics, and journeys, and air, and exercise, and am absolutely forbidden to "work" until I am well again.

Personally, I disagree with their ideas.

Personally, I believe that congenial work, with excitement and change, would do me good. But what is one to do?

I did write for a while in spite of them; but it *does* exhaust me a good deal—having to be so sly about it, or else meet with heavy opposition.

I sometimes fancy that in my condition if I had less opposition and more society and stimulus—but John says the very worst thing I can do is to think about my condition, and I confess it always makes me feel bad.

So I will let it alone and talk about the house.

The most beautiful place! It is quite alone, standing well back from the road, quite three miles from the village. It makes me think of English places that you read about, for there are hedges and walls and gates that lock, and lots of separate little houses for the gardeners and people.

There is a *delicious* garden! I never saw such a garden—large and shady, full of box-bordered paths, and lined with long grape-covered arbors with seats under them.

There were greenhouses, too, but they are all broken now.

There was some legal trouble, I believe, something about the heirs and co-heirs; anyhow, the place has been empty for years.

That spoils my ghostliness, I am afraid; but I don't care—there is something strange about the house—I can feel it.

I even said so to John one moonlight evening, but he said what I felt was a draught, and shut the window.

I get unreasonably angry with John sometimes. I'm sure I never used to be so sensitive. I think it is due to this nervous condition.

But John says if I feel so I shall neglect proper self-control; so I take pains to control myself—before him, at least—and that makes me very tired.

I don't like our room a bit. I wanted one downstairs that opened on the piazza and had roses all over the window, and such pretty old-fashioned chintz hangings! but John would not hear of it.

He said there was only one window and not room for two beds, and no near room for him if he took another.

He is very careful and loving, and hardly lets me stir without special direction.

I have a schedule prescription for each hour in the day; he takes all care from me, and so I feel basely ungrateful not to value it more.

He said we came here solely on my account, that I was to have perfect rest and all the air I could get. "Your exercise depends on your strength, my dear," said he, "and your food somewhat on your appetite; but air you can absorb all the time." So we took the nursery, at the top of the house.

It is a big, airy room, the whole floor nearly, with windows that look all ways, and air and sunshine galore. It was nursery first and then playground and gymnasium, I should judge; for the windows are barred for little children, and there are rings and things in the walls.

The paint and paper look as if a boys' school had used it. It is stripped off—the paper—in great patches all around the head of my bed, about as far as I can reach, and in a great place on the other side of the room low down. I never saw a worse paper in my life.

One of those sprawling flamboyant patterns committing every artistic sin.

It is dull enough to confuse the eye in following, pronounced enough to constantly irritate, and provoke study, and when you follow the lame, uncertain curves for a little distance they suddenly commit suicide—plunge off at outrageous angles, destroy themselves in unheard-of contradictions.

The color is repellant, almost revolting; a smouldering, unclean yellow, strangely faded by the slow-turning sunlight.

It is a dull yet lurid orange in some places, a sickly sulphur tint in others.

No wonder the children hated it! I should hate it myself if I had to live in this room long.

There comes John, and I must put this away—he hates to have me write a word.

•

We have been here two weeks, and I haven't felt like writing before, since that first day.

I am sitting by the window now, up in this atrocious nursery, and there is nothing to hinder my writing as much as I please, save lack of strength.

John is away all day, and even some nights when his cases are serious.

I am glad my case is not serious!

But these nervous troubles are dreadfully depressing.

John does not know how much I really suffer. He knows there is no reason to suffer, and that satisfies him.

Of course it is only nervousness. It does weigh on me so not to do my duty in any way!

I meant to be such a help to John, such a real rest and comfort, and here I am a comparative burden already!

Nobody would believe what an effort it is to do what little I am able—to dress and entertain, and order things.

It is fortunate Mary is so good with the baby. Such a dear baby!

And yet I *cannot* be with him, it makes me so nervous.

I suppose John never was nervous in his life. He laughs at me so about this wallpaper!

At first he meant to repaper the room, but afterwards he said that I was letting it get the better of me, and that nothing was worse for a nervous patient than to give way to such fancies.

He said that after the wallpaper was changed it would be the heavy bedstead, and then the barred windows, and then that gate at the head of the stairs, and so on.

"You know the place is doing you good," he said, "and really, dear, I don't care to renovate the house just for a three months' rental."

"Then do let us go downstairs," I said, "there are such pretty rooms there."

Then he took me in his arms and called me a blessed little goose, and said he would go down cellar if I wished, and have it whitewashed into the bargain.

But he is right enough about the beds and windows and things.

It is as airy and comfortable a room as any one need wish, and, of course, I would not be so silly as to make him uncomfortable just for a whim.

I'm really getting quite fond of the big room, all but that horrid paper.

Out of one window I can see the garden, those mysterious deep-shaded arbors, the riotous old-fashioned flowers, and bushes and gnarly trees.

Out of another I get a lovely view of the bay and a little private wharf belonging to the estate. There is a beautiful shaded lane that runs down there from the house. I always fancy I see people walking in these numerous paths and arbors, but John has cautioned me not to give way to fancy in the least. He says that with my imaginative power and habit of story-making a nervous weakness like mine is sure to lead to all manner of excited fancies, and that I ought to use my will and good sense to check the tendency. So I try.

I think sometimes that if I were only well enough to write a little it would relieve the press of ideas and rest me.

But I find I get pretty tired when I try.

It is so discouraging not to have any advice and companionship about my work. When I get really well John says we will ask Cousin Henry and Julia down for a long visit; but he says he would as soon put fire-works in my pillow-case as to let me have those stimulating people about now.

I wish I could get well faster.

But I must not think about that. This paper looks to me as if it *knew* what a vicious influence it had!

There is a recurrent spot where the pattern lolls like a broken neck and two bulbous eyes stare at you upside-down.

I get positively angry with the impertinence of it and the everlastingness. Up and down and sideways they crawl, and those absurd, unblinking eyes are everywhere. There is one place where two breadths didn't match, and the eyes go all up and down the line, one a little higher than the other.

I never saw so much expression in an inanimate thing before, and we all know how much expression they have! I used to lie awake as a child and get more entertainment and terror out of blank walls and plain furniture than most children could find in a toy-store.

I remember what a kindly wink the knobs of our big old bureau used to have, and there was one chair that always seemed like a strong friend.

I used to feel that if any of the other things looked too fierce I could always hop into that chair and be safe.

The furniture in this room is no worse than inharmonious, however, for we had to bring it all from downstairs. I suppose when this was used as a playroom they had to take the nursery things out, and no wonder! I never saw such ravages as the children have made here.

The wallpaper, as I said before, is torn off in spots, and it sticketh closer than a brother—they must have had perseverance as well as hatred.

Then the floor is scratched and gouged and splintered, the plaster itself is dug out here and there, and this great heavy bed, which is all we found in the room, looks as if it had been through the wars.

But I don't mind it a bit—only the paper.

There comes John's sister. Such a dear girl as she is, and so careful of me! I must not let her find me writing.

She is a perfect, and enthusiastic housekeeper, and hopes for no better profession. I verily believe she thinks it is the writing which made me sick!

But I can write when she is out, and see her a long way off from these windows.

There is one that commands the road, a lovely, shaded, winding road, and one that just looks off over the country. A lovely country, too, full of great elms and velvet meadows.

This wallpaper has a kind of sub-pattern in a different shade, a particularly irritating one, for you can only see it in certain lights, and not clearly then.

But in the places where it isn't faded, and where the sun is just so, I can see a strange, provoking, formless sort of figure, that seems to sulk about behind that silly and conspicuous front design.

There's sister on the stairs!

•

Well, the Fourth of July is over! The people are gone and I am tired out. John thought it might do me good to see a little company, so we just had mother and Nellie and the children down for a week.

Of course I didn't do a thing. Jennie sees to everything now.

But it tired me all the same.

John says if I don't pick up faster he shall send me to Weir Mitchell in the fall.

But I don't want to go there at all. I had a friend who was in his hands once, and she says he is just like John and my brother, only more so!

Besides, it is such an undertaking to go so far.

I don't feel as if it was worth while to turn my hand over for anything, and I'm getting dreadfully fretful and querulous.

I cry at nothing, and cry most of the time.

Of course I don't when John is here, or anybody else, but when I am alone.

And I am alone a good deal just now. John is kept in town very often by serious cases, and Jennie is good and lets me alone when I want her to.

So I walk a little in the garden or down that lovely lane, sit on the porch under the roses, and lie down up here a good deal.

I'm getting really fond of the room in spite of the wallpaper. Perhaps *because* of the wallpaper.

It dwells in my mind so!

I lie here on this great immovable bed—it is nailed down, I believe—and follow that pattern about by the hour. It is as good as gymnastics, I assure you. I start, we'll say, at the bottom, down in the corner over there where it has not been touched, and I determine for the thousandth time that I *will* follow that pointless pattern to some sort of a conclusion.

I know a little of the principle of design, and I know this thing was not arranged on any laws of radiation, or alternation, or repetition, or symmetry, or anything else that I ever heard of.

It is repeated, of course, by the breadths, but not otherwise.

Looked at in one way each breadth stands alone, the bloated curves and flourishes—a kind of "debased Romanesque" with *delirium tremens*—go waddling up and down in isolated columns of fatuity.

But, on the other hand, they connect diagonally, and the sprawling outlines run off in great slanting waves of optic horror, like a lot of wallowing seaweeds in full chase.

The whole thing goes horizontally, too, at least it seems so, and I exhaust myself in trying to distinguish the order of its going in that direction.

They have used a horizontal breadth for a frieze, and that adds wonderfully to the confusion.

There is one end of the room where it is almost intact, and there, when the cross-lights fade and the low sun shines directly upon it, I can almost fancy radiation after all—the interminable grotesques seem to form around a common centre and rush off in headlong plunges of equal distraction.

It makes me tired to follow it. I will take a nap, I guess.

I don't know why I should write this.

I don't want to.

I don't feel able.

And I know John would think it absurd. But I *must* say what I feel and think in some way—it is such a relief!

But the effort is getting to be greater than the relief.

•

Half the time now I am awfully lazy, and lie down ever so much.

John says I mustn't lose my strength, and has me take cod-liver oil and lots of tonics and things, to say nothing of ale and wine and rare meat.

Dear John! He loves me very dearly, and hates to have me sick. I tried to have a real earnest reasonable talk with him the other day, and tell him how I wish he would let me go and make a visit to Cousin Henry and Julia.

But he said I wasn't able to go, nor able to stand it after I got there; and I did not make out a very good case for myself, for I was crying before I had finished.

It is getting to be a great effort for me to think straight. Just this nervous weakness, I suppose.

And dear John gathered me up in his arms, and just carried me upstairs and laid me on the bed, and sat by me and read to me till it tired my head.

He said I was his darling and his comfort and all he had, and that I must take care of myself for his sake, and keep well.

He says no one but myself can help me out of it, that I must use my will and self-control and not let any silly fancies run away with me.

There's one comfort, the baby is well and happy, and does not have to occupy this nursery with the horrid wallpaper.

If we had not used it, that blessed child would have! What a fortunate escape! Why, I wouldn't have a child of mine, an impressionable little thing, live in such a room for worlds.

I never thought of it before, but it is lucky that John kept me here after all. I can stand it so much easier than a baby, you see.

Of course I never mention it to them any more—I am too wise—but I keep watch of it all the same.

There are things in that paper that nobody knows but me, or ever will.

Behind that outside pattern the dim shapes get clearer every day.

It is always the same shape, only very numerous.

And it is like a woman stooping down and creeping about behind that pattern. I don't like it a bit. I wonder—I begin to think—I wish John would take me away from here!

It is so hard to talk with John about my case, because he is so wise, and because he loves me so.

But I tried it last night.

It was moonlight. The moon shines in all around, just as the sun does.

I hate to see it sometimes, it creeps so slowly, and always comes in by one window or another.

John was asleep and I hated to waken him, so I kept still and watched the moonlight on that undulating wallpaper till I felt creepy.

The faint figure behind seemed to shake the pattern, just as if she wanted to get out.

I got up softly and went to feel and see if the paper *did* move, and when I came back John was awake.

"What is it, little girl?" he said. "Don't go walking about like that—you'll get cold."

I thought it was a good time to talk, so I told him that I really was not gaining here, and that I wished he would take me away.

"Why darling!" said he, "our lease will be up in three weeks, and I can't see how to leave before."

"The repairs are not done at home, and I cannot possibly leave town just now. Of course if you were in any danger I could and would, but you really are better, dear, whether you can see it or not. I am a doctor, dear, and I know. You are gaining flesh and color, your appetite is better, I feel really much easier about you."

"I don't weigh a bit more," said I, "nor as much; and my appetite may be better in the evening, when you are here, but it is worse in the morning when you are away."

"Bless her little heart!" said he with a big hug; "she shall be as sick as she pleases! But now let's improve the shining hours by going to sleep, and talk about it in the morning!"

"And you won't go away?" I asked gloomily.

"Why, how can I, dear? It is only three weeks more and then we will take a nice little trip of a few days while Jennie is getting the house ready. Really, dear, you are better!"

"Better in body perhaps—" I began, and stopped short, for he sat up straight and looked at me with such a stern, reproachful look that I could not say another word.

"My darling," said he, "I beg of you, for my sake and for our child's sake, as well as for your own, that you will never for one instant let that idea enter your mind! There is nothing so dangerous, so fascinating, to a temperament like yours. It is a false and foolish fancy. Can you not trust me as a physician when I tell you so?"

So of course I said no more on that score, and we went to sleep before long. He thought I was asleep first, but I wasn't—I lay there for hours trying to decide whether that front pattern and the back pattern really did move together or separately.

On a pattern like this, by daylight, there is a lack of sequence, a defiance of law, that is a constant irritant to a normal mind.

The color is hideous enough, and unreliable enough, and infuriating enough, but the pattern is torturing.

You think you have mastered it, but just as you get well under way in following, it turns a back somersault and there you are. It slaps you in the face, knocks you down, and tramples upon you. It is like a bad dream.

The outside pattern is a florid arabesque, reminding one of a fungus. If you can imagine a toadstool in joints, an interminable string of toadstools, budding and sprouting in endless convolutions—why, that is something like it.

That is, sometimes!

There is one marked peculiarity about this paper, a thing nobody seems to notice but myself, and that is that it changes as the light changes.

When the sun shoots in through the east window—I always watch for that first long, straight ray—it changes so quickly that I never can quite believe it.

That is why I watch it always.

By moonlight—the moon shines in all night when there is a moon—I wouldn't know it was the same paper.

At night in any kind of light, in twilight, candlelight, lamplight, and worst of all by moonlight, it becomes bars! The outside pattern I mean, and the woman behind it is as plain as can be.

I didn't realize for a long time what the thing was that showed behind, that dim sub-pattern, but now I am quite sure it is a woman.

By daylight she is subdued, quiet. I fancy it is the pattern that keeps her so still. It is so puzzling. It keeps me quiet by the hour.

I lie down ever so much now. John says it is good for me, and to sleep all I can.

Indeed, he started the habit by making me lie down for an hour after each meal.

It is a very bad habit, I am convinced, for, you see, I don't sleep.

And that cultivates deceit, for I don't tell them I'm awake—oh, no!

The fact is, I am getting a little afraid of John.

He seems very queer sometimes, and even Jennie has an inexplicable look.

It strikes me occasionally, just as a scientific hypothesis, that perhaps it is the paper!

I have watched John when he did not know I was looking, and come into the room suddenly on the most innocent excuses, and I've caught him several times *looking at the paper!* And Jennie too. I caught Jennie with her hand on it once.

She didn't know I was in the room, and when I asked her in a quiet, a very quiet voice, with the most restrained manner possible, what she was doing with the paper she turned around as if she had been caught stealing, and looked quite angry—asked me why I should frighten her so!

Then she said that the paper stained everything it touched, that she had found yellow smooches on all my clothes and John's, and she wished we would be more careful!

Did not that sound innocent? But I know she was studying that pattern, and I am determined that nobody shall find it out but myself!

•

Life is very much more exciting now than it used to be. You see I have something more to expect, to look forward to, to watch. I really do eat better, and am more quiet than I was.

John is so pleased to see me improve! He laughed a little the other day, and said I seemed to be flourishing in spite of my wallpaper.

I turned it off with a laugh. I had no intention of telling him it was *because* of the wallpaper—he would make fun of me. He might even want to take me away.

I don't want to leave now until I have found it out. There is a week more, and I think that will be enough.

I'm feeling ever so much better! I don't sleep much at night, for it is so interesting to watch developments; but I sleep a good deal in the daytime.

In the daytime it is tiresome and perplexing.

There are always new shoots on the fungus, and new shades of yellow all over it. I cannot keep count of them, though I have tried conscientiously.

It is the strangest yellow, that wallpaper! It makes me think of all the yellow things I ever saw—not beautiful ones like buttercups, but old foul, bad yellow things.

But there is something else about that paper—the smell! I noticed it the moment we came into the room, but with so much air and sun it was not bad. Now we have had a week of fog and rain, and whether the windows are open or not, the smell is here.

It creeps all over the house.

I find it hovering in the dining-room, skulking in the parlor, hiding in the hall, lying in wait for me on the stairs.

It gets into my hair.

Even when I go to ride, if I turn my head suddenly and surprise it—there is that smell!

Such a peculiar odor, too! I have spent hours in trying to analyze it, to find what it smelled like.

It is not bad—at first, and very gentle, but quite the subtlest, most enduring odor I ever met.

In this damp weather it is awful. I wake up in the night and find it hanging over me.

It used to disturb me at first. I thought seriously of burning the house—to reach the smell.

But now I am used to it. The only thing I can think of that it is like is the *color* of the paper! A yellow smell.

There is a very funny mark on this wall, low down, near the mopboard. A streak that runs round the room. It goes behind every piece of furniture, except the bed, a long, straight, even *smooch*, as if it had been rubbed over and over.

I wonder how it was done and who did it, and what they did it for. Round and round and round—round and round and round—it makes me dizzy!

I really have discovered something at last.

Through watching so much at night, when it changes so, I have finally found out.

The front pattern *does* move—and no wonder! The woman behind shakes it!

Sometimes I think there are a great many women behind, and sometimes only one, and she crawls around fast, and her crawling shakes it all over.

Then in the very bright spots she keeps still, and in the very shady spots she just takes hold of the bars and shakes them hard.

And she is all the time trying to climb through. But nobody could climb through that pattern—it strangles so; I think that is why it has so many heads.

They get through, and then the pattern strangles them off and turns them upside-down, and makes their eyes white!

If those heads were covered or taken off it would not be half so bad.

•

I think that woman gets out in the daytime!

And I'll tell you why—privately—I've seen her!

I can see her out of every one of my windows!

It is the same woman, I know, for she is always creeping, and most women do not creep by daylight.

I see her on that long shaded lane, creeping up and down. I see her in those dark grape arbors, creeping all around the garden.

I see her on that long road under the trees, creeping along, and when a carriage comes she hides under the blackberry vines.

I don't blame her a bit. It must be very humiliating to be caught creeping by daylight!

I always lock the door when I creep by daylight. I can't do it at night, for I know John would suspect something at once.

And John is so queer now, that I don't want to irritate him. I wish he would take another room! Besides, I don't want anybody to get that woman out at night but myself.

I often wonder if I could see her out of all the windows at once.

But, turn as fast as I can, I can only see out of one at one time.

And though I always see her she *may* be able to creep faster than I can turn!

I have watched her sometimes away off in the open country, creeping as fast as a cloud shadow in a wind.

If only that top pattern could be gotten off from the under one! I mean to try it, little by little.

I have found out another funny thing, but I shan't tell it this time! It does not do to trust people too much.

There are only two more days to get this paper off, and I believe John is beginning to notice. I don't like the look in his eyes.

And I heard him ask Jennie a lot of professional questions about me. She had a very good report to give.

She said I slept a good deal in the daytime.

John knows I don't sleep very well at night, for all I'm so quiet!

He asked me all sorts of questions, too, and pretended to be very loving and kind.

As if I couldn't see through him!

Still, I don't wonder he acts so, sleeping under this paper for three months.

It only interests me, but I feel sure John and Jennie are affected by it.

•

Hurrah! This is the last day, but it is enough. John is to stay in town over night, and won't be out until this evening.

Jennie wanted to sleep with me—the sly thing; but I told her I should undoubtedly rest better for a night all alone.

That was clever, for really I wasn't alone a bit! As soon as it was moonlight, and that poor thing began to crawl and shake the pattern, I got up and ran to help her.

I pulled and she shook. I shook and she pulled, and before morning we had peeled off yards of that paper.

A strip about as high as my head and half around the room.

And then when the sun came and that awful pattern began to laugh at me I declared I would finish it today!

We go away tomorrow, and they are moving all my furniture down again to leave things as they were before.

Jennie looked at the wall in amazement, but I told her merrily that I did it out of pure spite at the vicious thing.

She laughed and said she wouldn't mind doing it herself, but I must not get tired.

How she betrayed herself that time!

But I am here, and no person touches this paper but Me—not *alive!*

She tried to get me out of the room—it was too patent! But I said it was so quiet and empty and clean now that I believed I would lie down again and sleep all I could; and not to wake me even for dinner—I would call when I woke.

So now she is gone, and the servants are gone, and the things are gone, and there is nothing left but that great bedstead nailed down, with the canvas mattress we found on it.

We shall sleep downstairs to-night, and take the boat home to-morrow.

I quite enjoy the room, now it is bare again.

How those children did tear about here!

This bedstead is fairly gnawed!

But I must get to work.

I have locked the door and thrown the key down into the front path.

I don't want to go out, and I don't want to have anybody come in, till John comes.

I want to astonish him.

I've got a rope up here that even Jennie did not find. If that woman does get out, and tries to get away, I can tie her!

But I forgot I could not reach far without anything to stand on!

This bed will *not* move!

I tried to lift and push it until I was lame, and then I got so angry I bit off a little piece at one corner—but it hurt my teeth.

Then I peeled off all the paper I could reach standing on the floor. It sticks horribly and the pattern just enjoys it! All those strangled heads and bulbous eyes and waddling fungus growths just shriek with derision!

I am getting angry enough to do something desperate. To jump out of the window would be admirable exercise, but the bars are too strong even to try.

Besides I wouldn't do it. Of course not. I know well enough that a step like that is improper and might be misconstrued.

I don't like to *look* out of the windows even—there are so many of those creeping women, and they creep so fast.

I wonder if they all come out of that wallpaper as I did?

But I am securely fastened now by my well-hidden rope—you don't get *me* out in the road there!

I suppose I shall have to get back behind the pattern when it comes night, and that is hard!

It is so pleasant to be out in this great room and creep around as I please!

I don't want to go outside. I won't, even if Jennie asks me to.

For outside you have to creep on the ground, and everything is green instead of yellow.

But here I can creep smoothly on the floor, and my shoulder just fits in that long smooch around the wall, so I cannot lose my way.

Why, there's John at the door!

It is no use, young man, you can't open it!

How he does call and pound!

Now he's crying for an axe.

It would be a shame to break down that beautiful door!

"John dear!" said I in the gentlest voice, "the key is down by the front steps, under a plantain leaf!"

That silenced him for a few moments.

Then he said—very quietly indeed, "Open the door, my darling!"

"I can't," said I. "The key is down by the front door under a plantain leaf!"

And then I said it again, several times, very gently and slowly, and said it so often that he had to go and see, and he got it, of course, and came in. He stopped short by the door.

"What is the matter?" he cried. "For God's sake, what are you doing!"

I kept on creeping just the same, but I looked at him over my shoulder.

"I've got out at last," said I, "in spite of you and Jane! And I've pulled off most of the paper, so you can't put me back!"

Now why should that man have fainted? But he did, and right across my path by the wall, so that I had to creep over him every time!

Exercises:

- Try one of the experimental forms discussed in this chapter: square stories, illustrated stories, twenty-minute stories, a recipe, an object-as-story, a single-paragraph story, a ghost story . . . What do you find?

- Record a story you've written in your native language as a voice memo, then use Google Translate to render it into a different language. Then translate that text back to your home language. What do you hear now?

- Deliberately vague prompt: engage the internet in fiction. What do you find?

- Deliberately vague prompt: engage climate in fiction. What do you find?

- Find a place in your story where you over-/explain something to the reader, and cross it out. How does it feel to trust your reader instead?

- Write a single-scene story that starts with an image of something apparently unrelated that you have seen in the past week (maybe there's something in your notebook?) That real-life thing is seen by one of two people in a situation of tension between them. What subtext does the real-life image heighten, or not? What are you surprised to find yourself writing?

- *Contranym*—also called *auto-antonym,* or, wonderfully, a *Janus word* after the two-faced Roman god of doorways, transitions, and time—is a word that, according to Wikipedia, "has two directly or generally accepted meanings that contradict one another." (In ancient Greek, for instance, *pharmakon* means both *remedy* and *poison*.) They might also function as different words under different spellings, or as both verbs and nouns. In the energy of friction, opposition, and oddity can be the energy of a voice. What might you and your classmates discover if you share a list of contranyms (*raise/raze, oral/aural, awful, cleave, dust, execute, fast, hew, inflammable, like hell, put out, ravel, reservation, sanction, seed, strike, splice, trigger, weather, wicked*) and use one as the spark for flash fiction?

- Write a scene that makes you feel uncomfortable. What do you notice?

CHAPTER 4
WRITING IN COLOR
CULTURE, IDENTITY, AND ART[1]

What I do in writing of any character is to try to enter into the mind, heart, and skin of a human being who is not myself. Whether this happens to be a man or a woman, old or young, with skin black or white, the primary challenge lies in making the jump itself. It is the act of a writer's imagination that I set most high.

—Eudora Welty[2]

Imagining yourself into the body and mind of someone who isn't just like you—as Welty famously observed in the previous quote—is what writing fiction's all about. That's a given. But what if you and your character differ in gender, race, disability, age, sexuality, class, or other marker of social identity? How might you imagine them without meanness or stereotype while upholding fidelity to "reality as the character understands it" *and* exercising artistic freedom?

Let's think back to this book's first question: Why do we write? To travel beyond the boundaries of what we know. To write aspects of ourselves into characters and, in doing so, expand our selves. To explore other lives and questions that challenge us. To feel the sheer joy of imagining and creating, including the pleasure of freedom and exploration. To bear witness to voices and stories that might otherwise be forgotten. Novelist Jordy Rosenberg quotes author Samuel Delaney, who "has said that 'the fiction writer is trying to create a false memory with the force of history.'"[3] And that "false memory" can provide insightful truths: "[i]n an introduction to a reading of *Beloved*, Toni Morrison once said that she wrote her novel about slavery to find out 'what it must have been like.'"[4] Yet with that word—"history"—another ghost enters the room: the ways that human beings have dominated one another throughout time, the ways those acts of domination still shape the way we understand and imagine one another today, and the reality of all of it as we live each day, trying, in spite of everything, to do the right thing by one another, even as we're also following our imaginations and our hearts.

Therefore, here in the twenty-first century, many writers are asking: How might we write outside the boundaries of our own social identities, "crossing into" the skin of protagonists different from ourselves and representing a range of diverse perspectives—race, class, gender, culture, sexuality, embodiment, religion, politics on the page? My students want to write beyond their own identities and populate their fictional worlds with a range of characters, but they're uncertain about how, or whether, they might claim the authority to do so.

And it's the question of *authority* that I want to explore now. Sure, fiction writing is about imagining characters who are not necessarily me and not necessarily from my time and place. But can I imagine and write about these people without being racist or sexist or homophobic or clichéd or just plain embarrassing? Can I be an ethical citizen *and* an artist who takes risks? What if I get it wrong without meaning to? All the questions seem to circle back to one big one: *How far is* too *far for me to go?*

Starting the Conversation: Showing Up

First, let's admit that talking about culture and identity feels risky sometimes. Like writing itself, these conversations ask you to put your own vulnerabilities out there. People may not get where you're coming from. They may dismiss your words as a product of your skin color or ethnicity or class or region or gender or embodiment and, therefore, nothing they should bother to read. They may call you names, which can prompt a particularly painful blend of anger and humiliation. They may suggest that your particular social position has limited your ability to understand what you're talking about—and sometimes they may be right. "One of the hard things about writing," says the writer Leslie Jamison, "is that you have to show up, but you don't know what you're showing up for."[5] This feels true of writing and of conversations about culture and identity, together and separately. But with the voice I have, I'll do my best to help you, as fellow writers, through them.

What does it mean to "have a voice," though? What builds the perspective we have, the words we choose, the corners we investigate and the lives we imagine? I think we start out as writers from the same home base we start from as people—the set of experiences, memories, observations, and intersecting identities we accumulate by living in our particular bodies in our particular times and places on earth. Therefore, identity is always communal and personal at the same time, so, perhaps, is the voice in which you speak of it. "There is no way to write X character because not all X people are the same," writes "Writing with Color" blog founder and moderator Colette Aburime. "People of color are, well, *people*. We're *influenced* by family and our cultural aspects, yes, and also where we live, social status, who our friends are . . . and yet none of it *defines* us to the bone; influence is the key word here. This obviously goes for any person, any character."[6] While you may share the stories and histories of groups you're a part of, only you know what it's like to be *you*, living in the particular body and mind where all these experiences and stories mingle and grow, every day. This means that no one person is reducible to the broad outlines of her social group's story. And a fiction writer's first loyalty is always to the character as a complex *individual*.

Furthermore, every individual is part of the tapestry of what scholar, bioethicist, and disability-studies pioneer Rosemarie Garland-Thomson calls "human variation." "The human variations we think of as disabilities," says Garland-Thomson, "are part of the human condition that occur in every life and family and are a theme in all art and culture."[7] Once we expand our concept of ourselves and our fellow humans away from *norms and deviations* toward *human variation*, we can expand our understanding of *diversity* as it actually describes ourselves and our world and see it as not only a valuable thing but—in multiple ways—a natural one.

When I think of what builds variety and beauty in the natural world, I think of *color*—a word humans have used in neutral and not-so-neutral ways. The writer Zora Neale Hurston (born in Notasulga, Alabama, near my own hometown) published an essay in 1928 called "How It Feels to be Colored Me." While "colored" was the sometimes-derogatory language of Hurston's time to describe Black people like herself, I wonder if (in typical Hurston fashion, flipping the script on would-be detractors) she wasn't also making a play on the word to reclaim it. Perhaps, following that thought, we are "colored" as ourselves by the contexts we inherit and the social and bodily experiences that revise them from within, like a flower in a painting is colored magenta or orange or yellow by the pigment the artist chooses. Therefore, when we write, we are writing from within that particular color field—all the aspects of identity and life, some inherited and some new, that have colored us *ourselves.* We're writing from inside a body whose skin has a color unlike anyone else's, no matter what names people outside our bodies may give to those colors at different times. And so as we think about representing bodies and lives in their beauty, variety, complexity, history, and difficulty, we might also think about *color* as a kind of imaginative ink that helps us write those bodies and lives onto the page.

Color, of course, also has shades that not everyone might see, including language, representation, visibility, and authority. Siyabonga Mabuza, an economics major and fiction writer at my college, has some valuable thoughts about these issues. A native of Swaziland studying in the United States, he has found that when he writes in his native language, Siswati, he writes differently than in English or in French, the other languages he speaks, because its structures of grammar open particular pathways of thought. (The prizewinning writer Jhumpa Lahiri, who learned Italian as an adult and now writes fiction only in Italian, has said that she, too, feels like "a different writer" in Italian than English.) Each culture, Siyabonga said to me, has a "subconscious structure" that stories, languages, and characters arise from. Therefore, a person shaped by that culture and aware of those "subconscious structures" will write and construct characters from that culture differently than someone who is not.

Yet—perhaps now more than ever, in our globalized, inter-wired world—cultures also blend and borrow from one another, a process anthropologists and linguists call *creolization.* "I give myself complete artistic licence to write from multiple perspectives and to inhabit different cultures across the perceived barriers of race, culture, gender, age, and sexuality," writes Booker-Prize-winner Bernadine Evaristo. "How can culture be owned by anyone when it is in a perpetual state of movement and metamorphosis, of permeability and responsiveness to global influences? [. . .] Any attempts to essentialize culture into notions of authenticity only succeed in doing the opposite and revealing the interconnectedness of our societies."[8]

Like cultures and their (inter)connections, people are also more complex than they seem. "I'm a trained theologian," observes writer Sarah Sentilles,

> and what I've kept from that education is a belief in transcendence—not in the idea that there is one being (God) who is transcendent, but in the idea that there is part of everyone that is uncapturable, resistant, unknowable, mysterious, free. There

is always more to everything—every tree, river, refugee, child, prisoner, social worker—than what we think we know, than what we write. How do you make room for the people you're writing about to exceed and to trouble the language you use? How do you let your characters be more than what you say they are?[9]

Let me repeat those excellent questions: *How do you make room for the people you're writing about to exceed and to trouble the language you use? How do you let your characters be more than what you say they are?*

So, when you write, consider these things. You have a unique testimony to offer from the place where your own combination of body, history, and subjectivity meets the world. You have a right to your own experiences, and to the conclusions about the world you draw from them. You have a right to imagine and write about people different from you (that's the nature of fiction). You have the responsibility to consider that other people's life experiences may have led them to different conclusions about the world, and that the cultures from which they arise may have "subconscious structures" that you may not be able to see or write from if you aren't part of those cultures. You have the responsibility to represent human experiences on the page to the best of your ability, learning about what you don't know and striving for the same humanity and complexity you hope to be granted yourself. You also have the responsibility to consider that your ideas may change (and probably *will* change) as more information arrives, in the form of more life experiences, "mileage," time, and encounters with new people and things. You have the responsibility, as an artist, to experience the work of other artists in other times and places, widening your view of the way humans talk to one another and ourselves about our world and our lives. And for artists, that process of change and discovery is glorious. "Keep your language," said the Brazilian liberation-theology priest Dom Hélder Câmara. "Love its sounds, its modulation, its rhythm. But try to march together with [people] of different languages, remote from your own, who wish like you for a more just and human world."[10]

Writing across Difference: It's for Everyone

Okay, you may be thinking, *but I usually just write about characters like me—do I need to read this chapter?* Even if these issues don't seem relevant now, you *will* find yourself engaging with them if you keep writing and if you try to publish your work.

First, "writing across difference" begins as soon as you pick up a pen—your character *is* a character, after all, and not exactly like you, unless you're trapped in an author-narrator-character merge (see Chapter 5). Secondly, storytelling is about traveling beyond the boundaries of what you already think you know, being curious, taking risks. But it's also about acknowledging a range of possible readers, and their responses, in the characters you bring to the page. If you seek publication, you accept the reality that people of *every* demographic category buy books and magazines, carry library cards, design syllabi, and download audiobooks—because human variation is our world's reality. Fantasy and historical fiction writers will find it impossible to avoid all forms of "crossing" and writing difference (especially since, as in Octavia Butler's magnificent work, they are imagining bodies that may reflect *and* challenge our "normal" ones). Overall, we may all have been ignoring the reality of what it's like to occupy bodies different from our own, even if we're supposed to know better. As the scholar and writer Stephen Kuusisto, who is blind, wrote in 2017:

> [P]rofessors by and large don't view disability as a matter of diversity like race, gender, or sexual orientation, and imagine that it's a rehabilitative issue—a 19th century view to be sure—but one that's widespread. . . . That disability is a matter of culture; that the cripples are among the concert goers, the literate, the citizenry is hard for academics to fully grasp.[11]

Finally, as discussed in my previous chapter, intellectual and artistic freedom are built into writing itself: playing it *too* safe may mean sapping the good kind of risk from your work. Science-fiction author Nisi Shawl felt shocked when a white classmate declared that she would never even try to write a nonwhite protagonist or character. "I think this sort of misguided caution is the source of a lot of sf's monochrome futures," writes Shawl. "You know the ones I mean, where some nameless and never discussed plague has mysteriously killed off everyone with more than a hint of melanin in their skin. I wonder sometimes what kind of career I'd have if I followed suit with tales of stalwart Space Negroes and an unexplained absence of whites."[12] When writers stop "crossing" and "writing the other" in all the ways we do it, literature itself dies. ("Madame Bovary, c'est moi," Gustave Flaubert famously declared.) Yet ignoring some basic questions, or relying on too-arrogant an idea of "artistic freedom," can lead to cringe-inducing work. By discussing these issues, I hope to help you arrive at a responsible artistic position that moves you forward along your own writing path, in curiosity, generosity, and joy.

Writing the Other, or Writing in Color

"Writing the other" has been a term for the artistic practice I'm describing in this chapter: writing a character or protagonist who occupies a different bodily or social position than you do yourself. ("Writing in color," in my chapter's title, may be another way to say it; the "Writing with Color" blog invokes the concept too.) In using this term, I'm following the lead of Nisi Shawl and Cynthia Ward in their book *Writing the Other: A Practical Approach* (2005). But, as you can see, "writing the other" may take two forms:

1) Writing from *inside*: immersing yourself in the perspective of "the other" in order to write *from* that perspective, as narrator or point-of-view character (I will call this *crossing*), and

2) Writing from *outside*: writing *about* a non-point-of-view character who occupies a social position that you (and, perhaps, your narrator or point-of-view character) do not share.

To be sure, these categories aren't neat. Both do involve a type of imaginative travel outside your own experience, which, again, is basic to fiction writing. Yet the degree of travel may feel greater when "crossing" *into* a protagonist's identity than when writing a non-point-of-view character. Crossing requires you to immerse yourself in "reality as your character understands it" and write from *inside* that character's perspective, which in turn requires you to understand that reality well enough to do so believably.

Crossing can be controversial, especially the idea of a majority-population writer crossing into a minority-population perspective. Some might say that only writers from inside a particular group can accurately bear testimony to that group's experience, and that a writer from outside that group risks *cultural appropriation* by trying to cross in. (Appropriators risk seeming to imply, in the words of Ojibwe professor and author Anton Treuer, that they "know better than Natives what it's like to be Native."[13]) They may also be seeming to borrow another culture's stories, touchstones, images, or objects for decorative purposes, which can feel particularly infuriating and insulting—especially since writers of non-dominant cultures can feel connected to their stories, and to how audiences will receive those stories, in particular ways. "I never wanted to write fiction that was rooted in where I came from," writes Thea Lim. "That *where* is overexposed, like a stripped nerve. This is a problem for writers of color—or for anyone who knows there's a narrative attached to their body, a narrative over which they have no control."[14] To have something woven so closely and inescapably to you "borrowed" by someone else can feel as if it busts up into your life, and not in a welcome way.

Others might say that if you don't at least try to write outside yourself in one way or another (even if you aren't writing directly from another socially marked point of view as a protagonist), you're not writing fiction, and you're not stretching yourself as an artist, pushing yourself to learn and connect and try to understand something you didn't before. Even a sketch written in your notebook can help you challenge yourself in a way that's good for your art. Success in "crossing" can depend very much on the writer and the project. Yet art progresses because in every generation artists do things no one before them could have predicted, blending and transforming elements of culture from all over the world in new ways. Monet, Manet, and Stravinsky caused riots. In the twenty-first century, Kehinde Wiley and Kerry James Marshall have transformed painting by applying sumptuous traditional techniques and iconography to a range of Black subjects, including President Obama. Artists doing the hard work of building their craft and bringing it to bear on each new artistic risk—that's what moves art, and society, forward. (And, as James Baldwin notes, "every artist has an effect on every other artist, you know."[15]) Similarly, students Levi Bird and Ian Wreisner sparked constructive conversations with classmates and themselves when they took risks (see Student Craft Studios in Chapter 3 and this chapter). The injunction to "stay in your lane" can kill good books as well as bad ones.

So what does "crossing" (authors writing from the perspective of protagonists who occupy at least one different social category from themselves) look like in published fiction? Taking a quick look at literary fiction of the last few decades, I can make some inevitably limited but interesting speculations.

- *Racial/cultural identity* and *sexual orientation* seem to be lines authors cross the *least* when writing their narrators or point-of-view characters—but it does happen.

- Crossing lines of *gender* and historical, cultural, or alternate-world *place and time* seems to be *more* common.

- *Point of view* (first, second, third, or even multiple perspectives) seems closely connected to how and where writers "cross," or not. As discussed in Chapter 5, your choice of point of view and verb tense can enable particular kinds of access to, and comfort with, your representation of characters' consciousness on the page.

  - If the protagonist is similar to the author, a first-person "I" might reflect that "insider status" and an authority that comes from it. (A compelling first-person voice, like the young queer narrator of Sebastian Barry's *Days Without End*, can carry both author *and* reader through a "crossing," which Barry constructs in multiple ways.)
  - Second-person points of view (see p. 100) enable a certain confessional yet self-protective quality that can help a writer draw a specific yet inclusive line around themselves *and* readers, no matter who their readers are.
  - If the author is crossing boundaries of difference, a third-person point of view might reflect (and support) a bit of distance while still allowing the author to cross. Marlon James and Colson Whitehead, Black men, write third-person Black female protagonists in *The Book of Night Women* (James) and *The Intuitionist, John Henry Days*, and *The Underground Railroad* (Whitehead).
  - Multiple narrative perspectives can help represent a community in space and time, as in Toni Morrison's *Beloved* (1987), Jordy Rosenberg's *Confessions of the Fox* (2018), and Tommy Orange's *There There* (2018; see anthology), where narrative expansiveness echoes the forms of diaspora or a continuity of identity through time.

Of course, writers do choose point-of-view perspectives for a variety of reasons, and authors can draw successfully on a variety of life experiences shared across boundaries of race, gender, or other categories to "cross" in different ways. Read widely and you'll see!

Figure 1 is a brief chart designed to show you that "crossing" *does* happen, and it *can* be done successfully, depending on choices the author makes. The "x" marks categories the author "crosses" in writing a protagonist, determined by what I know of the author's own biography. If there's no X in a box, the author and protagonist share those traits, as far as I can tell (Figure 1).

But Who Are You?

Thinking about crossing and writing diverse characters starts with thinking about your own position. In *Writing the Other*, Nisi Shawl and Cynthia Ward introduce the idea of *the unmarked state*—the default character template within our heads that many of

Title, author, POV (1st, 2nd, 3rd person)	Gender	Sexual orientation	Time period/alternate world	Race/culture	Ability	Nationality	Age (more than 20 years)
Valerie Martin, Property (1st)			X				X
Sebastian Barry, Days Without End (1st)		X	X			X	X
Jonathan Lethem, Motherless Brooklyn (1st)			X		X		
Kazuo Ishiguro, The Remains of the Day (1st)			X	X		X	X
Cristina Henriquez, The Book of Unknown Americans (1st)							X
Francibe Prose, Lovers at the Chameleon Club, 1932 (3rd)		X	X			X	
Madison Smart Bell, All Souls Rising trilogy; (3rd)			X	X		X	
John Wray, Lowboy (3rd)					X		X
Colm Toibin, Brooklyn (3rd)	X		X			X	X
Rebecca Makkai, The Great Believers (3rd)	X	X	X				
Colson Whitehead, The Underground Railroad (3rd)	X		X				X

Figure 1.

us may fall back on when deciding who is "normal" and who is "other" in our fictional worlds and in life. "A character in the unmarked state has a certain transparency," they write, "he (and we use the pronoun advisedly) allows readers to read the action of the story without coloring it with his particularity."[16] In American society, especially among white Americans, the "unmarked state," the person we might imagine (often unconsciously) when we are asked to imagine an "average person," may be white, middle-to-upper-middle-class, heterosexual, non-disabled, and male. There's nothing inherently wrong with being any of these things. But it is a problem to view other characters (and readers) primarily as *deviations from this norm* rather than as *individuals in their own right*. In the words of anthropologist Wade Davis, "The world in which you were born is just one model of reality. Other cultures are not failed attempts at being you; they are unique manifestations of the human spirit." As professor and writer Jan Grue, who uses a wheelchair, writes, "At some point or another I stopped thinking about myself as someone who needed repairing."[17] And as disability scholar Jonathan Sterne muses, "Nothing works exactly like it is supposed to. If almost everyone and everything has some degree of impairment (though not in the same way), then impairment is a quality of experience. Impairment is always already there."[18] So who, exactly, is even "normal?" Much less "unmarked?"

Getting past the unmarked state starts with the general question: What haven't you been seeing about others' experience, and how might you come to see it more clearly? Learning and thinking into those experiences can help you achieve the goal of any fiction writer: creating a character who comes to life on the page as an *individual* (including complex and unlikeable traits), not as a stereotype, since successfully imagining and artistically rendering the experiences of people different from ourselves is basic to our work. "A writer's work is impossible if he or she cannot conjure up the lives of others," writes Viet Thanh Nguyen, "and only through such acts of memory, imagination, and empathy can we grow our capacity to feel for others."[19]

Stereotypes: Beyond the Magical Negro, Tiny Tim, and the Gay Best Friend

So now you're ready to move one step closer to the page, but beware—a vast unconscious inheritance of *stereotypes* may await. I define stereotypes as *received images of a social position that remove full humanity and agency from the person occupying it*. Stereotypes caricature people as one-dimensional heroes, villains, victims, buffoons, or saints, often locked in a particular historical stance or standard narrative arc. They can have an overtly prejudiced edge, like the "miserly Jew" (Fagin of Dickens's *Oliver Twist* or Shylock of Shakespeare's *The Merchant of Venice*), the "sexy Latina" (Carmen Miranda with her fruit-basket headdress and halter top), or the "real Indian" frozen in the nineteenth-century West. They may be associated with ethnic slurs. Crucially, stereotypes may exist *in spite of, or as signs of, the "good intentions"* of people using them, particularly because of a lurking *sentimentality*. Here are a few common ones.

Case Study 1: The "Magical Negro." This is a stereotypical image of a nonwhite person, often socially or economically subordinate to a white person, who offers moral truisms (and sometimes supernatural assistance) that "enlighten" or serve the white person while remaining, apparently cheerfully, in their subordinate position, which the text (and the author) leave unquestioned. One version of the "magical negro"—created with strong antislavery intentions, radically progressive in its own time, and, according to President Lincoln's wry remark, helping to spark the Civil War—is the martyred Uncle Tom in Harriet Beecher Stowe's *Uncle Tom's Cabin* (1852). "The magical negro" is satirized by comedy duo Keegan-Michael Key and Jordan Peele in their sketch "Magical Negro Fight" (2012) and, at greater (and more horrifying) length in Jordan Peele's first feature film, *Get Out* (2017).[20] The Magical Negro may not be of African descent; other "minorities" are often drafted into "magical Negro"-style positions too. People occupying economically subordinate positions sometimes get cast as "magical Negro"-style dispensers of wisdom: "Investment Banker Learns From Homeless Guy to Love Life, While Homeless Guy Remains Homeless" could be the headline of many a well-meaning student story. The satirical newspaper *The Onion* lampoons this kind of thing in one of its putative "advice columns" called "Ask an Elderly Black Woman as Depicted By a Sophomore Creative Writing Major."[21]

Closely connected to the "magical negro" is "the white savior," who achieves heroic status by, in part, using the "magical negro" as a stepping stone to a position of moral superiority. If you find yourself writing a perfect white character who receives the uncritical adoration of one-dimensional minority characters while the systems keeping them subordinate to the "savior" remain unquestioned (again, *by text* or *author*), then, perhaps, you have a white savior on your hands.

Case Study 2: The "Disabled Saint." Tiny Tim of Charles Dickens's *A Christmas Carol* (1843) is the poster child—pun intended—for this stereotype. He combines three of Victorian England's most beloved stereotypes: the grateful, humble poor; the uncomplaining, saintly person with a disability; and the sweet, inspiring child. Interestingly, all three of these stereotypes have a Magical-Negro-like function of "inspiring" those in more powerful positions without actually challenging entrenched social roles and structures. The "saint" never gets angry and never rebels, invalidating anger (among other feelings) among members of that community[22] and enabling "normal" readers to feel good about their own pity for him without taking any action *beyond* pity. Dickens is a great writer, and was a tireless progressive activist in his own time, but Tim never complains about his disability or his poverty, as well-off Victorians liked to believe (falsely) that the poor never did. (Look at histories of Victorian activism, such as feminist Josephine Butler's anti-prostitution and anti-human-trafficking campaigns, and studies such as Henry Mayhew's *London Labour and the London Poor*, first serialized in the 1840s, to see why that belief *was* false.)

Sentimentality is the real driver of this stereotype, and it's a pernicious flaw in writing about those considered vulnerable by those who consider themselves less so. The idea is found as far back as eighteenth-century aesthetic philosophy (see Edmund Burke's *A*

Philosophical Enquiry into the Origin of Our Ideas of the Sublime and Beautiful, 1757): contemplating the small, "weak" thing makes those who are "strong" feel secure in our own strength while also enjoying the virtuous thrill of our own ability to feel pity. But when it never leads to any action on behalf of or agency for the vulnerable being—indeed, when it relies on and reinforces our own "superiority"—that pity is really just emotional self-indulgence, a cheesy sentimentality also called *kitsch*. As Czech novelist Milan Kundera wrote in *The Unbearable Lightness of Being* (1984), "Kitsch causes two tears to flow in quick succession. The first tear says: How nice to see children running on the grass! The second tear says: How nice to be moved, together with all mankind, by children running on the grass! It is the second tear that makes kitsch kitsch."[23] James Baldwin goes further in his 1949 essay "Everybody's Protest Novel": "Sentimentality, the ostentatious parading of excessive and spurious emotion, is the mask of dishonesty, the inability to feel; the wet eyes of the sentimentalist betray his aversion to experience, his fear of life, his arid heart; and it is always, therefore, the signal of secret and violent inhumanity, the mask of cruelty."[24] (*Uncle Tom's Cabin* is his target here, by the way.)

To be clear, empathy isn't always a bad thing, although, as Leslie Jamison writes, it *is* "precariously perched between gift and invasion."[25] But sentimentalizing people in positions labeled "vulnerable" isn't really empathy—it's about enjoying your own desire, from your position of "superiority," to feel sorry for them. (This is why Kyla, a blind student I know, calls such writing "inspiration porn.") Thus, people get cast in what Jan Grue calls "a narrative that has already been written, and that is told by others."[26] Furthermore, sentimentalizing others means labeling them as "innocent" or "simple" relative to yourself, and inviting readers (assumed to be "normal people like you") to join you in standing apart from "them," looking on from a distance, rather than to enter reality as they understand it. Therefore, it denies these characters humanity and agency. In the words of philosopher Avishai Margalit, "Sentimentality is a double sin: it detracts from human dignity by presenting humans as basically victims, and it distorts by making them always appear innocent."[27]

Accordingly, sentimentality is a common thread in stereotypes of people our society, for various reasons, considers as *vulnerable deviations from an unquestioned ability- and agency-dependent norm* (with which we may unconsciously identify ourselves) rather than as *individuals in their own right*. Children, the elderly, and people with disabilities are frequent targets of this misperception. But Nicola Griffith's novel *So Lucky* (2018), based in part on her own experiences with multiple sclerosis, shows how "saintliness" denies a range of emotion, experience, and sexuality (in a word, *humanity*) to a person living with a disability. Poet and activist Jillian Weise, who wears a computerized artificial leg, identifies as a "cyborg" and believes people may resist this identification "because it connotes something 'hot, cool, and advanced in a way that upsets our notions about what an amputee woman is.'"[28]

Consider, too, how an elderly person's emotions—including sexuality, loneliness, and anger—get more, not less, complex with time. Now consider how much those people know, the depth and range of the insights and experiences they've accumulated. Yet consider how (unintentionally) stereotyping even a supposedly "positive" word can be.

A *New York Times* headline (October 23, 2018) on former Federal Reserve chair Paul Volcker's memoir read "Paul Volcker, at 91, Sees 'a Hell of a Mess in Every Direction': The former Fed chairman, whose memoir will be published this month, had a feisty take on the state of politics and government during an interview."[29] *Times* commenters pointed out that "feisty" is a patronizing brushoff for the elderly—and as anyone paying attention to the news at that time can testify, "a hell of a mess" wasn't just a cute-grandpa effusion but an accurate description of reality.

Sentimentality is a big danger in writing about children, who may be depicted (like Tiny Tim) as one-dimensionally sweet, cute, and "innocent." There's an important distinction to be made between *childlike* (a desirable clarity and honesty signaled by Picasso's happy declaration at age seventy, "At last! I can paint like a child!") and *childish* (reductive sentimentality based on what adults think, usually falsely, that children think). Artist and bookseller Tamsin Rosewell has written, "It isn't cheery, saccharine hope that children necessarily look for, it is the recognition of their dark and burning sense of injustice . . . that desperate childhood anger of not being listened to by authority, or of adults not seeing the full picture, when they—the children—can see the way things really are."[30] Children's joys and angers and fears are real and often overwhelming in their immediacy, since children lack the life experience to know that "it's not *always* going to feel this way." Therefore, writing a successful child can depend on reproducing child-logic, including clues that will tip off adult readers to what's happening (the child can report, but not always understand), and rooting the child's perspective in their major means of knowledge, the senses and primary experience (see Chapter 7 and stories such as Jane McClure's "The Green Heart" [anthology], James Joyce's "Araby" [Chapter 1 Craft Studio], and Edward P. Jones's "The First Day"). Both these things, in turn, rely on your ability to immerse yourself in, and take seriously, reality as that child understands and experiences it—*not* just to regard your child character as vulnerable from a kitsch-producing standpoint of imagined superiority and stand to the side, smiling fondly, inviting your readers to join you in contemplating—rather than imaginatively *becoming*—the character.

Case Study 3: The Gay Best Friend. Campy, chatty, endless fount of *bons mots* and interior design wisdom, defined by his sexuality yet, curiously, never seeming to *have* any sex—welcome to the world of the gay best friend. Stanford on "Sex and the City," Jack on "Will and Grace," the wonderful Rupert Everett in the dreadful movie *My Best Friend's Wedding*: typically, film and television offer many examples, although with better recent offerings (such as "Pose") the GBF may be less common now. An ostensibly benevolent stereotype is still a stereotype, because it still reduces or denies the individuality and complexity of people who fit into a demographic category. While lesbians are often stereotyped as well, the gay best friend is usually male and found most often in the company of another stereotyped figure: the single heterosexual woman driven by the desire for romance with a man at any cost, including career, financial security, and self-respect. Perhaps that's what her creators imagine she has in common with her Gay Best Friend. Ugh. Try again.[31]

Writing across the Aisle: The Political Other

As the twenty-first century gets more heartbreakingly acrimonious, writers may enter a new area of difference: politics. You may find yourself writing from the perspective of characters who do, say, or believe things you yourself wouldn't, and doing so may require you to consider the places (however awkward) where you and they overlap. "If only it were all so simple!" wrote Russian dissident Aleksandr Solzhenitsyn in *The Gulag Archipelago* (1973). "If only there were evil people somewhere insidiously committing evil deeds, and it were necessary only to separate them from the rest of us and destroy them. But the line dividing good and evil cuts through the heart of every human being. And who is willing to destroy a piece of his own heart?"

This, I think, is a good insight to bear along with you as you navigate the writing of characters who do or say things you yourself would never support. What gives the murderous white male voice in Eudora Welty's story "Where Is the Voice Coming From?" its power to chill us is, at least in part, the sliver of ice in each of our own hearts, the spectre of hatred that stalks us as people and individuals, the fact that, when it comes to doing and thinking "bad things," none of us is immune. (Maybe that's why the title asks this particular, maybe-unanswerable question.) Magogodi oa Mphela Makhene, a young Black woman who grew up in Johannesburg, has written that her story "The Virus," winner of the 2017 Caine Prize for African Writing, surprised her with the "verkrampte Afrikaner [reactionary white] male voice that belched out to tell the story."[32] Yet growing up amid the legacies of apartheid in her particular place and time gave her familiarity with multiple embodiments of that legacy, including people who might seem, on the surface, to have nothing in common with her at all.

Rendering reality as your protagonist/narrator understands it means that you might need to think through and separate yourself *and* readers from beliefs that your *protagonist or character* holds that *you yourself* do not. Most readers will be able to tell when the *writer*, as opposed to a *character*, is asking us to accept a stereotypical view of the world, and we'll resist accordingly. If your own political opponents are simplistic caricatures in your work—straw men, in the debate-team sense—we won't buy it. Sure, you can write from the perspective of characters whose outlook on the world takes readers to difficult places: consider the highly unreliable first-person narrators of Vladimir Nabokov's novel *Lolita* (1955) or Eudora Welty's story "Where Is the Voice Coming From?" (based on the real-life murder of Medgar Evers in 1963). But you need to offer readers a place to stand apart from biased views when they enter the story, so it's obvious to them that *you, the author,* aren't expecting them to agree with everything the *character* says. (This starts with achieving the author-narrator-character separation described in Chapter 5.) Consider, too, an interesting proposition I've heard: many people don't vote based on *ideas and logic* so much as on *their own experience of the world.* Therefore, to help us see why a character believes some of what he does, show us something of the world as he has experienced it and give him an inner life the reader can recognize—vulnerability, fear, loss, love.

Student Craft Studio: Ian Wreisner, "The New Chicago"

The spring of 2021 was a tumultuous, tense time for my students and me. After the terrifying far-right-driven Capitol insurrection of January 6, the year ground on in struggles with the Covid-19 pandemic and the aftereffects of George Floyd's murder on May 25, 2020, on a Minneapolis sidewalk, a three-hour drive north of our campus. Student Ian Wreisner spoke to these realities in his story—with a twist. A self-described progressive white male from suburban Minneapolis, Ian crafted a protagonist whose outward identity broadly matched his own but whose politics couldn't be more different. Torn between his reactionary father and his progressive high-school friends (all of whom, unlike himself, have moved on from their small town), Richard packs a handgun on an evening excursion into Minneapolis, a city still reeling from the aftereffects of George Floyd's murder and the Covid-19 pandemic.

"The New Chicago"—drawn from a racist snub for Minneapolis—engaged our class in rich, supportive discussions about artistic risks and rewards, particularly the challenge of finding the right psychic distance (see Chapter 5). Ian wanted to separate his own stance from Richard's without caricaturing Richard as a character *or* seeming to promote his views to the reader. Key to this was exploring Richard's vulnerable spot: his unrequited love for his high-school friend Jess. Showing rather than telling (in dialogue and action) also helped, as did some well-deployed humor: "We're across the street from a Whole Foods," Richard's friend tells him, "what do you think is gonna happen to you? It's safe here." As Ian revised this story, he continued to build its strong foundation: a writerly voice that could contain both compassion and understated sarcasm, including a sharp self-satirical eye for "Minnesota nice" and for real-world significance, that feels distinctive, understated, and ready to help Ian build many more stories to come.

From "The New Chicago"

They sat down across from the bar. Hanging just behind the bartender was an American flag, and right next to that was a Pride flag, both displayed with prominence. *Dad would lose his shit*, Richard thought. He felt his own face tense. What would his dad say if he knew he was in a bar like this?

The waitress took their drink orders (piña colada for Nolan, to go with his sweater, Richard guessed), and Jaden took a look around the bar and smiled. "Man, this is a totally different scene than what we had a year ago," she said.

"Yeah, it's great to see so many people again, out and living life. Feels like it all never even happened," Jess added.

Richard spoke up. "It's so great to see places like this are still open after getting torn apart by those thugs. Half expected to see some plywood and graffiti coating this place," he said, with a chuckle. Nobody else returned it.

"Rich," Jaden said, "I was talking about COVID."

The table was silent for a moment. They all stopped and looked at Richard. Before he could think to pick up the pieces he had scattered, the waitress came up to get their meal orders. Conversation was sporadic until the food came. A comment on the game happening on the TV beside them. Someone's jam had just come on over the sound system. Boring catching-up questions. At least when they got their meals there was a reason for them to keep their lips shut and chew.

When most of the food was gone, Richard could see Nolan getting antsy. He kept looking over at Jess like he was trying to ask permission for something. *Total beta move,* Richard thought. She finally gave him a nod and his face erupted in a smile.

"So, guys," Nolan started. This couldn't be good. "You guys know Jess and I have been dating for a while, and since we're both graduating a semester early and all, well . . . We really wanted you guys to be the first to know, but . . .we're getting married!"

Jaden and Alex erupted in screams and laughter, and Jess held out her hand to show a modest gold band with a bright diamond gracing the top of it. Richard saw it and felt his stomach do a double backflip and land on its ass.

"I gotta piss," he said, and nearly knocked over his chair as he made a beeline for the restrooms. He threw open the door and braced himself on the sink. He splashed water in his face, trying to cool what felt like steam coming up from his heart and leaving through his pores. He always knew the day would come, but never quite like this. He thought he'd at least have a chance first.

Ian says: "I was inspired to write this story after a visit to a friend's house in the midst of the Covid pandemic and the weeks just after the death of George Floyd in Minneapolis. We both live around thirty minutes from the Minnesotan metropolis, but couldn't live more different lives: me in my suburb of 60,000+, him in a rural community where you can count the number of neighbors on one hand. The conversations I overheard while there were surreal and challenging, ranging from pushbacks to Covid response and 'the whole mask thing' to claims refuting the existence of police brutality and a lack of empathy for a city and nation in mourning. The conversation shocked me. I wanted to write about the subject as a means of understanding and working through these comments and exploring how outrageous they were to me and the lack of empathy at the root of them.

In my initial drafts and writing for this story, it was without a doubt more aggressive and the level of satire I tried to employ came off as 'trying too hard.' I had taken my original mission of trying to analyze and understand and turned it into criticizing and ridiculing, which was not my intention. Still, I wanted to have a healthy level of satire that showed the nature of the situation we found ourselves in, and since I was a liberal city boy of the Twin Cities, my view was always going to come off as skewed in one way.

That's when two things came my way that helped me get my story back on track: psychic distance and Corey Taylor of Slipknot. Bear with me here.

As I discussed my story with Dr. Weldon, she saw the issue I was having with putting too much of myself in the story and being overbearing with my own views. She talked me through the concept of 'psychic distance,' which has helped other students [see Ch. 5]. It's now helped me as well. No longer was I jumping levels from myself to Richard and back again. I was able to keep it consistent and present Richard as he is seen by himself and his world rather than how I want him to be seen.

I also ran across the book *America 51: A Probe into the Realities That Are Hiding Inside 'The Greatest Country in the World'* by Slipknot frontman and Iowa native Corey Taylor. In it, he uses his experiences of growing up in the rougher parts of Blackhawk County, Iowa to his time meeting every kind of person on the road with Slipknot to show just how out-of-bounds the right *and* the left can be in American politics. He also shows incredible empathy, reminding his readers that every person has a reason for believing what they do; it doesn't mean they're a bad person, they simply have never known the alternative. It's been an incredible building block for where I wanted to take this story, and he's achieved my goal of wanting to present the other side of the aisle to understand and analyze, and hopefully become a better-learned person. Was it a very academic read? I can't say it was. Do I recommend it? Most certainly."

Writing in Color: Starting the Process

In an interview about his 2021 film *The Power of the Dog*, actor Benedict Cumberbatch said, "One of the true joys of this job in general for me is obviously the elements you can experience outside of your lived experience. And everything about this role is as far away from me as possible."[33] Nevertheless, Cumberbatch prepared for the role of hostile, closeted cowboy Phil by immersing himself in it—riding horses, smoking cigarettes, learning to braid lariats, and going for days without a bath. Similarly, although imagining yourself into the lives of people who may be very different from you is basic to writing fiction, some preparation helps. Here are some questions to ask:

- Why do you want to write from this perspective in the first place? Why and how do you feel this story needs to be told, and told by you? "Because diversity sells" is not a good answer. Neither is "because I don't know what else to write about." Do you feel artistically drawn to a vision of a character who feels alive and unique to you, someone whose story you are eager to explore? Are you eager to challenge yourself? Hey, that's awesome. So take the next steps: thinking, investigating, asking. Rebecca Makkai took those steps as she began her novel *The Great Believers* (2018, see this chapter's Craft Studio), set in Chicago during the HIV/AIDS crisis of the 1980s and alternating between the third-person points of view of a gay man and a straight woman. "In order to write this," she says, "I had to satisfactorily answer two questions: Was I reinforcing stereotypes, or combatting them? And was I stealing attention from first-hand narratives, or shedding light on them?"[34]

- Do you have a "message" to convey? If so, then beware—you may be headed for one-dimensional work that will cheat readers, characters, and yourself, since, in Joan Didion's words, "fiction has certain irreducible ambiguities" and "is in most ways hostile to ideology."[35] "[W]hen artists allow ideology to become the work," critic Hilton Als says, "they sell our imagination cheap. They're not letting others have the experience of looking, of alchemy, of invention—they're rendering that unimportant."[36] If your "message" would look good on a billboard, then it's probably too simple a story-engine. Try asking instead, "Do I have an image of a *person* in a *place and time* about whom I'm curious, whose actions and motivations I can explore?" Let curiosity guide you beyond what Chimamanda Ngozi Adichie (see Chapter 5 Craft Studio) has called "the danger of a single story."

- What kinds of "crossing" or "writing the other" feel within your reach? While it's good to try new things and push yourself as an artist, you may find you have territories in which you're more comfortable traveling than you are in others, and that's okay. "Writing the other" that works feels driven by understanding, respect, and generosity. To get to this place, try what the novelist Claire Lombardo, author of *The Most Fun We Ever Had* (2019), refers to as doing your "emotional homework": reflecting on, researching, and fully imagining your characters' lives. "Having outside readers can show you how empathetically you're rendering your characters," Lombardo says. "You have to have love for your characters and give them their due. And it was important for me to have readers who were parents, since I don't have kids. I had to remind myself I'm allowed to write about things I don't know, like a forty-year marriage. I just had to do my emotional homework."[37]

- Have you done your research? This question is *crucial*. Are you rooting yourself in accurate, multidimensional sources, including history, art, current conversations, real people's experiences (across a range of times and places), and good writing?

  - In her article "How to Write Across Difference," novelist Rebecca Makkai describes the process of research that helped her build *The Great Believers*. "Setting out to write about a real time and a real place, I knew empathy wouldn't be enough," she writes. "I couldn't good-person myself into good writing." So, "[i]n addition to hours of in-person interviews, I read every back issue of Chicago's LGBTQ weekly *Windy City Times* from 1985 to 1992. I went to surviving gay bars from the era (okay, this wasn't a hardship), I watched footage of ACT UP protests, I walked the city carrying business maps from 30 years ago. Along the way, I encountered my own ignorance."[38] She dispelled this "ignorance" further by interviewing people with personal experience of the era: "In an early draft of my third chapter," she writes, "my main character walks down the street in 1985 searching for his friends, looking into the window of every gay bar he passes. If you're not already laughing, let me explain: The windows would have been blackened, or covered with heavy curtains. This wasn't information I found in a book. I learned it sitting across from a friend in

Dunkin Donuts, listening to his memories of the bar scene."* Makkai also took her laptop to the hospital wards in which AIDS patients were treated to capture details of the setting, which "helped [her] write with more nuance."[39]

— In the absence of meaningful experience with people of different identities, do you turn immediately to movies? If so, beware—movies and TV are *highly* susceptible to the kind of flattening and stereotyping you're trying to avoid. "Above all, don't rely on representations of minorities gleaned from popular culture," advises Nisi Shawl. "They're as true to life as Donna Reed's pearl-laden floor-waxing outfits."[40] By contrast, reading literature from that group—not only within but across genre lines, including history as well as fiction—gives you a rich sense of the "subconscious structures," in my former student Siyabonga's words, of lives and languages.

- Are you imagining your potential readership as *including* readers from the groups you're writing about? Are people from those groups a presence in your life *and* your imagination *as* people? Young-adult fantasy writer Justina Ireland spoke about this in a roundtable. "If you think your audience is nothing but white people," she says, "then you have no business writing a character of color. Because that tells me you don't know any people of color, and so you're already in the wrong park."[41]

- Is there more than one person of a "diverse" demographic category in your story? If not, does that single person conform to a stereotype of that group? In her novel *The Other Black Girl* (2021), Zakiya Dalila Harris satirizes a white male author whose book includes only one nonwhite character: a Black female opioid addict named Shartricia Daniels, "flatter than the pages she appeared on," with a voice "which read as a cross between that of a freed slave and a Tyler Perry character down on her luck."[42]

- Are you letting your characters be more than the broad outlines of their demographic's experience or standard narratives associated with it—particularly its pain? Are you writing their joy? Student Bunmi Omisore, quoted in a profile of young-adult novelist Jason Reynolds, said, "You need stories to not only prove to Black readers that they have an identity outside of Blackness but to prove that to white readers. Because a lot of my white teachers and classmates, their perception of the Black experience is so warped, because all they come into contact with are books of struggle and pain."[43] The "Writing with Color" blog identifies this trope about Black characters by asking, with plaintive sarcasm, "Why we always gotta be slaves?"[44] A user adds, "What about Black people during the Middle Ages, or during the time of Shakespeare?[45] . . . [C]an't we

---

*The sentence as it appears in the final book is, "He looked into each bar he passed—opening the door when the windows were mirrored or painted black—scanning for Charlie, for Fiona, for any of them" (Makkai, *The Great Believers*, 20).

just have period dramas about romance, class differences, daily life the way the white people do?"[46] (Shonda Rhimes's Netflix series *Bridgerton* may be, in part, a response to this.[47]) Writer and editor David Treuer, of Ojibwe descent, is similarly focused on representing Native life as what he calls, in his book *The Heartbeat of Wounded Knee: Native America from 1890 to the Present,* "something much more, much greater and grander, than a catalog of pain."[48] In an interview, he says, "I absolutely see my work as a call to liberate Native literature—and self-regard and even our collective identity—from overreliance on tragic narratives. Tragedy is *the* dominant narrative that has been used to imagine Native realities. And frankly the narrative of loss—the idea that we as Native people have a great future *behind* us—participates in our continued erasure. I'm not here for that."[49]

- Are you respecting difference as part of the texture of a world that may *not* always operate on the terms you know, and that has realities to which you need to be responsible? This may be particularly important when using actual historical or archival material or writing about real historical figures (see Chapter 6).

  - Alice Jolly's *Mary Ann Sate, Imbecile* (2019) is an imagined retelling of the life story of a woman described only as "Mary Ann Sate, Imbecile" in an actual nineteenth-century British historical record—that one word, next to her name, is all Jolly knew of her.[50] "Imbecile"—the deliberately dated and shocking word—challenges the writer and reader to look below and through it for the real person. But it also reminds us that, in E. P. Hartley's famous words, "the past is a foreign country and they do things differently there." Engaging this difference in a way that respects it *and* renders the character multidimensionally is an important challenge.
  - Poets Tracy K. Smith and Jay Bernard have spoken about building poems around actual voices—in Bernard's case, voices from the 2017 Grenfell Tower fire in London, and in Smith's case from archives of Black Civil War soldiers' letters.[51] Bernard said, "I'm not trying to speak on behalf of or for these people I came across in the archives, but kind of through and with and at the same time as . . . I think it's an exercise in humanity . . . it feeds the soul in a particular way." Smith, the former Poet Laureate of the United States, agreed: "History is still breathing," she said, "and it's still generating something urgent we can choose to listen to. . . . Poetry is one of those things that can restore us to our large, original selves," not just the identities we're born with or the commercial values of the society around us. Both these poets have thought deeply about their craft and have great experience with it, which increases their ability to write these other lives with sensitivity and nuance, "enlarging the selves" of all who read their work.

- Are you borrowing someone else's culture to have "something"/"something 'real'" to write about? (This is connected to the question of violence as authenticity in Chapter 6.) This is complicated, and as a writer of historical fiction, I get that. To one extent, history (and current events) belong to all of us. To another extent, historical and cultural pain are real. And if you aren't of the groups predominately subjected to them, you may not fully realize the ways these kinds of pain are borne on wavelengths you usually don't see. Your imagination may be genuinely stirred by something you learn from outside your own place and time. That's wonderful! Now deepen that first enthusiasm with meaningful research and reading.

- Plainly put: have you enough fiction-writing competency to build the supporting structures of a complex technical choice like "crossing" *around* that choice? Simplistically appropriative *and* sloppy, error-filled writing adds insult to injury. As Rebecca Makkai points out, good writing is something you *can* control.

  - The more complex your writing project is, the more your existing experience will help. In 2019, the Irish novelist Edna O'Brien, then aged eighty-eight, released her nineteenth novel, *Girl*, the narrator of which is modeled on one of the young Nigerian women kidnapped and raped by the terrorist group Boko Haram in 2014.[52] "It has been suggested to me," O'Brien wrote, "that as an outsider I am not eligible to write this story. I do not subscribe to that devious form of censorship. Theme and territory belong to all who aspire to tell it and the only criteria is the gravity in the telling. I was haunted by the plight of girls in north-east Nigeria, Chibok and others, thrust into servitude, their childhoods stolen, the leeching of hope day by day. I marvel at their magnificent fortitude. The world is crying out for such stories to be told and I intend to explore them while there is a writing bone left in my body."[53] Edna O'Brien did tremendous research for this book, including two trips to Nigeria, sixteen boxes of material, and interviews with "doctors, aid workers, a trauma specialist and local journalists," as well as the girls who survived the kidnappings.[54] Her own long history as a woman artist standing up against traditional patriarchal repressions (like those of her Irish Catholic 1950s girlhood)[55] gave me, as one of her longtime readers, confidence that she'd be able to write into emotional subtexts. Most of all, Edna O'Brien knows how to create complex and believable characters on the page.

- Do you have readers who know more about these experiences than you who might be willing to read your work and give you feedback? Many publishers employ "diversity readers" or "sensitivity readers," for this purpose. However, people might be tired of being called on as "expert witnesses." Professor Alisha Gaines tells how her seventh-grade teacher asked her, thirteen years old and the only African American student in class, to "explain to my classmates what slavery was really like."[56] Yet if you have friends from these groups who might be willing to read your work, consider asking them. "If you're thinking of approaching someone who's more an acquaintance than a friend," advises Nisi Shawl, "offer to buy them lunch, or dinner, and make the interaction a formal interview. This is what you'd do with anyone else you wanted to pump for valuable data. Cultural background is data. If you want it, and you don't have it, it's valuable; treat it that way."[57] This applies, also, to compensating any "sensitivity readers" for their work. (You can see shoutouts to "sensitivity readers" in the ending credits of N. K. Jemisin's *The City We Became*, for example.) Rebecca Makkai observes usefully, "I'd argue that if you have to hire a stranger, you should ask yourself why you don't have more friends like the people you're writing about."[58]

Putting It into Practice: Some Techniques for "Writing the Other"

Writing almost always starts with imagining from within *reality as the character understands it*. Then comes a range of ways to handle this on the page, at the level of the sentence.

Consider how learning about others' difference often arises in our daily lives: when we have reason to notice or become aware of it, like when we see someone for the first time. Try letting difference come up in your story on an "as-needed basis" for the reader in a way that feels natural to your particular story's world. Reading (including the stories in this anthology) will show you a range of ways to represent bodies and voices.

We build culturally inflected pictures of characters in our mind with several kinds of information:

- What we are directly told: this character has brown skin, this character's wife is texting her.
- The presence of culturally specific objects (like the drum in Tommy Orange's *There There* [anthology]).
- What the characters call themselves, from within that group: Indian, Nuyorican, redneck.
- How their voices sound—speech patterns, grammar, bits of other languages than English—although dialect can be a danger. (See later.)
- Names: Sunita, Nguyen, Maribel, Isaiah, Juan, Ricardo, Aislin, Mohammed, Kjerstin.
- What and who the characters pay attention to, and in what level of detail, including things other characters or readers might not.
- How others react to them in their world (what they overhear, what others say and do, where they do/n't go).
- What character Y sees when character Z appears for the first time.
- How they describe themselves, to others or us. Beware, though, this can feel quite stagy unless you are Hilary Mantel placing the Irish Giant on a platform, describing himself humorously and eloquently to a spellbound London audience (in *The Giant, O'Brien*).

- What they say, and whether or not the author expects us to agree with it (see *psychic distance* in Chapter 5). The grandmother in Flannery O'Connor's "A Good Man Is Hard to Find" is one of a long line of deluded white folks who clings to her delusion of superiority until, literally, the last minute of her life. O'Connor's irony, which burns like dry ice, helps us understand *the author herself* doesn't share that delusion.

- How characters operate in their own worlds, within "the norm" as *they* understand it. In Chinua Achebe's 1958 novel *Things Fall Apart*, for instance, the characters' names, actions, and language place them firmly in an Igbo world; so does Chimamanda Ngozi Adichie's "The American Embassy" (Chapter 5 Craft Studio) offering non-Nigerian readers a subtle but important defamiliarization. Experiencing "normal" from inside someone *else's* "normal" is an experience that's always waiting for you, inside every book. (Reading is amazing, isn't it?!)

Here are some examples of ways writers have successfully marked characters by race, sexuality, embodiment, and culture directly *and* by building a world around them that lets us infer their identity: gestures and observed details, as well as others' reactions to a character, are very powerful. We come to know the person through what they see and how they move in their world at a time their identity would be noticed—not through a label—in a way that makes them feel truer to life.

Surroundings (Physical and/or Social)

Colson Whitehead's first novel, *The Intuitionist* (2000), is set in a film-noirish alternate mid-twentieth-century Manhattan, where two schools of elevator inspectors, the Empiricists and the Intuitionists, are competing for dominance in a skyward-growing city, and a Black female elevator inspector, Lila Mae Watson (an Intuitionist), is framed for a crime she didn't commit. In the novel's early pages, Whitehead establishes Empiricists as the good-ol'-boys and the Intuitionists as the "others" in his world. Lila Mae's co-worker, "Big Billy Porter . . . one of the Old Dogs, and proud of it . . . regal[es] the boys about the glory days of the Guild, before. While his comments are never specific, it is clear to everyone just what and who Big Billy is referring to in his croaking, muddy voice." "Before" means before Black elevator inspectors, like Lila Mae, joined the Guild. In contrast to the regulation haircuts of the men, "Lila Mae's hair parts in the middle and cups her round face like a thousand hungry fingers." When Lila Mae arrives at the building due for inspection, the superintendent's "lips arch up toward his nose and Lila Mae understands that he's never seen an elevator inspector like her before." He asks her, "How come Jimmy didn't come this time? Jimmy's good people." Direct racial confirmation doesn't arrive until page 8 ("tiny pricks of blood speckle [the superintendent's] pink cheeks") when Lila Mae writes him up:

The super grins. "If that's the game you want to play," he says. "I guess you got me on the ropes." There are three twenty-dollar bills in his oily palm. He leans over to

Lila Mae and places the money in her breast pocket. Pats it down. "I haven't ever seen a woman elevator inspector before, let alone a colored one, but I guess they teach you all the same tricks."

The small moment deflates and shocks readers who have been getting to know Lila Mae from inside her own subjectivity—illustrating, unfussily but pointedly, how a Black woman is treated as less than she knows herself to be.

Heightened Observations (Pointing to Influence of Character's Identity on Way of Seeing)

The repeated phrase "Maybe it started . . ." propels the opening of Andre Aciman's novel *Call Me By Your Name* (2007), narrated by a seventeen-year-old boy, Elio, who falls in love with Oliver, a man almost a decade older. The lyrical particularity with which Elio describes Oliver, before we even know their names, signals a level of sensual interest on which the novel will build:

> Maybe it started soon after his arrival during one of those grinding lunches when he sat next to me and it finally dawned on me that, despite a light tan acquired during his brief stay in Sicily earlier that summer, the color on the palms of his hands was the same as the pale, soft skin of his soles, of his throat, of the bottom of his forearms, which hadn't really been exposed to much sun. Almost a light pink, as glistening and smooth as the underside of a lizard's belly. Private, chaste, unfledged, like a blush on an athlete's face or an instance of dawn on a stormy night. It told me things about him I never knew to ask.[59]

Part of "reality as Elio understands it" is his sensual awareness of Oliver, which the heightened sensory detail of the prose lets us experience as well. (As seen in our discussion of James Joyce's "Araby" in Chapter 1's Craft Studio, emotion heightens what we notice and remember.)

"What a Camera Could Record"

Screenwriter David Mamet has said that writing only "what a camera could record"—visual detail, action, and speech—is a great way to deflate fake drama in your work. In *The Giant, O'Brien* (1998), Hilary Mantel marks both pride and starvation—selfhood and agency as well as pregnancy and physical debility—in the body of a young woman the Giant encounters on the road. Notice that this description shows us the woman through the Giant's eyes as well as with the relative objectivity of what a camera could record:

> A woman appeared at the door of one of the cabins. She began to step towards them, skirting the puddles, though her legs and feet were bare and muddy already.

The Giant saw her large grey eyes, mild and calm as a lake in August: the fine carving of her lips, the arch of her instep, the freedom of her bones at the joint. Her arms were white peeled twigs, their strong muscles wasted; a young child showed, riding high inside her belly like a bunched fist.[60]

Notice that the details give us all the information we need to realize she is in danger of starving but still retains some pride and dignity. (Although her feet are already dirty, she still avoids the puddles, and her eyes are "mild and calm.")

Language and Speech

On the first page of her novel *The Book of Unknown Americans* (2014), Cristina Henriquez uses an untranslated bit of language to mark the perspective of a Mexican immigrant, Alma, who whispers to her daughter Maribel, "We're here, hija." She doesn't tell us that "hija" means "daughter" in Spanish—the context makes it clear, and even more, in this context the character would not be translating the word to herself or her child. We can see, too, that the language represents a comforting trace of home and reminder of family bonds in this new place. Chimamanda Adichie's "The American Embassy" (see Chapter 5 Craft Studio) uses untranslated Nigerian pidgin ("*abi*," or "am I right?") to the same effect.

While cringe-inducing dialect, á la nineteenth-century American novels at their worst, is a danger to avoid, you can represent speech on the page with small, careful alterations. Just a little bit goes a *long* way, but that little bit can unlock a character and show your knowledge of her in her world. Consider the Irish speech in James Joyce's "Araby" (see Chapter 1 Craft Studio), "my heart misgave me," and "it's well for you." The murderous Misfit of Flannery O'Connor's chilling classic "A Good Man Is Hard to Find" says (in a rural Georgia voice) "thown" for "thrown" (no, it's not a typo!) Ron A. Austin's Black American men in "Muscled Clean Out the Dirt" (anthology) say, "y'all don't listen no way" and are warned, in turn, not to "be on no bullshit." Word order, carefully chosen and infrequent misspelling, general rhythms and cadence—all these things can render speech on the page. In the Upper Midwest, I hear people refer to expensive things as "spendy" and qualify their remarks with "All's I'm saying is . . ." (A friendly Minnesotan, charmed by your outfit or hairstyle, may exclaim, "Oh, for cute!") Expository dialogue is particularly important to avoid here, since it signals the presence of an anxious outsider writer. "Would you like a *bao*, the traditional steamed bun of Chinese and Taiwanese culture?" Ouch.

Looking at the examples above, you can see a couple of techniques to try:

- Call upon screenwriter David Mamet's advice to "write what a camera could record," erring on the side of neutral, non-editorial visual descriptions of what another character can see (actions, skin color, hair) and giving us the information we need to build the picture of that character for ourselves when it becomes relevant. Think "light brown, freckled skin," "long gray dreadlocks," "pale red hair and blue eyes." The "Writing with Color" blog has an interesting section on skin color.

- Metaphors and similes may reveal unconscious biases, especially when those descriptions aren't part of conscious metaphorical schemes. A biracial student in one of my own creative writing classes once advised her classmates, very usefully, not to describe people of color in terms of food: cinnamon, mocha, chocolate, caramel. A white student once observed, also usefully, that in makeup ads and in fiction, whiter skin tends to be rendered in terms of delicate, expensive things—"porcelain"—while darker skin tends to be rendered in terms of less expensive things, like wood. These are biases worth noting and working against.

- Consider your choice of point of view, the intimacy or distance it allows, and what feels comfortable and appropriate for you and your relationship to your character. Even though first-person point of view is not inevitably the most intimate or third person the most distant, as discussed in Chapter 5, the point of view you choose will act as subtext for your rendering of reality as your character understands it.

Although the conversations around "writing in color" are ongoing and ever-changing, I do believe that writing beyond the boundaries of our own personal experience and identity is possible, important, and valuable—and, as my student Sea says, "inspires more to try!" Your testimony, well-crafted, can help create a space for others to offer theirs. One artist being honest and free, in the best ways, expands the opportunity for artists everywhere. "I began to write," Jan Grue says in his memoir, "because I needed a different language than the one I was offered."[61] Cyborg Jillian Weise advises:

> To any writer with a disability, I say: Write whatever you want. The movie theater is full but there's no movie. If you want to write the screenplay, write it. If you want to write the Great American Novel, write it. If you want to write a sonnet about the weather, write it. We are the last inclusion, and we are not obliged to follow the rules. Break them. Break type.[62]

In his brilliant essay "The Master's Tools," Jesse McCarthy tells the story of Juan de Pareja (c. 1606–70), the "enslaved African assistant" of Spanish painter Diego Velasquez, who is "quite likely the earliest black painter whose works still survive."[63] Trained in traditional "Old Master" techniques, McCarthy argues, Pareja nevertheless brings a detectable perspective of his own to his work. The essay and McCarthy's thoughtful interview on the *London Review of Books* podcast (well worth seeking out[64]) make the point that artists from all walks of life spot, pick up, blend, adapt, twist, repurpose, absorb, and represent (re-present) anything around them, bringing their own perspective to whatever they render and reenvision. "[T]he hand of the slave who wields the master's tools," McCarthy writes, "inevitably transforms them."[65] Cultures, and artists, *blend*—and travel—across boundaries put in front of them, or around them. That's just what cultures, and artists, do.

So, where can we go from here? We can all buy and teach and read work by a range of writers: the publishing industry, like any industry, recognizes dollars as a person's ultimate vote, and a writer's sales records can increase the industry's willingness (at least in theory) to increase other writers' access to it (see Chapter 8). Consider the voices and stories you *do* have to offer, and how you might take those risks with responsibility and hope to connect with people you might never meet. Remember the words of William Faulkner in his Nobel Prize address, suggesting that what will survive of the human race is our "puny inexhaustible voice, still talking." That voice, our art, is the thing that lasts, keeping us and our stories alive in times and places and people we will never see. Unless we take the risk to make the thing that obsesses us with its mystery, energy, and beauty, we'll never join in. We add our voice to that choir, and we try to do the right thing. We move our art forward as best we can, and, in doing so, little by little, we move the world.

Craft Studio: Rebecca Makkai, Chapter 1 of *The Great Believers* (2018)

Having read Rebecca Makkai's advice on researching and writing across social and demographic difference, here you can see how her own research, revision, and imagination shaped the first chapter of her award-winning novel *The Great Believers* (2018). Set in Chicago (Makkai's hometown), *The Great Believers* traces Yale Tishman and his lovers and friends through more than thirty years, from 1985, the early years of the AIDS pandemic, to 2015. I finished this book with a lump in my throat and deep admiration for Makkai's work in bringing to life a social reality of a time I lived through (I was eleven years old in 1985), but feel, now, as if I'm seeing for the first time.

Even in this excerpt, *The Great Believers* demonstrates some good techniques of scene-setting and character building. In her first chapter, Makkai subtly establishes her characters' personalities and the novel's social world (return to this chapter when you are reading in Chapter 7 about how to write longer fictional forms!). See how she's setting up threads to play out in what Colson Whitehead (Chapter 7) calls "novel time?" The mysterious aunt, Charlie's jealousy, Yale's job as a development director for an art gallery, his friendship with Fiona, the aftereffects of her charismatic brother Nico's death, Richard's photography—all will play out in the years up to and including 2015, the second layer of the novel's time frame. Larger social contexts (Ronald Reagan's reelection, the deepening shadow of AIDS, the prejudice encountered by Terrence at Nico's funeral) are interleaved subtly with backstory of families and friendships.

The novel keeps expanding as you read it, into the art world of prewar Paris, motherhood and friendship, the ethical conflicts of work and love, and an electric scene of a protest modeled on a real-life Chicago ACT-UP demonstration in 1990.[66] In Virginia Woolf's phrase, Makkai has "a deep cave of knowledge" behind each of her characters. But all this knowledge is worn lightly, and its seeds are planted subtly in the beginning of the book. We meet the members of the cast one by one, with clear visual and psychological pictures of each (Makkai makes this look much easier than it really is) and start the process of investing in them that will carry us all the way through the novel. And believe me—this story *will* carry you.

First Chapter of Rebecca Makkai's The Great Believers *(2018)*

1985

Twenty miles from here, twenty miles north, the funeral mass was starting. Yale checked his watch as they walked up Belden. He said to Charlie, "How empty do you think that church is?"

Charlie said, "Let's not care."

The closer they got to Richard's house, the more friends they spotted heading the same way. Some were dressed nicely, as if this were the funeral itself; others wore jeans, leather jackets.

It must only be relatives up at the church, the parents' friends, the priest. If there were sandwiches laid out in some reception room, most were going to waste.

Yale found the bulletin from last night's vigil in his pocket and folded it into something resembling the cootie catchers his childhood friends used to make on buses—the ones that told your fortune ("Famous!" or "Murdered!") when you opened a flap. This one had no flaps, but each quadrant bore words, some upside down, all truncated by the folds: "Father George H. Whitb"; "beloved son, brother, rest in"; "All things bright and"; "lieu of flowers, donatio." All of which, Yale supposed, did tell Nico's fortune. Nico been bright and beautiful. Flowers would do no good.

The houses on this street were tall, ornate. Pumpkins still out on every stoop but few carved faces—artful arrangements, rather, of gourds and Indian corn. Wrought iron fences, swinging gates. When they turned into the walkway to Richard's (a noble brownstone sharing walls with noble neighbors), Charlie whispered: "His wife decorated the place. When he was *married*. In '72." Yale laughed at the worst possible moment, just as they passed a gravely smiling Richard holding open his own door. It was the idea of Richard living a hetero life in Lincoln Park with some decoratively inclined woman. Yale's image of it was slapstick: Richard stuffing a man into the closet when his wife dashed back for her Chanel clutch.

Yale pulled himself together and turned back to Richard. He said, "You have a beautiful place." A wave of people came up behind them, pushing Yale and Charlie into the living room.

Inside, the decor didn't scream 1972 so much as 1872: chintz sofas, velvety chairs with carved arms, oriental rugs. Yale felt Charlie squeeze his hand as they dove into the crowd.

Nico had made it clear there was to be a party. "If I get to hang out as a ghost, you think I wanna see sobbing? I'll haunt you. You sit there crying, I'll throw a lamp across the room, okay? I'll shove a poker up your ass, and not in a good way." If he'd died just two days ago, they wouldn't have had it in them to follow through. But Nico died three weeks back, and the family delayed the vigil and funeral until his grandfather, the one no one had seen in twenty years, could fly in from Havana. Nico's mother was the product of a brief, pre-Castro marriage between a diplomat's daughter and a Cuban musician—and now this ancient Cuban man was crucial to the funeral planning, while Nico's lover of three years wasn't even welcome at the church tonight. Yale couldn't think about it or he'd fume, which wasn't what Nico wanted.

In any case, they'd spent three weeks mourning and now Richard's house brimmed with forced festivity. There were Julian and Teddy, for instance, waving down from the second-story railing that encircled the room. Another floor rose above that, and an elaborate round skylight presided over the whole space. It was more of a cathedral than the church had been. Someone shrieked with laughter far too close to Yale's ear.

Charlie said, "I believe we're meant to have a good time." Charlie's British accent, Yale was convinced, emerged more in sarcasm.

Yale said, "I'm waiting on the go-go dancers."

Richard had a piano, and someone was playing "Fly Me to the Moon."

What the hell were they all doing?

A skinny man Yale had never seen before bear-hugged Charlie. An out-of-towner, he guessed, someone who'd lived here but moved away before Yale came on the scene. Charlie said, "How in hell did you get younger?" Yale waited to be introduced, but the man was telling an urgent story now about someone else Yale didn't know. Charlie was the hub of a lot of wheels.

A voice in Yale's ear: "We're drinking Cuba libres." It was Fiona, Nico's little sister, and Yale turned to hug her, to smell her lemony hair. "Isn't it ridiculous?" Nico had been proud of the Cuban thing, but if he knew the chaos his grandfather's arrival would cause, he'd have vetoed the beverage choice.

Fiona had told them all, last night, that she wasn't going to the funeral—that she'd be here instead—but still it was jarring to see her, to know she'd followed through. But then she'd written off her family as thoroughly as they'd written Nico off in the years before his illness. (Until, in his last days, they'd claimed him, insisting he die in the suburbs in an ill-equipped hospital with nice wallpaper.) Her mascara was smudged. She had discarded her shoes, but wobbled as if she still wore heels.

Fiona handed her own drink to Yale—half full, an arc of pink on the rim. She touched a finger to the cleft of his upper lip. "I still can't believe you shaved it off. I mean, it looks good. You look sort of—"

"Straighter."

She laughed, and then she said, "Oh. *Oh!* They're not making you, are they? At Northwestern?" Fiona had one of the best faces for concern Yale had ever seen—her eyebrows hurried together, her lips vanished straight into her mouth—but he wondered how she had any emotion left to spare.

He said, "No. It's—I mean, I'm the development guy. I'm talking to a lot of older alumni."

"To get money?"

"Money and art. It's a strange dance." Yale had taken the job at Northwestern's new Brigg Gallery in August, the same week Nico got sick, and he still wasn't sure where his responsibilities started and ended. "I mean, they know about Charlie. My colleagues do.

It's fine. It's a gallery, not a bank." He tasted the Cuba libre. Inappropriate for the third of November, but then the afternoon was unseasonably warm, and this was exactly what he needed. The soda might even wake him up.

"You had a real Tom Selleck thing going. I hate when blond men grow a mustache; it's peach fuzz. Dark-haired guys, though, that's my favorite. You should've kept it! But it's okay, because now you look like Luke Duke. In a good way. No, like Patrick Duffy!" Yale couldn't laugh, and Fiona tilted her head to look at him seriously.

He felt like sobbing into her hair, but he didn't. He'd been cultivating numbness all day, hanging onto it like a rope. If this were three weeks ago, they could have simply cried together. But everything had scabbed over, and now there was this idea of *party* on top of everything else, this imperative to be, somehow, okay. Merry.

And what had Nico been to Yale? Just a good friend. Not family, not a lover. Nico was, in fact, the first real friend Yale had made when he moved here, the first he'd sat down with just to *talk*, and not at a bar, not shouting over music. Yale had adored Nico's drawings, would take him out for pancakes and help him study for his GED and tell him he was talented. Charlie wasn't interested in art and neither was Nico's lover, Terrence, and so Yale would take Nico to gallery shows and art talks, introduce him to artists. Still: If Nico's little sister was holding it together this well, wasn't Yale obliged to be in better shape?

Fiona said, "It's hard for *everyone*."

Their parents had cut Nico off at fifteen, but Fiona would sneak food and money and allergy medicine to the place he shared with four other guys on Broadway, taking the Metra and then the El there by herself from Highland Park. At the age of eleven. When Nico introduced Fiona, he always said, "This is the lady that raised me."

Nothing Yale could find words for was worth saying.

Fiona told him to check out the upstairs when he got a chance. "It's Versailles up there."

Yale couldn't find Charlie in the crowd. Despite exuding tremendous height, Charlie was only a bit taller than average—and Yale was always surprised in situations like this not to spot his crew-cut head, his neat beard, his droopy eyes, above everyone else.

But Julian Ames was beside him now, down from upstairs. He said, "We've been going since lunch! I'm sloshed!" It was five o'clock, the sky already inking itself out. He leaned against Yale and giggled. "We ransacked the bathrooms. He has *nothing*, or else he's hiding it. Well, someone found some old poppers in the back of the fridge. But is there any point to poppers if you aren't getting laid?"

"No. Jesus. *Poppers*?"

"I'm asking seriously!" Julian pulled himself straight. He had a lock of dark hair in front that Charlie maintained made him look like Superman. ("Or a unicorn," Yale would add.) He brushed it out of his eyes and pouted. Julian was too perfect, if anything. He'd had a nose job when he left for Atlanta—better for his acting career—and Yale wished he hadn't. He'd have preferred an imperfect Julian.

"I'm answering seriously. There's absolutely no point to doing poppers at a memorial."

"But this isn't a funeral, it's a *party*. And it's like—" Julian was close again, conspiratorial in his ear. "It's like that Poe story, the Red Death one. There's death out there, but we're gonna have a fabulous time in here."

"Julian." Yale drained the Cuba libre and spat an ice chip back into the glass. "That is not the point. That's not how the story ends."

"I was never one to finish my homework."

Julian put his chin on Yale's shoulder—a thing he was prone to do, one that always made Yale worry Charlie would glance over right then. Yale had spent the past four years reassuring Charlie he wouldn't run off with someone like Julian, or like Teddy Naples, who was now leaning out precariously over the railing, his feet off the ground, calling to a friend (Teddy was so small that someone could probably catch him if he fell, but still, Yale cringed, looked away). There was no reason for Charlie's insecurity, beyond both men's looks and flirtatiousness. Beyond the fact that Charlie would never feel secure. Yale had been the one to propose monogamy to begin with, but Charlie was the one who dwelt on its possible unraveling. And he'd picked the two most beautiful men in Chicago to affix his anxieties to. Yale shrugged Julian off his shoulder, and Julian smiled dopily and wandered away.

The room had loudened, the sound bouncing off the stories above, people flooding in. Two very pretty, very young men circulated with trays of little quiches and stuffed mushrooms and deviled eggs. Yale wondered why the food wasn't Cuban, too, to match the drinks, but Richard probably had just one plan for every party: Open the doors, open the bar, boys with quiche.

In any case, this was infinitely better than that strange and dishonest vigil last night. The church had smelled nicely of incense, but otherwise there was little about it Nico would have liked. "He wouldn't be caught dead here," Charlie had said, and then he'd heard himself and tried to laugh. The parents had carefully invited Nico's lover to the vigil, saying it was "an appropriate time for friends to pay respect." Meaning, don't come today to the actual mass. Meaning, don't really even show up for the vigil, but aren't we generous? But Terrence *had* gone last night, and so had eight friends. Mostly to surround Terrence, and to support Fiona, who, it turned out, had convinced her parents to issue the invitation; she'd told them that if Nico's friends weren't invited, she'd stand up during the service and say so. Still, plenty of friends had bowed out. Asher Glass had claimed his body would revolt at setting foot in a Catholic church. ("I'd start yelling about rubbers. Swear to God.")

The eight of them sat shoulder to shoulder in the back, a phalanx of suits around Terrence. It would have been nice if Terrence could have blended in anonymously, but they weren't even seated yet when Yale heard an older woman pointing him out to her husband: "That one. The black gentleman with the glasses." As if there were another black guy in this church, one with perfect vision. That woman wasn't the only one who kept glancing back throughout the service to observe, anthropologically, when and if this gay black specimen might start weeping.

Yale held Charlie's hand low down—not as a statement, but because Charlie was so allergic to churches. "I see kneelers and hymnals," he said, "and five tons of Anglican guilt lands on my neck." So, far below anyone else's sightline, Yale had rubbed his wide thumb over Charlie's bony one.

Family members told stories only about Nico as a child, as if he'd died in adolescence. There was one good one, told by Nico's stoic and ashen father: Fiona, when she was seven, had wanted twenty cents to buy a handful of Swedish Fish candy from the bin on the counter of the convenience store. Their father pointed out that she'd already spent her allowance. Fiona had started to cry. And Nico, who was eleven, sat down in the middle of the aisle and, for five minutes, twisted and yanked at his barely loose molar until it came out. It bled—and their father, an orthodontist, was alarmed at the jagged root still attached. But Nico pocketed the tooth and said, "The Tooth Fairy's bringing a quarter tonight, right?" In front of Fiona, Dr. Marcus couldn't say no. "So can you give me a loan?"

The crowd laughed at this, and Dr. Marcus barely needed to explain that Nico gave the money straight to his sister, that it was another year before the permanent tooth grew in.

Yale looked now for Terrence. It took a minute, but there he was, sitting halfway up the stairs, too surrounded for Yale to chat with him yet. Instead, Yale took one of the mini quiches off a passing tray and slipped it to him through the balusters. "You look stuck!" Yale said, and Terrence put the quiche in his mouth, held his hand out again, said, "Keep 'em coming!"

Fiona had wanted to trick her parents, to exchange Nico's ashes with fireplace ones and give the real ones to Terrence. It was hard to tell if she was serious. But Terrence wasn't getting any ashes, and he wasn't getting anything else either, besides Nico's cat, which he'd taken when Nico first went into the hospital. The family had made it clear that when they began dismantling Nico's apartment tomorrow, Terrence would be excluded. Nico had left no will. His illness had been sudden, immediately debilitating—first a few days of what had seemed like just shingles, but then, a month later, moon-high fevers and dementia.

Terrence had been an eighth-grade math teacher until this summer, when Nico needed him around the clock and Terrence learned he was infected himself. And how would Terrence get through the fall, the winter, with no Nico, no job? It wasn't just a financial question. He loved teaching, loved those kids.

Terrence had some of the vague early symptoms, some weight loss, but nothing serious yet, not enough to go on disability. He'd taken the test after Nico got sick—whether out of solidarity or just to *know*, Yale wasn't sure. It wasn't as if there were some magic pill. Yale and Charlie had, just on principle, been among the first to get tested that spring. Charlie's paper had been advocating for testing, education, safe sex, and Charlie felt he had to put his money where his mouth was. But on top of that, Yale had just wanted to get it over with. Not knowing, he figured, was bad for his health in and of itself. The clinics weren't giving the test yet, but Dr. Vincent was. Yale and Charlie opened a bottle of champagne when they got good results. It was a somber toast; they didn't even finish the bottle.

Julian was back at Yale's ear, saying, "Get yourself a refill before the slide show starts."

"There's a slide show?"

"It's *Richard.*"

At the bar Yale found Fiona talking to someone he didn't know, a straight-looking guy with a jaw. Twisting her blonde curls around her finger. She was drinking too fast, because that was an empty glass in her hand. And she'd gotten it since she gave Yale her half-drink, and Fiona weighed maybe a hundred pounds. He touched her arm. He said, "You remember to eat?"

Fiona laughed, looked at the guy, laughed again. She said, "*Yale.*" And she kissed his cheek, a firm kiss that probably left lipstick. To the guy she said, "I have two hundred big brothers." She might fall over any second. "But as you can *see*, he's the *preppiest*. And look at Yale's hands. Look at them."

Yale examined his palm; there was nothing wrong with it.

"No," she said, "The back! Don't they look like paws? They're furry!" She ran her finger through the dark hairs clustered thickly on the pinky side of his hand. She whispered loudly to the man: "It's on his feet too!" Then, to Yale, "Hey, did you talk to my aunt?"

Yale scanned the room. There were only a few women here, none much over thirty. He said, "At the vigil?"

"*No*, she can't drive. But you must have talked, because I *told* her. I told her, like, *months* ago. And she said she had."

He said, "Your aunt?"

"No, my *father's* aunt. She loved Nico. Yale, you have to know that. She *loved* him."

Yale said to the guy, "Get her some food," and the guy nodded. Fiona patted Yale's chest and turned away, as if he were the one whose logic couldn't be followed.

He got his refill, almost straight rum, and looked for Charlie. Was that his bearded chin, his blue tie? But the curtain of people closed again, and Yale wasn't tall enough to see over a crowd. And now Richard dimmed the lights and pulled up a projector screen, and Yale couldn't see anything but the shoulders and backs boxing him in.

Richard Campo, if he had any job at all, was a photographer. Yale had no idea where Richard's money came from, but it let him buy a lot of nice cameras and gave him time to roam the city shooting candid photos in addition to the occasional wedding. Not long after Yale moved to Chicago, he was sunbathing on the Belmont Rocks with Charlie and Charlie's friends, though this was before Yale and Charlie were an item. It was heaven, even if Yale had forgotten a towel, even if he always burned. Guys making out in broad daylight! A gay space hidden from the city but wide open to the vast expanse of Lake Michigan. One of Charlie's friends, a man with wavy, prematurely silver hair and a lime-green Speedo, had sat there clicking away on his Nikon, changing film, clicking again at all of them. Yale asked, "Who's the perv?" and Charlie said, "He might be a genius." That was Richard. Of course Charlie saw genius in everyone, prodded them till he discovered their passions and then encouraged those, but Richard really was talented. Yale and Richard were never close—he'd never set foot in the guy's house till today—but Yale had grown used to him. Richard was always on the periphery, watching and shooting. A good fifteen years older than everyone else in their circle: paternal, doting, eager to buy a round. He'd bankrolled Charlie's newspaper in the early days. And what had started as a strange quirk had become, in the past few months, something essential. Yale would hear the camera's click and think, "He got *that*, at least." Meaning: Whatever happens—in three years, in twenty—that moment will remain.

Someone messed with the record player, and as the first slide displayed (Nico and Terrence toasting last year at Fiona's twentieth birthday) the music started: the acoustic intro to "America," the version from Simon and Garfunkel's Central Park concert. Nico's favorite song, one he saw as a defiant anthem, not just a ditty about a road trip. The night

Reagan won reelection last year, Nico, furious, played it on the jukebox at Little Jim's again and again until the whole bar was drunkenly singing about being lost and counting cars and looking for America. Just as everyone was singing now.

Yale couldn't bear to join, and although he wouldn't be the only one crying, he didn't think he could stay here. He backed out of the crowd and took a few steps up Richard's stairs, watching the heads from above. Everyone stared at the slides, riveted. Except that someone else was leaving too. Teddy Naples was at Richard's heavy front door, slipping his suit jacket back on, turning the knob slowly. Usually Teddy was a little ball of kinetic energy, bouncing on his toes, keeping time with his fingers to music no one else could hear. But right now he moved like a ghost. Maybe he had the right idea. If he weren't trapped on this side of the crowd, Yale might have done the same. Not *left*, but stepped outside for fresh air.

The slides: Nico in running shorts, a number pinned to his chest. Nico and Terrence leaning against a tree, both giving the finger. Nico in profile with his orange scarf and black coat, a cigarette between his lips. Suddenly, there was Yale himself, tucked in the crook of Charlie's arm, Nico on the other side: the year-end party last December for Charlie's paper. Nico had been the graphic designer for *Out Loud Chicago*, and he had a regular comic strip there, and he'd just started designing theater sets too. Self-taught, entirely. This was supposed to have been the prologue of his life. A new slide: Nico laughing at Julian and Teddy, the Halloween they had dressed as Sonny and Cher. Nico opening a present. Nico holding a bowl of chocolate ice cream. Nico up close, teeth shining. The last time Yale saw Nico, he'd been unconscious, with foam—some kind of awful white foam—oozing suddenly from his mouth and nostrils. Terrence had screamed into the hallway for the nurses, had run into a cleaning cart and hurt his knee, and the fucking nurses were more concerned about whether or not Terrence had shed blood than about what was happening to Nico. And here on the slide was Nico's full, beautiful face, and it was too much. Yale dashed up the rest of the stairs.

He worried the bedrooms would be full of guys who'd been taking poppers, but the first one, at least, was empty. He closed the door and sat on the bed. It was dark out now, the sparse streetlights of Belden just barely illuminating the walls and floor. Richard must have redone at least this one room after the mysterious wife moved out. Two black leather chairs flanked the wide bed. There was a small shelf of art books. Yale put his glass on the floor and lay back to stare at the ceiling and do the slow-breathing trick Charlie had taught him.

All fall, he'd been memorizing the list of the gallery's regular donors. Tuning out the downstairs noise, he did what he often did at home when he couldn't sleep: He named donors starting with *A*, then ones starting with *B*. A fair number overlapped with the Art Institute donors he'd worked with for the past three years, but there were hundreds of new names—Northwestern alumni, North Shore types—that he needed to recognize on the spot.

Recently he'd found the lists disconcerting—had felt a dull gray uneasiness around them. He remembered being eight and asking his father who else in the neighborhood was Jewish ("Are the Rothmans Jewish? Are the Andersens?") and his father rubbing his chin, saying, "Let's not do that, buddy. Historically, bad things happen when we make lists of Jews." It wasn't till years later that Yale realized this was a hang-up unique to his father, to his brand of self-hatred. But Yale had been young and impressionable, and maybe that's why the reciting of names chafed.

Or no, maybe it was this: Lately he'd had two parallel mental lists going—the donor list and the sick list. The people who might donate art or money, and the friends who might get sick; the big donors, the ones names you'd never forget, and the friends he'd already lost. But they weren't close friends, the lost ones, until tonight. They'd been acquaintances, friends of friends like Nico's old roommate Jonathan, a couple of gallery owners, one bartender, the bookstore guy. There were, what, six? Six people he *knew* of, people he'd say hi to at a bar, people whose middle names he couldn't tell you, and maybe not even their last names.

He'd been to three memorials. But now, a new list: one close friend.

Yale and Charlie had gone to an informational meeting last year with a speaker from San Francisco. He'd said, "I know guys who've lost no one. Groups that haven't been touched. But I also know people who've lost twenty friends. Entire apartment buildings devastated." And Yale, stupidly, desperately, had thought maybe he'd fall into that first category. It didn't help that, through Charlie, he knew practically everyone in Boystown. It didn't help that his friends were all overachievers—and that they seemed to be overachieving in this terrible new way as well.

It was Yale's saving grace, and Charlie's, that they'd met when they had, fallen in love so quickly. They'd been together since February of '81 and—to the bemusement of nearly everyone—exclusive since fall of the same year. Nineteen eighty-one wasn't too soon to get infected, not by a long shot, but then this wasn't San Francisco, it wasn't New York. Things, thank God, moved slower here.

How had Yale forgotten he hated rum? It always made him moody, dehydrated, hot. His stomach a mess.

He found a closet-size bathroom off this room and sat on the cool toilet, head between his knees.

On his list of people who might get sick, who weren't careful enough, might even already be sick: Well, Julian, for sure. Richard. Asher Glass. Teddy—for Christ's sake, Teddy Naples, who claimed that once he managed to avoid checking out of the Man's World bathhouse for fifty-two hours, just napped (through the sounds of sex and pumping music) in the private rooms various older men had rented for their liaisons, subsisting on Snickers bars from the vending machine.

Teddy opposed the test, worried names could get matched with test results and used by the government, used like those lists of Jews. At least that was what he said. Maybe he was just terrified, like everyone. Teddy was earning his PhD in philosophy at Loyola, and he tended to come up with elaborate philosophical covers for terribly average feelings. Teddy and Julian would occasionally have a "thing" on, but mostly Teddy just floated between Kierkegaard and bars and clubs. Yale always suspected that Teddy had at least seven distinct groups of friends and didn't rank this one very highly. Witness his leaving the party. Maybe the slides were too much for him, as they'd been for Yale; maybe he'd stepped out to walk around the block, but Yale doubted it. Teddy had other places to be, better parties to attend.

And then there was the list of acquaintances already sick, hiding the lesions on their arms but not their faces, coughing horribly, growing thin, waiting to get worse—or lying in the hospital, or flown home to die near their parents, to be written up in their local papers as having died of pneumonia. Just a few right now, but there was room on that list. Far too much room.

When Yale finally moved again, it was to cup water from the sink, splash it over his face. He looked frightful in the mirror: rings under his eyes, skin gone pale olive. His heart felt funny, but then his heart always felt funny.

The slide show must be over, and if he could look down on the crowd he'd be able to spot Charlie. They could make their escape. They could get a cab, even, and he could lean on the window. When they got home, Charlie would rub his neck, insist on making him tea. He'd feel fine.

He opened the door to the hall and heard a collective silence, as if they were all holding their breath, listening to someone make a speech. Only he couldn't quite hear the speech. He looked down, but there was no one in the living room. They'd moved somewhere.

He came downstairs slowly, not wanting to be startled. A sudden noise would make him vomit.

But down in the living room was just the whir of the record, spinning past the last song, the needle arm retired to the side. Beer bottles and Cuba libre glasses, still half full, covered the tables and couch arms. The trays of canapes had been left on the dining table. Yale thought of a raid, some kind of police raid, but this was a private residence, and they were all adults, and nothing much illegal had happened. Probably someone had some pot, but come on.

How long had he been upstairs? Maybe twenty minutes. *Maybe* thirty. He wondered if he could've fallen asleep on the bed, if it was 2 a.m. now. But no, not unless his watch had stopped. It was only 5:45.

He was being ridiculous, and they were out in the backyard. Places like this had backyards. He walked through the empty kitchen, through a book-lined den. There was the door, but it was dead-bolted. He cupped his hand to the glass: a striped canopy, a heap of dead leaves, the moon. No people.

Yale turned and started shouting: "Hello! Richard! Guys! Hello!"

He went to the front door—also, bizarrely, dead-bolted—and fumbled till it opened. There was no one on the dark street.

The foggy, ridiculous idea came to him that the world had ended, that some apocalypse had swept through and forgotten only him. He laughed at himself, but at the same time: He saw no bobbing heads in neighbors' windows. There were lights in the houses opposite, but then the lights were on here too. At the end of the block, the traffic signal turned from green to yellow to red. He heard the vague rush of cars far away, but that could have been wind, couldn't it? Or even the lake. Yale hoped for a siren, a horn, a dog, an airplane across the night sky. Nothing.

He went back inside and closed the door. He yelled again: "You guys!" And he felt now that a trick was being played, that they might jump out and laugh. But this was a memorial, wasn't it? It wasn't the tenth grade. People weren't always looking for ways to hurt him.

He found his own reflection in Richard's TV: He was still here, still visible.

On the back of a chair was a blue windbreaker he recognized as Asher Glass's. The pockets were empty.

He should leave. But where would he even go?

Cigarette butts filled the ashtrays. None were half smoked, none smashed out in haste. Copies of some of Nico's comics had been laid out on end tables, the bar, but now they were scattered—probably more a product of the party than its end—and Yale plucked one off the floor. A drag queen named Martina Luther Kink. A silly punch line about having a dream.

He walked through every room on the ground floor, opening every door—pantry, coat closet, vacuum closet—until he was greeted with a cold air and descending cement steps. He found the light switch and made his way down. Laundry machines, boxes, two rusty bikes.

He climbed back up and then all the way to the third floor—a study, a little weight room, some storage—and then down to the second again and opened everything. Ornate mahogany bureaus, canopy beds. A master bedroom, all white and green. If this had been the wife's work, it wasn't so bad. A Diane Arbus print on the wall, the one of the boy with the hand grenade.

A telephone sat next to Richard's bed, and Yale grabbed it with relief. He listened to the tone—reassuring—and slowly dialed his own number. No answer.

He needed to hear a voice, any human voice, and so he got the dial tone back and called Information.

"Name and city please," the woman said.

"Hello?" He wanted to make sure she wasn't a recording.

"This is Information. Do you know the name of the person you wish to call?"

"Yes, it's—Marcus. Nico Marcus, on North Clark in Chicago." He spelled the names.

"I have an N. Marcus on North Clark. Would you like me to connect you?"

"No—no thank you."

"Stay on the line for the number." Yale hung up.

He circled the house one more time and went, finally, to the front door. He called to no one: "I'm leaving! I'm going!"

And stepped out into the dark.

Exercises:

- To get started thinking about "crossing," identify a scene in a story you've written in which the protagonist is the same gender as yourself. Now rewrite that scene (using place, time, and situation you already know) with the protagonist as a person of a different gender. What do you notice? What changes does this prompt in the scene, including in other characters' actions or reactions? Where do you find yourself confident or faltering, and why? If you have a class or writers' group, share the short scenes and talk about what you notice. Try this with other types of "markers" as well: race, sexuality, class, and more. Don't worry about polished writing; just think about how crossing feels.

- Write a short-short story (1,500 words or fewer) from inside the point of view of someone whose political views absolutely oppose yours—and make that character a real, believable person, not a monster or a caricature. (Grant the person full humanity, in other words; some hints of a backstory, or what life experiences they're drawing on.) You don't have to convert yourself, or readers. Just flex your difficulty muscles. It helps to give them a fear or disappointment you share, or a vulnerable spot (like Richard in Ian Wriesner's Craft Studio story) and see what they do with it.

- Make a table of "crossing" with books you've read. What do you notice?

- Read a novel written by a writer whose identity differs from yours in at least two ways: race, sexuality, disability, gender, national origin, class, and more. What do you notice about how that writer marks identity? What strategies might you adapt?

- Suggested by Noemi Lefebvre's *Poetics of Work*, which has an ungendered narrator: write a story in which you go as long as you can *without* giving your narrator a gender *yet still* giving them a sensory body rooted in a believable sensory world.[67]

- Gather photographs of people from magazines or websites and write brief descriptions of them that, while avoiding stereotype, still mark appearance and, if desired, cultural identity. This can be useful to do and discuss in a group. (Google "diverse stock photo" for some options.)

- Research and discuss some creative identity/"crossing"-related controversies:
  - William Styron, *The Confessions of Nat Turner* (novel, 1967):
    - Original historical texts in *The Confession of Nat Turner, With Related Documents*, ed. Kenneth S. Greenberg (2016)
    - *William Styron's Nat Turner: Ten Black Writers Respond* (1967)
    - Albert Murray, "William Styron and His Troublesome Property" (1967)
    - Sam Tanenhaus, "The Literary Battle for Nat Turner's Legacy," *Vanity Fair,* September 2016; this article also describes the involvement of James Baldwin, a friend of Styron's.
  - Dana Schutz, *Open Casket* (painting, 2017):
    - Calvin Tomkins, "Why Dana Schutz Painted Emmett Till," *The New Yorker* (April 3, 2017)
    - Namwali Serpell, "The Work of Art" (fiction: *Harper's*, September 2020)

- Aruna d'Souza, "Who Speaks Freely?: Art, Race, and Protest," *The Paris Review* Blog (May 22, 2018)
- Anders Carlson-Wee, "How-To" (poem, 2018):
  - Jennifer Schuessler, "A Poem in *The Nation* Spurs a Backlash and an Apology" (*New York Times*, August 1, 2018)
  - John McWhorter, "There's Nothing Wrong With Black English" (*The Atlantic*, August 2018)
- Amelie Wen Zhao, *Blood Heir* (2019) and what became three-book young-adult series:
  - Alexandra Alter, "She Pulled Her Debut Book When Critics Found It Racist. Now She Plans to Publish" (*New York Times*, April 29, 2019)
  - Keira Drake and Jonah Winter, "When Social Media Goes After Your Book, What's the Right Response? Two Authors Weigh In" (*New York Times*, February 6, 2019)
- Jeanine Cummins, *American Dirt* (novel, 2020):
  - Rebecca Alter, "Why Is Everyone Arguing about the Novel *American Dirt?*" (*Vulture*, February 7, 2020)
- Zadie Smith, "Fascinated to Presume: In Defense of Fiction" (*New York Review of Books,* October 24, 2019)

CHAPTER 5
INVISIBLE ENGINES
PURPOSE, PSYCHIC DISTANCE, AND POINT OF VIEW

Adults, waiting for tomorrow, move in a present behind which is yesterday or the day before yesterday or at most last week: they don't want to think about the rest. Children don't know the meaning of yesterday, or even of tomorrow, everything is this, now: the street is this, the doorway is this, the stairs are this, this is Mamma, this is Papa, this is the day, this the night.

— Elena Ferrante, *My Brilliant Friend*

Sometimes an image, a character, or event announces inside you that it's ready to become a story, and it's brought all its equipment along—you have a purposeful sense right away of what its personality is, what the narrative voice or point of view will be, in what order the episodes might unfold, and where it takes place. These technical features can feel as immersive and automatic as Elena Ferrante describes a child's perspective, in the epigraph— except when they don't. And when they don't, they can be *really* frustrating. So this chapter will help you assess and re/design the often-invisible engines of your fictional world.

What's This Really About? Drawing Your Story's Heart

Working on my novel *Creature: A Novel of Mary Shelley and Frankenstein,* an editor asked me a valuable question: "What's the real story here?" For my big draft, this was a helpful question: I'd written sideways excursions into the lives of Mary Shelley's colleagues Lord Byron and John Keats, unknown corners of Shelley's own life, and the just-plain-fascinating details of her Regency world (including boxing—ask me about it sometime!). All this formed a lavish picture in *my* imagination. But it wouldn't be coherent to a *reader* unless I could identify a clear narrative purpose (or "through-line") and take-away what didn't belong in the novel.

Then I remembered an exercise I do with my students: close your eyes, mentally inhabit your fictional world for a moment, then open your eyes and draw the most immediate, compelling visual image that comes up in your mind, which will often provide an answer. My image was Mary Shelley as a little girl, standing on a chair and bending forward to bring her face close to the portrait of her mother, Mary Wollstonecraft, who died giving birth to her—the closest physical contact she could ever have with the adventurous, brilliant mother she'd never meet. That longing drove Mary Shelley as I imagined her, and it drove the story.

Drawing also opens a gate in your imagination between emotion and detail. What do you draw first? What do you find easier or harder to draw? Is there a detail in the picture that might enflesh your written scene? Sketching young Mary Shelley helped me to imagine and then describe her, including the long braid hanging down her back and her feet in their holey stockings on the cold wooden seat of the chair. It was just a little stick figure in a dress, but it catalyzed a sense of what my story was *really* about and helped me move forward with confidence. It also gave me a touchstone to refocus myself whenever I wondered what I should keep or cut. Try drawing at different times in your writing process to clarify your story's purpose, to "see" a scene more clearly, or to clarify your narrative perspective.

Too Close? Too Far? Just Right: Psychic Distance

Sometimes, especially when writing something closely based on your own experience, you may have the weird sense that this closeness is *draining* energy from rather than *infusing* energy into it. You may have trouble crafting events different enough from "real life" to be artistically effective. You may feel the urge to interrupt the story to tell your readers things you want them to know. And the story just keeps getting worse—but why? Maybe it's because a fiction writer often needs the momentum of an imaginative leap to cross into an invented world. Maybe you're struggling to get enough distance from your character to imagine their story *as* a story. Maybe you're not "pretending to be your character" quite enough yet.

Frederick Reiken describes this problem in his essay "The Author-Narrator-Character Merge: Why Many First-Time Novelists Wind up with Flat, Uninteresting Protagonists." To address it, Reiken introduces the concept of *psychic distance*, or the level of closeness (or intimacy) readers (and the author) feel to a character's subjectivity, which has to do with "where the writer 'stands'" imaginatively in relationship to a character as the writer imagines and then depicts that character.[1] These five sentences Reiken quotes from John Gardner's *The Art of Fiction* demonstrate progressively decreasing psychic distance. The first sentence represents the greatest psychic distance between the narrative voice and the reader—where the prose is most focused on *objective* information, only "what a camera could record" (as David Mamet says in Chapter 4). We're looking at the character from a completely *external* point. The last sentence represents the shortest, rooted completely in the character's *subjective* experience, an *internal* standpoint.

1) It was winter of the year 1853. A large man stepped out of the doorway.

2) Henry J. Warbutton had never much cared for snowstorms.

3) Henry hated snowstorms.

4) God, how he hated these damn snowstorms.

5) Snow. Under your collar, down inside your shoes, freezing and plugging up your miserable soul.

Even based on this short list, you may notice techniques that decrease psychic distance: direct dialogue. First names or pronouns rather than full names. Fragments rather than complete sentences. "Filterless" observations (see Chapter 7). But how close, or how far away, do you and your reader really want to stand? To answer this question in class, students and I stand in a circle to read this list aloud, taking one step forward toward each other with each sentence. By the time we reach #5, we're laughing at what has become an uncomfortable physical closeness, reflecting the close psychic distance of #5. Then we read the sentences in reverse order, stepping backwards, and students stop when they've reached a more comfortable spot. Most students stop around level 3. And that's about where many find their comfortable psychic distance as writers, too—somewhere in the range of #2 to #4, with occasional excursions "farther out" to level #1 or "closer in" to level #5 depending on the mood of the scene. The mood of #1 may feel too objective and impersonal, while level #5 (which dominates Charlotte Perkins Gilman's "The Yellow Wallpaper" in Chapter 3's Craft Studio) works well in short bursts but is uncomfortable to sustain for long. But once you figure out "where you want to stand," both you *and* your reader can get comfortable and settle into your character's world.

Establishing a unified, comfortable range of psychic distance starts with asking yourself, "Who am I pretending to be—and am I 'pretending' enough (to make this person different enough from me) while *also* imagining and accommodating, as I craft my sentences, what my reader needs to know to be able to enter, and sustain their belief in, this person's point of view?" Where's the most comfortable place for you to "stand" as a writer in imagining and writing through your character? Often this starts with imagining the character as different enough from yourself (even if you do share some similarities) to be able to inhabit their perspective as *their* perspective, not your own. Imagine you're an actor, playing that character's role. Try changing one big thing about your character to impose a difference between you and them, like gender, place, or time. Put them in a situation or event you haven't experienced. This will help you *imagine* your story as its own world rather than simply "fictionalize" real life. And, as an editor once told me, "Feel free to make shit up!" Even if it prompts research, an imaginative leap can unlock what Reiken calls the "author-narrator-character merge" and give you some freedom to invent characters in their world, so you don't feel stuck too closely to your own. Feel free to *invent more*: with a greater imaginative leap can come more freedom, energy, and fun.

Once you've established some imaginative separation between you and your character, you can consider your psychic distance, too. Like a movie camera on a dolly track, you can move forward and back across relatively short psychic distances from sentence to sentence, but if you go from, say, level 1 to level 5 and back again in the same paragraph, you may be jumping across too great a distance too quickly—from external to internal—and disorienting readers, who can't find a stable point of focus. Sometimes this happens when a writer is not imagining the character fully enough yet to write from *within* that perspective, so in order to assuage their anxiety, the writer "jumps" from the character's voice to a voice more like their own to provide information they think will help readers out. But in doing so, they widen the gap and heighten the artifice of the story, kind of like the Wizard of Oz pleading, "Pay no attention to the man behind the curtain!" My students say that understanding psychic distance is challenging but is also one of their most important breakthroughs in advanced-level fiction writing.

Student Craft Studio: Andrew Tiede, "Till Death"

Andrew, a gifted actor and improvisational comic, struggled with his first-person point of view in his story "Till Death," a darkly funny tale narrated by a mortician. While his classmates and I enjoyed Andrew's humor (and the Pink Floyd references), his narrator's voice sounded weirdly formal in spots, as if Andrew were interrupting his own character to tell us what he wanted us to know. When we did this psychic distance exercise in class (complete with socially awkward giggles), Andrew exclaimed, "I get it! Jumping from Level 1 to Level 4 works great in improv, but not in writing." *Exactly*. In comedy, the distance and incongruity of the leap drive the joke. (Remember Dennis, the Marxist peasant in the classic movie *Monty Python and the Holy Grail*?) But in fiction, it can disorient readers. Committing to a particular psychic distance, which starts with rooting yourself in your character's consciousness, helps you "settle in," as Andrew says (later), and start to enflesh your story with detail. Once you feel rooted, you can play with some leaps and shifts of diction and psychic distance, like Paul Beatty does in his satirical Booker-Prize-winning novel *The Sellout* (2015). With revision, Andrew developed a first-person psychic distance that let his own humorous voice shine, and he published "Till Death" in the Canadian online journal *Haunted MTL* in June 2019.

Here's Andrew's Original Beginning

When I was young I hadn't wanted to be a mortician. Yet here I am, looking down on a metal table at what Joseph Ramsey left behind when he passed into the next life. On first glance it isn't a glamorous job. Scratch that, it isn't a glamorous job.

I ended up in the trade because it was a stable job that a solitary man with an appreciation for his solitude could manage. Most of my working hours were spent here at the table, working on the bodies, with Pink Floyd playing softly in the background. I came from a line of morticians, so was able to learn the trade younger than most.

Joseph here was probably quite alike me. Looking at his body he too was a middle aged man, though a few years older than I, who liked his drink. He had some distant relatives who had given iffy promises about attending the funeral, and no close relations to speak of. His wife, like my own, had left the picture; likely she was the last thing he cared about.

And Here's His Revision of Those Same Passages

As a kid, I thought this job was the stuff of nightmares. Yet there I was, pulling the metal tray from the cooler. On that tray was what Joseph Ramsey left behind when he passed, with my sandwich bag and a little bottle of champagne nestled between his feet. I wheeled the cart to my little operating theatre while whistling "Comfortably Numb." It wasn't a glamorous job. Not the kind of job that would help a recent divorcee get back out there. I entered the trade in part because of the money which gave me status and security, but really I did it to be the better son.

Most of my working hours were spent at the table, working on the slowly putrefying bodies that of late were my only company, with Pink Floyd playing softly in the background. The way I'd set it up, I worked from home. This was fine after I got used to the idea of sleeping a floor above my work.

Death was a funny business, it came in little bursts. I sometimes went a week or two without having anyone to work on, and at other times I'd have to double-stack them in the coolers. I hope they didn't mind. I know I hated having roommates. Even as a kid, I always pissed my brother off. I wasn't an easy person to live with.

As I sprayed and scrubbed his body, I saw that Joseph was quite like me. He too was a middle-aged man, a few years older than I, whose gut said he liked his drink. He had been a plumber—disgusting trade. His distant relatives had given iffy promises about attending the funeral, meaning rows of empty seats. He hadn't left a legacy that people would come to talk about. He hadn't inspired kids or taken care of his family. This made him more like me and less like the person I'd wanted to become when I grew up, my Grandpa.

Andrew says: "At the time I felt I had a really strong protagonist with a really interesting perspective, but I couldn't get my plot or my other characters to feel as alive or interesting, which resulted in it feeling like there was a man worth paying attention to doing nothing worthwhile. With revision, I believe I managed to keep the comedy about the situation while keeping a more steady hand on the perspective. Because I was able to settle into the perspective more, I was able to feel the flaws in my plot and other castings. The sudden changes in perspective when that perspective is your only window into the story make it harder to immerse yourself in the fiction, both as a writer and as a reader. I find that I need that immersion to stay focused and to keep my writing flowing."

Keeping Your Distance—by Accident

What can cause a problem with psychic distance? One big answer is what the writer Peter Rock describes:

> We must familiarize ourselves with the inside of the story, so we can write from within it . . . . The story speaks to us. Our relationship, whether writing or reading, is not with the author. I don't mind being interrupted or even frustrated by a narrator, but I cannot abide being reminded of an author. In fact, I've found it helpful to try to avoid thinking of myself as an author or even a writer, but rather to consider myself as a space or consciousness through which narrators and narrations pass.[2]

To get over an awkward psychic-distance gap, "familiarize [yourself] with the inside of the story, so [you] can write from within it." Again, think of acting: onstage, you don't break character to speak in your own voice. Rather, you get your mind around an overall understanding or concept of your character that may connect their emotions with yours, yet also perform and understand that character as someone, at a basic level, who is *not you* and whom you are pretending to be. Otherwise you may find yourself writing things like objectified descriptions ("The beautiful girl got out of the car and gazed around the park, looking for her friends") or stilted exposition ("She felt a sense of inclusion in their social group that assuaged the trauma of her bullied childhood") because at some level you haven't "familiarize[d yourself] with the inside of" the story and character yet and are telling the reader things that are really more like expository notes to yourself, in *your* voice, looking *at* the character, rather than speaking from inside *her* head. Pop quiz: What's the psychic-distance problem in describing your own character as "beautiful?" (See more about this in my book *The Writer's Eye*.)

Surprisingly, dialogue can be a psychic-distance block too. Dialogue can feel intimate and fun when you're writing it, because you can "hear" it from inside the story's world—you're the writer. But readers are *already* external to the story's world—we're not you, remember? And overusing dialogue can distance us even further, because dialogue is *external* to a character; spoken into the world beyond their heads and limited by what would be believable in that situation, it's therefore limited in what it can tell us about a character's interior life (unlike italicized "voiceover" thoughts, for example). And without access to that interior life, the psychic distance between the reader and the character grows. (See "violence" in Chapter 6). Overreliance on dialogue may also signal that you don't know enough about your fictional world yet to animate it through action, sensory detail, and other, non-dialogue modes of characterization. What you *don't* know, readers *can't* know.

This is why dialogue, especially if it isn't ballasted with actions and sensory detail, can feel so much like disembodied voices in space. Plus, long stretches of dialogue can give the feeling that the writer is impressed with the characters' cleverness and wants readers to be as well. (We feel shoved into sitcom studio-audience chairs, watching the characters on stage, invited to applaud at conversations that go on just a little too long.) "I want my readers to view this character as X"—without *imagining* that character *as* X to write the character *being* X in reality as they understand it—can be a recipe for psychic-distance weirdness.

Take a look at your paragraphs and your major scenes: Where does dialogue appear, and for how long? In many student stories, paragraphs begin with lines of dialogue, then move to exposition kind of grudgingly, then get back to dialogue as quickly as they can. Some also revert to dialogue (or long speeches by characters) to reveal important plot or backstory information. For a first notes-to-self draft, this is okay. In revision, try something else.* If your paragraphs fall into a dialogue-then-exposition pattern, reverse that order. If using dialogue, keep it short and interwoven with external and internal detail. If writing a longer scene (like an argument), keep your stakes high (and obvious to the reader), keep

---

*Unless you are James Baldwin writing "Sonny's Blues."

the external world present (someone's gripping that paperweight, ready to throw it), and be sure the characters' words could believably emerge from an actual, non-televised human's mouth in that situation. (Remember: high emotion often makes people *less*, not *more*, articulate.) All these things will help keep your psychic distance on track.

Keeping Your Distance—on Purpose

As an actor, Andrew knows about "getting in character," pretending to be someone else and sustaining that illusion. But what happens when you want to both inhabit "reality as your character understands it" *and* separate yourself from that character? As we saw in Chapter 4, writers may create characters with identities or beliefs they don't share.[3] When you want to insist, "this character's not me!" you may be tempted to break in with words that come from *you* rather than your *character*. But then the psychic distance— and the spell you're trying to cast—may be broken too. The challenge is to access and render the layers of your character's self, including where it overlaps with your own, while still imagining it as a *separate* self, operating by its own fictional rules. Ask, "is this really something my *character* would say, or is this something *I* want to tell readers?"

Ian Wreisner of the Chapter 4 Student Craft Studio faced this challenge in writing his character Richard in "The New Chicago." In early drafts, Ian couldn't resist some snarky comments about Richard's politics. Readers responded that those comments "broke the dream," in John Gardner's famous phrase, by shaking them out of reality as Richard understood it. Yet they also understood Ian's desire to separate himself and them from Richard, so that while they could feel complex emotions about him, they could also feel free to reject his confused far-right beliefs. Ian's solution was threefold. By imagining Richard more thoroughly, including his confusion and vulnerability (to which both readers *and* author could relate) and locating himself at a solid psychic distance, Ian also gave himself more stable access to Richard's subjectivity, including his thoughts and memories. And who's the main source of Richard's beliefs? His father. Therefore, when Richard finds himself thinking or saying something his father would approve of (but readers would not), Ian could point readers to a character who stands farther from us than Richard does. In that distance, readers (and writer) could find some breathing space. David Mamet's advice to "write what a camera could record" also helped, because we could see as Richard sees and then judge for *ourselves* how accurate his vision is. (This is why access to a character's interiority also increases our sympathy for that character; see Chapter 6). Thinking through *psychic distance* helped Ian solve a number of problems at once, because imagining yourself in relationship to your character and your readers gives all of you a clear place to stand as you navigate your story's world.

Who's at the Controls: Point of View

Each point of view (POV) choice involves putting yourself into your character's head, then framing, in different technical ways, the world you're seeing as you look out. Like an actor on stage, you have to speak, move, and even think from within your character's reality—within that role. The details you choose, the pronouns you use, the rhythms of your sentences and your voice—all these things and more are part of immersing your reader in your story. Therefore, your narrator, your psychic distance, and your point-of-view choice are all part of the same apparatus: your reader's window on your story's world. Using that apparatus, you can immerse yourself—and thus readers—in reality as that character understands it, looking through that character's eyes. The writer Maurice Carlos Ruffin describes point of view in musical terms: "My first-person and second-person narrators are singing. The narrators in my third-person stories are playing their instruments."[4]

Here are some examples and choices for points of view from this book:

First person ("I")
with present-tense verbs: Charlotte Perkins Gilman, "The Yellow Wallpaper"
with past-tense verbs: James Joyce, "Araby," Rick Bass, "Fish Story," Keith Lesmeister, "East of Ely"
Second person ("you")
with present-tense verbs: Jennine Capó Crucet, "How to Leave Hialeah"
with past-tense verbs: Tommy Orange, excerpt from *There, There*
Third person ("she, he, they"[5])
with past-tense verbs: Chimamanda Ngozi Adichie, "The American Embassy," Cynan Jones, "Sound," Jane McClure, "The Green Heart," Ron Austin, "Muscled Clean Out the Dirt"

Each can be inflected with a particular psychic distance, from omniscient or relatively objective to limited, close, or "partial" (I prefer the term "partial" for limited/close third person, because it signals not only the character's partial vision of events but also, with colloquial sweetness, the way that a writer can be "partial to" a character when writing from their point of view). Brit Bennett's novel *The Vanishing Half* (2020) starts in an omniscient third-person point of view, representing a kind of collective consciousness of the all-black town of Mallard, Louisiana, then zooms in closer to a limited-third POV as it focuses in on a single character, Desiree Vignes. Rarely, you may encounter a true third-person omniscient point of view: like certain extinct birds, this is more often spotted in the nineteenth century (think George Eliot's *Middlemarch*) than now. Yet two twentieth-century short-science-fiction classics—Ray Bradbury's "There Will Come Soft Rains" and Ursula LeGuin's "The Ones Who Walk Away From Omelas"—deploy omniscience to deliberately chilling effect.

Intimacy, Verb Tense, and Point of View

Each point of view and governing verb tense can be crafted to create a particular relationship between reader and character: surprisingly, first person ("I") is *not* necessarily the most intimate or honest, nor third person ("s/he, they") the most emotionally distant. Derailing a reader's assumptions about itself is *really* interesting for a point-of-view choice to do. Deborah Eisenberg dislikes her first story, written in first person, because she finds it "ingratiating. That's something one has to watch with first-person narrative, that special pleading for an 'I' who is automatically in the right, or is even automatically lovable—whom the reader can snuggle up with and whose plight the reader can sniffle over," she says. "Because snuggling and sniffling can derail a more complex relationship between the reader and the material."[6]

Consider Chimamanda Ngozi Adichie's story collection *The Thing Around Your Neck* (2009), which deploys a range of point-of-view choices and verb tenses to surprising psychic-distance effect. We know more about the nameless third-person protagonist in "The American Embassy" (see this chapter's Craft Studio) than about the first-person narrator of "Cell One," who keeps some of her motivations hidden from us. The collection's title story, written in a detailed, intimate second person, made my students ask, "what would *I* do in this situation?" This is because, shifting from companionable to uncomfortable, second person's closeness can implicate the reader in choices or confusions faced by the characters.

Third-person point of view can be amazingly elastic and flexible, allowing a wide range of motion, intimacy, and dramatic irony beneath an apparently calm surface. The writer Elizabeth von Arnim (1866–1941) drew upon her disastrous second marriage in her suspense novel *Vera* (1921), forerunner of Daphne DuMaurier's *Rebecca* (1938) and George Cukor's film *Gaslight* (1944). *Vera* is the story of young Lucy Entwistle, who tumbles into love, then marriage, with Everard Wemyss after her father's death, despite her loyal spinster aunt's increasing doubts. (Go read *Vera* for free on Project Gutenberg online; you won't be sorry!)[7] While giving us access to all three characters' perspectives with a flexible yet stable third-person point of view and psychic distance, *Vera* nevertheless creates a tense, suffocating atmosphere that echoes Lucy's marriage: readers are held *close* to the unfolding nightmare even as we increasingly long to draw *away*. If you're thinking, "This sounds like 'The Yellow Wallpaper'"—well, you're right!

Intimacy and implication suffuse the extremely intimate (and highly "partial") third-person child's point of view in Jane McClure's story "The Green Heart" (anthology), which has haunted me ever since I first read it in an anthology of stories from the British press Persephone Books. Despite my best efforts, I've been unable to find out anything about Jane McClure other than the title of her collection *The Sandwiches Are Waiting* (1955), in which "The Green Heart" appears, and the information on the book's back jacket flap:

Jane McClure was born in New York in 1924 and was educated there and in Washington, where she specialised in English, psychology and drama. Later she became in turn a chorus girl in the Earle theatre in Washington, a card filer in the Library of Congress, a code clerk at the State Department, a salesgirl and a speech teacher. She is married to a television news cameraman, with whom she has traveled widely in Alaska, Canada, the Middle East, and Europe.

I feel compelled to rescue this story from undeserved obscurity and share it with you to celebrate its total immersion in a child's perspective, close-up psychic distance, and sheer, heartbreaking dramatic irony, as readers are swiftly and deeply involved in a situation we're powerless to stop. With vivid detail and incredible subtlety, "The Green Heart" takes us into the chilly, Cheeverish heart of mid-twentieth-century gender norms, the mystery of a child's sensibility and logic, the feeling of not fitting into a world of opaque and arbitrary rules, and the reality that we're not always loved as we long to be, even by the people from whom we have the right to expect that love. Remember our discussion back in Chapter 4 of how children's emotions are so fierce because they have such a strong sense of injustice, hate, love, pain, joy, and other emotions *without* the judgment to know what actions to take in response, or the perspective to know those emotions will not always feel this way? Even as I grieve in advance for him as this story ends, I understand *completely*—because McClure has put me so completely on Julian's side—why he does what he does. And I'm forever grateful to Jane McClure, whoever, and wherever, she is.

The Sound of the Second Person

Let's pause here to talk about the second-person point of view ("you"), which it seems that writers either love or love to hate. I was pretty much in the latter category (sorry, y'all—and yes, that *is* the second-person plural) until I put the second-person selections in this anthology—Jennine Capó Crucet's "How to Leave Hialeah" and Tommy Orange's excerpt from *There There*—next to each other and took another look. Or, rather, a listen. Because, although it can be insufferably trendy, second person's particular combination of intimacy and distance (or disguise?) can also propel a writer forward with a distinctive kind of energy that you can also hear in a distinctive *sound* and *voice*. That voice may be motivated, at least in part, by autobiography—perhaps a similar source of energy to the one you discovered in "Why I Write" (Chapter 1).

For Tommy Orange, second person helped unlock the voice and psychic distance of this chapter from his multivocal novel *There There* (in which, he's said, all the characters, particularly Thomas Frank, are at least somewhat autobiographical). "This chapter came out pretty late in the writing of the book," he told Deborah Treisman, fiction editor of *The New Yorker,* which published a version of this chapter as "The State." "And it came out fast. I wrote a ten-page first draft in one afternoon, and felt this urgency for it to be a part of the book. I hadn't planned on it, so it kind of blindsided me." When asked about POV choices, he responded,

> I played around a lot with P.O.V. in writing this novel. Tried different P.O.V.s out on almost all the characters. Tedious work, but I wanted to be sure that the story felt—to me, anyway—like it was coming from the right place. Was told in the right way. This chapter first came out in third person, then first, then finally, when I tried it in the second person, something clicked. Revision became easier, and that's usually when I know I have the right P.O.V.: there's less resistance.[8]

That speed, focus, and cadence of Orange's sentences feel especially suitable for a story about a drummer—and if you read aloud (or listen, via newyorker.com[9]), you can hear that connection. "Less resistance" is a great way to describe the feeling of being *released into a voice and story* that a good POV choice can unlock—and perhaps that release is connected to something the writer really needs to say and the mental place they need to "stand" to do it.

Jennine Capó Crucet's "How to Leave Hialeah" has stayed with me ever since I first heard her read aloud from it at the Bread Loaf Writers Conference in 2010—in her voice, spoken and written, is a mixture of humor and vulnerability that helps the reader dwell, along with the narrator, in a complex space. Like her narrator, Crucet was a first-generation college student and resident assistant in upstate New York, a long way from home. In a *New York Times* essay, she wrote:

> The students like me who stayed [on campus at Thanksgiving] had certain similarities, I noticed. We mostly spoke a language other than English at home. We tended to be the first in our families to go to college, or we were the first in our families to be born in America—or we weren't Americans at all. We hadn't made good enough friends to get an invitation to some strange family's celebration, but that was mostly a relief. It meant we weren't going to be asked uncomfortable questions about our "heritage."[10]

Crucet's experience, which also shapes her novel *Make Your Home Among Strangers* (2015), is one my own first-generation and international students would recognize; her bittersweet humor makes loneliness and displacement feel both universal and particular. "With fiction, I find that using humor lets readers take in the hard stuff," she's said, "it's easier to digest that way."[11] The vulnerability and inclusiveness of second person, which includes the reader in an experience they might not otherwise think they share, feel central to that effect.

Atmospheres: Point of View as Subtext

Voice, verb tense, psychic distance, and POV are all connected to each other, and to your overall mental picture of your characters and their world. Sometimes, therefore, as Tommy Orange says (earlier), the right combination of voice, verb tense, and POV can unlock a story's or novel's whole personality. (This can come in revision, too: an editor advised me, rightly, to shift my novel *Eldorado, Iowa* [2019] to past tense.) When we read Adichie's story collection, one student, Arthur, astutely remarked, "I can see now how point of view is also used as *subtext*."

Consider two classic dystopian novels: George Orwell's *Nineteen Eighty-four* (1949; third person, past tense) and its feminist descendent, Margaret Atwood's *The Handmaid's Tale* (1986; first person, present and past tenses). How do their POVs and verb tenses sharpen their nightmare futures? And subtexts? Take a look at this passage from *Nineteen*

Eighty-four, in which protagonist Winston Smith contemplates his dreary workplace, the Ministry of Truth:

> The fabulous statistics continued to pour out of the telescreen. As compared with last year there was more food, more clothes, more houses, more furniture, more cooking-pots, more fuel, more ships, more helicopters, more books, more babies— more of everything except disease, crime, and insanity. Year by year and minute by minute, everybody and everything was whizzing rapidly upwards. As Syme had done earlier Winston had taken up his spoon and was dabbling in the pale-coloured gravy that dribbled across the table, drawing a long streak of it out into a pattern. He meditated resentfully on the physical texture of life. Had it always been like this? Had food always tasted like this? He looked round the canteen. A low-ceilinged, crowded room, its walls grimy from the contact of innumerable bodies; battered metal tables and chairs, placed so close together that you sat with elbows touching; bent spoons, dented trays, coarse white mugs; all surfaces greasy, grime in every crack; and a sourish, composite smell of bad gin and bad coffee and metallic stew and dirty clothes. Always in your stomach and in your skin there was a sort of protest, a feeling that you had been cheated of something that you had a right to. It was true that he had no memories of anything greatly different. In any time that he could accurately remember, there had never been quite enough to eat, one had never had socks or underclothes that were not full of holes, furniture had always been battered and rickety, rooms underheated, tube trains crowded, houses falling to pieces, bread dark-coloured, tea a rarity, coffee filthy-tasting, cigarettes insufficient—nothing cheap and plentiful except synthetic gin. And though, of course, it grew worse as one's body aged, was it not a sign that this was not the natural order of things, if one's heart sickened at the discomfort and dirt and scarcity, the interminable winters, the stickiness of one's socks, the lifts that never worked, the cold water, the gritty soap, the cigarettes that came to pieces, the food with its strange evil tastes? Why should one feel it to be intolerable unless one had some kind of ancestral memory that things had once been different?

How do Orwell's point of view and verb tenses make you feel? For me, they create a chilly, specific, somewhat objective pallor (like the atmosphere of Ingsoc, Orwell's nightmare state, itself) that illuminates this world while still being able to dip into Winston's own subjectivity for some sympathetic outrage (those bad smells, which Orwell himself hated, and the sudden "you" are eloquent, and warm). Readers move more or less from psychic distance level 2 to level 4 and back, with the simple past ("continu*ed*," "look*ed*") holding Winston's world at a relatively stable distance. Notice, too, Orwell's skill in moving between the simple past tense and the past perfect tense: "there *had* never been quite enough to eat," "one *had* never *had* . . ."). (Past perfect—sadly underused, in my view—expresses a state of being that's been going on since some undefined point in the past, up to and in the background of the present moment.) Since the *past* is contested as a site of meaning for individuals and the state, Winston must always toggle between what he sees around him and what he thinks he remembers. The tenses take us into that process.

The Handmaid's Tale (which I think of as *Nineteen Eighty-four's* feminist niece) is narrated in the first person by a woman known as Offred, a citizen of the former United States, now kidnapped into a cruelly conservative regime called Gilead. Verb tenses and sentence structures combine with point of view to introduce us to Offred's past (how did she get to this point?) and root us in her present (where is she now, and how is she to survive when she doesn't know what will happen next?) The first chapter begins in simple past, with elegant excursions into the conditional past ("would have"), casting it as a rueful, longing memory that nevertheless stirs the reader with unease: if it "had once been" thus, why did it change? Like Orwell, Atwood relies on physical detail to draw readers into the novel's world and its central concern: feminine sensuality, ghostly yet real. Here's the first paragraph of the first chapter, which is only two pages long:

> We slept in what had once been the gymnasium. The floor was of varnished wood, with stripes and circles painted on it, for the games that were formerly played there; the hoops for the basketball nets were still in place, though the nets were gone. A balcony ran around the room, for the spectators, and I thought I could smell, faintly like an afterimage, the pungent scent of sweat, shot through with the sweet taint of chewing gum and perfume from the watching girls, felt-skirted as I knew from pictures, later in miniskirts, then pants, then in one earring, spiky green-streaked hair. Dances would have been held there; the music lingered, a palimpsest of unheard sound, style upon style, an undercurrent of drums, a forlorn wail, garlands made of tissue-paper flowers, cardboard devils, a revolving ball of mirrors, powdering the dancers with a snow of light.

And here's the first paragraph of the second chapter:

> A chair, a table, a lamp. Above, on the white ceiling, a relief ornament in the shape of a wreath, and in the center of it a blank space, plastered over, like the place in a face where the eye has been taken out. There must have been a chandelier, once. They've removed anything you could tie a rope to.

The fragmentary sentences and present tense help the reader wake up into the present with the same slow horror Offred herself feels, as both character and novel-world come into focus. Throughout the novel, Atwood alternates tenses in different chapters: for Offred's richly remembered backstory, she uses lush, tumbling sentences in the past tense (and longer paragraphs), and for her tense, circumscribed imprisonment as a Handmaid, she uses short, present-tense sentences (and shorter paragraphs). But throughout, Offred's first-person voice draws readers in and holds us there. And because the alternation of tenses is consistent and logical, it feels purposeful to readers. In *Frankenstein* (1818), Mary Shelley does this too: Robert Walton's letters, unfolding in the "now" of the novel, appear in present tense, while Victor's and the Creature's stories, recounting events gone by to Robert and to one another, are in past tense.

Orwell and Atwood both show that verb tenses are markers of a *consciousness as it moves through time*. Readers need to have a character's consciousness and its location in time established before they can fully "join up with it" and use it to navigate the fictional world. And, like psychic distance, verb-tense use and logic need to feel *consistent* in order to feel purposeful enough for readers to trust.

Verb Tenses and You: Shifts and Options

So why might you find yourself shifting tenses in the middle of a story—or even a sentence? "Sally **opens** the door and **sees** Rick standing there, but she **didn't** know how **he got** into the building so quietly" (my emphasis). In speech, we do this all the time. In writing, this is sometimes less about grammatical ignorance than basic uncertainty: What is your story really trying to be, and in what frame of time and psychic distance does it really want to live? Where are you as a writer most comfortable?

Past tense has some advantages: It keeps the reader close but not too close, giving us the psychic distance necessary to form our own pictures of the character while avoiding the claustrophobic closeness that present tense can bring. For a novel, it tends to feel trustworthy, encouraging readers to settle in and go on the voyage. Yet depending on your project, you might not like the slightly more traditional feel and distance this can impart (although past tense and experimental effects aren't incompatible). Present tense gives a sense of action unfolding *right now*—readers experience it at the same time the character does. Therefore, it can enable startling effects in prose and very close psychic distance. Yet the reader can feel held too tightly, as by Elaine's close-talking boyfriend on *Seinfeld*.[12] (But if you're Charlotte Perkins Gilman writing "The Yellow Wallpaper," from Chapter 3's Craft Studio, suffocating psychic closeness is your goal!)

Regardless of what you choose for your story, keep your tense-logic consistent. A story that keeps shifting verb tenses unexpectedly is like a car that keeps popping out of gear—it stalls between dimensions of time while the reader repeatedly tries to readjust her mental framework to figure out where she is now. Plus, they feel careless—not purposeful.

Just like my students standing in our psychic-distance circle, you may find that you have certain writerly standpoints in which you're most comfortable, certain frequencies of voice to which you like to tune in. Language sounds, sentence rhythms, verb tenses, points of view, psychic distances—all may add up to a characteristic writerly stance and voice that you and your readers come to recognize over time. For example, I feel most comfortable writing a close/partial third-person point of view, with present-tense verbs for shorter pieces and past-tense verbs for longer ones (although, lately, everything I write wants to be present tense). Your writerly stance and voice will be personal and distinctive, because *you* are a distinct person, from a distinct time and place.

Staging Significance: What's at Stake?

As you get a clearer sense of your character and her frame of place, time, and verb tenses, you may ask: What are the events of the story, and what makes characters react to them the way they do? What are the consequences of these actions? How are ongoing and immediate pressures (see Chapter 1) interrelated over time, and how might time affect or add to them? Basically, do you have enough going on, with enough at stake, to make a story? It's useful to remember, though, that as the great *How Not to Write a Novel* advises, "Characters should have serious problems. But one character should not have every serious problem known to mankind."[13]

To explore this concept, jot notes in this grid for a story that you'd like to write or revise:

Character (including personal traits like age, race, class, gender—which can also add to pressures)	Where are we, and when?	Who else is here?	What does character want? Fear? Love?	What happens if character doesn't get what character wants?	Immediate pressures (from inside and outside character)	Ongoing pressures (from inside and outside character)	Obstacles: what's in character's way? (In general and in particular?)	What tools (actual or potential, external and internal) does character have (or seek) to address obstacles?

Potentially, every item in the chart can interrelate with every other (for instance, a character's race, gender, class, or sexual orientation may exert different kinds of pressures depending on place and time). What do you notice? Do you see relationships among the items in each column? A lot of information in one column? Not enough in another? What don't you know yet? Circle the most interesting item in each column: what do you see now? Then, to get yourself thinking, start putting things together. Rank the top two forces of ongoing pressure and the top two forces of immediate pressure. How/are they interrelated? How do they connect to or challenge something in the character, personally?

This is a place where students writing stories (or me, writing a novel) find it helpful to remind ourselves that sometimes the only way to make discoveries is to keep asking questions and writing ourselves into the answers, building them in layers over time—responding, kind of like improv actors, to the images and realizations that pop up as we build the scene underfoot. It's okay not to know where you're going; sometimes the only way to find out is to write yourself there, maybe even completing an entire draft (or two) before you have a sense of what your story wants to be.

Moving through Time: Structure, Diagrams, and Subliminal Coordinates

As your path forward starts to develop, you may consider your story's relationship to time, and how that will determine its structure. Where are you actually spending time in your story—and is your story actually set in the layer of time you dwell in most? And what scenes will you invite the reader to move through, in what order, and according to what overall logic?

First, let's remind ourselves of common strategies—and mistakes. As Peter Rock writes, the simplest markers of time ("Two weeks later," "One year after her marriage") are often best.[14] You can also use the section break, the cinematic equivalent of a dissolve or a cut-away, as seen in many of our Craft Studio and anthology stories. Flashbacks ("She remembered the disastrous night of the party, one year ago") can also be useful. But if you love flashbacks (like I do), beware: they can slow your story's momentum, if there are too many of them and they go on too long.

To literally see this mistake, draw it like a graph, with horizontal and vertical axes to represent layers of time and points to represent individual scenes. Here's a chart I drew of one of my own early stories, with a passive main character doing little in the present moment but reminiscing about the (much more interesting) past. You can literally see the problem—the present time frame of the story's like a little fishing boat trying to drag a heavy net through deep water. The story's present time frame doesn't move forward well, since the past is where my own interest *and* the story's action obviously is. When I tried to make this story into a novel (Chapter 7), the problems got worse. Colson Whitehead, as my workshop leader, helped me see I should go ahead and set the story in the past, so both I and my reader could settle into that world (Figure 2).

Looking at the diagram, and thinking about that story now (coming up on twenty years later!), the problem and solution seem obvious. So why'd I write it that way? Maybe because I thought I "had to" build a story with lots of flashbacks because "real writers" did. The same thing can be true of multiple narrative perspectives. It's fun to try, but it can fall apart if the characters aren't distinct enough from one another or don't have different enough information to justify cutting away from your existing scene or POV. (Plus, in a short story, you may not have the literal space to settle into each character's POV in a way that satisfies readers.)

So how can you make moving through time feel purposeful? Consider Chimamanda Ngozi Adichie's "The American Embassy" (this chapter's Craft Studio). A rough diagram

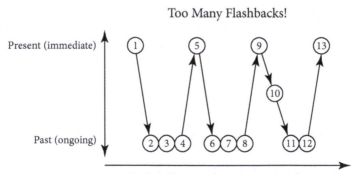

Too Many Flashbacks!

Reader's direction of travel–sequence of scenes

Figure 2 "Too Many Flashbacks" diagram by Michael Bartels.

Chimamanda Ngozi Adichie's "The American Embassy"

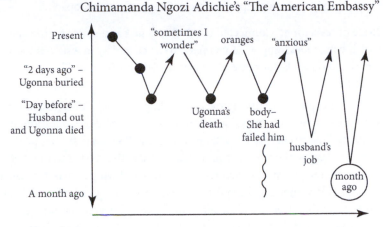

Figure 3 Moving through time in Chimamanda Ngozi Adichie's "The American Embassy." Diagram by Michael Bartels.

of its structure, with the story's time frame on the vertical axis and the story's forward motion through our own time on the horizontal axis, might look like as shown in Figure 3.

You can see how the flashbacks proceed in an orderly, alternating way between the narrator's present moment and her immediate past—the story inches forward, step by step, bearing information at *both* temporal levels, just as she does in the embassy line. Most of all, this structure gives readers information in an order we can use to understand what follows. You can flash forward (Stuart Dybek does this in "The Start of Something"), flash back, tell a story in reverse, whatever. But at the end, have these effects contributed to an experience of your story's world that feels satisfying and purposeful? Drawing diagrams like this for your own story can help you study the structures of anything you read—or write.

The writer Jim Shepard teaches his students about "subliminal coordinates," a phrase adapted from Vladimir Nabokov, which he has described as the thematic and imagistic patterns that reveal a character's personality and motivations and a story's central concerns. (Another word for these might be *leitmotifs,* which are technically patterns of sound or tones associated with themes or characters in music.) They may also be opposing forces around which images and pressures cluster, like the ones Professor Judy Troy (Chapter 1 Craft Studio) taught me to discern in James Joyce's "Araby" (1914): the sacred and the profane. To spot them and to think about their role in a story's structure, Shepard suggests a four-step process:

1) Read through a story once as a civilian.

2) Next, read it again, marking anything that stands out for you.

3) Next, read the end again and then go back to the beginning, reading it with the ending in mind. Mark as you read what drives toward the end.

4) Ask yourself: Is the story continually enlarging the reader's understanding of the character? What is the amount you are learning at any given moment?[15]

To this, I will add another couple phrases from Shepard's workshops:[16]

5) "Rate of revelation." Connected to #4, this is just as it sounds—the pace at which you are learning what you need to learn to stay invested in the story's forward motion. Is your rate of revelation proceeding steadily enough, or is it stalled out?

6) "What's the question?" Each novel, says Shepard, has a "question to which it keeps obsessively returning," which may be connected to a question he asks students: "Every character is selling something. What's that sales pitch trying to hide?" Maybe the two are connected: What is the risky question with which you (and/or your character) are obsessed, trying to avoid, trying to understand? Writer Elizabeth Eslami describes "the question" well: "You must have something deeper and richer than a single character or a clever idea. You must have something inexhaustible, a fire that will burn even if you tear away all the kindling, a fire that will keep you warm for the years you will spend stacking these words. That thing is your question, and only you know what it is . . . . The question is a live wire, connected to everything, providing juice for the whole body of the novel."[17] For example, one question might be central to the great science-fiction writer Octavia Butler's whole body of work: "the viability of the human enterprise. Will we survive our worst habits? Will we change? Do we want to?"[18]

Craft Studio: Chimamanda Ngozi Adichie (b. 1977), "The American Embassy" (2003)

Chimamanda Ngozi Adichie (b. 1977 in Enugu, Nigeria) had published two novels by the time her story collection *The Thing Around Your Neck* appeared in 2009. As I've mentioned, the collection combines the imaginative range of a novel with the technical precision of short fiction, encompassing multiple psychic distances, verb tenses, and points of view. "The American Embassy," which won an O. Henry Award in 2003, still surprises me, enmeshes me in a rich emotional experience, and teaches me and my students everything from rendering a story world in detail to building intimacy with a guarded, fiercely private character, even as we mourn with her for the gradually revealed tragedy at the heart of the story—the murder of her son. And "The American Embassy" always surprises students by showing just how intimate a third-person narrative voice can be.

By the story's end, we know almost everything about this character except her name. The details she notices and remembers immerse us in her subjectivity and give us a sense of her personality (stubborn, loyal, private, self-possessed) as they also teach us, gradually, why, exactly, she's standing in the embassy line. She knows that other people (perhaps even we readers) get her wrong, but she doesn't care, and we come to respect her and her great and private grief. Paradoxically, she's more intimate with us, in the private world of her memories, than with those around her physically in space. And

Adichie's flawlessly maintained third-person point of view builds intimacy and trust in all directions. Just as in coming to know a real person, we catch glimpses of ongoing conflict that are later revealed in full, yet the story trusts us to put the pieces together on our own. It also, unfussily, asserts its nonwhite, non-American context as "normal"—notice, here, who the "outsider" is, and how that person is marked.

If you look at the diagram on p. 107, you can see how the story's structure unfolds in orderly, deepening flashbacks that return us regularly to the present—it moves forward step by step, just like the story's unnamed narrator standing in line, inching toward the Embassy window but drawn elsewhere by painful memories of her little boy Ugonna's murder. The pressure builds as her interior world (thoughts of Ugonna's death) comes closer to collision with the exterior world (will she reveal everything she, and we, know about Ugonna when she reaches the end of the line?) But unlike many flashback-heavy stories, "The American Embassy" moves forward with grace and momentum, driven by a clear rate of revelation and an issue that matters, to the writer and reader: what decisions we make in our lives, and what those decisions may cost ourselves and others.

"The American Embassy" by Chimamanda Ngozi Adichie

She stood in line outside the American embassy in Lagos, staring straight ahead, barely moving, a blue plastic file of documents tucked under her arm. She was the forty-eighth person in the line of about two hundred that trailed from the closed gates of the American embassy all the way past the smaller, vine-encrusted gates of the Czech embassy. She did not notice the newspaper vendors who blew whistles and pushed *The Guardian*, *Thenews*, and *The Vanguard* in her face. Or the beggars who walked up and down holding out enamel plates. Or the ice-cream bicycles that honked. She did not fan herself with a magazine or swipe at the tiny fly hovering near her ear. When the man standing behind her tapped her on the back and asked, "Do you have change, *abeg*, two tens for twenty naira?" she stared at him for a while, to focus, to remember where she was, before she shook her head and said, "No."

The air hung heavy with moist heat. It weighed on her head, made it even more difficult to keep her mind blank, which Dr. Balogun had said yesterday was what she would have to do. He had refused to give her any more tranquilizers because she needed to be alert for the visa interview. It was easy enough for him to say that, as though she knew how to go about keeping her mind blank, as though it was in her power, as though she invited those images of her son Ugonna's small, plump body crumpling before her, the splash on his chest so red she wanted to scold him about playing with the palm oil in the kitchen. Not that he could even reach up to the shelf where she kept oils and spices, not that he could unscrew the cap on the plastic bottle of palm oil. He was only four years old.

The man behind her tapped her again. She jerked around and nearly screamed from the sharp pain that ran down her back. Twisted muscle, Dr. Balogun had said, his expression awed that she had sustained nothing more serious after jumping down from the balcony.

"See what that useless soldier is doing there," the man behind her said.

She turned to look across the street, moving her neck slowly. A small crowd had gathered. A soldier was flogging a bespectacled man with a long whip that curled in the air before it landed on the man's face, or his neck, she wasn't sure because the man's hands were raised as if to ward off the whip. She saw the man's glasses slip off and fall. She saw the heel of the soldier's boot squash the black frames, the tinted lenses.

"See how the people are pleading with the soldier," the man behind her said. "Our people have become too used to pleading with soldiers."

She said nothing. He was persistent with his friendliness, unlike the woman in front of her who had said earlier, "I have been talking to you and you just look at me like a moo-moo!" and now ignored her. Perhaps he was wondering why she did not share in the familiarity that had developed among the others in the line. Because they had all woken up early—those who had slept at all—to get to the American embassy before dawn; because they had all struggled for the visa line, dodging the soldiers' swinging whips as they were herded back and forth before the line was finally formed; because they were all afraid that the American embassy might decide not to open its gates today, and they would have to do it all over again the day after tomorrow since the embassy did not open on Wednesdays, they had formed friendships. Buttoned-up men and women exchanged newspapers and denunciations of General Abacha's government, while young people in jeans, bristling with savoir faire, shared tips on ways to answer questions for the American student visa.

"Look at his face, all that bleeding. The whip cut his face," the man behind her said.

She did not look, because she knew the blood would be red, like fresh palm oil. Instead she looked up Eleke Crescent, a winding street of embassies with vast lawns, and at the crowds of people on the sides of the street. A breathing sidewalk. A market that sprung up during the American embassy hours and disappeared when the embassy closed. There was the chair-rental outfit where the stacks of white plastic chairs that cost one hundred naira per hour decreased fast. There were the wooden boards propped on cement blocks, colorfully displaying sweets and mangoes and oranges. There were the young people who cushioned cigarette-filled trays on their heads with rolls of cloth. There were the blind beggars led by children, singing blessings in English, Yoruba, pidgin, Igbo, Hausa when somebody put money in their plates. And there was, of course, the makeshift photo studio. A tall man standing beside a tripod, holding up a chalk-written sign that read EXCELLENT ONE-HOUR PHOTOS, CORRECT AMERICAN VISA SPECIFICATIONS. She had had her passport photo taken there, sitting on a rickety stool, and she was not surprised that it came out grainy, with her face much lighter-skinned. But then, she had no choice, she couldn't have taken the photo earlier.

Two days ago she had buried her child in a grave near a vegetable patch in their ancestral hometown of Umunnachi, surrounded by well-wishers she did not remember now. The day before, she had driven her husband in the boot of their Toyota to the home of a friend, who smuggled him out of the country. And the day before that, she hadn't needed to take a passport photo; her life was normal and she had taken Ugonna to school, had bought him a sausage roll at Mr. Biggs, had sung along with Majek Fashek on her car radio. If a fortune-teller had told her that she, in the space of a few days, would no longer recognize her life, she would have laughed. Perhaps even given the fortune-teller ten naira extra for having a wild imagination.

"Sometimes I wonder if the American embassy people look out of their window and enjoy watching the soldiers flogging people," the man behind her was saying. She wished he would shut up. It was his talking that made it harder to keep her mind blank, free of Ugonna. She looked across the street again; the soldier was walking away now, and even from this distance she could see the glower on his face. The glower of a grown man who could flog another grown man if he wanted to, when he wanted to. His swagger was as flamboyant as that of the men who four nights ago broke her back door open and barged in.

Where is your husband? Where is he? They had torn open the wardrobes in the two rooms, even the drawers. She could have told them that her husband was over six feet tall, that he could not possibly hide in a drawer. Three men in black trousers. They had smelled of alcohol and pepper soup, and much later, as she held Ugonna's still body, she knew that she would never eat pepper soup again.

Where has your husband gone? Where? They pressed a gun to her head, and she said, "I don't know, he just left yesterday," standing still even though the warm urine trickled down her legs.

One of them, the one wearing a black hooded shirt who smelled the most like alcohol, had eyes that were startlingly bloodshot, so red they looked painful. He shouted the most, kicked at the TV set. *You know about the story your husband wrote in the newspaper? You know he is a liar? You know people like him should be in jail because they cause trouble, because they don't want Nigeria to move forward?*

He sat down on the sofa, where her husband always sat to watch the nightly news on NTA, and yanked at her so that she landed awkwardly on his lap. His gun poked her waist. *Fine woman, why you marry a troublemaker?* She felt his sickening hardness, smelled the fermentation on his breath.

Leave her alone, the other one said. The one with the bald head that gleamed, as though coated in Vaseline. *Let's go.*

She pried herself free and got up from the sofa, and the man in the hooded shirt, still seated, slapped her behind. It was then that Ugonna started to cry, to run to her. The man in the hooded shirt was laughing, saying how soft her body was, waving his gun. Ugonna was screaming now; he never screamed when he cried, he was not that kind of child. Then the gun went off and the palm oil splash appeared on Ugonna's chest.

"See oranges here," the man in line behind her said, offering her a plastic bag of six peeled oranges. She had not noticed him buy them.

She shook her head. "Thank you."

"Take one. I noticed that you have not eaten anything since morning."

She looked at him properly then, for the first time. A nondescript face with a dark complexion unusually smooth for a man. There was something aspirational about his crisp-ironed shirt and blue tie, about the careful way he spoke English as though he feared he would make a mistake. Perhaps he worked for one of the new-generation banks and was making a much better living than he had ever imagined possible.

"No, thank you," she said. The woman in front turned to glance at her and then went back to talking to some people about a special church service called the American Visa Miracle Ministry.

"You should eat, oh," the man behind her said, although he no longer held out the bag of oranges.

She shook her head again; the pain was still there, somewhere between her eyes. It was as if jumping from the balcony had dislodged some bits and pieces inside her head so that they now clattered painfully. Jumping had not been her only choice, she could have climbed onto the mango tree whose branch reached across the balcony, she could have dashed down the stairs. The men had been arguing, so loudly that they blocked out reality, and she believed for a moment that maybe that popping sound had not been a gun, maybe it was the kind of sneaky thunder that came at the beginning of harmattan, maybe the red splash really was palm oil, and Ugonna had gotten to the bottle somehow and was now playing a fainting game even though it was not a game he had ever played. Then their words pulled her back. *You think she will tell people it was an accident? Is this what Oga asked us to do? A small child! We have to hit the mother. No, that is double trouble. Yes. No, let's go, my friend!*

She had dashed out to the balcony then, climbed over the railing, jumped down without thinking of the two storeys, and crawled into the dustbin by the gate. After she heard the roar of their car driving away, she went back to her flat, smelling of the rotten plantain peels in the dustbin. She held Ugonna's body, placed her cheek to his quiet chest, and realized that she had never felt so ashamed. She had failed him.

"You are anxious about the visa interview, abi?" the man behind her asked.

She shrugged, gently, so as not to hurt her back, and forced a vacant smile.

"Just make sure that you look the interviewer straight in the eye as you answer the questions. Even if you make a mistake, don't correct yourself, because they will assume you are lying. I have many friends they have refused, for small-small reasons. Me, I am applying for a visitor's visa. My brother lives in Texas and I want to go for a holiday!"

He sounded like the voices that had been around her, people who had helped with her husband's escape and with Ugonna's funeral, who had brought her to the embassy. Don't falter as you answer the questions, the voices had said. Tell them all about Ugonna, what he was like, but don't overdo it, because every day people lie to them to get asylum visas, about dead relatives that were never even born. Make Ugonna real. Cry, but don't cry too much.

"They don't give our people immigrant visas anymore, unless the person is rich by American standards. But I hear people from European countries have no problems getting visas. Are you applying for an immigrant visa or a visitor's?" the man asked.

"Asylum." She did not look at his face; rather, she felt his surprise.

"Asylum? That will be very difficult to prove."

She wondered if he read *The New Nigeria*, if he knew about her husband. He probably did. Everyone supportive of the pro-democracy press knew about her husband, especially because he was the first journalist to publicly call the coup plot a sham, to write a story accusing General Abacha of inventing a coup so that he could kill and jail his opponents. Soldiers had come to the newspaper office and carted away large numbers of that edition in a black truck; still, photocopies got out and circulated throughout Lagos—a neighbor had seen a copy pasted on the wall of a bridge next to posters announcing church crusades and new films. The soldiers had detained her husband for two weeks and broken the skin on his forehead, leaving a scar the shape of an L. Friends had gingerly touched the scar when they gathered at their flat to celebrate his release, bringing bottles of whiskey. She remembered somebody saying to him, *Nigeria will be well because of you*, and she remembered her husband's expression, that look of the excited messiah, as he talked about the soldier who had given him a cigarette after beating him, all the while stammering in the way he did when he was in high spirits. She had found that stammer endearing years ago; she no longer did.

"Many people apply for asylum visa and don't get it," the man behind her said. Loudly. Perhaps he had been talking all the while.

"Do you read *The New Nigeria*?" she asked. She did not turn to face the man, instead she watched a couple ahead in the line buy packets of biscuits; the packets crackled as they opened them.

"Yes. Do you want it? The vendors may still have some copies."

"No. I was just asking."

"Very good paper. Those two editors, they are the kind of people Nigeria needs. They risk their lives to tell us the truth. Truly brave men. If only we had more people with that kind of courage."

It was not courage, it was simply an exaggerated selfishness. A month ago, when her husband forgot about his cousin's wedding even though they had agreed to be wedding sponsors, telling her he could not cancel his trip to Kaduna because his interview with the arrested journalist there was too important, she had looked at him, the distant, driven man she had married, and said, "You are not the only one who hates the government." She went to the wedding alone and he went to Kaduna, and when he came back, they said little to each other; much of their conversation had become about Ugonna, anyway. You will not believe what this boy did today, she would say when he came home from work, and then go on to recount in detail how Ugonna had told her that there was pepper in his Quaker Oats and so he would no longer eat it, or how he had helped her draw the curtains.

"So you think what those editors do is bravery?" She turned to face the man behind her.

"Yes, of course. Not all of us can do it. That is the real problem with us in this country, we don't have enough brave people." He gave her a long look, righteous and suspicious, as though he was wondering if she was a government apologist, one of those people who criticized the pro-democracy movements, who maintained that only a military government would work in Nigeria. In different circumstances, she might have told him of her own journalism, starting from university in Zaria, when she had organized a rally to protest General Buhari's government's decision to cut student subsidies. She might have told him how she wrote for the *Evening News* here in Lagos, how she did the story on the attempted murder of the publisher of *The Guardian*, how she had resigned when she finally got pregnant, because she and her husband had tried for four years and she had a womb full of fibroids.

She turned away from the man and watched the beggars make their rounds along the visa line. Rangy men in grimy long tunics who fingered prayer beads and quoted the Koran; women with jaundiced eyes who had sickly babies tied to their backs with threadbare cloth; a blind couple led by their daughter, blue medals of the Blessed Virgin Mary hanging around their necks below tattered collars. A newspaper vendor walked over, blowing his whistle. She could not see *The New Nigeria* among the papers balanced on his arm. Perhaps it had sold out. Her husband's latest story, "The Abacha Years So Far: 1993 to 1997," had not worried her at first, because he had written nothing new, only compiled killings and failed contracts and missing money. It was not as if Nigerians did not already know these things. She had not expected much trouble, or much attention, but only a day after the paper came out, BBC radio carried the story on the news and interviewed an exiled Nigerian professor of politics who said her husband deserved a Human Rights Award. *He fights repression with the pen, he gives a voice to the voiceless, he makes the world know.*

Her husband had tried to hide his nervousness from her.

Then, after someone called him anonymously—he got anonymous calls all the time, he was that kind of journalist, the kind who cultivated friendships along the way—to say that the head of state was personally furious, he no longer hid his fear; he let her see his shaking hands. Soldiers were on their way to arrest him, the caller said. The word was, it would be his last arrest, he would never come back. He climbed into the boot of the car minutes after the call, so that if the soldiers asked, the gateman could honestly claim not to know when her husband had left. She took Ugonna down to a neighbor's flat and then quickly sprinkled water in the boot, even though her husband told her to hurry, because she felt somehow that a wet boot would be cooler, that he would breathe better. She drove him to his coeditor's house. The next day, he called her from Benin Republic; the coeditor had contacts who had sneaked him over the border. His visa to America, the one he got when he went for a training course in Atlanta, was still valid, and he would apply for asylum when he arrived in New York. She told him not to worry, she and Ugonna would be fine, she would apply for a visa at the end of the school term and they would join him in America. That night, Ugonna was restless and she let him stay up and play with his toy car while she read a book. When she saw the three men burst in through the kitchen door, she hated herself for not insisting that Ugonna go to bed. If only—

"Ah, this sun is not gentle at all. These American Embassy people should at least build a shade for us. They can use some of the money they collect for visa fee," the man behind her said.

Somebody behind him said the Americans were collecting the money for their own use. Another person said it was intentional to keep applicants waiting in the sun. Yet another laughed. She motioned to the blind begging couple and fumbled in her bag for a twenty-naira note. When she put it in the bowl, they chanted, "God bless you, you will have money, you will have good husband, you will have good job," in Pidgin English and then in Igbo and Yoruba. She watched them walk away. They had not told her, "You will have many good children." She had heard them tell that to the woman in front of her.

The embassy gates swung open and a man in a brown uniform shouted, "First fifty on the line, come in and fill out the forms. All the rest, come back another day. The embassy can attend to only fifty today."

"We are lucky, abi?" the man behind her said.

•

She watched the visa interviewer behind the glass screen, the way her limp auburn hair grazed the folded neck, the way green eyes peered at her papers above silver frames as though the glasses were unnecessary.

"Can you go through your story again, ma'am? You haven't given me any details," the visa interviewer said with an encouraging smile. This, she knew, was her opportunity to talk about Ugonna.

She looked at the next window for a moment, at a man in a dark suit who was leaning close to the screen, reverently, as though praying to the visa interviewer behind. And she realized that she would die gladly at the hands of the man in the black hooded shirt or the one with the shiny bald head before she said a word about Ugonna to this interviewer, or to anybody at the American embassy. Before she hawked Ugonna for a visa to safety.

Her son had been killed, that was all she would say. Killed. Nothing about how his laughter started somehow above his head, high and tinkly. How he called sweets and biscuits "breadie-breadie." How he grasped her neck tight when she held him. How her husband said that he would be an artist because he didn't try to build with his LEGO blocks but instead he arranged them, side by side, alternating colors. They did not deserve to know.

"Ma'am? You say it was the government?" the visa interviewer asked.

"Government" was such a big label, it was freeing, it gave people room to maneuver and excuse and re-blame. Three men. Three men like her husband or her brother or the man behind her on the visa line. Three men.

"Yes. They were government agents," she said.

"Can you prove it? Do you have any evidence to show that?"

"Yes. But I buried it yesterday. My son's body."

"Ma'am, I am sorry about your son," the visa interviewer said. "But I need some evidence that you know it was the government. There is fighting going on between ethnic groups, there are private assassinations. I need some evidence of the government's involvement and I need some evidence that you will be in danger if you stay on in Nigeria."

She looked at the faded pink lips, moving to show tiny teeth. Faded pink lips in a freckled, insulated face. She had the urge to ask the visa interviewer if the stories in *The New Nigeria* were worth the life of a child. But she didn't. She doubted that the visa interviewer knew about pro-democracy newspapers or about the long, tired lines outside the embassy gates in cordoned-off areas with no shade where the furious sun caused friendships and headaches and despair.

"Ma'am? The United States offers a new life to victims of political persecution but there needs to be proof . . ."

A new life. It was Ugonna who had given her a new life, surprised her by how quickly she took to the new identity he gave her, the new person he made her. "I'm Ugonna's mother," she would say at his nursery school, to teachers, to parents of other children. At his funeral in Umunnachi, because her friends and family had been wearing dresses in the same Ankara print, somebody had asked, "Which one is the mother?" and she had looked up, alert for a moment, and said, "I'm Ugonna's mother." She wanted to go back to their ancestral hometown and plant ixora flowers, the kind whose needle-thin stalks she had sucked as a child. One plant would do, his plot was so small. When it bloomed, and the flowers welcomed bees, she wanted to pluck and suck at them while squatting in the dirt. And afterwards, she wanted to arrange the sucked flowers side by side, like Ugonna had done with his LEGO blocks. That, she realized, was the new life she wanted.

At the next window, the American visa interviewer was speaking too loudly into his microphone, "I'm not going to accept your lies, sir!"

The Nigerian visa applicant in the dark suit began to shout and to gesture, waving his see-through plastic file that bulged with documents. "This is wrong! How can you treat people like this? I will take this to Washington!" until a security guard came and led him away.

"Ma'am? Ma'am?"

Was she imagining it, or was the sympathy draining from the visa interviewer's face? She saw the swift way the woman pushed her reddish-gold hair back even though it did not disturb her, it stayed quiet on her neck, framing a pale face. Her future rested on that face. The face of a person who did not understand her, who probably did not cook with palm oil, or know that palm oil when fresh was a bright, bright red and when not fresh, congealed to a lumpy orange.

She turned slowly and headed for the exit.

"Ma'am?" she heard the interviewer's voice behind her.

She didn't turn. She walked out of the American embassy, past the beggars who still made their rounds with enamel bowls held outstretched, and got into her car.

Exercises:

- Try drawing your image—what's easier or harder to imagine? What details emerge first, most prominently?

- Do the "psychic distance" exercises above with your own story to help yourself establish a comfortable range:

  - Read your story aloud, stepping forwards or backwards to represent the psychic distances at which you're working from sentence to sentence. How much are you moving? Are you moving at all?

  - Circle the psychic distance on the list that feels most comfortable to you as a writer. Now write a paragraph in which you stay at that distance or, if you

travel, travel no more than a step or two away. (For example, go from 3 to 4 to 5 to 4, but not from 1 to 5).
  - Circle a sentence in that paragraph with a quality of voice and psychic distance that you really like, and try to tune in more of your story to that frequency.

- Look back at an old story or bit of fictional something and try rewriting it by hand with a new point of view, a new verb tense, or a new opening scene—let it go where it wants to go *now* and see what you get. (See Tommy Orange's remarks on second person mentioned earlier.)

- Try rewriting a page of your work-in-progress in a different POV and/or verb tense. What do you notice?

- Write a scene from a character's first-person point of view even if you *don't* intend to use that as your dominant POV in the story, then use something you learn from it or some quality of that voice elsewhere in your story.

- In *The Art of Subtext,* Charles Baxter writes that "we create a scene when we forcibly illustrate our need to be visible to others, often in the service of a wish or a demand that we seek to impose. Creating a scene is thus the *staging of a desire.*"[19] To think about plot, it helps to think about what your character wants, and what happens if they don't get it, and what other characters do in response to their desire. Write a scene in which your character stages a desire—does something that expresses what s/he wants or moves one step closer toward her/his goal. What information does it yield?

- Draw a diagram of your story's structure (like the one on p. 106). What do you see?

- Read your own story with the 4-step process Jim Shepard suggests to spot its "subliminal coordinates" (p. 107).

- *Hacking Your Structure:* Remember the "circle the most interesting thing" exercise from Chapter 2? A version of this can help you with the structure of a story in progress, or maybe even give you a new story. It's endlessly tweakable and adaptable to your own needs and ideas. Here's a place to start:
  - Print out a copy of a current draft or open your notebook pages to something you're working on.
  - Gather some scraps or slips of paper—bookmark-size or full-sheet-size is fine. So are multiple colors of paper, if you are a person who associates colors with moods and feelings.
  Circle a set number of "most interesting things" in your work, perhaps one thing from each of these categories:
    - Visual image
    - Line of dialogue (spoken)
    - Internal dialogue (character's unspoken thought)

- Physical object or architectural feature
- Natural-world/nonhuman object or creature
- Thematic keywords or "subliminal coordinates" (*body, land, child, money*)
- Something random (close your eyes and put your finger down on the page)

– Write each one of these things on a separate scrap of paper.

- If you have multiple colors of paper available—and/or colored pens—let your synesthetic self run free and write each of these things on/in the color that feels right for it. (Hard to explain—just try it!)

– Now, spread these out on a surface big enough for you to arrange and rearrange them, like a table or the floor. What do you see when you look at each new sequence or pattern? (I'm going to be deliberately vague here, for maximum writerly freedom.) What if you put them in a top-to-bottom sequence? What if you put them in a circle?

– If you see a new direction forward for your story now, try writing or typing "from scratch" on a fresh page with the first slip of paper in your sequence, and then follow what emerges, without stopping, for at least ten minutes.

- Disrupt an author-narrator-character merge by changing one big thing to separate you from your character.
- Jot notes to yourself in the "what's at stake" grid mentioned earlier. What do you discover?

CHAPTER 6
BUILDING A WORLD
FOR YOUR READERS AND YOURSELF

This tremendous world I have inside of me. How to free myself, and this world, without tearing myself to pieces. And rather tear myself to a thousand pieces than be buried with this world within me.

—Franz Kafka, *Diaries, 1910-1923*

But when you sit down to write . . . you think, ah, yes, the entire world and all its strange nuances, and subtleties, and inexpressibilities are about to surge through my arm into the pencil I'm holding. And then you look down at what you've written and it's something like, And so he walked to the grocery store . . .

—Deborah Eisenberg[1]

Once a student of mine—let's call him Tim—brought me the first chapter of his fantasy novel. The story opened right in the middle of a battle between two different nonhuman tribes, with missiles and weapons flying, and lots of different names flying, too. By the end of the first paragraph, I was lost. "So who are the Mixers again?" I asked. (I'm making up these details.) "And how are they different from the Manglers? Which one is using the swords, and which one is using the arrows?" Tim sighed. "My roommate asked me the same question," he admitted. "I don't get it. All my sentences are grammatically correct, I've spent a lot of time on worldbuilding and research, and I *know* the story is interesting. So why do readers still tell me they can't understand?"

Tim had just bumped against a reality that's surprisingly easy to forget: readers have never visited the fictional world that exists in your own mind. We know nothing about it except what we learn from the words on your page, encountered in the order you give them to us. "This, I think, is the difficulty of writing a book in general," says graphic novelist Liana Finck. "You need to make something that can be seen at a distance as a coherent object and that a reader can enter as its own universe, full of stand-alone details."[2] This prompts a mental process I call *imagining your reader*: envisioning their needs as a stranger to your fictional world and reverse-/engineering your prose to help meet those needs by welcoming the reader into it and helping them build their imaginative picture of your world while still creating the artistic experience you want them to have. (As the authors of the classic *How Not to Write a Novel* observe, this is "why your job is harder than God's."[3])

Tim would recognize the feelings expressed by both Kafka and Eisenberg, and the frustration when your words just won't connect with readers. To consider what stops your words from connecting, think of an acting exercise called the *mirroring technique*, in which you stand in front of another person and move slowly and predictably enough for them to make the same gestures: "you are helping them read you," the actor Alan Alda explains.[4] This image might help you picture the way that, as a writer, you give readers language cues so they can imaginatively enter your story-world, and then follow you through it. The more distant from them your story-world is (in place, space, or time), the more help they're likely to need. But never fear: you can accomplish this while still fulfilling your own artistic vision and helping the reader make discoveries.

Step One: What Do You Know—or Not?

Maybe you know too much about your fictional world (a big problem for—ahem—those of us writing novels about nineteenth-century England). Maybe you don't know enough (*why*, exactly, are the orcs fighting the elves?) Maybe you don't *want* to know what you *do* know ("the twenty-first century sucks—I want to write about something *else!*" Hey, I can relate). But successful worldbuilding starts by finding a balance between what *you* know and what your *readers need to know* to have an artistically satisfying experience with your work. This may involve paring back some of your knowledge (I cut my draft of *Creature,* my novel about Mary Shelley, down to 148,000 words from 236,000; Tim decided he didn't need the tribe of Malingerers in *addition* to the tribes of Mixers and Manglers). It may involve drawing pictures, making notes, and other forms of research (see Chapters 4, 5, and more in this chapter) to build up your own knowledge in your head. It may involve sharing your draft with readers to see what questions they have and where their interest goes. And it may involve getting honest with yourself about what you're really trying to say, and why.

Once again, look to climate dystopia. As I write this sentence, in July 2021, the West Coast is on fire, Minnesota is in drought, and my Alabama farmland home—like Europe, parts of China, and the New York subway system—is soaked with rain. The *New York Times* (July 18) reports that Napa Valley wine growers are spraying their grapes with sunscreen to try to stop them from baking to raisins in the 100+-degree heat.[5] In this deep grief, looking away feels self-protective. Yet as Cynan Jones's "Sound," in the anthology, shows, confronting that grief produces art that's sharp, urgent, and beautiful. When you *engage* rather than *evade* emotional work, your writing goes to a whole new level of artistry and significance. A student I quoted in my book *The Writer's Eye* expressed this brilliantly: "It's not about writing what I know how to *imagine,* it's about writing what I know how to *feel.*" And as writer Benjamin Percy advises, "Matters of the heart make your world worth occupying. Especially when it comes to high-concept storytelling."[6] As ever, ask "what is this really about?" Your answer centers the story with a weight that grounds readers and draws us in.

My student Katie, a biology major concerned about climate change, crafted a story in which the main character is a woman supervising a controlled prairie burn. Katie's fictional world is vaguely alt-medieval, with small eagle-like dragons as the source of the fire (a nifty touch), but the action of the fire through grass, the upward flight of the birds, and the sounds and smells are real, just as Katie has seen in controlled burns on our college's prairie land. In the story's first scene, the dragons' scales start to fall off; there is poisoning in the air and water, and the narrator must discover the source. Katie's knowledge of wildlife animates the story—the dragons land on their keepers' wrists and hunt fish in rivers just like real raptors—and her love for the natural world makes it compelling.

Chinese writer Hao Jingfang (b. 1984), a trained economist and writer of science fiction living in Beijing, is passionately concerned with three big twenty-first-century problems: economic inequality, environmental degradation, and omnipresent technology. As a new mother, she found herself awake and writing at 4 a.m., when an otherwise unseen army of garbage trucks enters the city. All these concerns shaped her novella "Folding Beijing," translated into English by Ken Liu, winner of the 2016 Hugo Award for Best Novelette (available online via *Uncanny Magazine*). In Hao's imaginary Beijing, the lower, middle, and upper classes are physically separated into Third Space, Second Space, and First Space, respectively, by a city that folds, turns, and locks into place again like a Rubik's cube. Unsurprisingly, the lower class gets the least amount of freedom yet does the most work—a situation challenged by Lao Dao, a Third Space sanitation worker who makes the dangerous journey to First Space in hopes of making enough money to change his life. Reading "Folding Beijing," students are quick to spot its ties to our world: income inequality, dangerous migrations, and robots threatening our jobs as they threaten Lao Dao's.[7]

Ron A. Austin's "Muscled Clean Out the Dirt" (anthology) has lingered in my mind ever since I heard him read it: strange, funny, and mysterious, it puts flesh (of a *very* particular kind) on the desire to build yourself a home. In his story, this universal longing has a magical edge rooted in the history of its particular place: a Black neighborhood not unlike Austin's hometown of St. Louis, Missouri. "I grew up in the neighborhood explored in 'Muscled Clean Out the Dirt,'" Austin says:

> My grandparents owned small businesses in the city which ended up being gutted and eaten up by urban blight despite their best efforts and hard labor. It's no secret that large segments of St. Louis city have been neglected and left to decay because of political, social, racist, and classist reasons. I can't lie—the more I read up on the systems that have worked to destroy communities and compare that research to my own experience, the more hurt, angry, and sad I become. The shit is scary and heartbreaking, but it's the truth. It's the reality I come from, and I can't look away. That'd be a real shame. And when I try to think of solutions, my mind turns to wishing for miracles, and in that way, I write to help process intense emotions and realizations.[8]

Austin is influenced by Gabriel Garcia Marquez, William Kennedy, Toni Morrison, and Jorge Luis Borges. "[These writers] developed a brand of magical realism that is both visceral and beautiful," Austin says, "that is engaged in both intense internal struggle and obligation to community. This method of stretching beyond reality by focusing on the strangeness of everyday life and distilling that feeling into breathing metaphor felt natural to me."[9] In this sparkling, Gothic-edged story, the sound that echoes in my ears beyond its ending is the sound of Miss Gail pounding the dirt, undefeated and out to get what's hers.

Take a look at the grid in Chapter 5. What don't you know yet? What's easier or harder to answer, and why? And what do you really want to be writing as the person you are, with the knowledge you have, *now*? "I've been writing this fantasy novel since junior high and this will give me time to finish it," some students tell me at the start of their senior-project process. A couple of weeks in, they often realize that it's time to reimagine their beloved junior-high story, or put it away and start something new. (There's no shame in having an unfinished novel in a drawer, believe me!) Especially since they were a *lot* more naïve about history, online-writing-community tropes, or stereotypes of "dark-skinned alien hordes" back in seventh grade.

Step Two: What Do You—And Your Readers—*Need* to Know?

Maybe you've read (or, ahem, even written) one of those historical novels that seem as if the writer did a ton of research and was determined to use every last bit of it. Or one of those science-fiction novels where every last feature of the spacecraft is lovingly described. Or, conversely, one of those novels where the writer isn't at home in his fictional world ("the samurai drew his gun from beneath his long flowy robe thing.") Research for writers, I think, can be guided by two key phrases: *establishing authority* and *a need-to-know basis*.

In her diaries, Virginia Woolf (1882–1941) described the writing of her novel *Mrs. Dalloway* (1925): the writer builds, and is aware of, a "cave" of knowledge behind each character, even if the reader only sees a little way into it.[10] As we've seen in Chapter 4, writing a believable character in a believable world means building up your own knowledge of that world. You won't be able to share with readers everything you know. But be assured: even if your readers never see your knowledge directly, they *will* feel its presence, and that's good.

Even F. Scott Fitzgerald (1896–1940) learned this the hard way. When he sent his editor, Maxwell Perkins, a draft of *The Great Gatsby* (1925) in the fall of 1924, Perkins replied,

> Among a set of characters marvelously palpable and vital—I would know Tom Buchanan if I met him on the street, and would avoid him—Gatsby is somewhat vague. The reader's eyes can never quite focus on him, his outlines are dim. Now everything about Gatsby is more or less a mystery, i.e., more or less vague, and this may be somewhat of an artistic intention, but I think it is mistaken.[11]

Fitzgerald squirmed but finally confessed: "I myself didn't know what Gatsby looked like or was engaged in & you felt it." His new description of Gatsby showed clearer, deeper knowledge: "His tanned skin was drawn attractively tight on his face and his short hair looked as if it were trimmed every day." Revisiting a real-world case of financial chicanery involving his own neighbor helped Fitzgerald sharpen Gatsby's occupation too: "after careful searching of the files (of a man's mind here) for the Fuller McGee case," he wrote Perkins, "and after having had Zelda draw pictures till her fingers ache I know Gatsby better than I know my own child . . . Gatsby sticks in my heart. I had him for awhile then lost him & now I know I have him again."[12]

So, how do you build your knowledge? First, read historical sources, biographies, other novels, and primary sources that will help give you the flavor of your characters' voices. Look at (and/or draw) pictures of your characters, or people like them, in their world. Draw maps (which William Faulkner did for his fictional Yoknapatawpha County, Mississippi, J. R. R. Tolkien did for Middle Earth, and Marlon James did for his sprawling *Black Leopard, Red Wolf* (2020). I made charts to hang above my desk for *Creature*: how old, and in what country, were Mary Shelley, Percy Shelley, John Keats, and Lord Byron each year? For her marvelous novel *Matrix* (2021) about the life of medieval abbess and mystic Marie de France (*c.* 1160–1218), Lauren Groff not only renewed her knowledge of French and read multiple histories of the period but spent time in a modern abbey, immersing herself in the rhythm of the nuns' daily work.[13] My friend Patrick Hicks, revising his novel about female guards (*Aufseherin)* and prisoners at the German Second World War concentration camp Ravensbruck, told me that he went to stay "in the same building the Aufseherin used," which is now converted to a youth hostel. But let your research emerge in ways that drive the plot. "I always want to strain history through my characters," says Namwali Serpell (anthology). "Whatever a character brings with them becomes something that I then pursue the history behind."[14]

Sometimes, learning a new thing—or finding a new object—sparks your existing knowledge. Each semester, my creative writing class visits the Luther College archives, full of cool objects, photographs, and documents to write about. Student Matt found himself holding an actual Second World War pilot survival kit, including chocolate bar, matches, needle and sewing thread, and benzedrine sulfate tablets to keep you awake (benzedrine sulfate, of course, is what we now call meth!) Matt himself has flown in small planes, knows a lot about the Second World War, and loves to hike and camp. In Matt's story, all these came together when a pilot crashes in the Himalayas and must fight off drowsiness, cold, and a snow leopard (which Matt also had to research: "I realized," he says, "that a snow leopard would not be like an African big cat; it would try to be elusive.") So the stranded pilot's fire smokes the cat out of the cave, provoking an inadvertent and believable confrontation rather than direct (and not-quite-believable) attack, as in Matt's first draft. And the scene in which the pilot fumbles for his survival kit and shakes out the matches had the satisfying ring of reality, for Matt and his readers.

Let me say just a bit more about the word "reality"; any fictional world, even speculative or "unreal," still needs to operate on a logic the reader can detect and follow. That's because every piece of writing asks the reader to enter into an implicit *contract*: "this is what I'm asking you to believe," it whispers, "and here are the rules this world follows, but you can trust them." When you use the name of a real historical figure or time period, your *contract with the reader* includes the promise that you're going to respect at least some of the historical reality we already know. Even Seth Grahame-Smith's *Abraham Lincoln, Vampire Hunter* (2010) and George Saunders's *Lincoln in the Bardo* (2017), which otherwise take fantastical liberties with the sixteenth US president, still check familiar boxes—black top hat, Emancipation, that famous axe. So do counterfactual historical novels, like Robert Harris's *Fatherland* (1992) and Philip Roth's *The Plot Against America* (2004). Therefore, even though that editor told me to "feel free to make shit up" in revising *Creature*—and I did—I didn't stray so far from Mary Shelley's actual life that readers would feel cheated rather than delighted.

For better or worse, readers *will* probably feel cheated if your story doesn't engage the big thing we know about your subject—even if only to subvert, tweak, or otherwise mess with it. (I say *Mary Shelley?* You say *Frankenstein.*) Sure, a writer who geeks out on a topic knows there's always more to tell, and wants to share that. Rightly so! But you may have to start with the one big thing *readers* know—which is definitely not as much as *you* know. My student Canon discovered this in writing his senior project in fiction, a short story from the limited-third-person point of view of King Herod the Great of Judea (37 BC–4 BC). A student of the Hebrew language and Biblical history, Canon knows a *lot* of really interesting things about King Herod—his rivalries with his sons, his epic building projects, his invention of a love potion that made him one of the wealthiest men in the world, his (shall we say) *interesting* relationships with his multiple wives. But most of Canon's readers (like me) know only that Herod tried to kill the infant Jesus. Therefore, Canon focused his story around the relatively limited time frame when Herod hears rumors of a young interloper born in Bethlehem and decides to take action. Stitched into this narrative are sideways glances and flashbacks that "teach" us other things we've never known about Herod's world—like a paragraph where a political challenger approaches Herod, dressed in a robe dyed "royal purple." This is a confrontational move, because this dye, generated from a spiky snail called the murex, could only be worn by people of a certain rank, like Herod himself. "I had to include that," Canon exclaimed, "just because it's so cool!" I agree—and learning cool things like this is deeply fun, for writer and reader.

Midrash—the Hebrew religious tradition of adding commentary to flesh out gaps and silences in a religious text—can be something fiction writers do, too, not only for history but for familiar stories from folklore, myth, or religious traditions, and even for other novels.[15] Such approaches, says scholar Wil Gafney, "reimagine dominant narratival readings while crafting new ones to stand alongside—not replace—former readings. Midrash also asks questions of the text; sometimes it provides answers, sometimes it leaves the reader to answer the questions."[16] In this way, Madeleine Miller's *Circe* (2018) reimagines the "witch" from the *Odyssey*, while her *The Song of Achilles* (2012), David Malouf's *Ransom* (2009), and Michael Hughes's *Country* (2018) reenter and relocate the *Iliad.* Kae Tempest's *Hold Your Own* (2015) queers the story of Tiresias in poetry. Mary Renault's novels, such as *The King Must Die* (1958), range through Greek history, myth, and the places they intersect. I've had students writing good stories from the perspective of Delilah (of Samson and Delilah fame) and a Roman soldier witnessing Christ's crucifixion, from the Bible; Geraldine Brooks's *The Secret Chord* (2015) revives King David, and my own story "The Serpent," discussed in Chapter 7, is a twist on Genesis and the phrase imperfectly translated as "virtuous woman" from Proverbs 31 ("woman of valor" is better). Fiction writers can find midrash-ist inspirations in classic works; Peter Carey's *Jack Maggs* (1997) is a brilliant take on *Great Expectations* (see Chapter 5), Sarah Hall's "Mrs. Fox" (2013) recasts David Garnett's short novel *Lady Into Fox* (1922), and my own novel *Creature* recasts Mary Shelley's world and the world of *Frankenstein* itself. Jean Rhys's *Wide Sargasso Sea* (1966) imagines a backstory of Charlotte Bronte's *Jane Eyre* (1847). Helen Oyeyemi and Angela Carter (see "The Tiger's Bride" in this chapter's Craft Studio) reinhabit fairy tales like Bluebeard, Red Riding Hood, and Beauty and the Beast.[17] (Be aware that characters under copyright—like "Star Wars" characters—are *not* fair game for this, even, perhaps, in online fanfiction communities.[18]) Like historical fiction, midrash can be appealing to readers and writers because it invites us to meet in a place of shared knowledge, then move forward in story.[19]

Step Three: Solve Your New Problems

In historical or other alt-world fiction, *anachronism*—a detail that doesn't belong in your story's place and time—can sneak in, because it's hard to separate yourself from the thought and language patterns of your own time and place. My student Carter wrote a nifty story in which a man time-travels back to a sci-fi convention in 1956 and sees "cosplayers." Whoops—this is a twenty-first-century term. In revision, Carter wrote, "Amateur costume designers sweated under layers of cardboard and tinfoil," which is non-anachronistic, more visual, *and* funnier. In a draft of *Creature*, I had a character cutting "rubbery" meat, around 1814. Whoops—rubber wasn't successfully mass-produced until around the 1890s.

Anachronism can run deep in political or cultural attitudes, too: if you're writing historical fiction, certain words, attitudes, rights, and social codes available to us now were simply not available in that time. Although people now called LGBTQIA+ have always existed, for instance, and have, of course, always possessed the same complex individual subjectivities as anyone you might write about, they weren't always called by that term—to say the least. In his story "The World to Come," Jim Shepard's rendering of two women in love still respects rural American nineteenth-century reality. How others label, view, and regulate a person affects the way they view themselves. Therefore, writing characters who feel full and lively to us but also true to their own place and time means doing research and, as in Chapter 4, imagining yourself carefully into reality as that character understands and experiences it, including the interplay between how they see themselves and are seen by others.

Building a world presents interesting problems where logic and technique intersect. For instance, in writing *Creature*, I had to ask: what did Mary Shelley *eat* during the summer of 1816, when *Frankenstein* was born? In April 1815, Mt. Tambora, an Indonesian volcano, erupted and spewed ash clouds that blocked the sun, creating rain, cold, and food shortages that lingered into the following year—including in Europe. Having planned a summer of sailing, hiking, and writing at Lake Geneva, Mary Shelley, Percy Shelley, Lord Byron, and John Polidori were forced to hole up indoors, amusing themselves with the famous "ghost story contest" that inspired *Frankenstein*. Every biographer tells that story, yet (perhaps due to lack of evidence) no biographer answers a basic question: in that food shortage, what did these people *eat*? So, in combination with books like Gillen D'Arcy Wood's *Tambora*, Miranda Seymour's *Mary Shelley*, and Daisy Hay's *Young Romantics*, I worked from known facts to invent some plausible answers. At other times I found myself looking up a detail I needed to move forward regarding physical textures of the period: shoes, carriages, menageries, or hot-air balloons. But the goal of my research in each case was the same: give myself solid ground underfoot to move forward with authority in my fictional world. And authority comes from accuracy as well as vivid imagining. "I think sloppiness is worth trying to avoid," says author Maggie Shipstead, "both out of pure principle (why get something wrong when you could get it right?) and because mistakes can be indicative of an author not pressing hard enough on the world she's building, not making it sturdy enough, settling for a facade."[20]

Student Craft Studio: Joel Murillo, *Cracker Jack*

When I think about a student building an alternate world successfully on the page, I think about Joel Murillo, who wrote a seventy-seven-page novella called *Cracker Jack* for his year-long senior project in creative writing. Set in a dystopian future where food is scarce, a whole underclass labors in slavery, and fights are staged for the entertainment of the rich, *Cracker Jack* follows an orphaned young man, Jack, as he trains for a fight he hopes will let him and his sister escape to freedom. Joel loves martial arts and had studied creative writing and literature, so he had a sense of how to build and drive a story. He was also following the news closely, so a lively connection to issues of race, labor, environment, and economic inequality electrified his process throughout. (Marking his characters' racial backgrounds is something else Joel was careful to do, aware that dystopias in particular speak to "real-world" inequalities.) A number of pitfalls await a writer working with this material: *Hunger Games* cliché, statically violent scenes that don't advance the plot, and—one of Joel's particular concerns—writing female characters without making them superficial (Jack has a sister and a love interest, a fellow fighter with a complex past). The challenges are significant, and I think Joel handled them well.

Looking at the opening scenes of Joel's first draft and his final draft, you can see some big changes. The first draft feels like Joel's notes to himself, centered on an *info-dump*; the final draft feels oriented to the reader, releasing information at a pace the reader can absorb—an *info-drip* (see p. 130). Right from the beginning of the final draft, Joel's rich knowledge of his fictional world is apparent but not overbearing. Crucially, it's staged in images, building our picture of this imaginary world and what's at stake here by showing rather than telling. (Joel wrote it more slowly than his first draft, stopping often to let the images develop in his mind's eye and then describe them.) The opening scenes sow the seeds of future conflicts and establish a secure narrative perspective and psychic distance that put us in Jack's shoes and on his side. (A character to attach to and follow, as well as a sensory, direct prose style, help readers enter a new fictional world.) Joel offers flashes of background information but delays full flashbacks until later (compare this with Jim Shepard's "rate of revelation" in Chapter 5 and Colson Whitehead's "novel time" in Chapter 7).

Of course, all this didn't happen overnight. Joel and I met every two weeks for the entire year, and Joel worked diligently to write and revise the work alongside his other classes and commitments, one scene at a time. *Cracker Jack* ultimately became a novella Joel's readers enjoyed, and of which Joel himself was justly proud.

Cracker Jack, *original beginning*

Jack chuckled, picking up a gold tooth. Maybe he and Kara would have a choice cut tonight, at the very least half a bread loaf. Normally people from The Pit could afford meat once a month. He rose, brow furrowed. Whoever lost the tooth definitely wasn't from The Pit—no one who lived there could have afforded one.

•

Y2K anxieties came to fruition when the largest solar storm since the Carrington Event of 1859 wiped out technology worldwide. The geomagnetic storm was the first of several, as more solar flares hurled electromagnetic pulses into the atmosphere. Lightning charred the earth and falling satellites streaked the sky. After the first day, people turned on each other. Wars and riots killed the hundreds of millions of people spared from the natural disasters. Within three months, all power sources ceased functioning. Civilizations crumbled. The world turned black.

Humanity started over. As years passed, communities banded together and rebuilt what was left of the world. Rib Mountain served as a hub for survivors in Wisconsin. Ron Whitfield, the former mayor of the nearby city, Wausau, was chosen by his peers to lead the community of Rib Mountain. The governing elite claimed homes at the peak called Summit. Whitfield's family resided in a European Manor House that had been largely spared from catastrophe. The wealthier the person, the higher up Rib Mountain one lived. Middle class citizens inhabited Alpine and lower class lived in Foothill. Impoverished people lacking possessions lived in The Pit. In exchange for protection and lodging, these citizens labored beneath the other levels, cultivating food and mining for metals to supply the community.

To keep The Pit subservient, Whitfield further molded a culture of violence with his elite squad, the Peacekeepers. Peacekeepers in Summit were allowed firearms, and the Alpine and Foothill Peacekeepers were supplied blades. If citizens in The Pit were discovered with weapons, assaulted a Peacekeeper, or incited an insurrection, they were led to the Hanging Tree. Keeping extra rations, thievery against an upper level, outstanding debt, and trespassing meant the Whipping Post. In cases involving offenders who jeopardized Rib Mountain, the Peacekeepers were allowed creativity in their methods of execution. One such case was Jack's uncle. 10 years after the establishment of Rib Mountain, an uprising led by Jack's uncle, an elder named Thomas, was quelled after a group of 500 Pit civilians attempted to storm Summit. Despite clearing Foothill and Alpine, the group was still massacred by firearm-clad Peacekeepers. Whitfield ordered Thomas captured alive and forced him to watch as Peacekeepers burned alive his wife and sons before being executed himself. His nephew and niece, Jack and Kara, were left without any living relatives.

Despite Whitfield's four-tier system's rigid discipline, exceptions were made. An exceptionally bright child could be educated in either the Alpine or Foothill, finding a valuable profession at the cost of permanent isolation from its birth family. Some Summit men would hire Peacekeepers to bring prostitutes to their homes. Occasional meetings would be held between elders of The Pit and the respective tiers to address quota and law. The other method for escape was Pankration. Named for the first type of mixed martial arts, fighters won by any means necessary, aside from biting, low blows, and eye gouges. Whitfield had been enamored with the UFC before Y2K and insisted on holding leagues and tournaments throughout the tiers. Gambling was the link that connected all on Rib Mountain. From The Pit to Summit, thousands of men and women placed bets toward fight results. Winning fighter sponsors would take 20% of the winning bets and distribute leftovers to fighters. Therefore, talented fighters, no matter the tier, would be able to support not only their families, but their communities as well.

Cracker Jack, *revised beginning*

Jack chuckled, picking up a gold tooth off the cracked earth. Maybe he and Kara would have a choice cut tonight, something sliced fresh off the hog. Perhaps a bread loaf, still radiating heat from the oven, not like the coarse cardboard they usually ate. People from The Pit could afford real meat once a month, living off canned foods for weekly rations. He rose, brow furrowed. Whoever lost the tooth wasn't from The Pit—no one who lived there could have afforded one.

He slipped the tooth into the secret pocket inside the waistband of his shorts. No one would find it there. Wandering hands had taken valuables from him in the past, a shoulder bump distracting him long enough for a day's rations to go up in smoke. Even worse would be if the Peacekeepers found it and imprisoned him for theft, taking it for their own bartering. Who would keep Kara out of trouble then?

Jack walked through the marketplace, dirt kicking up around his tattered sneakers. He scanned the faces inside the makeshift stands of rusted metal and rotting wood. A squash farmer peered back with sunken, dull eyes. The shallow red soil yielded little, especially during dry spells. A wrinkled elderly woman followed him with beady eyes, hunkering over her clay bowls. Jack trod on, stepping over a withered girl with hollowed cheeks. Defeated and emaciated people could contort into ravenous fiends. He knew from experience, though the potential thieves took only beatings from him. Last week three teenagers had received concussions after demanding he hand over a bag of noodles, and one time, a man tried bashing his head in with a rock for a strip of jerky. Jack had ended up hosting the man and his wife for dinner: pregnant women need protein. He couldn't blame the guy: he would've done the same. Just as he fought for himself and Kara, the deprived never stopped struggling to support their loved ones.

Jack reached the end of the marketplace and started up the hill, heading toward the red brick gym on Whitfield's property. Ron Whitfield controlled everything in The Pit. He and a handful of others owned all the livable land in the vicinity, placing roofs over heads in exchange for a lifetime of labor. Debts were always left unsettled after death, and the dead's next of kin would assume them, as was the case with Jack and Kara. Whitfield's Peacekeepers tallied bi-weekly labor statistics, raising the quota to prevent anyone from gaining freedom. Those who cheated Whitfield found themselves exposed by their neighbors in exchange for a chicken. Bodies were sold to him for liquor: Whitfield possessed an insatiable appetite. He was a puppeteer, and he could cut strings at will.

Jack saw Marvin looming alongside two Peacekeepers, arms crossed and frown on display, and upped his pace to a jog. Marvin worked as fighter trainer for Whitfield and never needed to worry about going hungry, his corded body a product of three square meals a day that energized him enough to spar with fighters half his age. Whitfield's affinity for violence was shared amongst the other land owners and even the masses, a night of blood and sweat in a ring erasing a day of blood and sweat in a field. He had enjoyed a decade of victorious fights when Marvin had fought, a period that abruptly ended; laborers whispered of a wager prior to Marvin's final fight—he had made Whitfield so much money that he had earned freedom for his whole family. However, when he returned home, his wife and twin daughters were gone, their cabin ravaged by a struggle. Jack knew Marvin had suspected Whitfield, but because he believed his family to be living, Marvin yielded and began to coach Whitfield's fighters, which had ushered in a period of unsuccessful bets until Jack arrived. Marvin never forgot the fragility of his station. Jack had seen the knobby cross stitch pattern across Marvin's brown skin, every layer marking each failed fighter: Ron Whitfield hated losing. His fighters were the only ones under him to be spared the lash, Marvin absorbing the floggings until Whitfield deemed a fighter disposable. Yet, Marvin's back had been spared from scourging ever since Jack became the number one fighter, and he planned to keep it that way.

Joel Says . . .

Pacing: "I struggled mightily with *Cracker Jack*'s pace. As an avid fan of martial arts films, I believe these films' pacing, generally speaking, is a very poor working model for writing an action story. Unfortunately I learned the hard way by having my first draft torn apart in an instant—out of 17 pages, only a 3-sentence paragraph was acknowledged as a building point. This feedback was of course completely correct. I was in a rush—I wanted to cover a world that could span 1,000 pages within 17. Given the time frame of the project combined with my senior year's course load, I needed to take a more realistic approach. I chose to refine a few scenes that showed promise and slowed my pace significantly. This allowed me to 'show' instead of 'tell' the story."

Showing vs Telling: "Action films generally have very thin plots—they focus more on the fight sequences than character development, and the dialogue receives minimal attention. This was the exact opposite of what my approach needed. I learned through my project reading list (other dystopic stories and books on fiction writing) that my world would be best built by focusing on the world *around* the fights. Why does Jack fight? The answer lies in his world. I found that when I looked through Jack's eyes, the world became not only clear but immersive."

Power via Omission: "I only used the word 'slaved' once—it was on the penultimate page and refers to the effort Jack and Kara would put forth when planting and harvesting crops. Slave, slavery, enslavement: I never mentioned these because there was no need. I provided images that evoked slavery—human beings without rights, working not for wages but sustenance, their own bodies belonging to Ron *Whitfield*. Through these methods, I avoided shoving a message into readers' faces; rather, I provided puzzle pieces that readers could connect to arrive at their own conclusions. I respected my readers and trusted them to form their own connections."

Flexibility: "I would read my drafts numerous times prior to submitting them to Dr. Weldon, and without fail she would always identify parts that simply did not belong. However, I only realized that I was forcing together the story when I took a step back. Through thoughtful outside critique, I was able to understand how other people understood the world that existed within my head. I distanced myself from the draft during a part of January 2017 and found that when I returned I saw the story in a different way. Events took place in the real world that stayed with me, and I felt compelled to react. I changed my ending and incorporated four scenes arbitrarily. These additions resulted in a far more cohesive draft that flowed logically and left far fewer holes. I learned that I was my biggest hindrance within the process—once I stopped trying to force the writing and let them happen organically, my world wrote itself into existence."

Step Four: Start the Info-Drip: Establish Figure and Ground

Joel's first draft is centered on an *info-dump*—he tells us everything he wants us to know in one big chunk. In a first draft, that's fine—it helps him get his story straight.[21] But in revision, imagining the reader's needs helped him craft a beginning that enacts an *info-drip*, allowing information to enter the story at a pace that readers can absorb. As with IV medicine or a garden irrigation system, a steady drip of information is easier for readers to absorb than a giant blast. And a character whose perspective readers can connect with (through the common language of our senses) and follow into the story delivers that information. (It is OK to write beginnings later, or last, after the rest of your draft, don't forget!)

Leslie Marmon Silko's *Ceremony* (1977) begins with four pages of what can be called short poems, on four different pages, framing the novel's world as a specifically Native and perhaps not-quite-realistic or even metafictional one. ("Ts'its'tsi'nako, Thought Woman, / is sitting in her room / and whatever she thinks about / appears" are the first words we read.) On the fifth page, we read the first prose paragraph of the novel, in the third-person perspective of a Second World War veteran. Notice how the sentences, in increasing length and complexity, walk readers step by step into the character's inner world while still conveying Silko's distinctive vision and voice:

Tayo didn't sleep well that night. He tossed in the old iron bed, and the coiled springs kept squeaking even after he lay still again, calling up humid dreams of black night and loud voices rolling him over and over again like debris caught in a flood. Tonight the singing had come first, squeaking out of the iron bed, a man singing in Spanish, the melody of a familiar love song, two words again and again, "Y volveré." Sometimes the Japanese voices came first, angry and loud, pushing the song far away, and then he could hear the shift in his dreaming, like a slight afternoon wind changing its direction, coming less and less from the south, moving into the west, and then the voices would become Laguna voices, and he could hear Uncle Josiah calling to him, Josiah bringing him the fever medicine when he had been sick a long time ago. But before Josiah could come, the fever voices would drift and whirl and emerge again—Japanese soldiers shouting orders to him, suffocating damp voices that drifted out in the jungle steam, and he heard the women's voices then; they faded in and out until he was frantic because he thought the Laguna words were his mother's, but when he was about to make out the meaning of the words, the voice suddenly broke into a language he could not understand; and it was then that all the voices were drowned by the music—loud, loud music from a big juke box, its flashing red and blue lights pulling the darkness closer.

To help sort out your main character from the world around her, consider the artistic concept of *figure and ground*.[22] What's your main figure, the focus of attention, and what are the details that build the "ground," or the background, around them? Joel's first draft puts the ground first, with Jack, his figure, in the background—his revised draft brings Jack forward, allowing the ground to recede supportively behind him. Readers get to know a world by watching a character move around in it. So identify a clear "figure" that matters to you, get the reader immersed in their perspective, and hold back the mass of other research and knowledge like liquid cell contents behind a permeable membrane; the details can seep in on an as-needed basis out of the wealth of knowledge you have, based on what the character thinks and sees. You may write slowly; that's okay. And feedback from readers always helps. During a workshop, I asked my students about my draft of *Creature*'s opening, which began:

Villa Magni
Lerici, Italy
10 July 1822

Ten days ago, Shelley sailed away with Edward Williams and the boy. He's not been heard of since. This silence isn't like him. But Mary wouldn't know what he's like anymore. She's only his wife, abandoned in their house at the edge of the world.

My student Gideon pointed out that while this put him into a world, it didn't attach him clearly to a person he could *follow* into that world, so it left him floundering at a vulnerable place: the novel's first sentence. The header of place and date (a big clue for Mary Shelley nerds, and a frequent tool for historical fiction) wasn't doing as much work as I thought. When Gideon read it aloud, I could hear the problem: figure and ground. (We'll talk more about beginnings in the next chapter.) So I revised and sharpened it:

Villa Magni
Lerici, Italy
10 July 1822

Mary paces before the tall windows, looking out to sea. Shelley sailed away ten days ago with Edward Williams and the boy, and he's not been heard of since. This silence isn't like him. But Mary wouldn't know what he's like right now. She's only his wife, abandoned in this drowning house at the edge of the world.

Step Five: Build a Real Character—from the Inside

We write about particular alt-worlds or historical worlds because they speak to something in *us*, and building psychologically believable worlds starts with discovering what that is. Early on in the process of writing what became his smash-hit musical *Hamilton* (2015), Lin-Manuel Miranda received some good advice: "Whatever attracted you to Hamilton is the spine of the story. Don't worry about getting it all. Because you can't. No one can. So forgive yourself in advance for not getting it all and start to dramatize the moments that make you think this thing sings. And that begins to form its own kind of spine."[23] Therefore, Lin-Manuel Miranda's version of Alexander Hamilton is *his* Alexander Hamilton, the character he creates based on what he sees in that real historical figure. My Mary Shelley is *my* Mary Shelley: a biographer, or another novelist, would write a different version. But in following my own answer to "What is this really about?," I build my own version of her.

Adam Guettel, the composer of the musical based on Elizabeth Spencer's 1960 novella *The Light in the Piazza* (see Chapter 7), took this approach in adapting her book to the screen. He says that he read the novella only once and then never went back to it in detail, because—as Lin-Manuel Miranda said of Alexander Hamilton—to adapt an existing historical reality or creative work into your own project, you have to attend to what makes that thing come to life *for you*. In talking about musical composition in a July 2021 online event, Guettel described "a heat that is generated by some situations" and not others—those situations tend to attract the kind of energy that helps them become songs. Then, regarding the question of motivation and what makes a good musical, you have to ask, in Guettel's words, "what gives these characters a reason to sing?" This is a version of the same question writers ask: What's this really about? What's the spine of the story, and its emotional heart?[24] Why am I doing this? As Joel Murillo (Student Craft Studio, above) asked himself, "Why does Jack fight?"

My student Grace explored this connection by writing about the Black Plague in the Covid-haunted spring of 2021. In her story, a medieval French boy leaves his family to travel to a church on an island and pray for healing; like Geraldine Brooks in *Year of Wonders* (2001), Grace created a fictional person in a real historical time of plague. While Grace had to look up distances, tidal patterns, and other details (like names and clothing), in the Covid-19 pandemic she could imagine all too well what it felt like to be under threat from disease, which gave her story a shiver of reality that brought her words to life.

To enliven your character, try an exercise inspired by writer Jim Shepard. "I tell my students," he says, "that one reason fiction writers are attracted to nonfiction and/or historical material is that it's a way of enlarging our contact with the world. It's also a way of enlarging the arena of our autobiographical obsessions."[25] Yet research alone won't do it: "Arcana without some emotional stake in the arcana was just trivia," he's written of the real-life Hindenburg disaster that inspired his story "Love and Hydrogen."[26] Shepard has also been known to draw a Venn diagram of two overlapping circles, explaining that one circle is his character (even a nonhuman character like the Creature from the Black Lagoon of 1950s movie-monster fame), the other circle is himself, and where they overlap in the middle is where the story is.

Try this now: sketch a Venn diagram of your relationship to your character. One circle is your character, and the other is you. What lies in your shared, or intersecting, space where they overlap? That's the knowledge you'll draw on in developing your story and its emotional significance. And as you adjust your point of view and psychic distance, you can find ways to let your own emotional stake show through your character's thoughts, observations, and words.

Here's another way to get deeper into your character and to practice "enlarging the arena" of your own "autobiographical obsessions." Students and I like to do this exercise together in class. It works best if you cover up each step with a piece of paper, so you do the steps in order and don't skip ahead:

1) Think of a mythical beast or character from fairy tales or legends (one that will be common knowledge, like a unicorn, the Minotaur, or Rumpelstiltskin). This could also work for a historical figure you're writing about.

2) List at least five physical features of that beast/character.

3) Write a paragraph of straight-up emotional exposition: What does this character love, fear, feel? What's it like inside that head/body? Don't be afraid to tell rather than to show. "I love . . ." "I fear . . ."

4) Circle one sentence in that paragraph you like best.

5) NOW write two to three sentences in which this character does something. NO DIALOGUE YET.

6) NOW write two to three more sentences in which a second character reacts. NO DIALOGUE YET.

7) One of these two characters says one thing. "DIALOGUE."

8) The other character responds with either dialogue OR a gesture.

9) Write two to three more sentences of action or exposition. No dialogue.

10) Look at your whole paragraph and put your circled sentence wherever you think it needs to go.

11) Add one more sentence (of any kind) if you think you need it.

12) Read us what you've got.

   – Talk with your classmates:
      • Why this character? What's in the overlapping space between you and it? What makes your beast human, or your historical figure attractive to you? What is in your "shared emotional genealogy," in Shepard's words?
      • What is harder or easier to imaginatively "enflesh?" Why?
      • What might you find if you kept writing?

I designed this exercise to push writers to imaginatively "enflesh" the character's body in its environment rather than leaping immediately to dialogue, which is easy for many of us to write but not that helpful for readers in picturing where we are and who we're with. (See my discussion of psychic distance and dialogue in the last chapter.) Don't worry if this takes time: I always feel myself slowing down when I am "enfleshing" the character's appearance or actions, waiting for the detailed picture to develop in my mind so I can write from it, and that's okay.

The Room Where It Happens: Place and Its Pressures

Having invoked *Hamilton* earlier, I can't resist borrowing its signature song here: the place where a story happens—real or imagined—can drive its pressures, inside and outside your characters' minds. *Setting* is simply "the physical surroundings in which a story happens," yet *place* means something more—a confluence of social mores, geography, weather, economic pressures, and more that mean "this story's events could only happen this way, here." Think of the urban Nigeria of Chimamanda Ngozi Adichie's "The American Embassy" (Chapter 5 Craft Studio) or the magical St. Louis of Ron Austin's

"Muscled Clean Out the Dirt" (anthology), just to name two. Investing some detail and revision time in your story's place—even if that place is semi-imaginary, like the nineteenth-century, fairy-tale Europe of Angela Carter's "The Tiger's Bride" (discussed later)—can heighten the richness of the ground across which your figures move. Can you see its buildings and trees, feel its summertime heat, know where everyone goes on a Friday night? (See exercises at the end of this chapter.)

Place is a powerful, organic source of meaning and often a character in its own right, as Bonnie Friedman writes: "When the conditions are right," she says,

> live things creep up. . . . The most potent meaning arises indigenously. It looks like earth, like mud, like a log. The more your eyes discern the particulars of the physical world and its inhabitants, the more meaningful your work becomes. This is the meaning that, when it's laid dormant in the sun long enough, strikes with devouring force.[27]

Remember that weather can be an aspect of place, building subtext: "Christopher Sykes once asked his good friend Evelyn Waugh how it was that one of his earlier novels, apparently light and humorous, had an undertow of melancholy," writes critic and novelist John Lanchester. "Waugh said he had done it by keeping the weather in the book grey and rainy."[28]

Consider that good description drawn from the sensory surroundings of a place can appeal to more senses than just the visual ones. Kyla, a blind creative writing student of mine, remarked very usefully that visual descriptions of people and things are less lively for her than textures, smells, sounds, and tastes. In class, when we did the "feature of your crush" exercise in the next chapter, Kyla said, "I think about the sound of someone's voice, how it feels when they hold my hand. Tightly or loosely? Are their palms sweating?" This is a great reminder that good description can build your fictional world's sensorium—a whole environment appealing to all five senses of a variety of human bodies, reaching a range of readers where they are.

Student Craft Studio: Kari Myers, "Fields of Ash"

As a new professor in the Upper Midwest, I never knew someone could drown in corn— until I read this elegant, elegiac story by Karoline (Kari) Myers, an Iowa native whose senior project in creative writing was one of the first I ever supervised. "Fields of Ash" is narrated by Izzy, a fourth-grader dealing with the death of her classmate Billy and her mother's affair with Billy's father in a farm town much like Kari's own. "All the kids in school knew about the accident," Izzy tells us, "had been warned for ever afterwards about never playing in bins or wagons of grain that could suddenly suck you to the bottom like quicksand and leave you for dead. Like Billy." Kari's work reminded me of Alice Munro, who also writes with quiet, devastating effect about women in rural worlds. Kari's sense of place lets her select small details that give the story a subtle authority: the "burn barrel," the strawberry-patterned tablecloth, the smell of line-dried sheets—and grains still clinging to Billy's small body.

Midwestern students, with typical modesty, sometimes demur writing about their own home: "it's boring." But as Kari shows, place is not only about *what would only happen this way here* but *what could go wrong here, and how would people respond*—the classic instigation for many an effective story like hers. And she shows how looking closely at any place, and its inhabitants, can make it less boring after all.

Excerpt from "Fields of Ash"

That night, when I was supposed to be in bed, I crouched beneath the window where I could hear Mama and Uncle Pete talking on the porch.

"Oh, Pete," said Mama. "It just broke your heart."

And she told him about Mrs. Barth, how after she had picked Billy up from the ground and carried him into the house, she had laid him on top of the kitchen table, right on top of the tablecloth. As Mama's voice floated up to me, I imagined the scene—Mama watching as Mrs. Barth removed Billy's shoes and set them side by side on the floor. She rolled the socks down from his ankles, gently revealing each heel, the pink sole, the toes. "Grace?" said Mama, but Mrs. Barth did not look at her. Slowly, she removed Billy's glasses, then his shirt and pants, folding each article of clothing until he lay on the table naked as the day he came into the world. She wet a rag and began wiping away the dirt from when they had laid him on the ground and tried to breathe for him, wiping away each particle of grain that had lodged itself in the creases of his flesh, his bellybutton, the folds in his hands, in between his toes. She did not cry. Her hands continued to wipe with the rag, as steady as they were when she drove the tractor, pushing seeds deep into the earth. When she finished, she carried him to his bedroom. She laid him in his bed, covering him with the sheets she had just washed fresh the day before, hanging them out in the sun to dry so they smelled like wind. She returned to the kitchen and gathered the tablecloth by its four corners into a bundle, trapping the loose grains.

Together with the men, Mama and I had watched Mrs. Barth come outside, drop the cloth into the burn barrel, and strike a match. The pattern of strawberries smoldered.

Kari says: "People and place are inextricably linked. The environment in which you place a character exerts its own unique set of pressures. I like to ask myself 'could this character or set of circumstances take place anywhere else at its most heightened possibility?' From there, creating that immersive sense of place becomes both a challenge and an opportunity. Often I find in my early drafts that my efforts to create a sense of place are fueled simply by the desire to give believability to my character's world. What objects, sounds, and specific actions or behaviors fill this place as experienced through the character's eyes? Later, I love the opportunity to revisit those 'place makers' and see if there are ones that can be brought more clearly into focus or deepened, that, more than sensory, point to a deeper layer of truth or theme in the story. Finding a way to bring those out and further heighten their connection within the story is one of my favorite undertakings as a writer. Writing this passage from 'Fields of Ash' was one of those euphoric moments in which I remember feeling both of those layers click into place almost simultaneously—in part, I suspect, because the world of Iowa fields and farmhouses, of neighbors and quiet fortitude, was one with which I was intimately familiar."

Why Are You Hurting Me? Violence and Fiction

We live in a culture that equates violence with authenticity—on and off the movie screen—and that's a problem. Because writers always have to consider how, and whether, our readers will follow us into our story's world, violence presents a special case for us. The line is delicate. Violence on the page can indicate writerly conviction and serious engagement with the world and its troubles. But too much violence can also make you feel snarled in the writer's own grim preoccupations (at too close a psychic distance) and send you hunting for the exit. Because of our mirror neurons, readers will at some level be feeling the violence you inflict on your characters in our *own* bodies as we read—so, remember, when you hurt your character, you are hurting us too.

In her book *The Art of Death*, novelist Edwidge Danticat says that writers must give their characters' lives *and* deaths moral weight and appropriate dignity. What if we imagine their deaths, in other words, as reflecting the lives we have also richly imagined? "Whether we love or hate them," she writes, "the people dying on the page must somehow reveal themselves to us. We must be invested in their fate, whether we want them to live or die."[29] Her words make me reflect on how I might imagine characters' accidents, pains, and deaths—as well as their lives—with dignity and depth. Kari Myers's "Fields of Ash" is a beautiful example of how a child's untimely death is given moral weight.

Representing violence and trouble with appropriate moral weight can be a purposeful way of highlighting difficult—and, yes, violent—realities that readers might not otherwise see. In an interview with *The Paris Review*, Jesmyn Ward, author of *Salvage the Bones* (2011), was asked, "Do you think of your writing as political?" Ward responded:[30] "After I finished my first draft of *Salvage the Bones*, I felt that I wasn't political enough":

I had to be more honest about the realities of the community I was writing about. After my brother died in the fall of 2000, four young black men from my community died in the next four years—from suicide, drug overdose, murder, and auto accidents. My family and I survived Hurricane Katrina in 2005; we left my grandmother's flooding house, were refused shelter by a white family, and took refuge in trucks in an open field during a Category Five hurricane. I saw an entire town demolished, people fighting over water, breaking open caskets searching for something that could help them survive. I realized that if I was going to assume the responsibility of writing about my home, I needed narrative ruthlessness. I couldn't dull the edges and fall in love with my characters and spare them. Life does not spare us.

Ward's perspective is echoed by Benjamin Percy in his essay "There Will Be Blood: Writing Violence": "The author (whether a writer or filmmaker) is a servant of memory and must make certain the reader never forgets, must hold up a mirror to truths we would rather not acknowledge."[31] Colson Whitehead's novel *The Nickel Boys* (2019) lifted up just such a hidden truth: the story of the real-life Dozier School in Florida, where boys (particularly Black boys) were tortured and killed. Douglas Stuart's novels *Shuggie Bain* (2020) and *Young Mungo* (2022) depict the grim realities of life for queer teenage protagonists growing up, like Stuart himself, in working-class Glasgow.

As Levi Bird mentions in his Student Craft Studio (Chapter 3), including violence in your story can be personally challenging. Novelists Ethan Rutherford and Colson Whitehead have both described how becoming a parent makes writing violence harder for them. "[W]hat is the worst thing that could happen?" Rutherford writes. "That's not a question I'm interested in anymore, it provides no more fertile soil. Violence, for me, is no longer pleasurably abstract, a means to a story's end. Everyone is somebody's mother; everyone is somebody's son."[32] Whitehead echoes this in an interview about *The Underground Railroad*: "Thinking about the loss of a child, about how my own children would feel if they saw me beaten to death in front of them, made writing this book very different than it would have been if I had tried it when I was 30."[33] Crime novelist Don Winslow, warning against "crossing a line into the pornography of violence," says, "If you've ever seen someone die of a gunshot wound you know there's nothing pretty or romantic about it."[34]

Responding to real-world concerns of harm, the Staunch Book Prize was established in 2018 for thrillers that don't use violence against women to advance its plot. Yet crime writer Sophie Hannah noted that this may not adequately represent the realities of the world or of storytelling conflict. "If we can't stop human beings from viciously harming one another, we need to be able to write stories in which that harm is subjected to psychological and moral scrutiny, and punished," she writes. "There is no life-changing experience that we should be discouraged from writing and reading about."[35] This feels crucial for writers: let us not only render the harm on our pages where appropriate but *subject that harm to psychological and moral scrutiny*, even if it's just opening a space between us and the violent (or potentially violent) character, as Eudora Welty does in "Where Is the Voice Coming From?" and as Elizabeth Von Arnim does in *Vera* (see Chapters 4 and 5).

Violence can be a kind of necessary shock, a way of "going there," that suits your work as an artist. The theological discussion between the Misfit and the grandmother in Flannery O'Connor's "A Good Man Is Hard to Find" slings a kind of moral weight only O'Connor—a devout Catholic convinced of human folly and fallenness—could deploy. "When you can assume that your audience holds the same beliefs you do, you can relax and use more normal means of talking to it"; she wrote in her essay "The Fiction Writer and His Country," "when you have to assume that it does not, then you have to make your vision apparent by shock—to the hard of hearing you shout, and for the almost-blind you draw large and startling figures."[36] But how "startling" is *too* startling? How weird and dark is *too* weird and dark? (See "Dr. Weldon's Fiction Prescriptions" at the end of this textbook for ideas.)

Here are some questions to consider:

- Are you relying on stereotypical tropes of violence against [insert person here] to move the plot forward?[37] Conversely, is your story stalling because you're making things *too* easy on your characters?

- Writing violence well starts with remembering that readers may be coming to that violent moment from a range of perspectives and experiences you don't know. Sure, your characters must have troubles for a story to move. Violence will be a reality of (for instance) the world of many historical novels and dystopias, and it can suffuse acknowledged literary masterpieces like Cormac McCarthy's *Blood Meridian* (1985), Toni Morrison's *Beloved* (1987), Rick Bass's "Fish Story" (anthology), or pretty much anything by Flannery O'Connor. Imagining a range of experiences is basic to being a writer. But still, empathy, humility, and responsibility are *crucial* here—especially since through our mirror neurons, readers literally experience the pain you evoke. So consider how you will actually render violence on the page—including where you will *not* go.

- As in Chapters 3 and 4, representing people multidimensionally on the page can avert *many* problems. In fiction and in life, removing someone's agency and their capacity for choice, dignity, complexity, beauty, and joy—even as you can *also* acknowledge constraints on them—removes their full humanity. Jesmyn Ward's fiction (for example) is also full of moments of beauty and resilience alongside violence: her characters are never *merely* anything.

So how might you write violence responsibly? And believably?

- In fiction which features violence, look at how the author *prepares* readers for its possibility by gradually building pressures within the story's world (rendered in place-based textures) to which the characters respond. (*Nobody* "just snaps.")

- Consider how to link violence with *consequence*, and please don't glamorize it or treat it casually or cartoonishly. As Benjamin Percy writes, "So many of my students—mostly young men egged on by I don't know what: Xbox, Hollywood, Axe body spray? —prolong suffering and splash buckets of blood across their stories without principle and with peculiar malice and glee."[38] Yet in an era of school (and church, and synagogue, and concert, and shopping mall, and Wal-Mart, and nightclub, and parade . . .) shootings, and more, violence feels anything but casual to people all over America and the world right now. So if readers feel you are using violence casually in your work, we will turn away. And rightly so. This goes double, I think, for violence against animals. That said, Rick Bass's "Fish Story" (anthology) has haunted me since I read it more than a decade ago, and it still rocks me with its great honesty, mystery, and grief. Dogfighting bears this weight in Jesmyn Ward's *Salvage the Bones*. These writers challenge me to ponder how humans "do not spare," in Ward's words, each other, or other beings, without merely exploiting pain.

- Beware *victimhood*: deprive someone of agency and personal complexity and you'll get a stereotype rather than a real character. That is not to say you can't render the severity of what happens to them. But is your character merely on the receiving end of violence—a passive person without agency, which, as we've seen in Chapter 4, can nudge that person perilously close to stereotype? Or does that character's relationship with violence and resistance—and your own imagining of that character—flow in more than one direction? Kristina in Deborah Eisenberg's great domestic-violence story "Window" is kind of a drifting, small-town Pretty Girl until she has to make a hard decision—increasing our respect for her, since we know how risky that decision is.

- *Interiority* leads to *empathy*. Giving reader's access to a character's interiority heightens our sympathy for them; decreasing or denying it hardens our hearts against them. Movies use this principle: we never see "into" serial killer Michael Myers in *Halloween* (1978) or brutal Edwin Epps in *Twelve Years a Slave* (2013). Basically, people don't do things for no reason, even if that reason makes sense only to them. If you want us to "get closer" to a character, let us see their reasoning process, or the capacity for it—leading, perhaps, to the magnificent discomfort of a novel like *Lolita* (1955). (See my Chapter 5 endnote on "creepy first-person narrators" in the back of this book.)

- Offer readers an "out" or two from violent description, respecting our tolerance levels. Implying what happens next may be enough. As the films of Alfred Hitchcock show, there's great power in leaving some things to readers' imaginations—because given a chance, we'll script and film the action ourselves, in our heads. How graphic—and how extensive—does your description of violence *really* need to be? (Again, consider classic Gothic domestic drama like Von Arnim's *Vera*, DuMaurier's *Rebecca*, or Cukor's *Gaslight*, where just the *threat* of violence creates signature, persistent suspense.)

- If you look at the moment of actual shooting in two great stories—Tobias Wolff's "Bullet in the Brain" (1995) or Andre Dubus's "Killings" (1979)—you see the prose is clinical: only nouns and verbs. This reflects great advice from Anton Chekhov: write action of great drama or potential sentiment like a police report, to avoid importing fake emotion with puffed-up, purple language or—*cringe*—glamorizing violence.

- Above all, as in Chapters 1 and 4, ask *why you're writing this*. To explore believable consequences of believable actions and pressures on believable people in a believable world? To signal the truth that, alas, violence and discomfort *do* exist in life? To challenge yourself toward multidimensionality, empathy, and the good kind of risk? If readers feel these are the case, we'll likely follow. Or are you trying to haul in a feeling of "realness" or intensity that just feels fake? *But violence does not automatically confer authenticity or artistic seriousness.* It can be a way to avoid taking other beings seriously—and that's a problem, on and off the page.

Craft Studio: Angela Carter (1940–92), "The Tiger's Bride" from *The Bloody Chamber and Other Stories* (1979)

Angela Carter delighted in paradox. A deeply individualistic writer, she was also inspired by the communally historical, alive to the past's strange beauty but savvy about its misuse. "This past, for me, has important decorative, ornamental functions," she once wrote; "further, it is a vast repository of outmoded lies, where you can check out what lies used to be à la mode and find the old lies on which new lies have been based." A committed feminist, Carter also distrusted easy answers, especially about sexuality, which she explored with fearlessness, nuance, and humor. Direct and funny, her writerly voice is also stylishly ornate (who else can get away with words like "ciliate" and "gracile?"). Internationalist and time-traveling, she was also deeply English: her work rings with echoes of William Blake, John Keats, Charles Dickens, and the vast rackety circus of music halls, legends, and ballads that also inspired her generational peers the Beatles. Rooted in literature, folklore, and history, and alive to their enchantments and general bloodiness, she imaginatively metabolized them into a new kind of fruit, borne on a profuse and fascinating tree.[39]

"My father lost me to The Beast at cards": from the first sentence of "The Tiger's Bride," Carter twists a familiar tale to suspend readers in some space between a bygone world and our own. "Beauty and the Beast" is a familiar story, first published in written form in 1740 by Gabrielle-Suzanne Barbot de Villeneuve (1685–1755) and revisited ever since, including Jean Cocteau's gorgeous film *La Belle et La Bête* (1946) and, of course, Disney. As with Bluebeard and Red Riding Hood elsewhere in *The Bloody Chamber*, Carter makes "Beauty and the Beast" her own by finding its emotional heart and casting Beauty (otherwise unnamed) as a real, complex girl. Beauty's first bitter admission strikes a note on which Carter builds: her anger comes from betrayal, including betrayal of the dignity she knows herself to possess. Typically, Carter focuses sharply on patriarchy: Beauty's gender makes her a bargaining chip among men. Yet Beauty's desires are also a source of agency, leading her to the profoundly human place she and the Beast share: vulnerability, which shatters the shells of human forms and of the story itself. Sexy, shapeshifting, tender, wild—welcome to Angela Carter's world.

Near the end of her life, writing the introduction for her second anthology of international fairy tales, Carter left a fragmentary note: "fairy tales," she wrote, "—cunning and high spirits."[40] *Cunning and high spirits:* not a bad summary of Angela Carter's distinctive writerly presence, and her wise, joyful council to those of us who follow her.

"The Tiger's Bride" by Angela Carter

My father lost me to The Beast at cards.

There's a special madness strikes travellers from the North when they reach the lovely land where the lemon trees grow. We come from countries of cold weather; at home, we are at war with nature but here, ah! you think you've come to the blessed plot where the lion lies down with the lamb. Everything flowers; no harsh wind stirs the voluptuous air. The sun spills fruit for you. And the deathly, sensual lethargy of the sweet South infects the starved brain; it gasps: "Luxury! more luxury!" But then the snow comes, you cannot escape it, it followed us from Russia as if it ran behind our carriage, and in this dark, bitter city has caught up with us at last, flocking against the windowpanes to mock my father's expectations of perpetual pleasure as the veins in his forehead stand out and throb, his hands shake as he deals the Devil's picture books.

The candles dropped hot, acrid gouts of wax on my bare shoulders. I watched with the furious cynicism peculiar to women whom circumstances force mutely to witness folly, while my father, fired in his desperation by more and yet more draughts of the firewater they call "grappa," rids himself of the last scraps of my inheritance. When we left Russia, we owned black earth, blue forest with bear and wild boar, serfs, cornfields, farmyards, my beloved horses, white nights of cool summer, the fireworks of the northern lights. What a burden all those possessions must have been to him, because he laughs as if with glee as he beggars himself; he is in such a passion to donate all to The Beast.

Everyone who comes to this city must play a hand with the grand seigneur; few come. They did not warn us at Milan, or, if they did, we did not understand them—my limping Italian, the bewildering dialect of the region. Indeed, I myself spoke up in favour of this remote, provincial place, out of fashion two hundred years, because, oh irony, it boasted no casino. I did not know that the price of a stay in its Decembral solitude was a game with Milord.

The hour was late. The chill damp of this place creeps into the stones, into your bones, into the spongy pith of the lungs; it insinuated itself with a shiver into our parlour, where Milord came to play in the privacy essential to him. Who could refuse the invitation his valet brought to our lodging? Not my profligate father, certainly; the mirror above the table gave me back his frenzy, my impassivity, the withering candles, the emptying bottles, the coloured tide of the cards as they rose and fell, the still mask that concealed all the features of The Beast but for the yellow eyes that strayed, now and then, from his unfurled hand towards myself.

"*La Bestia!*" said our landlady, gingerly fingering an envelope with his huge crest of a tiger rampant on it, something of fear, something of wonder in her face. And I could not ask her why they called the master of the place, "*La Bestia*"—was it to do with that heraldic signature?—because her tongue was so thickened by the phlegmy, bronchitic speech of the region I scarcely managed to make out a thing she said except, when she saw me: "*Che bella!*"

Since I could toddle, always the pretty one, with my glossy, nut-brown curls, my rosy cheeks. And born on Christmas Day—her "Christmas rose," my English nurse called me. The peasants said: "The living image of her mother," crossing themselves out of respect for the dead. My mother did not blossom long; bartered for her dowry to such a feckless sprig of the Russian nobility that she soon died of his gaming, his whoring, his agonizing repentances. And The Beast gave me the rose from his own impeccable if outmoded buttonhole when he arrived, the valet brushing the snow off his black cloak. This white rose, unnatural, out of season, that now my nervous fingers ripped, petal by petal, apart as my father magnificently concluded the career he had made of catastrophe.

This is a melancholy, introspective region; a sunless, featureless landscape, the sullen river sweating fog, the shorn, hunkering willows. And a cruel city; the sombre piazza, a place uniquely suited to public executions, under the heeding shadow of that malign barn of a church. They used to hang condemned men in cages from the city walls; unkindness comes naturally to them, their eyes are set too close together, they have thin lips. Poor food, pasta soaked in oil, boiled beef with sauce of bitter herbs. A funereal hush about the place, the inhabitants huddled up against the cold so you can hardly see their faces. And they lie to you and cheat you, innkeepers, coachmen, everybody. God, how they fleeced us!

The treacherous South, where you think there is no winter but forget you take it with you.

My senses were increasingly troubled by the fuddling perfume of Milord, far too potent a reek of purplish civet at such close quarters in so small a room. He must bathe himself in scent, soak his shirts and underlinen in it; what can he smell of, that needs so much camouflage?

I never saw a man so big look so two-dimensional, in spite of the quaint elegance of The Beast, in the old-fashioned tailcoat that might, from its looks, have been bought in those distant years before he imposed seclusion on himself; he does not feel he need keep up with the times. There is a crude clumsiness about his outlines, that are on the ungainly, giant side; and he has an odd air of self-imposed restraint, as if fighting a battle with himself to remain upright when he would far rather drop down on all fours. He throws our human aspirations to the godlike sadly awry, poor fellow; only from a distance would you think The Beast not much different from any other man, although he wears a mask with a man's face painted most beautifully on it. Oh, yes, a beautiful face; but one with too much formal symmetry of feature to be entirely human: one profile of his mask is the mirror image of the other, too perfect, uncanny. He wears a wig, too, false hair tied at the nape with a bow, a wig of the kind you see in old-fashioned portraits. A chaste silk stock stuck with a pearl hides his throat. And gloves of blond kid that are yet so huge and clumsy they do not seem to cover hands.

He is a carnival figure made of papier mâché and crêpe hair; and yet he has the Devil's knack at cards.

His masked voice echoes as from a great distance as he stoops over his hand and he has such a growling impediment in his speech that only his valet, who understands him, can interpret for him, as if his master were the clumsy doll and he the ventriloquist.

The wick slumped in the eroded wax, the candles guttered. By the time my rose had lost all its petals, my father, too, was left with nothing.

"Except the girl."

Gambling is a sickness. My father said he loved me yet he staked his daughter on a hand of cards. He fanned them out; in the mirror, I saw wild hope light up his eyes. His collar was unfastened, his rumpled hair stood up on end, he had the anguish of a man in the last stages of debauchery. The draughts came out of the old walls and bit me, I was colder than I'd ever been in Russia, when nights are coldest there.

A queen, a king, an ace. I saw them in the mirror. Oh, I know he thought he could not lose me; besides, back with me would come all he had lost, the unravelled fortunes of our family at one blow restored. And would he not win, as well, The Beast's hereditary palazzo outside the city; his immense revenues; his lands around the river; his rents, his treasure chest, his Mantegnas, his Giulio Romanos, his Cellini saltcellars, his titles . . . the very city itself.

You must not think my father valued me at less than a king's ransom; but, at *no more* than a king's ransom.

It was cold as hell in the parlour. And it seemed to me, child of the severe North, that it was not my flesh but, truly, my father's soul that was in peril.

My father, of course, believed in miracles; what gambler does not? In pursuit of just such a miracle as this, had we not travelled from the land of bears and shooting stars?

So we teetered on the brink.

The Beast bayed; laid down all three remaining aces.

The indifferent servants now glided smoothly forward as on wheels to douse the candles one by one. To look at them you would think that nothing of any moment had occurred. They yawned a little resentfully; it was almost morning, we had kept them out of bed. The Beast's man brought his cloak. My father sat amongst these preparations for departure, staring on at the betrayal of his cards upon the table.

The Beast's man informed me crisply that he, the valet, would call for me and my bags tomorrow, at ten, and conduct me forthwith to The Beast's palazzo. *Capisco?* So shocked was I that I scarcely did "capisco"; he repeated my orders patiently, he was a strange, thin, quick little man who walked with an irregular, jolting rhythm upon splayed feet in curious, wedge-shaped shoes.

Where my father had been red as fire, now he was white as the snow that caked the window-pane. His eyes swam; soon he would cry.

"Like the base Indian," he said; he loved rhetoric. "'One whose hand / Like the base Indian, threw a pearl away / Richer than all his tribe . . .' I have lost my pearl, my pearl beyond price."

At that, The Beast made a sudden, dreadful noise, halfway between a growl and a roar; the candles flared. The quick valet, the prim hypocrite, interpreted unblinking: "My master says: If you are so careless of your treasures, you should expect them to be taken from you."

He gave us the bow and smile his master could not offer us and they departed.

•

I watched the snow until, just before dawn, it stopped falling; a hard frost settled, next morning there was a light like iron.

The Beast's carriage, of an elegant if antique design, was black as a hearse and it was drawn by a dashing black gelding who blew smoke from his nostrils and stamped upon the packed snow with enough sprightly appearance of life to give me some hope that not all the world was locked in ice, as I was. I had always held a little towards Gulliver's opinion, that horses are better than we are, and, that day, I would have been glad to depart with him to the kingdom of horses, if I'd been given the chance.

The valet sat up on the box in a natty black and gold livery, clasping, of all things, a bunch of his master's damned white roses as if a gift of flowers would reconcile a woman to any humiliation. He sprang down with preternatural agility to place them ceremoniously in my reluctant hand. My tear-beslobbered father wants a rose to show that I forgive him. When I break off a stem, I prick my finger and so he gets his rose all smeared with blood.

The valet crouched at my feet to tuck the rugs about me with a strange kind of unflattering obsequiousness yet he forgot his station sufficiently to scratch busily beneath his white periwig with an over-supple index finger as he offered me what my old nurse would have called an "old-fashioned look," ironic, sly, a smidgen of disdain in it. And pity? No pity. His eyes were moist and brown, his face seamed with the innocent cunning of an ancient baby. He had an irritating habit of chattering to himself under his breath all the time as he packed up his master's winnings. I drew the curtains to conceal the sight of my father's farewell; my spite was sharp as broken glass.

Lost to The Beast! And what, I wondered, might be the exact nature of his "beastliness"? My English nurse once told me about a tiger-man she saw in London, when she was a little girl, to scare me into good behaviour, for I was a wild wee thing and she could not tame me into submission with a frown or the bribe of a spoonful of jam. If you don't stop plaguing the nursemaids, my beauty, the tiger-man will come and take you away. They'd brought him from Sumatra, in the Indies, she said; his hinder parts were all hairy and only from the head downwards did he resemble a man.

And yet The Beast goes always masked; it cannot be his face that looks like mine.

But the tiger-man, in spite of his hairiness, could take a glass of ale in his hand like a good Christian and drink it down. Had she not seen him do so, at the sign of The George, by the steps of Upper Moor Fields when she was just as high as me and lisped and toddled, too. Then she would sigh for London, across the North Sea of the lapse of years. But, if this young lady was not a good little girl and did not eat her boiled beetroot, then the tiger-man would put on his big black travelling cloak lined with fur, just like your daddy's, and hire the Erl-King's galloper of wind and ride through the night straight to the nursery and—

Yes, my beauty! GOBBLE YOU UP!

How I'd squeal in delighted terror, half believing her, half knowing that she teased me. And there were things I knew that I must not tell her. In our lost farmyard, where the giggling nursemaids initiated me into the mysteries of what the bull did to the cows, I heard about the waggoner's daughter. Hush, hush, don't let on to your nursie we said so; the waggoner's lass, hare-lipped, squint-eyed, ugly as sin, who would have taken her? Yet, to her shame, her belly swelled amid the cruel mockery of the ostlers and her son was born of a bear, they whispered. Born with a full pelt and teeth; that proved it. But, when he grew up, he was a good shepherd, although he never married, lived in a hut outside the village and could make the wind blow any way he wanted to besides being able to tell which eggs would become cocks, which hens.

The wondering peasants once brought my father a skull with horns four inches long on either side of it and would not go back to the field where their poor plough disturbed it until the priest went with them; for this skull had the jaw-bone of a *man*, had it not?

Old wives' tales, nursery fears! I knew well enough the reason for the trepidation I cosily titillated with superstitious marvels of my childhood on the day my childhood ended. For now my own skin was my sole capital in the world and today I'd make my first investment.

We had left the city far behind us and were now traversing a wide, flat dish of snow where the mutilated stumps of the willows flourished their ciliate heads athwart frozen ditches; mist diminished the horizon, brought down the sky until it seemed no more than a few inches above us. As far as eye could see, not one thing living. How starveling, how bereft the dead season of this spurious Eden in which all the fruit was blighted by cold! And my frail roses, already faded. I opened the carriage door and tossed the defunct bouquet into the rucked, frost-stiff mud of the road. Suddenly a sharp, freezing wind arose and pelted my face with a dry rice of powdered snow. The mist lifted sufficiently to reveal before me an acreage of half-derelict façades of sheer red brick, the vast man-trap, the megalomaniac citadel of his palazzo.

It was a world in itself but a dead one, a burned-out planet. I saw The Beast bought solitude, not luxury, with his money.

The little black horse trotted smartly through the figured bronze doors that stood open to the weather like those of a barn and the valet handed me out of the carriage on to the scarred tiles of the great hall itself, into the odorous warmth of a stable, sweet with hay, acrid with horse dung. An equine chorus of neighings and soft drummings of hooves broke out beneath the tall roof, where the beams were scabbed with last summer's swallows' nests; a dozen gracile muzzles lifted from their mangers and turned towards us, ears erect. The Beast had given his horses the use of the dining room. The walls were painted, aptly enough, with a fresco of horses, dogs and men in a wood where fruit and blossom grew on the bough together.

The valet tweaked politely at my sleeve. Milord is waiting.

Gaping doors and broken windows let the wind in everywhere. We mounted one staircase after another, our feet clopping on the marble. Through archways and open doors, I glimpsed suites of vaulted chambers opening one out of another like systems of Chinese boxes into the infinite complexity of the innards of the place. He and I and the wind were the only things stirring; and all the furniture was under dust sheets, the chandeliers bundled up in cloth, pictures taken from their hooks and propped with their faces to the walls as if their master could not bear to look at them. The palace was dismantled, as if its owner were about to move house or had never properly moved in; The Beast had chosen to live in an uninhabited place.

The valet darted me a reassuring glance from his brown, eloquent eyes, yet a glance with so much queer superciliousness in it that it did not comfort me, and went bounding ahead of me on his bandy legs, softly chattering to himself. I held my head high and followed him; but, for all my pride, my heart was heavy.

Milord has his eyrie high above the house, a small, stifling, darkened room; he keeps his shutters locked at noon. I was out of breath by the time we reached it and returned to him the silence with which he greeted me. I will not smile. He cannot smile.

In his rarely disturbed privacy, The Beast wears a garment of Ottoman design, a loose, dull purple gown with gold embroidery round the neck that falls from his shoulders to conceal his feet. The feet of the chair he sits in are handsomely clawed. He hides his hands in his ample sleeves. The artificial masterpiece of his face appalls me. A small fire in a small grate. A rushing wind rattles the shutters.

The valet coughed. To him fell the delicate task of transmitting to me his master's wishes.

"My master—"

A stick fell in the grate. It made a mighty clatter in that dreadful silence; the valet started; lost his place in his speech, began again.

"My master has but one desire."

The thick, rich, wild scent with which Milord had soaked himself the previous evening hangs all about us, ascends in cursive blue from the smoke of a precious Chinese pot.

"He wishes only—"

Now, in the face of my impassivity, the valet twittered, his ironic composure gone, for the desire of a master, however trivial, may yet sound unbearably insolent in the mouth of a servant and his role of go-between clearly caused him a good deal of embarrassment. He gulped; he swallowed, at last contrived to unleash an unpunctuated flood.

"My master's sole desire is to see the pretty young lady unclothed nude without her dress and that only for the one time after which she will be returned to her father undamaged with bankers' orders for the sum which he lost to my master at cards and also a number of fine presents such as furs, jewels and horses—"

I remained standing. During this interview, my eyes were level with those inside the mask that now evaded mine as if, to his credit, he was ashamed of his own request even as his mouthpiece made it for him. *Agitato, molto agitato*, the valet wrung his white-gloved hands.

"Desnuda—"

I could scarcely believe my ears. I let out a raucous guffaw; no young lady laughs like that! my old nurse used to remonstrate. But I did. And do. At the clamour of my heartless mirth, the valet danced backwards with perturbation, palpitating his fingers as if attempting to wrench them off, expostulating, wordlessly pleading. I felt that I owed it to him to make my reply in as exquisite a Tuscan as I could master.

"You may put me in a windowless room, sir, and I promise you I will pull my skirt up to my waist, ready for you. But there must be a sheet over my face, to hide it; though the sheet must be laid over me so lightly that it will not choke me. So I shall be covered completely from the waist upwards, and no lights. There you can visit me once, sir, and only the once. After that I must be driven directly to the city and deposited in the public square, in front of the church. If you wish to give me money, then I should be pleased to receive it. But I must stress that you should give me only the same amount of money that you would give to any other woman in such circumstances. However, if you choose not to give me a present, then that is your right."

How pleased I was to see I struck The Beast to the heart! For, after a baker's dozen heartbeats, one single tear swelled, glittering, at the corner of the masked eye. A tear! A tear, I hoped, of shame. The tear trembled for a moment on an edge of painted bone, then tumbled down the painted cheek to fall, with an abrupt tinkle, on the tiled floor.

The valet, ticking and clucking to himself, hastily ushered me out of the room. A mauve cloud of his master's perfume billowed out into the chill corridor with us and dissipated itself on the spinning winds.

A cell had been prepared for me, a veritable cell, windowless, airless, lightless, in the viscera of the palace. The valet lit a lamp for me; a narrow bed, a dark cupboard with fruit and flowers carved on it bulked out of the gloom.

"I shall twist a noose out of my bed linen and hang myself with it," I said.

"Oh, no," said the valet, fixing upon me wide and suddenly melancholy eyes. "Oh, no, you will not. You are a woman of honour."

And what was *he* doing in my bedroom, this jigging caricature of a man? Was he to be my warder until I submitted to The Beast's whim or he to mine? Am I in such reduced circumstances that I may not have a lady's maid? As if in reply to my unspoken demand, the valet clapped his hands.

"To assuage your loneliness, madame . . ."

A knocking and clattering behind the door of the cupboard; the door swings open and out glides a soubrette from an operetta, with glossy, nut-brown curls, rosy cheeks, blue, rolling eyes; it takes me a moment to recognize her, in her little cap, her white stockings, her frilled petticoats. She carries a looking glass in one hand and a powder puff in the other and there is a musical box where her heart should be; she tinkles as she rolls towards me on her tiny wheels.

"Nothing human lives here," said the valet.

My maid halted, bowed; from a split seam at the side of her bodice protrudes the handle of a key. She is a marvellous machine, the most delicately balanced system of cords and pulleys in the world.

"We have dispensed with servants," the valet said. "We surround ourselves, instead, for utility and pleasure, with simulacra and find it no less convenient than do most gentlemen."

This clockwork twin of mine halted before me, her bowels churning out a settecento minuet, and offered me the bold carnation of her smile. Click, click—she raises her arm and busily dusts my cheeks with pink, powdered chalk that makes me cough; then thrusts towards me her little mirror.

I saw within it not my own face but that of my father, as if I had put on his face when I arrived at The Beast's palace as the discharge of his debt. What, you self-deluding fool, are you crying still? And drunk, too. He tossed back his grappa and hurled the tumbler away.

Seeing my astonished fright, the valet took the mirror away from me, breathed on it, polished it with the ham of his gloved fist, handed it back to me. Now all I saw was myself, haggard from a sleepless night, pale enough to need my maid's supply of rouge.

I heard the key turn in the heavy door and the valet's footsteps patter down the stonepassage. Meanwhile, my double continued to powder the air, emitting her jangling tune but, as it turned out, she was not inexhaustible; soon she was powdering more and yet more languorously, her metal heart slowed in imitation of fatigue, her musical box ran down until the notes separated themselves out of the tune and plopped like single raindrops and, as if sleep had overtaken her, at last she moved no longer. As she succumbed to sleep, I had no option but to do so, too. I dropped on that narrow bed as if felled.

Time passed but I do not know how much; then the valet woke me with rolls and honey. I gestured the tray away but he set it down firmly beside the lamp and took from it a little shagreen box, which he offered to me.

I turned away my head.

"Oh, my lady!" Such hurt cracked his high-pitched voice! He dexterously unfastened the gold clasp; on a bed of crimson velvet lay a single diamond earring, perfect as a tear.

I snapped the box shut and tossed it into a corner. This sudden, sharp movement must have disturbed the mechanism of the doll; she jerked her arm almost as if to reprimand me, letting out a rippling fart of gavotte. Then was still again.

"Very well," said the valet, put out. And indicated it was time for me to visit my host again. He did not let me wash or comb my hair. There was so little natural light in the interior of the palace that I could not tell whether it was day or night.

You would not think The Beast had budged an inch, since I last saw him; he sat in his huge chair, with his hands in his sleeves, and the heavy air never moved. I might have slept an hour, a night, or a month, but his sculptured calm, the stifling air remained just as it had been. The incense rose from the pot, still traced the same signature on the air. The same fire burned.

Take off my clothes for you, like a ballet girl? Is that all you want of me?

"The sight of a young lady's skin that no man has seen before—" stammered the valet.

I wished I'd rolled in the hay with every lad on my father's farm, to disqualify myself from this humiliating bargain. That he should want so little was the reason why I could not give it; I did not need to speak for The Beast to understand me.

A tear came from his other eye. And then he moved; he buried his cardboard carnival head with its ribboned weight of false hair in, I would say, his arms; he withdrew his, I might say, hands from his sleeves and I saw his furred pads, his excoriating claws.

The dropped tear caught upon his fur and shone. And in my room for hours I hear those paws pad back and forth outside my door.

•

When the valet arrived again with his silver salver, I had a pair of diamond earrings of the finest water in the world; I threw the other into the corner where the first one lay. The valet twittered with aggrieved regret but did not offer to lead me to The Beast again. Instead, he smiled ingratiatingly and confided: "My master, he say: invite the young lady to go riding."

"What's this?"

He briskly mimicked the action of a gallop and, to my amazement, tunelessly croaked: "Tantivy! tantivy! a-hunting we will go!"

"I'll run away, I'll ride to the city."

"Oh, no," he said. "Are you not a woman of honour?"

He clapped his hands and my maidservant clicked and jangled into the imitation of life. She rolled towards the cupboard where she had come from and reached inside it to fetch out over her synthetic arm my riding habit. Of all things. My very own riding habit, that I'd left behind me in a trunk in a loft in that country house outside Petersburg that we'd lost long ago, before, even, we set out on this wild pilgrimage to the cruel South. Either the very riding habit my old nurse had sewn for me or else a copy of it perfect to the lost button on the right sleeve, the ripped hem held up with a pin. I turned the worn cloth about in my hands, looking for a clue. The wind that sprinted through the palace made the door tremble in its frame; had the north wind blown my garments across Europe to me? At home, the bear's son directed the winds at his pleasure; what democracy of magic held this palace and the fir forest in common? Or, should I be prepared to accept it as proof of the axiom my father had drummed into me: that, if you have enough money, anything is possible?

"Tantivy," suggested the now twinkling valet, evidently charmed at the pleasure mixed with my bewilderment. The clockwork maid held my jacket out to me and I allowed myself to shrug into it as if reluctantly, although I was half mad to get out into the open air, away from this deathly palace, even in such company.

The doors of the hall let the bright day in; I saw that it was morning. Our horses, saddled and bridled, beasts in bondage, were waiting for us, striking sparks from the tiles with their impatient hooves while their stablemates lolled at ease among the straw, conversing with one another in the mute speech of horses. A pigeon or two, feathers puffed to keep out the cold, strutted about, pecking at ears of corn. The little black gelding who had brought me here greeted me with a ringing neigh that resonated inside the misty roof as in a sounding box and I knew he was meant for me to ride.

I always adored horses, noblest of creatures, such wounded sensitivity in their wise eyes, such rational restraint of energy at their high-strung hindquarters. I lirruped and hurrumphed to my shining black companion and he acknowledged my greeting with a kiss on the forehead from his soft lips. There was a little shaggy pony nuzzling away at the trompe l'oeil foliage beneath the hooves of the painted horses on the wall, into whose saddle the valet sprang with a flourish as of the circus. Then The Beast, wrapped in a black fur-lined cloak, came to heave himself aloft a grave grey mare. No natural horseman he; he clung to her mane like a shipwrecked sailor to a spar.

Cold, that morning, yet dazzling with the sharp winter sunlight that wounds the retina. There was a scurrying wind about that seemed to go with us, as if the masked, immense one who did not speak carried it inside his cloak and let it out at his pleasure, for it stirred the horses' manes but did not lift the lowland mists.

A bereft landscape in the sad browns and sepias of winter lay all about us, the marshland drearily protracting itself towards the wide river. Those decapitated willows. Now and then, the swoop of a bird, its irreconcilable cry.

A profound sense of strangeness slowly began to possess me. I knew my two companions were not, in any way, as other men, the simian retainer and the master for whom he spoke, the one with clawed forepaws who was in a plot with the witches who let the winds out of their knotted handkerchiefs up towards the Finnish border. I knew they lived according to a different logic than I had done until my father abandoned me to the wild beasts by his human carelessness. This knowledge gave me a certain fearfulness still; but, I would say, not much ... I was a young girl, a virgin, and therefore men denied me rationality just as they denied it to all those who were not exactly like themselves, in all their unreason. If I could see not one single soul in that wilderness of desolation all around me, then the six of us—mounts and riders, both—could boast amongst us not one soul, either, since all the best religions in the world state categorically that not beasts nor women were equipped with the flimsy, insubstantial things when the good Lord opened the gates of Eden and let Eve and her familiars tumble out. Understand, then, that though I would not say I privately engaged in metaphysical speculation as we rode through the reedy approaches to the river, I certainly meditated on the nature of my own state, how I had been bought and sold, passed from hand to hand. That clockwork girl who powdered my cheeks for me; had I not been allotted only the same kind of imitative life amongst men that the doll-maker had given her?

Yet, as to the true nature of the being of this clawed magus who rode his pale horse in a style that made me recall how Kublai Khan's leopards went out hunting on horseback, of that I had no notion.

We came to the bank of the river that was so wide we could not see across it, so still with winter that it scarcely seemed to flow. The horses lowered their heads to drink. The valet cleared his throat, about to speak; we were in a place of perfect privacy, beyond a brake of winter-bare rushes, a hedge of reeds.

"If you will not let him see you without your clothes—"

I involuntarily shook my head—

"—you must, then, prepare yourself for the sight of my master, naked."

The river broke on the pebbles with a diminishing sigh. My composure deserted me; all at once I was on the brink of panic. I did not think that I could bear the sight of him, whatever he was. The mare raised her dripping muzzle and looked at me keenly, as if urging me. This river broke again at my feet. I was far from home.

"You," said the valet, "must."

When I saw how scared he was I might refuse, I nodded.

The reed bowed down in a sudden snarl of wind that brought with it a gust of the heavy odour of his disguise. The valet held out his master's cloak to screen him from me as he removed the mask. The horses stirred.

The tiger will never lie down with the lamb; he acknowledges no pact that is not reciprocal. The lamb must learn to run with the tigers.

A great, feline, tawny shape whose pelt was barred with a savage geometry of bars the colour of burned wood. His domed, heavy head, so terrible he must hide it. How subtle the muscles, how profound the tread. The annihilating vehemence of his eyes, like twin suns.

I felt my breast ripped apart as if I suffered a marvellous wound.

The valet moved forward as if to cover up his master now the girl had acknowledged him, but I said: "No."

The tiger sat still as a heraldic beast, in the pact he had made with his own ferocity to do me no harm. He was far larger than I could have imagined, from the poor, shabby things I'd seen once, in the Czar's menagerie at Petersburg, the golden fruit of their eyes dimming, withering in the far North of captivity. Nothing about him reminded me of humanity.

I therefore, shivering, now unfastened my jacket, to show him I would do him no harm. Yet I was clumsy and blushed a little, for no man had seen me naked and I was a proud girl. Pride it was, not shame, that thwarted my fingers so; and a certain trepidation lest this frail little article of human upholstery before him might not be, in itself, grand enough to satisfy his expectations of us, since those, for all I knew, might have grown infinite during the endless time he had been waiting. The wind clattered in the rushes, purled and eddied in the river.

I showed his grave silence my white skin, my red nipples, and the horses turned their heads to watch me, also, as if they, too, were courteously curious as to the fleshly nature of women. Then The Beast lowered his massive head; Enough! said the valet with a gesture. The wind died down, all was still again.

Then they went off together, the valet on his pony, the tiger running before him like a hound, and I walked along the river bank for a while. I felt I was at liberty for the first time in my life. Then the winter sun began to tarnish, a few flakes of snow drifted from the darkening sky and, when I returned to the horses, I found The Beast mounted again on his grey mare, cloaked and masked and once more, to all appearances, a man, while the valet had a fine catch of waterfowl dangling from his hand and the corpse of a young roebuck slung behind his saddle. I climbed up on the black gelding in silence and so we returned to the palace as the snow fell more and more heavily, obscuring the tracks that we had left behind us.

The valet did not return me to my cell but, instead, to an elegant, if old-fashioned boudoir with sofas of faded pink brocade, a jinn's treasury of Oriental carpets, tintinnabulation of cut-glass chandeliers. Candles in antlered holders struck rainbows from the prismatic hearts of my diamond earrings, that lay on my new dressing table at which my attentive maid stood ready with her powder puff and mirror. Intending to fix the ornaments in my ears, I took the looking glass from her hand, but it was in the midst of one of its magic fits again and I did not see my own face in it but that of my father; at first I thought he smiled at me. Then I saw he was smiling with pure gratification.

He sat, I saw, in the parlour of our lodgings, at the very table where he had lost me, but now he was busily engaged in counting out a tremendous pile of banknotes. My father's circumstances had changed already; well-shaven, neatly barbered, smart new clothes. A frosted glass of sparkling wine sat convenient to his hand beside an ice bucket. The Beast had clearly paid cash on the nail for his glimpse of my bosom, and paid up promptly, as if it had not been a sight I might have died of showing. Then I saw my father's trunks were packed, ready for departure. Could he so easily leave me here?

There was a note on the table with the money, in a fine hand. I could read it quite clearly. "The young lady will arrive immediately." Some harlot with whom he'd briskly negotiated a liaison on the strength of his spoils? Not at all. For, at that moment, the valet knocked at my door to announce that I might leave the palace at any time hereafter, and he bore over his arm a handsome sable cloak, my very own little gratuity, The Beast's morning gift, in which he proposed to pack me up and send me off.

When I looked at the mirror again, my father had disappeared and all I saw was a pale, hollow-eyed girl whom I scarcely recognized. The valet asked politely when he should prepare the carriage, as if he did not doubt that I would leave with my booty at the first opportunity while my maid, whose face was no longer the spit of my own, continued bonnily to beam. I will dress her in my own clothes, wind her up, send her back to perform the part of my father's daughter.

"Leave me alone," I said to the valet.

He did not need to lock the door, now. I fixed the earrings in my ears. They were very heavy. Then I took off my riding habit, left it where it lay on the floor. But, when I got down to my shift, my arms dropped to my sides. I was unaccustomed to nakedness. I was so unused to my own skin that to take off all my clothes involved a kind of flaying. I thought The Beast had wanted a little thing compared with what I was prepared to give him; but it is not natural for humankind to go naked, not since first we hid our loins with fig leaves. He had demanded the abominable. I felt as much atrocious pain as if I was stripping off my own underpelt and the smiling girl stood poised in the oblivion of her balked simulation of life, watching me peel down to the cold, white meat of contract and, if she did not see me, then so much more like the market place, where the eyes that watch you take no account of your existence.

And it seemed my entire life, since I had left the North, had passed under the indifferent gaze of eyes like hers.

Then I was flinching stark, except for his irreproachable tears.

I huddled in the furs I must return to him, to keep me from the lacerating winds that raced along the corridors. I knew the way to his den without the valet to guide me.

No response to my tentative rap on his door.

Then the wind blew the valet whirling along the passage. He must have decided that, if one should go naked, then all should go naked; without his livery, he revealed himself, as I had suspected, a delicate creature, covered with silken moth-grey fur, brown fingers supple as leather, chocolate muzzle, the gentlest creature in the world. He gibbered a little to see my fine furs and jewels as if I were dressed up for the opera and, with a great deal of tender ceremony, removed the sables from my shoulders. The sables thereupon resolved themselves into a pack of black, squeaking rats that rattled immediately down the stairs on their hard little feet and were lost to sight.

The valet bowed me inside The Beast's room.

The purple dressing gown, the mask, the wig, were laid out on his chair; a glove was planted on each arm. The empty house of his appearance was ready for him but he had abandoned it. There was a reek of fur and piss; the incense pot lay broken in pieces on the floor. Half-burned sticks were scattered from the extinguished fire. A candle stuck by its own grease to the mantelpiece lit two narrow flames in the pupils of the tiger's eyes.

He was pacing backwards and forwards, backwards and forwards, the tip of his heavy tail twitching as he paced out the length and breadth of his imprisonment between the gnawed and bloody bones.

He will gobble you up.

Nursery fears made flesh and sinew; earliest and most archaic of fears, fear of devourment. The beast and his carnivorous bed of bone and I, white, shaking, raw, approaching him as if offering, in myself, the key to a peaceable kingdom in which his appetite need not be my extinction.

He went still as stone. He was far more frightened of me than I was of him.

I squatted on the wet straw and stretched out my hand. I was now within the field of force of his golden eyes. He growled at the back of his throat, lowered his head, sank on to his forepaws, snarled, showed me his red gullet, his yellow teeth. I never moved. He snuffed the air, as if to smell my fear; he could not.

Slowly, slowly he began to drag his heavy, gleaming weight across the floor towards me.

A tremendous throbbing, as of the engine that makes the earth turn, filled the little room; he had begun to purr.

The sweet thunder of this purr shook the old walls, made the shutters batter the windows until they burst apart and let in the white light of the snowy moon. Tiles came crashing down from the roof; I heard them fall into the courtyard far below. The reverberations of his purring rocked the foundations of the house, the walls began to dance. I thought: "It will all fall, everything will disintegrate."

He dragged himself closer and closer to me, until I felt the harsh velvet of his head against my hand, then a tongue, abrasive as sandpaper. "He will lick the skin off me!"

And each stroke of his tongue ripped off skin after successive skin, all the skins of a life in the world, and left behind a nascent patina of shiny hairs. My earrings turned back to water and trickled down my shoulders; I shrugged the drops off my beautiful fur.

Exercises:

- Try the "Jim Shepard Venn Diagram"
- Try the exercise on page 133 (the step-by-step, exquisite-corpse-like game).
- Inspired by Angela Carter's tiger, even if your character isn't in a fairy tale, ask: if they were an animal, what would they be? Could you borrow a detail for characterization?

- Find an interesting, odd detail about a historical period you already know something about and write a scene that starts with that detail: How far can you get before you have to stop and look up more?

- Take a sensation or observation from your everyday life right now (especially a bodily or natural one) and blend it into your story's alternate/historical world, whatever it is.

- Complete this sentence with the name of your place, and keep going: "On a Friday night in . . ."

- Something goes wrong in your place: What happens next, and why? What tools, resources, and choices do your characters have available?

- Can you add to your descriptions of your place some appeals to a sense you have *not* yet touched? For example, if everything is visual, might you enrich your world with sound? Texture? Taste? Smells?

- The question of discovering a place by discovering what could go wrong in it is linked for me with a great exercise by the writer Sarah Shun-lien Bynum: based on Denis Johnson's novella *Train Dreams*, in which objects inside a burning cabin are destroyed one by one, Bynum's exercise asks you to imagine and describe a beloved place by "detailing its destruction."[41]

- Find a passage in your historical or alt-world work where you sharpen a description in such a sensory way that it shortens the distance between that time and our own, as in George Garrett's *Death of the Fox* (p. 173): Use the common language of the senses, which human (and nonhuman) bodies share across place and time.

CHAPTER 7
TRUST THE PROCESS
REVISING, EDITING, AND WRITING AT LENGTH

All music is what awakens from you when you are reminded by the instruments.

—Walt Whitman, *Leaves of Grass*

On a January day at Carnegie Hall, a nervous young soprano, Amalia Avilán Castillo, takes the stage with Joyce DiDonato, a Kansas native, opera star, and inspiring teacher. They're working through Mimi's aria "Donde lieta usci" from Puccini's *La Boheme* (1896). Step by step, DiDonato helps Castillo toward a freedom that comes from control—a cycle of breath through the body for a radiant, flexible sound. After several tries, Castillo strikes a note of astonishing beauty. The audience applauds as Castillo smiles in flustered surprise. "Don't recreate what just worked," DiDonato advises, smiling too. "Analyze the *process* you went through to create that result. You go for the *result*, it ain't gonna work. It might, but it's luck. It's not technique. *Process*."[1]

Students and I watch this moment together on YouTube to absorb this wisdom: there's a big difference between "recreating what just worked" and "analyzing the process you went through to create that result" so that you can repeat that process to achieve the same *qualities* of "what just worked." Maybe this is another difference between beginning and advanced writers. "Beginning writers look for rules, guidelines, clever sayings that can be posted on a mirror," Rick Bass (anthology) writes, "and these things are important, or at least they were for me."[2] Beginning writers may also still be stuck in the praise- or success-seeking mode we mentioned back in Chapter 1: *if my teacher liked this trick, I'll do it exactly the same way, again!* Advanced writers—while we still love clever sayings on the mirror—have learned to trust the *process* more than just focusing on the end result. Because it's the process that lets us chase the beautiful, maddening, compelling thing that sometimes only we can see: the work we're trying to make, through rounds of writing and revision, even when that work seems out of reach, being "reminded by the instruments," as Whitman says earlier, of where we want to go. "You will never make it," DiDonato said in her commencement address to the Julliard class of 2014. "'It' doesn't exist for an artist. The work will never end. . . . It will always be there for you—even if in some moments you lack the will to be there for it. All it asks is that you show up, fully present."[3]

Being able to show up and trust the writing and revision process every day—including how it takes you into and out of your own head, and may lead you from writing in shorter forms to longer ones—starts with accepting its mix of get-it-done realism and mysterious emotion. "Writers need to learn to calibrate editing's singular blend of mechanics and magic," says Susan Bell in her wonderful book *The Artful Edit* (2007). "For if writing builds the house, nothing but revision will complete it. One writer needs to be two carpenters: a builder with mettle, and a finisher with slow hands."[4] Here are some practical strategies to get you there.

More Like This/This Stops Me

As I described in my book *The Writer's Eye,* my students and I use two phrases to guide our revision: "*more like this*" and "*this stops me.*" "*More like this*" is something you can say to classmates and yourself to identify places where the writing feels precise, compelling, and alive, immersing readers in the experience you, and they, want them to have. (The writer Wells Tower compares this to tapping and finding "the real wood behind the fiberboard."[5]) "*This stops me*" is just like it sounds—a place where readers (or you) feel "stopped" by imprecision, authorial bossiness, weird psychic distances, or something else. Each phrase asks the writer to identify within herself *the mental conditions that helped create those words on the page,* the particular presence/attentiveness or absence/ inattentiveness, in order to produce the effects on the reader that she wants. Then she can re-enter or reproduce that mental state or tap into that particular "more-like-this energy" to revise or reproduce her words from within.

Sure, *editing* can be striking through typos or removing obvious filters. But to get into true *re-vision*—actually *re-seeing* and re-entering your writing process—it helps to go back to the place in your mind where the story, voice, and/or image started, and where they live now. As Walt Whitman wonderfully writes in *Leaves of Grass*, let yourself be "reminded by the instruments" of technique, observation, and practice on how to move forward. Here's an exercise to help you tune into "more like this" feelings and experience this.

Seeing a Character: Description as Process

Remember what your first crush looked like? I sure do, because my kicked-up fifteen-year-old emotions stamped him into my memory (crisp haircut line under faded baseball cap, birthmark on his neck). Heightened emotion heightens our physical memories too, so "going there" in memory helps us remember and write that specific detail—especially if we're trying to get past cliché. Paying good attention can start with imagining your subject fully enough to "see" it, then describe it. And heightened emotion heightens *attention*, so you can bring your best (or "more like this") energy to your work.

Once, my students got interested in a technical challenge: how to describe a character another character finds romantically interesting *without* crudely sexualizing them (a psychic-distance nightmare!) So we returned to an emotional place where that detail is stored. In class, I asked each student to pick a (safe-for-class-consumption) physical feature of their first crush—which can be done gender-neutrally—and share it aloud, then write that feature into a short description of a romantically appealing character. A mood of wistfulness filled the room, sweet with humor and shared vulnerability, as marvelous details tumbled out: eyes with little chips of gold in them, large hands, crooked nose, freckles, crisp curls, "ears that turned red when she blushed," "he smiled with all his teeth." The laughter and shared emotion helped the students write *really* good descriptions, precise and poignant: transporting themselves to a particular tender, specific mental place transformed their words by heightening the words' precision, sensuality, and focus.

Even if your character's not a romantic lead, sharpening your mental image of them sharpens your description too—especially when readers see your character for the first time. Here's a brilliant description from Imogen Hermes Gowar's *The Mermaid and Mrs. Hancock* (2018), which is set in eighteenth-century London. Merchant Jonah Hancock hurries downstairs to answer a late-night knock:

> As he opens the door, there is a little crescendo of light as Sukie puts the taper to the last of the candles, and here is Captain Tysoe Jones, ruggedly lit. He is in his sea clothes still, a jacket so faded by salt and sun that it appears dove-grey except for wedges of its old blue preserved under the lapels and the cuffs. His person is equally stained and faded: his face brick-coloured and tough as the soles of feet, with white creases about his eyes and mouth. The stubble on his cheeks twinkles as if a light frost has settled there. He clutches a canvas sack and looks mightily irritated.

Of all the things to admire here—the clarity and specificity of the language, the steady third-person psychic distance and point of view inflected just enough with eighteenth-century cadences—my favorite moment is the "wedges of its old blue preserved under the lapels and the cuffs." Only a writer totally at home in her novel's world and observant about our own world, too, would notice and report this contrast between faded and unfaded cloth. (And because he's a merchant, Mr. Hancock notices it too.) This gives her the precision and authority readers trust.

Here's nine-year-old orphan Pip's first sight of Miss Havisham, the rich lady who's summoned him to her eerie house, in Charles Dickens's novel *Great Expectations* (serialized 1860–1, published in book form 1861). Technically, adult Pip is the narrator, yet here, in Vivian Gornick's phrase, child-Pip is "the self in whom the story resides," so his eyes—frightened, fascinated, honest—are our windows on the scene:[6]

> We went into the house by a side door—the great front entrance had two chains across it outside—and the first thing I noticed was, that the passages were all dark, and that [Estella] had left a candle burning there. She took it up, and we went through more passages and up a staircase, and still it was all dark, and only the candle lighted us.
>
> At last we came to the door of a room, and she said, "Go in."
>
> I answered, more in shyness than politeness, "After you, miss."

To this, she returned: "Don't be ridiculous, boy; I am not going in." And scornfully walked away, and—what was worse—took the candle with her.

This was very uncomfortable, and I was half afraid. However, the only thing to be done being to knock at the door, I knocked, and was told from within to enter. I entered, therefore, and found myself in a pretty large room, well lighted with wax candles. No glimpse of daylight was to be seen in it. It was a dressing-room, as I supposed from the furniture, though much of it was of forms and uses then quite unknown to me. But prominent in it was a draped table with a gilded looking-glass, and that I made out at first sight to be a fine lady's dressing-table.

Whether I should have made out this object so soon, if there had been no fine lady sitting at it, I cannot say. In an arm-chair, with an elbow resting on the table and her head leaning on that hand, sat the strangest lady I have ever seen, or shall ever see.

She was dressed in rich materials—satins, and lace, and silks—all of white. Her shoes were white. And she had a long white veil dependent from her hair, and she had bridal flowers in her hair, but her hair was white. Some bright jewels sparkled on her neck and on her hands, and some other jewels lay sparkling on the table. Dresses, less splendid than the dress she wore, and half-packed trunks, were scattered about. She had not quite finished dressing, for she had but one shoe on—the other was on the table near her hand—her veil was but half arranged, her watch and chain were not put on, and some lace for her bosom lay with those trinkets, and with her handkerchief, and gloves, and some flowers, and a prayer-book, all confusedly heaped about the looking-glass.

It was not in the first few moments that I saw all these things, though I saw more of them in the first moments than might be supposed. But, I saw that everything within my view which ought to be white, had been white long ago, and had lost its lustre, and was faded and yellow. I saw that the bride within the bridal dress had withered like the dress, and like the flowers, and had no brightness left but the brightness of her sunken eyes. I saw that the dress had been put upon the rounded figure of a young woman, and that the figure upon which it now hung loose, had shrunk to skin and bone. Once, I had been taken to see some ghastly waxwork at the Fair, representing I know not what impossible personage lying in state. Once, I had been taken to one of our old marsh churches to see a skeleton in the ashes of a rich dress, that had been dug out of a vault under the church pavement. Now, waxwork and skeleton seemed to have dark eyes that moved and looked at me. I should have cried out, if I could.

"Who is it?" said the lady at the table.

"Pip, ma'am."

"Pip?"

"Mr. Pumblechook's boy, ma'am. Come—to play."

"Come nearer; let me look at you. Come close."

It was when I stood before her, avoiding her eyes, that I took note of the surrounding objects in detail, and saw that her watch had stopped at twenty minutes to nine, and that a clock in the room had stopped at twenty minutes to nine.

"Look at me," said Miss Havisham. "You are not afraid of a woman who has never seen the sun since you were born?"

I regret to state that I was not afraid of telling the enormous lie comprehended in the answer "No."

"Do you know what I touch here?" she said, laying her hands, one upon the other, on her left side.

"Yes, ma'am." (It made me think of the young man.)

"What do I touch?"

"Your heart."

"Broken!"

She uttered the word with an eager look, and with strong emphasis, and with a weird smile that had a kind of boast in it. Afterwards, she kept her hands there for a little while, and slowly took them away as if they were heavy.

"I am tired," said Miss Havisham. "I want diversion, and I have done with men and women. Play."

Dickens built this distinctive first-person voice for his earlier, semi-autobiographical novel *David Copperfield* (1849–50; 1850). As an adult tells his story, he draws closer in memory to the child he used to be, which turns up the flame of his child-self's emotions like a gas jet on a parlor wall.[7] All of us have sore spots and preoccupations that brighten that flame, heightening the details that stick to our minds. For Charles Dickens—like Pip—that sore spot was a bright boy's humiliation at feeling powerless and poor. In 1824, his father, John Dickens, was imprisoned for debt in the Marshalsea Prison, and young Charles went to work in a factory—a sting that even Dickens's tremendous success never quite healed. Here, Pip is dimly aware that this strange lady is important to his future because she's rich and he is not, which he's never quite realized before. Riskily but skillfully, Dickens keeps both child *and* adult in his psychic-distance frame, capitalizing on the child's sensory sharpness and the adult's hindsight, with that halo of heightened emotion brightening them both. (James Joyce does this in "Araby," in Chapter 1's Craft Studio.)

What if your character isn't human? In Allan Gurganus's great story "It Had Wings," an angel falls out of the sky into a widow's backyard on an ordinary Tuesday. Gurganus renders our first sight of the angel with similes from the widow's own homely world and a stranger, fiercer one: the feathers on the angel's wings are like "machetes." Right away, those similes redirect readers from sentimental clichés of angels toward Rainer Maria Rilke's famous line, "every angel is terrifying." I've read that Gurganus often draws his characters and has a great visual sense—maybe he drew this one too. (Try the exercise on p. 133 to help you describe your imaginary creature.)

All three of these passages are ones I read when I need a tune-up—when I feel my writing and the mindset I'm working in is boring or cliched, or when I want to bring my best attention to my work. If we can identify passages like this, and what kind of "more like this" qualities they spark in us, then we can identify sources of that same energy, attention, and intention in our own minds. Returning to these will help us home in on our best work as we write and revise. Like the young singer in Joyce DiDonato's master class, tuning into your best and truest sound can help you revise. But even as you have your ideal note in mind, consider, also, the pacing and tempo of the whole opera, and the people listening in the seats. What information will your readers need, and when, to enflesh in their minds the fictional atmosphere you want them to enter? Here's how I revised a story with these questions in mind.

Teacher Craft Studio: Amy Weldon, "The Serpent"

First, let me be clear: I'm *not* putting myself in a class with James Joyce, Angela Carter, and Chimamanda Ngozi Adichie. But I can tell you about revision from the inside. So I'll follow the example of my brave students, who've shared their process in Craft Studios throughout this book.

My short story "The Serpent" is a kind of Biblical midrash drawn from my rural Alabama upbringing and based on a strong memory of a very particular farm (and, I see now, an unconscious Eudora Welty homage—where *is* that voice coming from?). I finished a draft I was happy with and sent it to an environmental-writing journal called *The Hopper.* The editor accepted it for publication but asked for more revisions (this often happens—see Chapter 8). Here is an image of the first document page, with her comments; I'll only include the first page, because that's where most of the problems are (Figure 4).

When I opened this Word document with the editor's suggested changes in pink to the right, at first I was taken aback, as writers often are in our secret hearts: "what do you *mean,* I need to revise this?!" But her comments pried the lid off my stubbornness so I could see what was inside the story: a great love of a world, time, and place I knew well (which is good) but had not yet imagined with my *readers* in mind and unpacked for them in an order they could follow (not so good). Remember how we talked about this in Chapter 6? Eager to get information into the story (like Joel Murillo in *Cracker Jack*) I'd crammed it all in, too close to the start. Take a look at that first sentence. I ran out of breath while reading it aloud; that should have told me something!

This sent me back to revision's first question: *What do my readers need to know, and when, to have the experience I want them to have?* So I rearranged and tightened my draft with that question in mind. Snakes need to be mentioned earlier—on Alabama farms, they tend to motivate things—and the Adam figure ("Adam" means "clay" in Hebrew, by the way) doesn't need so many lines. Overall, I calmed down a bit (which you can see in the prose) but kept the underlying intensity and heart: it still feels, very much, like the story I wanted to write. Since I wanted readers to know the story's source material,

1

The Serpent   *Genesis / Proverbs 31*

Amy Weldon

When he left her there alone in what used to be their garden, with all the animals bawling to be fed and the maypop vine and blackberries thronging over the falling-down fences and the sweetgums sneaking out into the pastures, she had to try and put it back the way it was, although he'd cursed her when he left. *You'll never survive here without me. Every move you make will be in pain. Every single step.*

Luckily the roof is good. At least he saw to that. This is still her home, with its fig tree and garden patch she hopes will do all the better for being let to rest a year. Even such a terrible year as this may yield that one good thing, despite his drinking and his raging and his jealousy. (*Sit here with me, stay here, I made this house for you.*) She spent whole days just hunkered there with him next to his sleeping couch, her hand limp in his fists. No matter the jars on the pantry shelves and the smokehouse hams diminishing: three left, two left, one.

But now, dDown the red dirt road he'd gone to something else. *There are people out there,* he shouted, *there have to be, even though we've been living out here at the end of this road like there's nobody else on earth.* That was in February, on a bright cold day. She watched him weaving away, his clay-colored hair all bristly, his shirttail flapping, his knapsack pooched-out like a burst mushroom. Devil's sSnuffbox, she'd learned to call those mushrooms as a girl. Step on it and the dark gray spores drift out to ride the wind to what could be anywhere.

Even as she watched him walk away, her eyes were drifting to the garden patch. It had that sunken, scraggly look a garden gets when a woman has her mind on something else. The rickety wooden winter-bleached tomato frames still cradling brittle white vines, a few cold-leathered orange fruits still clinging. Blue-gray collards, all leaf and yellow flower. Pepper plants smashed flat where some small creature had rummaged through. Maybe it was the possum that laid waste that last melon over by the fence, its striped hull cracked and teethmarked, its faded heart open bare.

At least the fence——ten feet high, too high even for the deer——is still intact. The metal discs he cut for soaring are still shimmering and bouncing in the wind. She can see the evil little face etched into each one; they'd done that together, laughing, trying to outdo each other in charming a protection for their food against the crows and deer and dangers threatening this garden that would surely feed them both together for all time.

Good thing she'd kept her seeds in their brown twists of paper, upright in their box. *Ole Timey Blue. Cow Horn. Cherokee Purple. Trail of Tears. Arkansas Traveler. Mortgage Lifter. Hill Country Red. Yellow Gold. Moon and Stars.* Once When February got into March——an early season, thankfully——she could get out in the garden and ripped out the old tomato vines and the tall fierce weeds just starting to bud their seed-heads and hauled them to the place where the other garden skeletons were melting down to next year's food. She stropped the razor and

Commented [JG1]: The move between past and present tense is a little confusing on the first read. I wonder if giving an idea of "when" he left sooner (and when "February" is in relation to "now") will help the reader make more sense of the shifting of tense.

Something else that might help is putting a first sentence in present tense, since most of the story is in the present moment, and she's reflecting on the past. Beginning it in the past tense makes us want to read the rest of it in past tense, which makes the transition to present a little more abrupt than it should be.

Commented [JG2]: Later, you make the point that the fence is still intact. Maybe use a different adjective to describe the fence?

Commented [JG3]: Do you think we need an explanation for why this doesn't seem to be dwindling?

Commented [JG4]: Using "living" instead of "livin'" makes it more consistent with the rest of his dialogue.

Commented [JG5]: A paragraph break here helps with the switch in tense.

Commented [JG6]: I think the "once" and the "could" made it sound like she "would" do this—but really this is something she did before the present moment of the story, correct?

Figure 4.

I included the biblical citation as an epigraph, which signals a homage to another text when you want to let readers know that you are—to paraphrase Dolly Parton—"doing it on purpose."[8] Here's the revised and published version (in *The Hopper,* 2018), with my "source material" as the epigraph and with a couple more little tweaks added for this book, four years later (still revising!).

"The Serpent" by Amy Weldon

Genesis/Proverbs 31

He left her alone in what used to be their garden, with blackberry brambles clotting the fencerows and all the animals bawling to be fed. All winter he'd drunk and raged and watched her.* The jars on the pantry shelves and the smokehouse hams diminished: three, then two, then one. When February dawned, bright and cold, he wobbled away down the red dirt road with his knapsack on his back, his clay-colored hair bristling. *You'll never survive here without me*, he shouted back at her. *Every move you make will be in pain.* Never, once, could she have dreamed that she'd be glad to see him go. But left alone, she could put the garden back the way it was.

So she took stock. The tin roof on the house: still good. The well still drew, the fig tree and the plum and peach trees were setting fruit.† The vegetable patch, however, had that sunken, scraggly look a garden gets when a woman has her mind on something else. Rickety wooden winter-bleached tomato frames still cradled brittle white vines, where a few cold-leathered orange fruits still clung. Blue-gray collards burst up into yellow flower. Pepper plants were smashed flat where some creature had rummaged through. A possum had laid waste one last melon over by the fence, its striped hull cracked and teeth-raked, its faded heart laid bare. At least the deer fence, ten feet high, was still intact. The metal discs he had cut to scare them still shimmered and bounced in the wind. An evil little face was etched into each one; they'd done that together, laughing, charming a protection for their food against the crows and deer and dangers threatening this garden that would surely feed them both together for all time.

Without him, the milk cow lost a tendency to kick. The chickens clustered back around the house. The big yellow cat came out from under the porch. She replanted the seeds, upright in their twists of brown paper. *Ole Timey Blue. Cow Horn. Cherokee Purple. Trail of Tears. Arkansas Traveler. Mortgage Lifter. Hill Country Red. Yellow Gold. Moon and Stars.* She ripped out the old tomato vines and the tall fierce weeds and hauled them to the place where the other garden skeletons were melting down to next year's food. She sharpened the scythe and swung it through the grass to cut it all down.‡ Because in the warm weather coming on, snakes would be moving.

He had hated snakes beyond reason, ever since he opened the chicken coop and found a brown-and-gold rat snake stretching its mouth§ around a fresh white egg. *Don't bother them and they won't bother you*, she'd argued. *They keep the mice away.* She'd stopped up every hole in the coop and reburied the fence wire and thought that was the end of it. But in his bad time, as the grass feathered high and the garden grew wild and withered and the chickens got feral and experienced, she came to fear what might be out there: the panicked muscle writhing to life under her foot, the hot needle to her calf. Overgrown and wild and forlorn, this was not the happy garden they'd been given anymore. She'd die out here, no one to bury or to mourn.

But now, on a summer morning, the first tomato-ripening heat just taking hold, she lets herself release those fears. The garden is hers again. The seeds are up and flourishing.

---

*Here I omitted the sentence "She'd spent whole days hunkered there next to his sleeping couch, her hand limp in his fists" from the published version. Adds abusive-marriage subtext (okay) but feels a bit overdramatic now.
†Here I changed "bloom and leaf" to "fruit," which is more accurate.
‡Original sentence: "She stropped the razor and sharpened the scythe and swung it through the high grass to cut it all around the house, the garden, the fig tree." Too wordy.
§Omitted the word "open" here. If a snake's stretching its mouth around an egg, that mouth is, by definition, open.

The melon-hills are crowned with glory, the beans climbing their cornstalks right on time. Green baby crabgrass bristles between the new collards and the lettuces. If she lets crabgrass go, she's in for a war, gripping giant clumps of it and heaving it out. Gripping is a problem for her now. At night her hands ache, down in the joints. So big-knuckled and rough they are, so different from the slender fingers she held up before her own eyes as a girl, marveling *This is my body, all of this is me.* Deep in her hip is a grinding of bone on bone that freezes her in place, howling, if she catches it wrong. So she stretches and she takes a rest and she tries to ignore the way her body is no longer fully hers. Traitorous and tired, it's been swelled and split by both her sons. The one son's dead. The other—she doesn't know where he is. It's a pain worse than her swollen hands to think on them. So she chooses the pain that feeds her. She rubs the pig fat against her joints at night to keep them as supple as they can be for the next day in the garden. For a woman, keeping herself fed in this world is a full-time job. And now there's only her, out here at the end of the world, to see to it.

She chops the young crabgrass with her hoe, turning the roots over to bake in the sun. Then something rustles in the squash vines, slow, low against the ground. She freezes. There's only one thing that sound can be. But she can't just back away or it'll find her sometime she's less ready for it, like when she's barefoot on the porch steps, walking out into the yard at night to see the stars. This is her garden. She has to be free to move in it.

She steps back and slams the hoe into the soil. *I tell you to come out.* The air thickens with a heavy liquid hush of skin on skin. She chops the dirt. *Come out.* Slowly a rattlesnake unfurls itself into the light. Black birdwing shapes on its back, bird after bird after bird, loop toward her in the dirt. Its thick midsection is as wide as her right arm. Its black tail ends in a long cluster of rattle-beads. Its head is as big as her own outstretched hand, fingertip to wrist. And its lidless eyes are open, watching her.

Cold fear shoots down her spine, locking her to the dirt. Words scramble in her head: *be still, it'll strike, oh why oh why did—* She stares at the flat spade-shaped head and marshals her lost man's counseling words: *big snake is less to be feared than a small one, big snake knows what to use his venom on, little snake's just like a shirttail boy, lash out at anything he can.* Wild shirttail boy. Lost son. So much fear and grief now all undone in her. Why, oh, why did she command this beast out into the light?

The black eyes watch her. *Snake venom takes away the joint pain.* Whose voice is this? *Sure it does.* Longing rises in her chest, coloring the fear like wine in water. No more pain. Dizzily she pictures it. Step forward. Grasp this rope of muscle around its throat. Slip her right hand underneath the belly scales—it will be heavy—and lift it toward her heart. The flat eyes stare through her at nothing. *I'll be still.* Where is that voice coming from? *You'll pick me up and I'll be quick. Just one little bite. You won't hardly feel it. And all your pain will then be gone.*

Inside a pure cold emptiness opens, waiting, humming like her lost sons in their sleep. It is the place from which fear reaches for her in the night.[*] It is not-knowing. It

---

[*]Cut the sentence "The space in which her thoughts chased around and around as her lost man gripped her hand between his own." With the earlier hand-imprisoning reference gone, this can go too. Plus, now, at a moment of climactic tension, we're focused on her.

is intolerable. It is inescapable. It is where she must live now, on her own. She cannot run. And the doing and the caretaking of each day—the clothespins on the line, the sharp edge of the blade against the dirt, and the red skin of the fruit her own hands have brought forth—is the sturdy warm force that sends the fear back into its hole.

She lifts the blade and swings it down. The big snake bunches backward in a self-protective coil, rattle-buzz slicing the air. It's not a hiss, it's a harder sound, silver-edged and mean. Mean? Afraid. All down its neck is a split in the black-and-tan scales her blade has opened. It's bleeding. It is red meat and nerve and hunger, like any other thing.

She steps back and the rattlesnake whips away under the wide sunlit leaves. The fence quivers as it hits what must be a hole,** back there, in the wire. It's out in the pasture now, seedheads swaying as it passes. With her hoe upright in her hand, she stands and watches it. Rustle, rustle, away and out of sight.

Thinking about revision feels better when you consider that it helps your story, or your book, become what it really wants to be. A senior editor I know at an American university press says that great feedback offers "book-building takes"—assessments that focus on what the writer is really trying to do help build the book into what it has the potential to become. So think about revision and feedback as getting, and giving, "book-building takes." Revising is not just about "cutting"—it's about examining what's currently blurring the story's real shape so you can see how you want to keep building it from what we saw in Chapter 1—the wellspring of its best energy.

Information Order: When Do We Need to Know What?

Take a look at "The Serpent" draft and you can see how I needed to rearrange information. The garden is front and center—that's good, since it's the center of everything my character wants and needs (surviving, thriving, feeling at home in her world). For ongoing pressure, readers learn quickly about the marriage and catch a glimpse of the time it was happy (which we need to see in *any* story about a marriage gone bad). But—in a story called "The Serpent"—where's a snake? Not until my earlier draft's page 2, when, in my general tour of the farm, I describe the chicken house and the rat snake. I want to use the tensions of this super-short, midrashic form and of this world's dangers: my protagonist moves from the danger of her abusive husband to the dangers of the natural world. (Shorter forms have to "sparkle harder," remember?) So I bring the snakes forward to increase their pressure within the story. Let's be real: once the word "snake" gets into your story's (or your movie's) title, your dramatic imperatives become very clear. Just ask Samuel L. Jackson.

Literary agent Nicole Aragi, who represents Colson Whitehead, Tommy Orange, Nathan Englander, and Rebecca Makkai, among others, helped her client Jonathan

---

**Revised from a "hidden hole." Delete "hidden" as redundant—the sentence makes it clear the snake is leaving through a hole the narrator can't see.

Safran Foer perform this kind of revision on his novel *Everything Is Illuminated* (2002).[9] "There was a historical section right at the beginning," she told *Guernica* magazine, "and we shifted that back so that the book started with the modern-day voice. I have a reliance on that 'Hook people with the first paragraph' thing. Perhaps it's a cheap instinct, but I have an idea that people in bookshops will do what I do, which is to pick up a few books and read the first paragraph and see what they're grabbed by."

To revise, ask: What images and information do you need now to hook readers in and set them up for what happens later? What could you add or reintroduce to build up significant through-lines? What about your "rate of revelation," in Jim Shepard's words? Cutting a manuscript apart with scissors and moving the pieces around can help you make this decision.

"I'm Bored Here": What to Cut, and Why

Reducing, removing, or shrinking—making something *less*, in any form—is literally difficult for human brains to think of doing when presented with a problem in need of solutions.[10] But for writers, alas, it can be necessary. Sometimes writing must be shortened—or cut.

Matt Weiland, vice president and senior editor at W.W. Norton, has some signature editing marks. One he writes in a manuscript's margins: "BORED HERE." (Sometimes this becomes "REALLY BORED HERE.") Another comes from a waiter. "I often channel the memory of a waiter at an Italian restaurant in south Brooklyn," Matt has said, "who years ago paused when I repeated my order (thinking he hadn't heard me) and said, 'Yeah. You said dat already.'"[11]

Matt's a nice guy from Minneapolis, Minnesota, and when he told us these stories at the Bread Loaf Environmental Writers Conference a few years back, we laughed—and learned. "I'm bored here." "Ya said dat already." They sound harsh, but, especially once you let your first draft rest a bit, their truth shows through: what seemed essential at first may be things to let go.

Overexplaining, or showing the presence of an *anxious author*, may be the main thing that makes cuttable things cuttable. Writer Peter Rock calls this "bad telling": "Bad telling happens when we betray our anxiety about not knowing enough, when we stand outside the story and try to control it, when we simplify and, in so doing, condescend to our readers, and, worse, to our characters," he writes. "We worry when we ourselves don't believe, so we scramble to explain, we cast nervous asides, we become 'Authors.'"[12]

Sometimes this looks like explaining your own dialogue ("'I am furious!' she exclaimed angrily") or diluting a great sentence with a second one that explains it. Writer Rick Bass (anthology) calls this phenomenon "the Echo Sentence," or "when the same thought, or concept, has been said better—often brilliantly—in the previous sentence." For instance, he writes,

in the following student's scene, a young boy is upset, having been given some bad news by his father. The passage is as follows: "I rushed from the house, oblivious to the cold air that hit me when I opened the door. I crossed the yard and started to circle the barn, my hands in my pockets, the frozen grass crunching under my boots, anger clawing inside me."

This is okay. But listen to the next sentence—listen to the buzz go off, the Echo Sentence: "I felt helpless, then, and upset."

Writing a story is like crossing a minefield. You cross the field, with the story loosely in your arms, and you try not to step on any of the mines.[13]

Filtering—presenting sensory information through the direct "filter" of a character's perception—can feel like it draws you and readers closer to a character, but the opposite is true. Consider:

She peered down into the street and saw a yellow taxi pull up to the curb, then saw a tall man get out, clutching a brown grocery bag.

"She saw" is the "filter" here. Just present the thing the character sees:

She peered down into the street. A yellow taxi pulled up to the curb and a tall man got out, clutching a brown grocery bag.

In his story "The New Chicago" (see Chapter 4), student Ian Wreisner found a "filter" he could remove:

Dad would lose his shit, **Richard thought. He felt his own face tense as he thought about what his dad might say if he knew he was in a bar like this.**

Minus the "filter," the line's more active and the psychic distance closer:

Dad would lose his shit, **Richard thought. He felt his own face tense. What would his dad say if he knew he was in a bar like this?**

In his book *Refuse to Be Done: How to Write and Rewrite a Novel in Three Drafts* (2022), Matt Bell offers many ideas for what to cut during revision. One I really like is to cut the weakest sentence (or clause) from every single paragraph. He also differentiates between "backstory that *explains* your character," which "can go," and "backstory that *complicates* your character, [which] is likely doing better work."[14]

Writerly anxiety can produce *too much distraction*: What takes away from the narrative momentum and major through-line? What is this really about? Maybe you've got too much description, or too many characters, too much alike, with names that sound too similar. Maybe it's scenes you just don't need. Maybe it's a place where "you weren't sure what a character was implying when they made some elliptical statement, so you gave an answer."[15] Maybe it's long passages of dialogue where all the action around them just stops. This, too, can come from authorial anxiety: *please believe my novel's world is interesting!* It comes from that particular love you feel for your characters and their world. But unless the plenitude of a voice, and a world, is your point (as in James McBride's *Deacon King Kong*), and unless you can clearly control that plenitude and keep cutting a clear forward path through your material, readers might be distracted rather than enchanted by it. Matt Bell helps us cut through overexplaining by pointing out, "mostly the reader does not want your logic":

What the reader wants to do is to connect the dots for themselves, to figure out your characters' motives, to make connections between one scene and another, to explore and solve the mysteries of your novel. If you get in their way by leaving your logic [aka overexplanation] on the page, then you're taking away some of the joy of reading fiction.[16]

Beginnings and Endings: Establishing Authority

If *anxiety* can tell us what to cut, *authority* can tell us what to leave in—especially at the beginning, a vulnerable point for both writers and readers. Rob Spillman, writer and founding editor of *Tin House*, uses the word "authority" to describe what hooks him into the beginning of a story or novel and can mean the difference between a successful and unsuccessful submission. Here are three authoritative fictional openings he offered my students and me when he visited our campus:

> He speaks in your voice, American, and there's a shine in his eye that's halfway hopeful.
>
> It's a school day, sure, but he's nowhere near the classroom. He wants to be here instead, standing in the shadow of this old rust-hulk of a structure, and it's hard to blame him—this metropolis of steel and concrete and flaky paint and cropped grass and enormous Chesterfield packs aslant on the scoreboards, a couple of cigarettes jutting from each.
>
> Longing on a large scale is what makes history. This is just a kid with a local yearning but he is part of an assembling crowd, anonymous thousands off the buses and trains, people in narrow columns tramping over the swing bridge about the river, and even if they are not a migration or a revolution, some vast shaking of the soul, they bring with them the body heat of a great city and their own small reveries and desperations, the unseen something that haunts the day—men in fedoras and sailors on shore leave, the stray tumble of their thoughts, going to a game.
>
> The sky is low and gray, the roily gray of sliding surf.
>
> (from *Underworld* by Don DeLillo, 1997)

> At first, our pack was all hair and snarl and floor-thumping joy. We forgot the barked cautions of our mothers and fathers, all the promises we'd made to be civilized and ladylike, couth and kempt. We tore through the austere rooms, overturning dresser drawers, pawing through neat piles of the Stage 3 girls' starched underwear, smashing light bulbs with our bare fists. Things felt less foreign in the dark. The dim bedroom was windowless and odorless. We remedied this by spraying exuberant yellow streams all over the bunks. We jumped from bunk to bunk, spraying. We nosed each other midair, our bodies buckling in kinetic laughter. The nuns watched us from the corner of the bedroom, their tiny faces pinched with displeasure.
>
> (from "St. Lucy's Home for Girls Raised By Wolves" by Karen Russell, 2006)

Drummond opened the shop every morning at seven so he and his boy could eat breakfast while the first dropoffs were coming in. The boy liked cereal and sat at the workbench in back, slurping his milk, while Drummond occasionally hustled out to the curb to help a secretary haul a cumbersome IBM from the back seat of a car. The front of the store was a showroom for refurbished machines, displayed on shelves, each with a fresh sheet of white bond rolled into the platen, while the back was a chaos of wrecked typewriters Drummond would either salvage or cannibalize for parts someday. There were two stools and two lamps at the workbench for the rare times when the son felt like joining his father, cleaning the keys, but generally after breakfast the boy spent the rest of the day sitting behind Drummond in an old Naugahyde recliner, laughing to himself and saying prayers, or wandering out to the sidewalk to smoke a cigarette. That he step outside to smoke was the only major request Drummond ever made of his son.

(from "Drummond & Son" by Charles d'Ambrosio, 2002)

Each of the foregoing three beginnings establishes authority by establishing what Rob calls "forward lean," a strong, intriguing voice with a sense of musicality and uniqueness, an engaging point of view, a narrative momentum, and what Rob described to my students and me as "good mystery." *Good mystery*, he explained, is when the reader wonders, "Will she find her way? Will she find love? Will she find water before it's too late?" *Bad mystery* is, "What the hell is going on?"

No wonder, then, that beginnings are challenging. This starts with identifying where your story really begins. Frequently, Rob says, he's seen stories that really begin on page 3; pages 1 and 2 are just "throat-clearing." What opening image is the one that will make your reader want to keep reading, and strike the first note of your story's particular song in a way that helps them imaginatively enter its world?

Perhaps for this reason, it's really hard to begin successfully with a line of dialogue. Unless you're E. B. White, beginning *Charlotte's Web* (1952) with the question, "Where's Papa going with that ax?," it's hard to give a voice the forward lean that a whole story needs. Readers may be intrigued by a voice, but as I described in Chapter 6, we also need a sense of a person in a place, a person next to whom we can locate ourselves, a figure against the ground.

Revising toward this may take a while. The first beginning of my novel *Creature* was a dreamlike swirl of images, kind of cool but also confusing. At the Bread Loaf Environmental Writers Workshop in 2017, my workshop leader, novelist Megan Mayhew Bergman, mused, "This opening is killer . . . but I feel like it needs to be in *scene*. What if we begin at the *end*? Mary Shelley is waiting for Percy Shelley to come sailing back home, except we know what she doesn't know yet—that he's drowned?" After I finished the book and got more feedback (including from students), I wrote the beginning I believe in—the one you see on p. 132—that follows her advice. And the most important image from that first beginning did re-enter the novel later, where it really belonged. (Did I mention it *is* okay to write your beginning last?)

Endings may seem easier than beginnings; writers can often tell when we get to a point at which we can think, "It's okay to leave [character] here." (A good ending does not necessarily have to tie up all possible loose ends.) Some thinking about authority and anxiety can help you here, too: Have you followed through on the plot/character arcs of your story, and, therefore, on the promises your story is making to the reader? If there are unanswered questions, are these the "good mystery" or "bad mystery" kind? Are you clinging on, writing more scenes, because you don't want to let your character go? In his introduction to *Best American Short Stories 1984,* novelist John Updike remarks,

> The ending is where the reader discovers whether he has been reading the same story the writer thought he was writing. . . . A narrative is like a room on whose walls a number of false doors have been painted; while within the narrative, we have many apparent choices of exit, but when the author leads us to one particular door, we know it is the right one *because it opens.*

The First Sentence: Packing and Unpacking

"Opening sentences yank us out of our lives and into other lives," writes novelist Edwidge Danticat. "They are, as many writers have said, anchors, hooks, handshakes, embraces, pickup lines, promises, and, as science fiction writer William Gibson told the *Atlantic's* Joe Fassler, 'something like filing, from a blank of metal, the key for a lock that doesn't exist, in a door that doesn't yet exist.'"[17]

No wonder, then, that we may tackle the job of writing a sentence like we tackle the job of packing a suitcase, thinking, "how can I find a place, in this sentence, for everything I know, to **deliver** it to the reader and be done?" But you aren't only unloading what you know onto the page—you're crafting a version of what you want readers to see that helps them build that picture in their own heads. Unlike you, readers are starting from zero. Therefore, it's smart to heed the advice of the great comic writer P. G. Wodehouse: beware "a great slab of prose right at the start"[18] and consider how sentences can start and design a successful info-drip. Compare these two beginnings:

1. ORIGINAL: "At age thirteen, perched in her mother's parlor in the chateau on the Loire where her ancestors had lived for the last four hundred years, Antoinette Devereaux met the man who would become her husband, although she could not know that yet since, unlike her ancestors, she had no power of divination, although the blood of witches still ran in her veins, waiting to be reawakened."

2. REVISION: "At age thirteen, perched in her mother's gold-and-white parlor, Antoinette Devereaux met the man who would become her husband. However, she had no way of knowing this. Unlike her ancestors—four hundred years'

worth, living in this chateau at a bend of the Loire—she had no power of divination. Yet their blood still ran in her veins, waiting to be reawakened."

How might these revised sentences be easier to absorb for a reader brand-new to the story's world than that first massive one? And can you apply this lens to the "info drip" in your draft as a whole? Looking back at "The Serpent" and the beginning of *Creature* (p. 132), you can see how I revised with this idea in mind.

The novelist Jonathan Lee (p. 173) says, "If writing fiction is a process of playful problem-solving, the problem to solve with opening lines may be this: If the entryway is found to be too creaky, or too tricky to unlock, no one is going to bother to walk through it. But the opposite is a problem too. If the opening line to a book seems *overly* inviting—a door not just ajar, but flung open to the elements—the reader smells desperation instead of freshly baked bread." Therefore, Lee describes a great first line as "a perfect balance between resistance and invitation."[19]

Energy and Sound: Weaving a Writerly Voice

Every writer brings to the page a particular kind of energy that has much in common with the kind of sound a singer like Joyce DiDonato produces—an energy writers also call *voice*, arising from an intangible combination of language, cadence, rhythm, information, and preoccupation that shapes the words you choose and the order in which you write them down. Reading a writer's words, you may also hear their voice as a distinctive sound. But how might you get here? Practice, sure—writing lots of sentences over time. But there's more. In her memoir *Priestdaddy* (2017), Patricia Lockwood writes:

> I thought a voice had to be about what you could do. It wasn't until I heard Billie Holiday that I realized a voice could be a collection of compensations for things you *couldn't* do.[20] It could be an ingenuity—in the same way some writers wrote books that coursed between the boulders of what they couldn't do, and went faster, tumbled over, fell in rills and rushed breathingly over the stones.
>
> The great singers were also the great interpreters. She had just a single octave, and she made it her lifelong subject.
>
> I thought a voice had to be about your fluency, your dexterity, your virtuosity. But in fact your voice could be about your failings, your falterings, your physical limits. The voices that ring hardest in our heads are not the perfect voices. They are the voices with an additional dimension, which is pain.

"Style is a very simple matter: it is all *rhythm*," wrote Virginia Woolf to her onetime lover Vita Sackville-West (March 16, 1926). "Once you get that, you can't use the wrong words."[21] Style and voice aren't always clearly separable from "content," as writer Becca Rothfeld says about religious philosopher Simone Weil: "The point is the violent originality of the idea, and the striking personality that produced it, and the bright chime of the language . . . in this instance the glove is much of what lends the hand its interest and its elegance."[22] Style, voice, content, and personality—all are intertwined. And all are marked—no matter how different—by a quality of heightened attention: the writer is deeply alert, alive, present with their work. In writing about Joan Eardley's paintings, Andrew O'Hagan renders that sensation: "There's a newness in that, painting what you feel in a way that engages the nervous system of the viewer."[23] (This nicely echoes what critic Margo Jefferson has called writing, and building the network of influences that builds your writerly sensibility and voice: "constructing a nervous system."[24]) How is your prose engaging your reader's "nervous system"—and your own?

So here are some questions to ask as you're considering your own writerly voice:

What voices inspire you on the page, and why?

Take a look at passages from writing you love to learn some features you may use. Style and sentence structures, for instance, may evoke particular sensory immediacy and thus collapse time—especially important in historical fiction. Let's start with George Garrett's dazzling, unfairly neglected epic *Death of the Fox* (1971), centered on Sir Walter Ralegh's 1618 imprisonment in the Tower of London. Here, Ralegh, an old man, departs the Tower for his execution at the Palace of Westminster:

> Clinging to the cudgel, he rises. All move in quickstep through the presence chamber and, following the yeoman, through the long council chamber and down the turning inner stairs.
>
> Feeling his way more carefully now. Needing the staff to steady himself.
>
> It would have been quicker to descend by the scaffold of wooden stairs outside. But they go down the old stairway.
>
> Past the armory, where useless armor rusts and cannon from the time of Henry VIII—Great Harry, Long Meg, Seymour's Gun—lie idle, oddly comic in repose.
>
> Down and across the hall and at last outside.
>
> Dawn air chill, ghosting breath, but sweet after the sorrows of old stone. Breathing it. Taste and odor, in keen chill, of October's falling, dying leaves, of woodsmoke and coalsmoke from houses and towers. And always faint salt of the river and the sea. All around the yard is sprinkled, leaved with October blood. From houses and walls and in the yard there are watchers. Who have turned to stone.[25]

And this passage from Jonathan Lee's *The Great Mistake* (2021), set in nineteenth-century New York City:

> Andrew believed in walking more firmly than he believed in a higher being. Was even more hungry for motion here than he had been at home. So he walked to the Presbyterian churches and the Episcopalian churches, to the Baptist churches and

the Methodist churches, to the Wesleyan and Independent churches, to the Dutch Reformed and the Roman Catholic churches, to the Universalist and Orthodox and Quaker churches, to the Hicksite and Congregationalist and Unitarian churches, to the Lutheran and Moravian and Swedenborgian churches, and, on one swiftly regretted occasion, even the German Reformed. A sermon was much cheaper than the theatre. It was also a lesson in the way city gentlemen moved. Their phrases, gestures. An opportunity to watch and imitate, which had to be the first stage of possession? In the rearmost pews his lips moved in mimicry. Performance. And sometimes desire. He loved the energy of the hymns, the sense of belonging they seemed to offer. He memorized words in foreign languages, faithful only to their sounds, and wondered if his own occasional doubts about the existence of God might in some way be mutual. Did anyone in the heavens really believe in him, Andrew Green, this awkward boy below, his spirit, his potential for good? His own question frightened him into muteness, the kind of silence the living rarely know, the moon hanging sullied by smoke in the sky, filthy with the expulsions of men.

Like Hilary Mantel's justly famous trilogy on Thomas Cromwell's life and death—*Wolf Hall* (2009), *Bring Up The Bodies* (2012), and *The Mirror and the Light* (2020)—both these passages draw readers into a believable past by crafting a voice that exemplifies what the novelist David Mitchell has called "bygone-ese." "If you get [historical speech] too right," Mitchell has said,

> it sounds like a pastiche comedy—people are saying "thou" and "prithee" and "gadzooks," which they did say, but to an early 21st-century audience, it's laughable, even though it's accurate. So you have to design a kind of "bygone-ese"—it's modern enough for readers not to stumble over it, but it's not so modern that the reader kind of thinks this could be out of "House" or "Friends" or something made for TV.[26]

Both these passages embody features that close the distance between readers in the present and characters in the historical past—specifically the sentence fragments and the sensory, direct language ("taste and odor . . . woodsmoke and coalsmoke," capitalizing on the common language of the senses—we, George Garrett, and Sir Walter Ralegh all have human bodies). Can you tell how clearly each writer is imagining his character in his place and time? Yet each writer is also heeding the cadences and details *of* that place and time. Note the authoritative terminology ("presence chamber," names of churches and cannons, "whale-oil illumination") and the nineteenth-century cadences of Lee's sentences (like that beautiful periodic sentence at the end of this excerpt). I hear a seventeenth-century stance in Garrett, too, particularly in the double meaning of that verb-turned-adjective "leaved" (leaves of books, leaves of gold, leaves of trees, all layered like time itself), which also bears a ghost of the religious verb-turned-adjective "leavened."[27] The impression is of a careful writer not only imagining his character energetically in his own present moment (including twentieth-century skepticism about state executions and organized religion) but also letting himself be held in check by the caution of *what could my character realistically think, see, know, or say here?* That tension gives an energy to each writer's voice that, for me, is the real engine of successful bygone-ese.

"Do you like sentences?"

A well-known writer got collared by a university student who asked, "Do you think I could be a writer?"

"Well," the writer said, "I don't know . . .. Do you like sentences?"

The writer could see the student's amazement. Sentences? Do I like sentences? I am twenty years old and do I like sentences? If he had liked sentences, of course, he could begin, like a joyful painter I knew. I asked him how he came to be a painter. He said, "I liked the smell of the paint." (from Annie Dillard, *The Writing Life*)

[T]he real fun of writing, for me at least, is the experience of making a set of givens yield. There's an incredibly inflexible set of instruments—our vocabulary, our grammar, the abstract symbols on paper, the limitations of your own powers of expression. You write something down and it's awkward, trivial, artificial, approximate. But with effort you can get it to become a little flexible, a little transparent. You can get it to open up, and expose something lurking there beyond the clumsy thing you first put down. When you add a comma or add or subtract a word, and the thing reacts and changes, it's so exciting that you forget how absolutely terrible writing feels a lot of the time. (Deborah Eisenberg)

To think about cadences, words, and voice, of course, you first have to think about sentences, and whether you "like them" enough (as Annie Dillard says) to geek out on, play with, craft and recraft, "make the givens yield" (as Deborah Eisenberg says) and tweak—because without good sentences, you have no story. Nor do you have the trust of your readers. *New York Times* book reviewer Parul Sehgal asks this pointed question: "To see language treated so shabbily shakes the reader's confidence; if a writer can't work her way around a sentence or land a metaphor, what assurance have we that she can parse her subjects' traumas, their complex, sometimes inchoate yearnings?"[28] Writing good sentences starts with bringing good attention to your work, focusing, considering, and tightening the relationship between your words, your readers, and your story's world. And, most of all, it starts with reading.

One day, I asked my excellent mechanic, Jeff Burke, about what I thought was moisture buildup behind the headlight lenses of my car. He showed me that it wasn't fog—years of road grit had abraded the once-clear plastic. If, as George Orwell wrote, "good prose is like a windowpane," then messy prose is like my car's headlights, clouded by a million little mistakes. In general, the more advanced you get as a writer, the more important it is to be able to proofread your own prose, since readers (and editors) will cut you progressively less slack. Control what you can—verb tense shifts (p. 104), misplaced modifiers, commas, and all the rest. For an idea of where to start, look back at comments you've received on your written work: Does your annoying teacher (like me) keep writing "Misplaced modifier?" Maybe that's a clue.

In my book *The Writer's Eye*, I included a chapter on metaphors, similes, modifiers, compound sentences, and other sentence-level concerns, so I won't repeat all of that here; y'all are advanced writers. But I will repeat and build on an exercise I offered students there: the graph. Here are the steps:

1) Find a passage of writing you love, written by someone else, with a quality of voice you want to replicate.

2) Copy that passage on paper by hand, exactly, to get inside its spirit and rhythms.

3) Jot a few words to name the things about it you like—the kind of energy it has.

1) Now plot its sentence lengths on the graph in Figure 5.

2) Connect the dots and look at the shape the line makes. What do you see?

3) Now graph a "more like this" AND a "this stops me" moment in your own prose. What do you see—and do you have ideas for how to revise your sentences and words? Do longer or shorter sentences, for instance, or variations between them, create particular kinds of momentum you can use?

4) Consider the relationship between the pattern you see and the mood you want. Are the sentence lengths and word choices you're using helping to set or defuse that mood?

This may seem obsessive, but for sentence geeks, it brings the same deep joy and attentiveness that editing can. "While we write into a void," says Susan Bell, "we edit into a universe, however ravaged it may be . . . the reassurance we feel at having something to

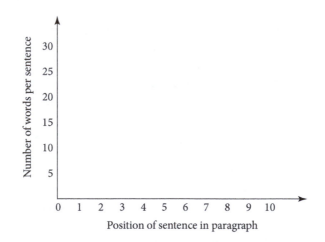

Figure 5.

work with goes far to explain why editing is, in one important sense, easier than writing: being somewhere is less lonely and frightening than being nowhere."[29]

Can you see what you're saying? Or: do you know what you're writing about?

As we've discussed, building a world—and writing good sentences about it—can start with slowing down enough to imagine and understand what you're building. Anne Lamott compares letting an image bloom in your mind to "letting a Polaroid develop," letting the image come into mental focus. As you see the image more clearly, you can track back and forth between that picture and the language on the page, adjusting your words more precisely to the thing you see. You may draw pictures, as we've mentioned. You may also slow down more than you're used to. And that's fine.

Here's another exercise from *The Writer's Eye* that helps bring an image, and a writerly voice, into focus. Think of a moment of tension or dramatic action in your story. Now write that moment under the following prose constraints:

1) Sentences of no more than fifteen words each.

2) Words of no more than two syllables each.

3) No adverbs (-ly words).

4) Adjectives of the five senses only (sight, sound, taste, touch, smell)—not editorial (beautiful, amazing, awful).

5) Take a moment to read through, notice what you've got, and think about this experience. What *new* information or detail did it yield?

6) Now ask yourself: Which of these rules annoyed you most as you wrote, or made the writing hardest? Go back into this passage and break that rule, in any single place you like. That may be a clue into your own writerly voice: What do you find yourself with the impulse to put on the page at particular times, and why? Do your sentences expand or contract at moments of tension? Where do your adjectives and details get clear?

What embarrasses you or pleases you about your old work, and why?

In my advanced creative writing class, I ask students to bring in a piece of their writing that's at least two years old (or more), and, together, we talk about what we see. Always, the students trace some aspect of their younger self's voice to their younger self's mindset: "I was trying to please my teacher," "I was trying to write about something I didn't know at *all*," "I wasn't really paying attention to my own work—I was phoning it in." Sadly, some students also marvel, "I used to have so much *fun* when I wrote. What happened?!" Don't beat yourself up—just open the channel between your writerly voice and your mindset in a way that helps you now.

Do you need a fresh start?

As I mentioned back in Chapter 6, writers can get really bound up with a project they've been working on for a while. If you find yourself struggling in the mire of an "old project you want to fix up," then hoist yourself out by putting the old document aside—closing it out on your computer, putting your marked-up manuscript in a drawer, whatever—and starting from the top, with the image or voice uppermost in your mind, from the place you are *now*. Just start writing (or typing) on a totally fresh page or in a totally fresh document, and keep going for at least fifteen minutes, or until you've solidified your new voice and stance. Start closer to where the action really is (as Rob Spillman advises), try another character's point of view (as Tommy Orange advises), envision a different image or place or start in a different scene (as Megan Mayhew Bergman advised me to do with *Creature*). You still have the old manuscript to consult if you need it, but what really belongs in the novel (for instance) will usually migrate into the new draft on its own. Lauren Groff, author of *Matrix* (2021), told an audience (including me and my students) that she writes first and second drafts by hand, setting written pages aside as soon as she completes them and trusting the right material to resurface in the next draft as she begins it from scratch.[30] A great technique is to literally cut out the "most interesting thing" from a previous draft, tape it to the top of a new page, and continue writing from there—starting fresh.

Writing (and Revising) at Length: Moving from Stories to Novels

At some point, you might feel ready to try writing something longer than a short story—like a novella/short novel or a full-length novel. But what makes them different? How might you get started? Experiences vary, but here's what I learned when I made this move:

1) Some people are just more comfortable writing stories or writing novels, although you can do both. You don't "have to write novels" to be a great writer (hello, Alice Munro!) "In my opinion, there's only one mind or another at work in a piece of fiction," says Deborah Eisenberg, "and it's the mind, not the length, that most accounts for the piece's properties."[31]

2) Your material itself often tells you what it wants to be (story, novella, or novel).

3) Writing about the same material in a new form means re-imagining it *for* that form—not just "making it longer" or "making it shorter."

4) You can relax a bit in a novel as opposed to a story, because you have a larger timescale on which to release your "info drip." But novel length is *not* just an excuse to ramble and sprawl—except in your first draft.

5) Wherever you go, there you are: when you move from one form to another, your strengths, weaknesses, preoccupations, habits, and signature sounds will usually come along too.

6) But different forms, like types of exercise, can strengthen you and teach you how to listen to the material—not only to your own goals for it.

I say this a lot, but for me, at least, it's true: as you begin a piece, it's okay, even normal, not to know exactly what shape it's trying to be or what will happen by the end or what its motivating questions are. Sometimes, not knowing is even *preferable*, because *discovery* can also light up a book, for writer and reader. In her *LitHub* essay on "writing without a plan," Aimee Bender (anthology) says, "There isn't necessarily a perfect image or story or moment [in your head] you are transmitting to the page. I kept trying to force [an early, abandoned] novel into a shape I had imagined for it, and it simply didn't work":

> For me, [she continues], the page is all I get, and the page is what makes the soup of the mind into something tangible. If there is no book in my mind, then the only way I can find a book is by writing it. This act of writing is how I get access to the material I might not readily know about. We cannot read each others' minds, and the truth is, we often cannot really read our own.
>
> There's something sad in this—that we cannot replicate our idea, our perfect, imagined book in there, our brilliant ideas that seem so full and glorious when walking past the autumn leaves. But the amazing side, the truly amazing side, is that we might write something else, something surprising.[32]

A Workshop Story: Colson Whitehead, Novel Time, and My Real Main Character

When I was admitted to the Tin House Summer Writers Workshop in 2008, I was thrilled. Writers' workshops like this (including the Sewanee Writers Conference and the Bread Loaf Writers Conference) are kind of like summer camp for writers. You spend two weeks at a campus-style site where you divide your time among craft lectures and readings by famous writers, advisory talks and meetings with editors and agents, and daily workshops (led by one of the famous writers) in which you and about a dozen strangers read and discuss each other's work. I'd be joining a workshop led by Colson Whitehead for writers working on novels. Although I was humbled, and excited, and nervous, I also thought I knew what I was doing, because I was (ahem) going to be *turning my short story into a novel*.

Back in graduate school, I'd published and won an award for a short story, "Mansions," in which Rex, the younger brother of a rural white Southern family, tries to cope with his older brother Byron's suicide. Since then, I'd imagined a Black woman, Janie, who grows up alongside them. In 2008, I was also going through a third-year review in my tenure-track college teaching job (thank God). And I figured it was time to step up my game from short stories to novels, so I could be a "real writer." Accordingly, I opened a document, called it "Mansions: A Novel," and started typing. But it wasn't working, and I didn't know why. Like the frustrated student at the beginning of Chapter 6, I cared about my characters, I could write good sentences, and I knew, basically, what happened. I wrote more than a hundred pages, yet energy leaked out through some invisible pinhole, and the more I worked, the worse it got. Surely, a writer I admired could help.

And I admired—yet was intimidated by—Colson Whitehead. By that time, he'd published three novels (*The Intuitionist*, which I'd taught at Luther, *John Henry Days*, and *Apex Hides the Hurt*) and one book of nonfiction (*The Colossus of New York*) and won a Whiting Award and MacArthur "Genius Grant." And he was just five years older than me! Turned out, he was a quiet, low-key person, really thoughtful, funny, and kind.

On that first day, at the head of our table of fourteen people, Whitehead sketched a simple diagram on the board.[33] "Novels play out over a different time frame than short stories," he said.

In "novel time," you can settle in a bit, take your time, think about what you want to set up first, because you're going on a journey. Let's take *The Intuitionist* as an example. Here's the first chapter, and its major notes: Lila Mae Watson is a black woman elevator inspector, so here's the place we see her doing her job, on site

—he sketched a quick vertical chalk mark on the board, describing the scene I quoted in Chapter 4—"and here she is, back at her office, with her co-workers. Then at home, that evening." He sketched two more lines to the right of the first. "And here's the accident." One more line, the incident that kicks off the novel's mystery plot. "So now we have to think: where do we want to give the readers more information about the two kinds of elevator inspectors, the Empiricists and the Intuitionists?" He moved his hand about four inches to the right and made another mark. "Maybe we don't really need to unpack them fully until a little later on, although we can see them at work in the meantime, because they do drive the conflict. And eventually we need to see a relevant scene from Lila Mae's childhood in Texas"—he made a mark about six inches further still to the right—"but that can wait."

Watching and listening, as a chronological chart of *The Intuitionist* grew on the board, I began to see that writing a novel means imagining and discovering (via drafting, too) a whole world, with an even deeper "cave of knowledge," as Virginia Woolf would say, behind each character than I'd thought. And then it means organizing a structure to deliver that information to readers in a way that allows for discovery *and* the novel's unique relationship to time (as Joel Murillo does in Chapter 6's Student Craft Studio). One of Whitehead's comments on my manuscript read, "Scenes occur without some large design." And he was right: I was still in story-mode of bundling small scenes together, not yet in novel mode of imagining, then reverse-engineering, a bigger picture. I needed to think in novel-time and re-imagine my short story's world accordingly.

In conference on my manuscript, Whitehead identified a second problem: Rex, the main character I'd brought from my story, was too passive to carry a novel. Everyone around him was interacting and sparking action and consequence, but he was offstage, or bystanding, for much of it. This led to the same problem you saw in my diagram of the story on p. 108: lots of scenes of flashback or "imagining" or "wondering" that dragged the momentum backwards. "Things really start cooking when Janie enters on p. 9," he wrote. "Do you find her more interesting than Rex? How come?" *Oh, wow,* I realized.

I've had the wrong main character! All this time! And once I knew that, I could really think about where the novel should root itself: the characters' adulthood or their childhood.

Once I got home, bearing the warmth of our workshop community and a new certainty, I sat down and restarted the whole novel in a fresh document. Its first image tipped me right into Janie's perspective, with a third-person-limited point of view. In a month, I'd rewritten 150 pages, interrupted by the image that became my first published novel, *Eldorado, Iowa* (2019), where Rex Wainwright's ancestor appears in a supporting role. *Mansions* might always remain my training-wheels novel, but I'll never forget what I learned from its process, and from Colson Whitehead, whose work I've read and honored ever since.

Pitfalls and Signposts: More Revision Problems

I tell this story to show you some of the pitfalls that can show up at the advanced level and/or in the transition from stories to longer forms. "Wrong main character" is surprisingly common—like Rosalind Russell as the pushy stage mom in *Gypsy*, writers can pick the wrong kid to promote. Maybe you aren't quite imagining your material for the unique requirements of its form—story, novella, or novel. Here are some other issues you may encounter:

- Switching up your structure or POV as an evasion technique, rather than as an attempt to find its real voice. To be sure, there's nothing inherently wrong with multiple narrators or time frames. But, as Susan Bell asks, "Are you wandering in order to stimulate a work that's staid? Or to avoid the apparent tedium of moving straight ahead? In other words, are you being inspired or undisciplined?"[34]

- "The Clone Entourage" (as described in *How Not to Write a Novel*[35]): Do you have too many characters too alike? Or too many varieties of beasts in your fantastical world? Problem is unless they are part of an authoritative design (like James McBride's), they start to blur together, and the reader finds themselves wondering, "Now wait a minute . . . who's *this* guy, again?" (Especially if their names look or sound similar. Bill, Tom, Jim, and Mike will be hard for the reader to tell apart—hear the monosyllables? But Bill, Isaiah, Lorenzo, and Clint feel like four *different* people.)

- Stuck on repeat: Do you have too many plot-loops or scenes that are too similar? This is a particular challenge in novels that alternate among multiple characters and/or locations; we can feel like we're reading the same five scenes over and over while the novel spins like a stuck tire in mud, digging itself down instead of forward.

- Pause for a tennis match: Long passages of dialogue where the writer, loving her clever characters, hands them the mike—and then nothing else happens for a while. (See Chapter 5.)

- "I don't trust myself": It's really hard to know when you are editing and when—like a raccoon with a sugar cube—you're wearing away the sweetest, most mysteriously unique things about your work by obsessively washing it.[36] "When you edit," writes Susan Bell, "determine what is mystery and what is muddle; the first to be respected and left alone, the second to be respected and cleaned up."[37] Novelist Ann Patchett describes this feeling: "The moment at which I really feel like I've begun a novel is the day that I sit down and start writing without going back and rereading the thirty pages I've already written. The first two chapters of this book that I'm writing now are like patent leather because I was completely floundering and stuck trying to move onto the third and fourth chapters. I kept going back and polishing."[38] This is a version of what literary agent Anna Sproul-Latimer calls "the rubber band ball you have fled the rest of the book to add to every time you felt uncertain or anxious."[39]

For me, an antidote to obsessive over-editing is an opportunity for *discovery*—writing toward and into something new and fun rather than going back over something I know well. So let's talk about some opportunities that longer forms can offer.

Linked Story Collections

Also known as a novel-in-stories or story cycles, a linked story collection is just like it sounds: a group of stories explicitly linked by a common setting, a common set of characters, a common theme, or some other kind of logic the writer's set forth. While each story can stand on its own as a self-contained unit, a linked story collection is also designed to provide a similar kind of cumulative effect that comes from reading all the stories in sequence, like a novel. Some book-length examples are Alice Munro's *Lives of Girls and Women* (1971), Eudora Welty's *The Golden Apples* (1949), and Elissa Schappell's *Use Me* (2000). Cynan Jones's *Stillicide* (2020), from which "Sound" (anthology) is drawn, is woven together by intersecting character arcs from different stories about water scarcity in a climate-challenged future. You may also find mini-linked-story-collections tucked within larger ones: Amy Bloom's "Silver Water" is the centerpiece of a three-story cycle about the same family that can be found in Bloom's collection *Come to Me* (1993).

Novellas: Not Too Long, Not Too Short . . .

Writers often complain (or confess) that it's hard to respect the novella as a form in its own right, neither a story that goes on too long nor a novel that stops too soon. It's even hard to agree on how long a novella is—most of them clock in at between 10,000 and 40,000 words, or about 50 to 125 manuscript pages. But read a good novella and you'll appreciate its particular shapeliness and interesting constraints. A good novella really does feel as if its content has been imagined for its form and no other; any shorter and it would leave us with "bad mystery" questions and confusions, any longer and it would lose the particular bittersweet tang it derives from its refusal to overexplain. Each of my favorite novellas exemplifies this: David Garnett's *Lady Into Fox* (1922), Nella Larsen's *Passing* (1929), Marghanita Laski's *The Victorian Chaise-Longue* (1953), Truman *Breakfast at Tiffany's* (1958), Elizabeth Spencer's *The Light in the Piazza* (1960), Jim Harrison's *Legends of the Fall* (1978), Denis Johnson's *Train Dreams* (2002), Hao Jingfang's *Folding Beijing* (2012; translated into English by Ken Liu in 2015), and Danielle Evans's *The Office of Historical Corrections* (2020). Each is built on a significant concept or character, and each happens in a significant and richly evoked place that also has dramatic weight—a short story wouldn't do justice to the way a reader needs to be immersed in the combination of these things for full artistic payoff. Yet each also benefits from the way its form *denies* a reader any over-explanation of its themes and events: in each case, readers are left wondering, "Wow—how do I feel about what I just saw play out?" I think a novella's combination of brevity and depth invites readers to ponder that question in a special way.

Is This Really a Novel?

Only you can tell whether your image or idea really wants to be a novel. It helps to think about the "caves" that start opening behind characters and images as you ask questions. I began my novel *Eldorado, Iowa* (2019) with an initial image of a pregnant woman standing on the porch of her house in the town she's moved to, in what was then Iowa Territory, sometime after the Civil War. Immediately I wondered: who's the baby's father? Then, how'd she get here? (She's not one of the Native people moved on from that same area just a few years before.) The Civil War was such a massive upheaval for the entire country: How'd it affect her? She's from Alabama. A second young woman her age, formerly enslaved by her family, has come West with her after the war ends and the family's entire economic and social world changes. And with that, I know I have a big cave of backstory, which also means I have a significant structure of past *and* present time frames. I also feel that it all does belong together, and I need a novel's length to tell the whole story. That only became more true when I started asking what the "push" forces or pressures were—what does she want, fear? Who does (or did) she love?

The only way to find out whether you've got a novel, ultimately, is to go ahead and try to write it. Start with your point of strong energy (which, for me, happened to be its opening scene) and follow it from scene to scene. See whether, and how, you feel led by the energies and questions of your characters—and, if so, toward what. "I think writing takes you where you need to go," the critic Hilton Als has said, "and that my new writing is leading me."[40] This is definitely the feeling I've gotten in my novels. As your novel leads you forward, you'll probably also find your structure developing too. When do the natural energies of scenes and actions rise and fall? When do you need backstory? When do your chapters, or even sections, begin and end?

Unfortunately, you may discover (as I did with *Mansions*) that what you thought was going to work as a novel really *doesn't*. Therefore, it's not unusual to write several novels (complete or fragmentary) before finishing and/or publishing one. Novelist Alexander Chee describes this well:

> I have a theory of the first novel now, that it is something that makes the writer, even as the writer makes the novel. That it must be something you care about enough to see through to the end. I tell my students all the time: writing fiction is an exercise in giving a shit—an exercise in finding out what you really care about. Many student writers become obsessed with aesthetics, but I find that is usually a way to avoid whatever it is they have to say. My first novel was not the first one I started. It was the first one I finished. Looking at my records, I count three previous unfinished novels; pieces of one of them went into this first one. But the one I finished, I finished because I asked myself a question. What will you let yourself know? What will you allow yourself to know?[41]

Therefore, to get into, and to the end of, your novel, you have to ask not only "what is this about" but "why do I care—*really* care." But getting to the end of your novel is not only going to be one long slog. Aside from the forward motion of discovery, you'll find lots of fun things to do—of which this is one.

Little Arias: Handing Off the Mike in Novel Time

Some novels do a risky, cool, and under-celebrated thing: even as they move their story forward, they will stop and sing what feels to me like one of Joyce DiDonato's arias, exploring and expanding their world in a celebration of pure imagery and voice. In such passages, you can see a novel's whole, expansive world of character, time, and place in miniature, even though that passage—like a character's aria in an opera—breaks the frame, just a little bit, to add in an extra flourish of performance. For this to work, the novel in general, and the author, have to have built an authoritative sense of a world on that scale. This effect is particularly easy to see in three passages I'll discuss here.

Virginia Woolf (1882–1941) is one of the writers who forever changed the novel's shape and possibilities by developing the modernist technique of "stream of consciousness." This term doesn't mean simply "rambling"—it means tracking a character's thoughts as they flow in a stream of images, memories, and urges that have a purposeful interior logic. Following the character's perceptions from one moment to the next invites readers to think about perception itself. You can see this very clearly in *Mrs. Dalloway* (1925), which moves among the minds of loosely related characters on a single London day. The middle section of *To the Lighthouse* (1927) explores its characters' relationship to time by detailing the slow decay of their beloved vacation house, to marvelous and haunting effect. The protagonist of *Orlando: A Biography* (1928) (a playful homage to Woolf's then-lover Vita Sackville-West) lives for five hundred years and changes gender from man to woman halfway through. With a blend of the historical and the magical, the novel whisks Orlando and the reader from one time period to another to tease our notions of history and gender. Here's my favorite passage, from Chapter Four, a love letter to Woolf's favorite city and mine:

At length [Orlando] came home one night after one of these saunterings and mounted to her bedroom. She took off her laced coat and stood there in shirt and breeches looking out of the window. There was something stirring in the air which forbade her to go to bed. A white haze lay over the town, for it was a frosty night in midwinter and a magnificent vista lay all round her. She could see St Paul's, the Tower, Westminster Abbey, with all the spires and domes of the city churches, the smooth bulk of its banks, the opulent and ample curves of its halls and meeting-places. On the north rose the smooth, shorn heights of Hampstead, and in the west the streets and squares of Mayfair shone out in one clear radiance. Upon this serene and orderly prospect the stars looked down, glittering, positive, hard, from a cloudless sky. In the extreme clearness of the atmosphere the line of every roof, the cowl of every chimney, was perceptible; even the cobbles in the streets showed distinct one from another, and Orlando could not help comparing this orderly scene with the irregular and huddled purlieus which had been the city of London in the reign of Queen Elizabeth. Then, she remembered, the city, if such one could call it, lay crowded, a mere huddle and conglomeration of houses, under her windows at Blackfriars. The stars reflected themselves in deep pits of stagnant water which lay in the middle of the streets. A black shadow at the corner where the wine shop used to stand was, as likely as not, the corpse of a murdered man. She could remember the cries of many a one wounded in such night brawlings, when she was a little boy, held to the diamond-paned window in her nurse's arms. Troops of ruffians, men and women, unspeakably interlaced, lurched down the streets, trolling out wild songs with jewels flashing in their ears, and knives gleaming in their fists. On such a night as this the impermeable tangle of the forests on Highgate and Hampstead would be outlined, writhing in contorted intricacy against the sky. Here and there, on one of the hills which rose above London, was a stark gallows tree, with a corpse nailed to rot or parch on its cross; for danger and insecurity, lust and violence, poetry and filth swarmed over the tortuous Elizabethan highways and buzzed and stank—Orlando could remember even now the smell of them on a hot night—in the little rooms and narrow pathways of the city. Now—she leant out of her window—all was light, order, and serenity. There was the faint rattle of a coach on the cobbles. She heard the far-away cry of the night watchman—"Just twelve o'clock on a frosty morning." No sooner had the words left his lips than the first stroke of midnight sounded. Orlando then for the first time noticed a small cloud gathered behind the dome of St Paul's. As the strokes sounded, the cloud increased, and she saw it darken and spread with extraordinary speed. At the same time a light breeze rose and by the time the sixth stroke of midnight had struck the whole of the eastern sky was covered with an irregular moving darkness, though the sky to the west and north stayed clear as ever. Then the cloud spread north. Height upon height above the city was engulfed by it. Only Mayfair, with all its lights shining. burnt more brilliantly than ever by contrast. With the eighth stroke, some hurrying tatters of cloud sprawled over Piccadilly. They seemed to mass themselves and to advance with extraordinary rapidity towards the west end. As the ninth, tenth, and eleventh strokes struck, a huge blackness sprawled over the whole of London. With the twelfth stroke of midnight, the darkness was complete. A turbulent welter of cloud covered the city. All was darkness; all was doubt; all was confusion. The Eighteenth century was over; the Nineteenth century had begun.

In *Death of the Fox* (1971; see p. 173), his novel about the life, times, and execution of Elizabethan adventurer Sir Walter Ralegh, George Garrett takes a big risk: handing over two different chapters to two different first-person voices, a soldier and a sailor from two of Ralegh's campaigns, who appear nowhere else in the book. Oddly, I think it works. Perhaps this is because (a) *Death of the Fox* is a 739-page, big-canvas novel that, like the film *Citizen Kane*, shows us the protagonist through other people's eyes as well as his own, (b) the sailor and soldier really do add value to our picture of Ralegh's world, and (c) they appear in the narrative at structurally well-judged points, not too close together or far apart. Cynically, I'll add a fourth item (d): this novel was published thirty years before the internet fractured our attention spans, and editors' willingness to trust them.[42] But anyway. Here's the soldier from Chapter 2 of Part 3, 297 pages into the book, concluding his tale where his and Ralegh's stories meet:

There he dozes. Who else but an old soldier could nap in the shadow of the heading ax?

Why not? He has lived a long time and far beyond the use of king and kingdom. His time was really done when the King made peace. For a soldier in peace is a chimney in summertime.

One thing more and then I am done.

Somewhere in the fields of France a stranger wheeled horse and fired at the lad from a dozen paces and the wind and heat of the bullet singed his ear. Then the lad fired his pistol and saw a man gasp, go white-eyed, and topple out of the saddle to lie spurting blood on grass while the riderless horse galloped away. Somewhere, then and there, Walter Ralegh gave up his ghost with a shudder. And as a good hunter honors the fallen stag, so he, looking down at a dying stranger, partook of death himself.

A man can only die once. A soldier dies early, and he lives, if he lives, on time that is given him, nothing he ever earned.

Every soldier is the ghost of the man he was. He can never shed fear until he sheds flesh and bones. But he need not be fearful.

What does a ghost have to be afraid of?

Take it all, wars and glory and riches and fame, and stuff it down the privy.

I'll settle for one more night in a certain Irish tower by the burning fire.

James McBride's *Deacon King Kong* (2020) is set in a Brooklyn housing project in 1969, with a vast cast of characters—human and nonhuman—mirroring the world of McBride's own childhood. In the first half of Chapter 7, readers tour the social and physical landscape of the novel's world by following a line of red ants, "big, red country ants with huge backsides and tiny heads" and ferocious appetites. An Alabama farm kid, I recognize these ants from life, and from their literary ancestor: the macabre, magical tall tale of Matt Bonner's yellow mule in Zora Neale Hurston's *Their Eyes Were Watching God* (1937). That great novel also playfully, purposefully stretches the boundaries of the human, the nonhuman, and literary form. Winding in, out, up, down, around, and through the Cause Houses, McBride's sentences—like the path of the ants—tour readers through 1969 New York City, their energy building and building and even breaking the fourth wall with a nod to his real-life collaborator, director Spike Lee:

> And there [the ants] stayed, a sole phenomenon in the Republic of Brooklyn, where cats hollered like people, dogs ate their own feces, aunties chain-smoked and died at age 102, a kid named Spike Lee saw God, the ghosts of the departed Dodgers soaked up all possibility of new hope, and penniless desperation ruled the lives of the suckers too black or too poor to leave, while in Manhattan the buses ran on time, the lights never went out, the death of a single white child in a traffic accident was a page one story, while phony versions of black and Latino life ruled the Broadway roost, making white writers rich—*West Side Story, Porgy & Bess, Purlie Victorious*—and on it went, the whole business of the white man's reality lumping together like a giant, lopsided snowball, the Great American Myth, the Big Apple, the Big Kahuna, the City That Never Sleeps, while the blacks and Latinos who cleaned the apartments and dragged out the trash and made the music and filled the jails with sorrow slept the sleep of the invisible and functioned as local color.

Spanning 187 words, this sentence also spans an entire city's life, then and now. Like one of the saxophone riffs McBride (also a musician) plays, it teeters beautifully on the edge of chaos but never spills over. Here's a writer—like his fellow Brooklynites Walt Whitman and the Beastie Boys—completely in control of his nimble, expansive verbal technique.

One more thing: each of these moments arrives at least a third of the way through the novel, after the reader is wise to its particular logic and energies. The famous composer Stephen Sondheim said that the first ten minutes of any musical should introduce audience members to its "rules of engagement": at what points will the characters sing, and why will they *want* to?[43] To build a little aria like this in your own novel, consider: What energies within its world will make that song feel like a natural highlight, rather than anxious excess?

Doing the Thing: Writing Novels in the Real World

Writer Lorrie Moore once wryly pointed out that the difference between the two forms is that stories need to be written, or at least mapped out, in a single sitting, while, with a novel, "you can just go in and write a paragraph and then go away." She continued, "This is why some people think the novel is the perfect form for the busy single working mom."[44]

I can recognize the truth (and the humor) of this: I've found the pace of writing a novel to be more relaxed than that of a story, because you have more time over which to keep adding scene after scene, bit after bit, faithfully. But how *does* the process of novel-writing work? Some writers like to just move forward without quite knowing where they're going. Some writers like to have a detailed outline. And some writers fall in between. The question is, what enables *you* to move forward on your novel with the particular kinds of energy, discovery, and confidence that motivate you? And how do *you* need to work to feel as if you're making sufficient progress—how many pages per day? Per week?

Back in 2008, my Tin House workshop-mates and I asked Colson Whitehead about his process. Then and now, he sets himself a quota of eight pages a week. "A year is full of a lot of eight-page weeks," he observed in a November 17, 2020, talk online,[45] "and it adds up." Asked about outlining, he said that he likes to outline a novel enough to know the beginning and the end, although "the middle can be fuzzy." He develops a list of things that need to happen in the book and works his way through them: "I have to have an assignment every day," he said about writing *The Nickel Boys* (2019), "describe the Nickel Academy grounds, describe Superintendent Spencer." Yet building the book is not always strictly sequential: "I'm always going forward and back, forward and back," he said, although the overall trajectory is always forward. If he writes ten pages, he'll go back and revise pages 1–5; if he writes pages 11–12, then he'll revise pages 6–10. And if he gets a new idea on page 200, he said, he'll go back and plant the seed of it earlier in what he can see as the "now-prevailing structure."

This respects what I've found myself: writing a novel means you're in the process long enough to watch the novel change shape underneath you, but also to change with it. In writing novels, I've found myself settling into a rhythm of waking up early (or taking whatever time I can find), at least five days a week, and writing (at best 3–5 shitty-first-draft [SFD] pages a day) until I feel that particular sense that, for today, the tank is empty. (I stop when I still know the first thing that comes next—which makes it easier to start writing the next morning.) My goal is to get to the end of a complete SFD ASAP, so I can then begin multiple rounds of revision. The challenge is to keep moving forward without endlessly revising the opening pages (as Ann Patchett says on p. 182). This can be an assignment too: *until I have written the following two scenes, I won't look back at earlier material*. But I don't think you have to write your novel (or anything else) in order. If a scene's developing in your head but you think it might end up coming toward the middle or the end, go ahead and write it anyway. You can always rearrange.

My process has evolved over time, as I've taught myself to write novels by flailing around and doing the thing. Mostly, I start by gathering scraps, pictures, bits, phrases, or scenes in notebooks and computer files (see Chapter 2), which are attracted to that energy field of potential story like iron filings to a magnet. When they've reached a certain critical mass, I start to see the shape of a novel rising from them, and then its ghostly face whispers *go.* Only then can I start writing with confidence what I'd call a *novel manuscript,* more or less moving forward one page after another.

"How long does it take to write a novel," students ask, "start to finish?" Well . . . depends on what you mean by *start.* With both *Creature: A Novel of Mary Shelley* and *Eldorado, Iowa*—the two novels I've finished—the answer is something like *ten years,* over *twelve* complete drafts. I can identify a clear starting point and date for the initial image that became *Eldorado, Iowa*—a beautiful October day in 2008, as described in *The Writer's Eye*—and I submitted a finished, revised version to my publisher in 2018 for publication in 2019. I have notes and scraps for *Creature* going back ten years and more, although it was finished in 2021, then rewritten in 2022. But between the time *Eldorado, Iowa* was born and was finished, I wrote and published two nonfiction books, each of which busted into my life and begged *Write me now!* (If it were a computer screen, my writing life would be one of those download windows with three or four bars of varying lengths creeping forward at the same time.) Writers who are working on one book at a time (as Whitehead tends to do) can move faster; as you can see above, he finishes a novel in about a year. So I don't think there's a right answer—only what works for you, your life, and what you need to get your writing done, or, in the words of my wise student Kira, "what you have to do to *make the thing exist!*"

Exercises:

- Work through the exercises on pp. 176–7 (graph, old work, fifteen words, copying, etc.).

- Think about your work overall and current project. What are "MLT" and "TSM" moments for you? What tends to produce your MLT moments?

- Do exercise on p. 158: give a feature of your own first crush to a romantic character.

- A la Vivian Gornick, think of a sensory memory from some past time in your own life, then write from the POV of the "self in whom story resides."

- Find a congested beginning (like the first draft of my story "The Serpent") and unpack it.

- Reorder your information in a way the story needs. Identify something that plays an important role later in the story (like the snake in "The Serpent") then bring it in closer to the beginning so readers can see it.

- Take out a piece of your writing that's at least two years old and identify something you wouldn't write that way now. Why not? Reflect in writing: When you look at your old work, what do you see?

- Here is an exercise on beginnings (novels or stories) to do in a class or group. It's really tough, but it really works. Everyone brings the typed first page of their story, with a title and without their name. They put their pages on the floor and everyone picks up a page that doesn't belong to them, returns to their seats, and reads the title and first paragraph aloud in turn. On the board, I make a chart of the following information: the story's title, "what's at stake," and then a score, 1–3, arrived at in an instant vote by the class. 1 means "I'd definitely keep reading," 3 means "I probably wouldn't keep reading." Hearing your story's beginning in isolation *really* helps evaluate its "forward lean" and good or bad mystery. Small groups can also read and compare each person's pages, then nominate one effective beginning to read and discuss with the class.

- Try writing a longer piece than you ever have—and see what happens.
- If you have a novella or novel manuscript, apply to it the set of questions Jim Shepard asks on p. 107.

CHAPTER 8
CREATIVE WRITING AND YOUR FUTURE

Hope is invented every day.

—James Baldwin

Congratulations—you've made it almost to the end of this book and, maybe, all the way through at least one advanced creative writing class. So what's next? In this chapter, I'll offer some advice that can help you move ahead, even if your dream career doesn't have "writer" in its name. Our world's changing faster than I can type, so I'll try to be both specific and general enough to be useful. Mostly, I'll focus on actions you can use to propel yourself forward—"inventing hope," in James Baldwin's words in the epigraph, "every day" by renewing it—whether you're seeking an agent and publication or looking to land your first job in any field.

Thinking about the Future: Build Your Foundations

On November 3, 2020, students and I had a little trouble focusing. Not only were we sitting six feet apart, wearing Covid masks (still in the pandemic), but we were also waiting for the results of (ahem) a very important presidential election. So that day, we tried to feel at least a little less panicked and powerless by controlling what we could. Together, we wrote about the following quote and questions:

> *If you have built castles in the air, your work need not be lost; that is where they should be. Now put the foundations under them.* **Henry David Thoreau, from Walden: or, Life in the Woods (1854)**
>
> **What is my "castle in the air"—something I dream of doing or becoming?**
>
> **What are three capacities I will need to have / show / demonstrate to be competitive for this—now or in the future?**
>
> **What are three concrete things I can do in the next three weeks to take steps toward my castle's door?**
>
> **If I needed someone to write me a positive, specific professional reference to get into my castle, a) who might I reach out to, and b) when will I schedule a conversation with that person to talk about what that reference might look like and how I might position myself for it?**
>
> **"A year from now, what will I wish I had done now?"**

After writing and talking through some of our answers (which students said *did* make them feel better—although not as good as that election's results!), we looked at an actual job ad:(see Figure 6).

If you have a "castle" like this job in mind, how might you move forward?

PublishersMarketplace Keywords or location | search jobs

<<Job Board Tweet Like 28 Share

Job opening detail :

Full-time research assistant to Bob Woodward ***posted*** **: Oct. 9, 2020**

Offered by: Bob Woodward

Benefits: Health; Dental

Duration: Full Time

Location: Washington, DC

Requirements:

Bestselling author and Washington Post reporter Bob Woodward is seeking a motivated, energetic person with a can-do approach to assist with research, transcribing, editing, and assorted administrative tasks for upcoming projects.

The strongest candidate will be someone with a demonstrated interest in news and current events and eager to learn about journalism or publishing. The role calls for strict confidentiality and an openness to being a jack of all trades. Attention to detail and a high standard of accuracy are a must.

Administrative work will overlap with high-level, heavy-duty research and editorial work. There will be some long hours and a lot of transcribing. (Please be prepared to take a test of your transcribing ability as part of the application process.) This is a fabulous opportunity for the right person, and is definitely a job a person can grow their writing and reporting skills in.

The position is based in Woodward's home office in Northwest Washington D.C. and remote work is not available. While we've adapted to accommodate some remote work due to Covid-19, the confidential nature of the work means it's largely in-house.

Competitive salary, health insurance, and vacation time are provided.

About Our Company:

Bob Woodward is an associate editor of The Washington Post, where he has worked since 1971. He has shared in two Pulitzer Prizes, first for the coverage of the Watergate scandal with Carl Bernstein, and second as the lead reporter for coverage of the 9/11 terrorist attacks.

Woodward has written #1 best-selling books on the last nine presidents—Nixon, Ford, Carter, Reagan, George H.W. Bush, Clinton, George W. Bush, Obama and Trump—as well as the CIA, the Joint Chiefs, Hollywood and the Supreme Court. His approach is aggressive but fair and nonpartisan reporting.

He has authored or coauthored 20 books, all of which have been national non-fiction bestsellers. Fourteen have been #1 national bestsellers, including his most recent book, Rage, which was Woodward's second book on the Trump administration. More information is available at www.BobWoodward.com

Contact: Evelyn Duffy

E-mail: assistant3027@gmail.com

Special Instructions:

Please send a cover letter, resume, and a writing sample to Evelyn Duffy at assistant3027@gmail.com.

Figure 6.

1) *Build capacities, relationships, and awareness of the world—these give you freedom to move.*

What capacities would you need to show if you were applying to be Bob Woodward's assistant? I say "*capacities*" because while "skills" mean things like typing ability, "capacities" mean inner qualities that can be developed. Like curiosity, writing flair, initiative, tenacity, ability to seek good information from a variety of sources, and—with the very name *Bob Woodward*—an eager ability to join in the major political and cultural conversations of the last fifty years.

What steps could you take right now? Start a habit of reading *The New York Times* and/or the *Washington Post*—maybe your school, like ours, has free subscription options through its library. Identify an opportunity on campus related to this job (see later). Check out one of Bob Woodward's books, browse his website, and watch the 1976 film *All the President's Men*, starring Robert Redford as Woodward and Dustin Hoffman as his reporting partner, Carl Bernstein. Each one of these things could be done within a week and would move you concretely toward your goal.

Think about your relationship with your writing community, and who might testify to your qualities as a reliable member of that community in *professional references*. Colleagues and I need people who write tenure letters or vouch for us when we reach out to editors and agents. Students need people who can write recommendation letters. And good recommendations start in good relationships (including that dreaded word "networking"). Therefore, many professors, including me, will decline to write references unless we can write positive, specific ones.

Sounds harsh, but that rule goes for everyone. When writer and editor Rob Spillman visited my class in person, after several years of Skyping with us about his journal *Tin House*, students asked him for advice. Surprisingly, he turned to me, with a smile. "Be a nice person," he said. "When Amy asked me to come here, I was glad, because I know she's a nice person. The writing world is really small, and if you're an asshole, people will find out." I also like critic Hilton Als's response, when asked if he was "ambitious":

> [A]mbition was what I equated with people who would use others to get what they wanted, or who stepped over the dead body without a second thought, once they got what they wanted. I don't mind the word anymore, but the word to describe me is *determined*—determined to get better as a man and a writer. A determined person doesn't court favor, discount, or hurt other people to get what they want, whatever that want is.[1]

Let me tell you a story about that mysterious thing, *networking*: if you put yourself out there politely and appropriately, people will, amazingly often, be glad to help. Once, at the Association of Writers and Writing Programs conference (AWP), I was visiting the book-fair table for Graywolf Press. As a reviewer for *Orion* magazine, I introduced myself to Graywolf's publicity director so that I could ask her for an ARC (advance reviewer's copy) of Paul Kingsnorth's *Confessions of a Recovering Environmentalist*, which Graywolf was about to publish.[2] A young woman nearby edged politely into my field of vision, said hello, and introduced herself as a student in an MFA program. Her voice was shaking—obviously, she was nervous—but she was still moving ahead, politely, and that was fine with me. "I hope this isn't presumptuous," she said, "but I heard you say you wrote reviews for *Orion*. If you don't mind, can you tell me how you got started with that?" Better yet, I said, I'll take you to meet them. We talked for a moment, and I gave her my business card. Then I walked her over to the *Orion* book-fair booth, where all the editors were sitting, and introduced her to them. We legacy-media GenXers have our flaws, but we know how lucky we are to have gotten into this world, and we like to help other people get here too. It starts with Rob Spillman's advice—be a good person, and be sincere. And if you follow through by sending a polite thank-you email, this will set you above 99 percent of humans. Just saying.

Maybe now's a good time to address a classic networking question: What do you call someone you're meeting for the first time? Sometimes the person will give you the cue (as the poet Danez Smith kindly did for a student of mine, extending a hand and saying, "Hi, I'm Danez"), but sometimes it's less clear. Talk to trusted advisors about this, since regional and cultural manners can vary. I advise students to err on the side of formality— an honorific plus last name—in any professional or academic situation, particular for someone older or professionally senior to you ("Ms. Ramirez," "Dr. Gupta," "Professor Lee," "Dean Craft"). No matter how innocent, a twenty-year-old student *automatically* addressing a fifty-year-old professional by her first name, as if they were peers, is going to grate on some people—with good reason.[3] As you see in my sample agent letter (below), I still default to a formal salutation when reaching out to a stranger. My students call me "Dr. Weldon" while they're still my students, and it's a nice social milestone when, after graduation, I can warmly invite them to call me "Amy." If the person's pronouns or honorifics aren't clear and they haven't provided you a cue after you've talked a bit, I do think it's okay to ask, "how would you prefer to be addressed?" Overall, the message you'll send is a good one—*I'm showing respect for you and for our social context.*

Alongside in-person networking, build *awareness*: look at the landscape you want to enter and join the conversations of people in that field. A common question on a literary press's internship application is "What are the last three books you read?" This really means, "Do you read books like we publish?" The young-adult fantasy trilogy you binged over Christmas break (hey, no shame) won't help you at a press that publishes adult literary fiction in translation. Get and read their books now (interlibrary loan can help). Browse what the staff members like to read (some websites have fun little bios, like bookstores have "staff recommendations") and investigate some of those titles, too.

This is where students protest, "I don't have time!" Classes, jobs, activities, family caregiving—I get it. But out of (tough) love, I have to share some good advice I got in graduate school, when I was overcommitted and unfocused: don't let the *important* (long-term) be sacrificed to the *urgent* (short-term). If you really want to finish your novel, if you really want to be competitive for an internship at a literary press, you may have to re-evaluate how you're spending your time now. Taking a hard look at extracurriculars and media consumption (especially social media) can help. A year from now, what will you wish you had done now?

2) *Read and tell the story—for yourself and others.*

Curiosity gets you interested in other people, just as if they were your characters. As smartphones and Zoom proliferate, students may feel awkward when talking face to face with possible employers or colleagues. But use the questioning skill you have as a writer to build a conversation: What happens next? Why did this person do that? A question opens a door for your interlocutor to tell you more, and then for you to identify a note within it: "Sounds like your company's growing, and there are good opportunities for . . ." "Sounds like you have a lot of new ideas for . . ." As a writer, you know how to do this: read (or listen), detect a through-line, and say, "tell me more." Plus, questions open doors for you to learn about the other person—not just talk about yourself.

Consider what capacities, experiences, and secret superpowers you may already have. For instance, video game design, arts/nonprofit management, fundraising, university development, and marketing all involve storytelling and close reading. So do patient care and diagnosis in medical fields (which involve more intuition and creativity than non-physicians ever see, as Reed Johnson, MD, says further on). Jennifer Acker, novelist and founding editor of *The Common,* advised my students, "You may think you want to work at a literary magazine, and that's great. But there are other possibilities than editorial ones. Marketing, web design, social media, fundraising—all these things are also part of your work." [4]

To start thinking about your secret superpowers, think of your own resume like a draft of a story in progress: What is it really about? What's its through-line or major note? Once, a sophomore student named Susie came to my office, plopped down in my battered armchair, and confessed, "I have no idea what I want to do with my life—can you help?" So we started putting pieces together. Susie was an English major who sang in the school's prestigious choir and spent weekends volunteering for a rape crisis hotline. A common through-line, therefore, was *amplifying women's voices.* Once Susie could see that her own life and interests did have a story, she was able to focus on what she really cared about without getting overinvolved on campus. She also felt a sense of relief and focus about where she was going that helped her identify a new area of interest: counseling and social work. (Careers grow out of skills and interests, not always precisely matching majors and minors—you know that, right? Good.)

Your storytelling experience can boost your professional life in lots of ways. Say that an employer looks at your transcript and says, "I see you studied abroad for a semester! Tell me about it." Resist the urge to rattle off tourist checkpoints. Instead, think, "What is the question I'm really being asked?" (Hint: it's probably "How will that experience help you contribute to this organization?") And craft a (true) story in response. Share a few points on what you got better at (curiosity, resilience, understanding cultural difference and historical perspective in non-superficial ways), and then a specific anecdote to illustrate that. Say that you spend your summers working road construction. This can say a *lot* about your ability to work hard on a team with a variety of people to accomplish a real and important goal—and I'm guessing you've also got great characters and details from that experience. ("Manual" jobs are nothing to be ashamed of—in fact, they give you stories and skills that people really respect.) Say that you're a single parent pursuing your college degree and your dream of writing a novel. What does this say about your ability to balance long-term goals *and* daily stresses—but also joys, which you know in a way many people don't? Your experiences as a writer and a person make you capable of building fictional worlds *and* real organizations like the one you're interviewing for.

3) *Identify what helps you or holds you back—including online habits.*

Given the ambient shittiness of the twenty-first century, controlling what you can is a matter of survival, emotionally and professionally. And by now, there's no denying it: social media, YouTube, and their ilk are adding to that shittiness, in every way. This is true even if you aren't a disinformed Capital insurrectionist. Sure, social media does help witnesses and activists get the word out (like TikToks from Ukraine after Russia invaded that country on February 24, 2022). It can help writers find community. But it's also terrible for physical, social, mental, and economic health. Even so, many students rely on it as their portal to the world, often to the exclusion of legitimate news sources, face-to-face relationships, and printed words on a page. This is, and will be, a real professional problem: as your range of media consumption, reading ability, and social interaction narrows, your range of motion in the world beyond your peer group narrows too.[5] So: how should you manage or control your habits, especially electronic ones?

Pause while I dodge tomatoes from people under thirty complaining (rightly) about the economic and ecological dystopia their elders are foisting on them, the refuge social media offers them (well, kind of), and the okay-Boomer tiresomeness of people like me. (Will anybody even know what "okay, Boomer" *means* by the time this book comes out?) My students point out that quitting all social media (as I've done) will harm their professional opportunities in ways it won't for me. Maybe so. But we can't stay hooked, uncritically, on this thing that's killing us. And, yes, social-media-made myopia and disinformation (see the January 6, 2021, insurrection, Covid-19 vaccine denial, and climate emergency) *are* literally killing us. The internet has already killed a lot of opportunities, for artists and others, in our Amazon-dominated world as algorithms and robots edge out human workers.[6] Since, as Jaron Lanier says, "attention is the new oil,"[7] whatever draws attention on the internet—particularly anger, outrage, and fear—makes its creators money, whether or not it's good for humans, nonhumans, and our world. As I've taught college since 1998, I've seen that as students get more screen-focused, they often become *less*, not more, aware of the world offscreen. Sometimes people don't know where to look for information. But sometimes they just aren't *looking*.

At first, this just seems naïve. But naivete becomes embarrassing when a college senior can't join a conversation about current events during a dinner with potential employers. It's ironic when a creative writing student "active on Twitter" doesn't know about #PublishingPaidMe. And it's tragic when a creative writing student seeking a literary internship doesn't recognize the names of Booker Prize or National Book Award shortlist authors *or* the presses that publish them. Yet every student in my classroom has a smartphone. And every student in my classroom is hoping that being there will help them navigate the challenging world to come. So, ask yourself: How am I *actually* spending my precious attention, and is it getting me the results I want? Again, as in Chapter 2, ask: **One year from now, what will I wish I had done now?**

Now that the tough-love interlude is over (thanks for listening—y'all know it's because I care about your success, right?), let's identify professional resources around you, starting with your campus and community.

Level One: Your Information Ecosystem

Get savvy about the professional world you want to enter by entering the ecosystem of reputable information around it and voting with your attention and your dollars (however limited) to support its health. For writing students, this might look like this:

- Get at least a rough draft of your resume and a job letter in your computer ASAP, to be added to and updated so it's ready to go. Your college's Career Center can help with this and more.

- Develop a calendar and reminder system that works for you—and *do* try a system on paper (and a non-smart wristwatch) to reduce attention-fracturing screens.

- Build real-life relationships with professors and peers, who may be letter writers—or future colleagues.

- Listen to National Public Radio and read a newspaper like the *New York Times*. Subscribe if you can, to support reputable news and the people who gather it. Your school may also provide free online access through its library.

- Read writing-world-specific newsletters like *Literary Hub* (lithub.com) and "Publishers Lunch," the newsletter of Publishers Marketplace; presses and magazines also have their own newsletters and podcasts. *Poets and Writers* magazine (pw.org) is a good source of writerly news, interviews, submission opportunities, and professional guidance. So is "Don't Write Alone" at Catapult.co. And, yes, scanning Twitter (which even I sometimes do) can help you listen in on conversations without having to sign up.

- Broaden your cultural and media consumption to develop your mature tastes. Take some risks. For example, good films like those curated by the Criterion Collection (see Student Career Studio, in this chapter) offer rich cultural perspectives and ways to tell stories. Go to events and talks on campus. In a Zoom conversation, Andrew Chan, web editor at Criterion, advised my students, "Take more classes in things you don't know anything about." Ask professors for recommendations—like those I've given in this book's endnotes.

- Use your library—it's free! In addition to print and online access to books and films, your library will also have a Current Periodicals section, where magazines and newspapers wait on open, browsable shelves. (Subscribing to *The New Yorker* as a college sophomore changed my life.) If they don't have a book, they can usually get it for you via interlibrary loan. And librarians love to help people!

- Vote with your dollars and attention for the writerly ecosystem that supports us. Buy books from an independent store or an online independent-supporting source like bookshop.org. (Aside from the obvious benefit to local economies, sales figures—including pre-orders—from these stores help writers get their next book contracts.) I subscribe to Scribd, an e-book and audiobook service that costs me about $10 a month. If I want to buy a cheap used book or splurge on a first edition, I can often find it at abebooks.com. And even when you can't buy books, keep using libraries—what libraries buy and subscribe to also matters.

Level Two: Writing-Related Jobs and Publication Credits on Campus

Here are some places to look on campus for writing-related opportunities:

- Marketing, publication, athletic communication, development/alumni-communications, and/or departmental offices. One English Department student worker started a weekly newsletter for our students and faculty. Every department chair I know *longs* for help with social media and webpages.
- Newspapers or literary magazines. (As seen in Shannon Baker's Chapter 1 Student Craft Studio, there are also national and regional undergraduate literary magazines, including those from honor societies like Sigma Tau Delta). You can write for these, join their staffs, or both.
- Academic support centers—tutoring is a great foundation for an editing career.
- Libraries and/or archival collections (library and information science and museum studies are great career fields for writers!)
- Alumni connections: Which alumni of your school are working in a field you want to join? (Hint: say *please* and *thank you,* early and often!)
- Named scholarships: Fulbright, Marshall, Rhodes. These offer students focused, prestigious academic honors and experiences that can become powerful parts of your professional story.
- Campus career center: from resumes to internship and employment connections, a career center can help everyone, at any stage.
- Campus events: as the co-director of the Luther College Writers Festival, I recruit students as volunteers, which can include writing website and printed materials, introducing writers at the mike, and talking with them.
- Conversations and research with professors. Especially at small liberal arts colleges, that's why we're here. If professors feel able to vouch for you, they may write you recommendation letters or connect you with other opportunities, professionals in their fields, or research assistantships (see Annika Dome in "Student Career Studio"). But this process starts with you. Make that appointment, have that conversation, and, again, say *please* and *thank you*. Please.

Level Three: The Wider Writing World

Here are some ways to move into the writing world beyond your campus:

- Seek publication opportunities (no matter how small) in magazines and newspapers. Book reviews are a classic place to start; so are community newspapers (where Ian Wreisner of Chapter 4's Student Craft Studio got a summer job). For creative work, journals and presses will have submission guidelines on their websites. The website and print journal of *Poets & Writers* are full of opportunities.

- Start a workshop group (online or in person) with fellow students after your class is over.

- Attend readings and events at local bookstores.

- Investigate writing classes at community arts centers like the Loft in Minneapolis.

- Internships can be found in many places, including on the websites of presses and journals you admire. These may be in-person or remote opportunities, paid or unpaid, and you need not always be a student to take advantage of them. For example, literary journals often call for manuscript readers—people willing to spend three to five hours per week reading and evaluating submissions.

- Job boards like the one at Publishers Marketplace, bookjobs.com, Poets & Writers, or NYFA (New York Foundation for the Arts), which Andrew Chan recommends, can be places to look. Industry professionals often post openings on their social media accounts.

- Writers' festivals and gatherings (like my own Luther College Writers Festival) are great ways to mingle with other writers, learn new things, and get inspired over a weekend or so. Most of these are focused on readings and panel discussions rather than workshops (see later), but they're fun and relatively inexpensive.

- Writers' conferences—like Tin House Summer Writers Workshop (the one I described in Chapter 7), Sewanee Writers Conference, and Bread Loaf Writers Conference—are fabulous "summer camps for writers" that offer you focused workshop experience and professional advice. They do have an application process, and they do require an investment of time and money. But based on my own experiences with all three of those listed earlier, I can say the return on that investment is *stellar*. And many offer active outreach to, and scholarships for, students. More of these are listed in *Poets and Writers* magazine.

- Writers' residencies—which offer housing and financial support for writers for a defined period of time—are another opportunity to apply for. Writer R. O. Kwon says, "I also always point people to the backs of books in the acknowledgments—especially in people's first or second books—in which most people will list everyone who's ever given them money or a space to write. That helps a lot." (This is also a good place to find agents' names, by the way.)

- The Association of Writers and Writing Programs (AWP) has an annual conference that takes place in a large city over four to five days and draws crowds of as many as 15,000 people. Yep, it's huge, and it can be expensive, by the time you factor in lodging, transportation, food, and registration. But depending on your goals, AWP may be worth a try. It's built around readings and panel discussions on every topic you can imagine (the printed program is the size of a small town's telephone book!) and a book fair—a cavernous space full of display tables at which the staff of presses and magazines sell their wares and talk with writers. As you can imagine, the networking opportunities are considerable (remember the earlier MFA student at the Graywolf table?) As an organization, AWP offers resources for writers; see their website at awpwriter.org.

- Resources on the internet and Twitter offer honesty about different aspects of writing, publishing, and supporting yourself financially. A full-time job and a writing life are not necessarily incompatible, as Richard Mirabella describes in his essay "On Writing (With a Day Job)."[8] Yet novelist Raven Leilani describes honestly how writing is "more challenging when you arrive at the page already spent" and says her novel *Luster* was fueled by "that tension between having this art inside you, the will and the capability, and how that grind to survive frays the bandwidth you need to do it."[9] In July 2020, *New York* magazine's "The Cut" asked six women with recent books "how they make writing work financially":[10]

  - **Samantha Irby**: "Any time I talk to anyone and they're like, 'I want to be a writer,' I'm like, 'Get a regular job.' Try not to depend on your writing to fund your life because it, uh, won't."

  - **R. O. Kwon**: "For most of the time before I sold *The Incendiaries*, I favored freelance jobs that I could do from home. I very quickly realized that I'm very introverted and it's hard on me to engage with people every day except with the one person I'm living with. So that is something I often try to tell people, especially students. It can help to figure out what kinds of jobs will leave you more energy at the end or start of the day, whenever it is you can write. And once you figure that out, it helps a great deal."

- For years, I've recommended Meg Jay's *The Defining Decade: Why Your Twenties Matter and How to Make the Most of Them Now* (2012; updated 2021) to my students. She advises: Don't wait for the "perfect" opportunity while you spin your wheels, inert and anxious—get moving, even in a new direction, because it could lead to something good. Julie Lythcott-Haims's *Your Turn: How to Be an Adult* (2021) has awesome advice on relationships, money, life design, and more. As yoga teachers say, "any amount"—a step forward, no matter how small—is good. Because one step leads to another.

Student Career Studio: Andrew Chan (University of North Carolina-Chapel Hill Class of 2008): Web Editor at The Criterion Collection and Freelance Writer (*The New Yorker* and Others)

I first met Andrew Chan at the University of North Carolina-Chapel Hill in 2004, when he was an incoming first-year student and I was finishing my PhD in literature. Andrew was the third-ever winner of the Thomas Wolfe Scholarship in creative writing, the application for which includes a "Why I Write" essay like those in Chapter 1. As a selection-committee member, I got to meet Andrew in person: funny, smart, and kind, he also knew more about film, even in those pre-Netflix days, than anyone I'd ever met. At Carolina, Andrew minored in creative writing, including extensive coursework in poetry, fiction, and creative nonfiction. Now, he's Web Editor at The Criterion Collection, which preserves, streams, and educates viewers about world cinema. His writing appears in its newsletters, Lincoln Center's *Film Comment* Magazine, and *The New Yorker*,[11] among others, and he's currently writing a book on 1990s pop and R&B. Over email, Andrew and I discussed how studying creative writing can be a springboard into your post-college professional and intellectual lives.

Can you describe your path from Thomas Wolfe Scholar to New York film critic: What were some concrete steps you took to move from one level to another?

I'm not sure how conscious I was of the steps I've taken; what I remember most is the uncertainty. At the time that I graduated college, in 2008, the economy was in freefall, and film criticism had already been pronounced dead several times over, at least as a profession that could offer a financially secure life. So I have to admit that the path I took was probably the most cautious one available; I'm sure bolder, more ambitious people have found it easier to get a foothold than I did in my early years in New York.

The key to it all was actually moving to the city, where all the viewing and reviewing opportunities were (and still are). I got an internship at the Museum of Modern Art's film department in my junior year of college, and I used that as an opportunity to meet some of the film critics I most admired. Then I went to NYU's cinema studies graduate program and interned for *Film Comment,* a magazine I revered, for about two years. The world of magazines (what few of them are left!) can seem elite and opaque to anyone who's young and on the outside, but I was lucky enough to find generous editors who opened the gates to me, and I just began writing, pretty relentlessly. I knew I probably couldn't ever rely on film criticism to pay the bills, but the more I wrote and the more I published, the more I wanted to keep it going.

At a certain point I had to pare down the writing; I couldn't sustain that pace, nor was I interested anymore in trying to drum up semi-interesting things to say about movies I cared nothing about. There were years when I wrote no criticism. But having day jobs within New York's film world—as a marketing manager in the film department at BAM (a performing arts venue in Brooklyn) and as an editor at the Criterion Collection—gave me the financial security that then opened up more mental space. I began to carefully consider what it was I wanted to be writing and the subjects I wanted to tackle. And it was when I started becoming extremely selective about my subject matter (a luxury that I realize most freelance critics and journalists do not have) that I regained my self-confidence and people started paying more attention to my work. There's no question in my mind that my writing got better.

That's a short way of conveying the twists and turns of my writing life over the past thirteen years!

What does a typical day look like for you?

As a writer, I'm constantly wrestling with the finite resource that is time. Most of my hours during the workday are taken up with my work as an editor at the Criterion Collection. It can be incredibly intellectually energizing; I'm helping writers figure out how to make their pieces better, and often I feel like I'm figuring it out right alongside them. Having come to the editorial profession as a writer first, I think I have a certain perspective in the job: I am on the writer's side, and my solutions are rooted in and informed by my own experiences tinkering and laboring over sentences.

It can be hard to cobble together the hours (and the energy) to write when you spend so much time working on other people's writing. So, much of my writing life is project- and deadline-based: I have freelance work that I do on weekends, and now I have a book project that is churning away in my brain. There's a lot of journaling and note-taking and trying to capture the ideas and phrases that will make it easier for me to get the job done when I'm lucky to have a solid day or two just for composition.

How do you think studying creative writing helped you build your life and career—tangibly and intangibly?

Like a lot of young writers, I really did not know how to revise. Either I would be so enamored of what I'd done that I couldn't see alternatives to the words that were on the page, or I was so embarrassed of my failure that I couldn't see a path to salvation or improvement. Workshops can be grueling when you are so emotionally invested and take your writing so seriously. If the study of creative writing taught me anything, it's the joy in refining and sometimes radically reenvisioning a piece. It reshaped my ideas about where the pleasures of writing lie: if you can find pleasure in wrestling with what's on the page, and relinquishing your perfectionism, you will set yourself up for a much happier writing life. The focus becomes less on initial inspiration and more on the process (and the time and the devotion) it takes to create something worthwhile for the reader.

As a gifted critic, what are your thoughts on how criticism relates to other kinds of "creative writing?"

Criticism of all kinds is bound up in the magic of the art that it describes. Great critics have shaped how I experience the art forms that I love—whether or not I actually agree with their positions and assessments. When you don't grow up around a lot of people who are passionate about the arts, you rely on these writers to share in that experience with you, and to guide you. And of course aesthetic experience is as profound as any other kind of human experience, so in a sense I don't see any fundamental division between "creative writing" and "criticism"—they are both trying to render, in sentences, what it's like to be a human being undergoing an experience.

Your career has tracked in really interesting ways with the rise of the digital realm, which is reshaping the way film, writing, and other arts get produced and marketed. Yet you obviously occupy and love the world of old[er]-school art forms too. How might current college students think about balancing these in their own artistic and professional lives?

Digital publishing has certainly made it easier for writers to get bylines and put together a portfolio, but it has become harder and harder for anyone to make a living off freelance writing. Not to paint too bleak a picture, but the drive for more and more content has created a publishing ecosystem in which content is churned out on the cheap and then, often, forgotten. Most freelance writers I know who write for primarily digital outlets are working from assignment to assignment, with no real certainty that their next pitch will be greenlit. You have to be aware of these realities in order to keep your spirit and curiosity as a writer alive. The obstacles and the challenges often have nothing to do with your skill or talent. I realize this is not what a lot of people want to hear, but I encourage caution: if you love writing, you have to be prepared to do it on your off-hours, often for little pay and little fanfare. Use the opportunities created by the digital landscape's endless hunger for "content" to stand out: just because outlets are looking for something quick and disposable doesn't mean you can't turn the assignment into something timeless.

What advice would you give your student self? And students reading this book right now?

I'm not sure how much stock someone should put into my advice because my path has been a bit unorthodox. Looking back on my career, I realize how fortunate I've been, and at the risk of sounding disingenuous, I have to say that some of it was unintentional on my part. I've always been a risk-averse person—the classic result of second-generation American financial and social insecurity, perhaps—and so I never really allowed myself to take on the identity of "writer" or to pursue my creative dreams with naked ambition.

But that doesn't mean I didn't put a lot of time, work, and patience into every piece I've published. And because of my lack of a clear path, I opened up myself to covering a pretty wide range of subjects: not just film but also literature, music, and other kinds of culture and art. Even though some of what I've shared here might sound a bit discouraging, my final message—both to readers of this book and to myself, because I'm in constant need of hearing it—is that if you're faithful to your curiosity and your love of the written word, they will take you places you never expected. Open those windows; walk through those doors. Do it for the love of it, not for money or attention. Those things may not arrive on the schedule you have in mind; they are not promised. But if you nurture your relationship to language, if you immerse yourself in the art of the phrase and the line and the sentence, and (even more crucially) if you continue to find pleasure and excitement in the themes and subjects you're tackling in your work, you will be giving yourself something that money can't buy: something to live for.

Wow—I love that, and I need to hear it too! Any closing words?

It's important to create space in your writing life for play, improvisation, and failure. This is something I didn't understand in my perfectionist, somewhat masochistic early years as a published writer. I would spend hours on single sentences. And I would imagine that there was inherent nobility to that kind of rigor. Sure, there can be... but that approach can also engender what I inelegantly refer to as "writer's constipation." You become so afraid of the wrong word, the false sentiment, the poorly constructed sentence that you can't move, you can't think. A few years ago I retaught myself how to write longhand, and while it wasn't any kind of cure-all (nothing is), I found it helped. I could write in a journal and accumulate material more casually, without the pressures of having to deliver perfectly sculpted sentences on a computer screen. When your writing life is dictated by assignments and deadlines, as mine has been for many years, a desire to maintain the appearance of professionalism can take hold, and you forget how to take risks; you lose your relationship to the strangeness of language. I've gradually had to find my way back to the possibilities that risk creates, and while I'm still struggling with it, that process has helped me to build in time in my daily life for imperfection.

Other Former Creative Writing Students Say . . .

Derek Lin: Founding Editor and Editor-in-Chief, *The Starter* (Luther College Class of 2020) [https://issuu.com/the_starter]. Former student co-editor at *The Oneota Review* (Luther's undergraduate literary journal).

In March 2020, the world changed. The edges of the world suddenly became my bedroom walls and possibility shrunk with it. But in September 2020, I lit a flame and began to nurture a fire. With a global pandemic severely limiting my job search, I found myself sitting around with the skills to write, to edit, to design, and a burning need to create, but no work for those skills. And I wasn't the only one. Friends all around me were in the same boat. So, I went with something I knew to forge something new. In September, I pitched the idea of launching a literary and art journal to a graphic designer, who was one of my best friends from high school. We could craft something that blended our strengths and simply, craft something. Something that would attract and allow our friends and others a space to share creative work. A space within their reach that would seek to provide emerging creatives professional experience at a launchpad level. A space that would allow all involved to hone their skills, staff and contributors alike. Proof that our studies mean something.

Consider why we learn writing. We learn writing to help us communicate, to record thoughts and pass them to one another visually. Creative writing is a continuation of that concept, with the focus for study on the creative aspect—the aspect of creation. As such, creative writing serves as the foundation for when I design or work on social media posts for *The Starter*. I'm a user of written words, even in those alternative communication formats. I create stories and journeys, even there. It's enrichment, it's meaning. The thing about studying creative writing is that it teaches you ways to focus your creative energy so others may read it. Put together your poems, your short stories. Then keep going.

Reed Johnson, MD: Internist (Luther College Class of 2016)

It continues to amaze me how many writers first trained as physicians. Recently, I learned William Carlos Williams was also a general practice doctor. At the core of being a good physician and being a good writer is the ability to pay attention and notice. Unfortunately, in the age of numbers, it is very easy for physicians to not be as good at noticing the small details on a physical exam. Previously, physicians had to notice the most minute details in order to make informed decisions about treatment, but that is no longer the case with all of the imaging and lab results that are now available every day in medicine. But I hope to be able to continue to emphasize learning these observation skills and carry on this time-honored ritual of medicine.

Vocation is something I have been thinking about recently too because in the last month I have been quite busy. This has increased my level of fatigue, which makes it harder to enjoy what I am doing. I have been thinking about it along the lines of passion. When I was in high school and at Luther, I remember feeling pressure to "find my passion." But I never really felt that any of my interests fully met the intensity threshold to be called a passion. The more time I spend learning medicine, the more I realize that "passion" is something that must be learned and cultivated over time. Part of this realization came to me when I asked a more senior physician if he'd seen any interesting patients recently. He replied by saying, "all your patients are interesting once you know enough." The more I learn about medicine, the more I realize that it is an art. And I think the "passion" that I was told to find when I was in undergrad actually comes from learning to love the practicing of an art form. To clarify, this is not the same as being good at an art form. It is learning to love the journey inherent to developing and nurturing the art and beauty of what you do. It is not about the destination.

Annika Dome: (Luther College Class of 2022): Production Assistant to Amy Weldon, *Advanced Fiction: A Writer's Guide and Anthology* (this book!) Work-study position paid for through Luther College Provost's Office. Fulbright Scholar, 2022–3.

A lot of people ask me what I want to do with an English major once I'm done with college, and all I know is that I want to work with stories. In my last semester on Luther College's campus, I worked with Dr. Weldon to help locate and negotiate permissions for the stories contained in the craft studios and the anthology section of this book!

Every morning when I knocked on Dr. Weldon's door to check in, I felt like I needed a tweed cloak or a pipe of some kind, because for a few weeks, I did nothing but detective work. Locating authors or their representatives, tracking rights from the US to the UK and beyond, locating the right person to email—it was sometimes a challenge, but worth it. I kept a running tally of the permissions requested and the general correspondence and documents associated with the project, helping keep everything organized.

And of course, it was an absolute joy to banter with Dr. Weldon all the while. The printer would whir to life and she would come down the hall, and we would exchange whatever updates necessary. Occasionally, these updates were instead running jokes, one of which was all of the potential secondary jobs that I could take on: fashion consultant, copy runner, coffee fetcher, or MI-6 agent.

Working on this project and getting to be in contact with so many accomplished authors, agents, and publishers has been amazing. I hope to one day write my own books and publish them, but working on the inside of the publishing industry has opened my eyes to how books are made, as well as the sheer number of people involved in that process.

MFA Studio: Keith Lesmeister (MFA from Bennington Writing Seminars, 2014; Author, *We Could've Been Happy Here;* Editor, *Cutleaf* Journal (cutleafjournal.com); Co-Director, Luther College Writers Festival; Instructor of English at Northeast Iowa Community College)

As you think about your future, you may be considering advanced degrees. For creative writers, this may be an MFA (Masters of Fine Arts) in creative writing or perhaps even a PhD in creative writing. (Graduate programs in publishing also exist; see resources at Publishers Weekly.[12]) *Poets & Writers* Magazine (pw.org) has a great collection of MFA-related resources, updated regularly, and an annual special issue on MFAs. I don't have an MFA myself (I applied for my teaching job with a PhD in literature and publications in scholarly and creative work) so will hand the mike to Keith Lesmeister.

Keith has been my friend since 2006, when he signed up for the very first community writing class I ever taught, in a little room above a Mexican restaurant. Discovering a love for writing, Keith took more classes from me and my colleague David Faldet at Luther College while holding down a full-time job and raising a family. In 2011, he made the decision to apply to the low-residency MFA program at Bennington College, which, as I said in my recommendation letter, is tailor-made for a talented working adult like him. Keith received his MFA from the Bennington Writing Seminars in 2014. Now we codirect the Luther College Writers Festival. He's also a founding editor of the literary journal *Cutleaf* (cutleafjournal.com). You can read more about him at https://keithlesmeister.com.

When, and why, did you decide to pursue an MFA?

In the summer of 2011, I attended the Iowa Summer Writing Festival in order to take a fiction workshop with Andrew Porter. I had signed up for the class because I wanted to know from a short story writer who didn't know me from Adam if anything I was writing was worth a shit. All along, without getting into too much detail, I was trying to transition from my career in college admissions to a high school English teacher, but the financial aspect wasn't working out. Meaning: the financial reality of having to quit my full-time job in order to student teach (and pay a semester's worth of tuition to do so) smacked me in the face, so I was in the process of figuring out other options. Now, circle back to 2011 in Iowa City. After that fiction workshop, Andrew Porter, in our one-on-one meeting, asked if I'd ever considered low-residency programs. He explained that they were intended for people like me—people with full-time jobs and families, and who didn't want to uproot those families in order to pursue writing. While I was in my MFA program at Bennington College, I wanted to learn and practice the craft of writing, certainly, but I also wanted to use my MFA as a means to teach. It worked out well. I now teach at the local community college.

What did you like about that experience? What surprised you?

I pretty much loved everything about my MFA experience: the people, the place, the work, the reading, and of course the writing. I enrolled at Bennington just after my 32nd birthday, and even then, in my thirties, I was surprised by how much sheer joy the program brought me, both then and now. I was so happy to be around people who loved books and words and talking about writing and literature as much as I do.

Any advice for students thinking about pursuing an MFA?

Find writers/teachers who you respect and admire. If they teach at an MFA program, apply. Consider both full-residency and low-residency programs, and if there's a particular place you'd like to live or travel to, I think that's a perfectly fine consideration for where to attend grad school. If you're just out of undergrad, try working in the "real world" for a while. Gain experience and figure out what you might want. Writing isn't a job so much as a vocation, and if it's something you must do to feel alive and whole and completely yourself, and if you feel that your way of contributing to your community is through writing, then that will happen whether you attend an MFA or not. And you'll also write regardless. After a couple of years distance from undergrad, if you still feel the desire to go, then by all means, go. We only get one shot at this life, so you may as well make the most of it and pursue those passions that make life the most meaningful.

Keith's story "East of Ely" appears in his collection *We Could've Been Happy Here* (Midwestern Gothic Press, 2017) and was first published in the journal *Flyway: A Journal of Writing and Environment* at Iowa State University in 2015; other stories have appeared in journals, including *Gettysburg Review, Meridian,* and *American Short Fiction.* I love this story's sly, quintessentially Midwestern humor and subtle sense of place—and the unexpected sweetness of the journey on which it takes us, beginning to end.

"East of Ely" by Keith Lesmeister

We stopped caring about how we actually felt toward one another a long time ago because our feelings fluctuated like spring temperatures in the Midwest. Instead, we devoted ourselves to each other in the old-fashioned way of loyalty and partnership. It wasn't a sexy, Hollywood endeavor—our marriage—but that was all about to change.

I should tell you now that I won't get into the specifics of our actual lives. That is, our names, jobs, etc., but as we get to the part I really want to tell you about, I think—I hope—you'll understand why.

What I will tell you, though, is that we married under what you might call societal pressures. She was pregnant before we were married, and really, there's not much else to say about it. We went on about our lives and everything was more or less fine until a month before our twenty-fifth wedding anniversary, when I lost my job and she decided we needed something different.

"We need an adventure," she said to me while gardening in the backyard.

"What do you have in mind?"

"I have ideas," she said, "but I don't think you have the stomach for them."

"Try me." I looked up from the push mower. I was changing a spark plug.

"Why have I always felt attracted to banks?" she said.

"Oh, Lord," I said.

Here's the other thing you need to know about my wife: she was, and is, a kleptomaniac. We can't go into a gas station without her walking out with some ornament or pin, something small enough to conceal in her palm.

"I've got it staked out," she said.

"Risk factor?"

"I wouldn't have brought it up if there was much of any."

"I was thinking a nice dinner, you know? Maybe a movie. Dinner and a movie? You ever heard of that?"

"You were always so predictable, darling."

We were both forty-five years old, empty-nesters. My wife was slender in an overworked sort of way, and I was just developing what my kids called a beer-belly, despite not drinking much anymore.

"What are you planting?" I was trying to change the subject.

"Transplanting," she said. "Raspberries. Damn things are like weeds and I don't want them next to the garage anymore." The bandana around her forehead was wet. The sun was out and the sky was a perfect blue. "We should start taking our country drives again, too," she said. "I always liked those sleepy afternoons on the open road."

"All of a sudden we need to spend more time together?"

"Seems like a nice thing to do, that's all," she said. "Seems like a thing any married couple might do."

•

What wasn't a thing any married couple might do was rob a bank. But that's exactly what we did. On June 12th, the day of our twenty-fifth anniversary, we walked into the

Ely Credit Union wearing masks, holding canvas bags, and clutching plastic pistols that we purchased at the Dollar Tree, and we used them to paralyze the bank staff while a teller—previously designated by my wife—unlocked the tills of money.

It was a beautiful spring day, lush trees and soft grasses that made you want to sing songs from your childhood. Ely was a village just outside of Cedar Rapids, surrounded by large swaths of timber. The actual village was just a few houses and as many abandoned buildings, but there was this one, lone bank in the middle of nowhere on some county road that connected to nothing, just a few miles outside of Ely. Apparently, my wife had staked out the place for two months prior, hiding behind trees across the street, observing which days and times were busiest. She even knew which teller she wanted to mark. She said she chose the woman because of her predictable nature: parked in the same spot, chewed gum, wore her hair and carried her purse the same way, and always—always—held an unopened bottle of Diet Coke while walking into the bank.

The predictability, my wife argued, was a sign of some due diligence on her part to create a life of least resistance—that if she was put to a task, like helping us unlock money tills, she'd surely not fight or talk back, but instead do what she was told to do, and with efficiency. She was blond, and reasonably attractive, but only by virtue of her effort. Makeup, nails, hair fashion. My wife pegged her for a Target shopper, fake-baker, college Business major who slept around with endless frat boys in the hopes that one would eventually be fond enough to take her as a spouse. My wife was unusually perceptive about these things, and once, while we were on the last stakeout before our heist (the only one I attended), I spotted the woman walking into the bank and I knew right away she was the mark. I thought: my wife is exactly right.

My wife brandished her toy pistol, requested that all bank employees move to one corner of the room. "Nobody panic," she said. "We're not gonna hurt you. Now move." She was speaking in this faux British accent that she failed to warn me about. I thought it a deft move and chimed in with my own.

"Move quickly," I said, but it sounded more Australian than British.

"You," my wife said, sticking the pistol in the back of the mark, "come with me." The mark squealed a little, but obeyed, just as my wife had figured. Up close, I realized the woman wasn't in fact good-looking at all. She was all show. Not an ounce of natural beauty. Just fake nails, fake tan, and poorly highlighted hair, and it occurred to me at that very moment how deeply grateful I was that my wife—my partner—didn't feel a need for such show.

The other bank employees cowered toward the ground, moving like snails. "Quickly," I said again, trying to adjust my accent to match my wife's.

I walked over to where the other employees were commanded to wait and kept an eye on the three who squatted down, huddled against the corner, facing the wall. No one whispered a word, cried, or whimpered, and while my adrenaline surged, I became so hyper-focused that every movement of every person, even just the slightest slide of a finger or a leaning one way or the other, etched itself permanently into my memory. I can recall, even today, with great accuracy, every second we were actually inside the bank: the nervous twitch under an eye; the hostages shifting weight from one knee to the other; the bead of sweat that ran down one's cheek; the smell of flowery hand soap; the dark stain on the carpet next to one of the chairs (probably coffee); the unused look of the leather couch; the way the teller's ponytail curled at the end, swaying slightly with every nervous movement.

The one male hostage was wearing gray slacks and a navy blue shirt, and I remember thinking that he looked quite dapper, dressed up in a way to make himself appear more competent than he actually was. Maybe not so different from our mark in this way. The other two employees—women of about forty—were dressed like our mark, except both were brunettes, and both wore nondescript sets of earrings, and some low-heeled shoes. The practicality of which didn't go unnoticed, and I was glad that my wife had picked who she picked, because the others—more practical, more prepared women—might've out-flanked us, might've made a move for which we weren't ready. And I think that's the thing about life. Even at our most spontaneous we're still doing things within the realm of what we're fit for, and in this case our mark's always been fit for compliance, the path of least resistance. My wife, on the other hand, has always been fit for thievery. Like Michael Jordan's jump shot, or Magic Johnson's ability to dish out the ball, my wife was a natural born thief, and watching her work was a thing of beauty: the way she so elegantly glided around, giving orders. This was her most ambitious take yet, and I knew, after we got out of there, it wouldn't be our last. And it wasn't.

"Scoot your ass over to the corner with the others," my wife said. She shooed the mark away. The tills were open and she was filling bags. I signaled our mark with a motion of my toy gun to hustle. Her high heels tapped the wood floors. My wife stuffed the canvas bags full of bills. I knew, for her, it didn't matter if they were ones or one-hundreds; this take was about so much more than the money.

As our mark walked past me, she looked back at my wife, turned toward me, and tripped over the threshold between the wood floor and carpet. She fell head-first into a desk. The collision made a loud, unsettling smack. And instantly there was blood everywhere—on her face, the floor.

"What the hell happened?" my wife said, still in her best British accent. I knelt down to the woman who was crying and clutching her head. "Ouch," I said. "That doesn't look good."

"Let me help," one of the women next to the wall said.

"Nobody moves," my wife said. She was back to her normal voice. A slight Midwestern drawl.

The blood pooled quickly. I knew this from my days in basketball. A guy gets elbowed in the face, the head, and it bleeds. I mean, bleeds. And that's what our mark was doing.

"She'll be fine," I said to no one in particular. "Just a lot of blood."

The woman squirmed and made noises on the ground, tiny whimpers, and I felt an uncommon urge to reassure her that she would in fact be okay. I reached out and touched the woman's leg. She flinched, flung her right arm at me as if she were trying to simultaneously shoo me away and backhand me. As she did this, she accidentally slapped my right hand, the one holding the pistol, and dislodged the plastic gun from my grip, sending it flying across the lobby. It sailed—the pistol—in an arch, toppling sideways over itself, until finally it hit the counter that my wife stood behind. As it connected with the counter a less-than-sufficient thud filled the room, and when that happened, all four of the hostages looked at me, then my wife, then back at me, and there was for a moment this palpable breach in conduct. All of a sudden, I was simply a guy in a bank with no weapon, no gun, therefore no power, and the looks on the hostages' faces told a hundred different stories all at once. I glanced at my wife and the story I told her, without speaking of course, was to get the fuck out of there as soon as possible. Which we started to do.

But that didn't stop the guy dressed in gray slacks, blue shirt and tie, from confronting me. He didn't address the fake gun issue because there was no need. We all knew. Instead, he emerged slowly while the other employees stayed on the floor, and stepped toward the bleeding woman, checked on her, then leveled his gaze at me. I can't tell you now that I felt completely in control. I didn't. But I wasn't altogether scared either. I was mostly calm, and as he approached me, with my wife still behind the counter, now moving toward the door, I remembered my pocket knife and pulled it out: four-inch blade, stainless, spring-loaded, so it flipped open with ease.

"You come near us," I said, "and I'll slice your throat." The guy stopped. My hand shook. My heartbeat quickened. This, of course, wasn't part of the plan. We were improvising. We were establishing a new path. When I said this, my wife stopped, stood next to me, clutching three canvas bags, each of which ballooned out to the size of a soccer ball.

Then, instead of walking straight out the door, she turned toward the bank employees. "Nobody moves for five minutes," she said.

"Yeah, right," the guy said. "Second you morons walk out, cops are on your ass—you'll never get away with this, you and your fake guns."

She leveled her toy pistol on the guy's forehead with an unwavering confidence. The action made everyone in the room momentarily wonder if hers was fake or real. You could see a definite moment of hesitation reorient his face.

"Like I said," my wife said. "Stay put for five minutes, or I will torch each of your houses." Then, in yet another surprising move, she started reciting the names and addresses of each of the employees. Actually, she only got through the names of the other two women. Then she said to those women, "I'll come to your homes and fuck your husbands, kill your children, and burn everything to ash if you even so much as think of moving before five minutes are up."

It was her best British accent yet.

We hustled out the glass door. A wave of fresh, spring air. "Nice speech," I said, trying for my best Brit, but it sounded more Irish this time. We hopped into our Taurus—which we no longer own—and drove off.

My wife drove, and I rode shotgun with the money at my feet. For a while we didn't talk, just enjoyed the drive, the open road. The windows were down and her gray brown hair flew all around her, some of it wrapping around her face. I could tell by her silent look of satisfaction that she was as pleased with this day as any other we'd shared.

We maneuvered onto some gravel roads, kicking up dust behind us, the sun high and strong, and the fresh air infusing everything around us with the promise of a beautiful summer.

"Where to?" I said, breaking our silence.

"East of Ely," she said. "To a land of lush forests and vast prairie—a place where no one will bother us." She leaned over, patted me on the knee. "Good work, darling."

We pulled into an abandoned farmstead, which was yet another surprise. It was an old turn-of-the-century Victorian that butted up against a wooded hillside in back, and a field of prairie grass out front, just as she'd said.

She got out, lifted a dilapidated garage door. She got back in, pulled the car inside. Then she led me into the empty house where she had already set up an air mattress, picnic basket, blanket, three bottles of wine (which I considered at that moment a bit excessive), and a handheld radio that she turned on to some jazz station that neither of us ever listened to before. She grabbed me then, brought me close, and we danced to some musician's sad saxophone.

We made love that night in a way that I can only describe as reckless and desperate—the way we sloppily kissed and clung to each other, the way we flopped around on that air mattress, and later, outside in the still spring night, on a bed of thick grass.

And later still, in the wee hours of the night, we lay in bed, sipping wine, whisper-talking about our dreams, how some of them had come true, while others had not. She also confessed to me all the times she'd thought about leaving, and I confessed to her the same. We talked about moments when we fought or ignored each other, stretches of our lives when we were simply enduring the daily grind, and she told me she used to occasionally pick fights with me just to feel something more than what she described as my "cruel indifference." I told her then that I'd never loved her more than I did at that exact moment. And that was true. And I made a promise to myself that night that I'd be a different person, for her and for me.

As the sun came up over the eastern tree line, filtering first-light through cloudy glass windows, I asked her what she wanted to do with the money. It was the first time either of us had thought to discuss it. Her head was propped on my shoulder as we lay naked under the quilt.

"I didn't have anything in mind," she said. "Nothing at all."

MFAs: Further Thoughts

As I described in *The Writer's Eye*, MFA programs have real benefits for writers, primarily dedicated time to focus on reading and writing and immersion in an environment that helps you discipline yourself as a professional. They also give you a ready-made writing community and connections. With publications, they can sometimes help you secure a teaching job after graduation, although in higher education, a PhD will often be the requested degree, since colleges usually need applicants to show that they can teach a wide range of courses in writing and literature, and an MFA program might not include teaching experience or training in writing pedagogy. Higher-ed teaching jobs are limited—which, unfortunately, does not seem likely to change.

Keith Lesmeister was an ideal candidate for an MFA. He was already building a writing life on his own, because he loved reading and writing. He thought about his goals and financial realities, did his research, and applied to programs accordingly. And he used his time in the program to hone his writing skills, to seek publications (below), and to build connections. Unless you're thinking this carefully about an MFA, it can be a very expensive decision that might not have the results you want. Sometimes, people go into MFA programs because they don't know what else to do: "well," they reason, "I *did* get good grades in my creative writing classes." Or they think, "This will really help me get serious about my writing." But, honestly, if you're not *already* serious about your writing (and reading!), an MFA might not be the answer.

So, now, the major question I ask students considering MFA programs is this: *Are you already doing your best, on your own, to make your writing happen and take advantage of opportunities?* Do you geek out on writing even when nobody's watching? Do you read widely and actively, support other writers, revise, and meet deadlines? Do you attend readings and lectures? And do these things energize you to do more? Because an MFA program will be more of the same—and while it can be a valuable boost to an existing writing and reading life, it can't create such a life for you from scratch. As Keith Lesmeister advises, if you're uncertain, wait a year or two past college and see how you feel.

Please know that you needn't have an MFA or work in a literary field to make writing a meaningful part of your life. In my experience, it's often living your life *beyond* a classroom (as Keith says earlier) that gives you something to say and a voice in which to say it—and that can lead to a book. If you really love writing and keep making it part of your life, writing will stay with you. Keep the faith and stay open to following the words wherever they lead.

Thinking about Publication: From Stories to Collection

As I described in *The Writer's Eye,* and as Derek Lin indicates earlier, advanced fiction writers may be ready to start sending out their stories and poems to literary journals. How do you know where to submit? Consult databases like those at *Poets and Writers,* the publication credits of writers and books you admire (this will tell you where their stories appeared), the lists of literary journals in the back of annual collections like *Best American Short Stories*, and journals that may be associated with universities you and your friends might know. Many have print and online versions; some are online-only. Try young journals like Derek's *The Starter* and those you find at places like the AWP Book Fair. When you gather a certain number of publications, you may craft them into a collection to submit to small presses. Like the rest of the writing process, this happens little by little, with a lot of patience, over time—but you can get where you're going if you don't give up.

Finding an Agent

As the publishing industry has contracted (due to corporate mergers and declining readership numbers—because, internet) yet the number of people submitting manuscripts keeps rising, many publishers will no longer accept submissions of fiction directly. Rather, they'll only accept submissions from literary agents. So, what this means for fiction writers is that agents are now the First Important Person to Impress (poets usually work directly with presses, and nonfiction is often pitched and sold on the basis of a proposal, without a complete manuscript, as described in Susan Rabiner and Alfred Fortunato's *Thinking Like Your Editor*).

Although some agents will represent story collections, most will prefer novels. So, if you finish and revise a novel until you believe it's ready to submit (draft numbers in at *least* the high single digits!), your next step will probably be to start querying agents. For ideas, look in the "acknowledgements" section of books you admire and/ or intend to compare to yours in your pitch letter. Other sources online (and via *Poets and Writers* magazine and Publisher's Marketplace) abound. Some agents also post at *manuscriptwishlist.com*. Reputable agents *never* ask you for a fee to read your work.

If you have writer friends, ask about their agents, who will also be named on their author websites or acknowledgments of their books. It's OK to ask a writer friend if you may use their name in querying their agent, but please remember three things: (1) you *must* ask that writer if it's OK with them before you do so, (2) you must not lie or exaggerate connections, which are easily checked, and (3) you must accept that the writer may need to say "no" to your request for reasons that are not only about you and your work, and that they may not be able to share with you (and anyway, this is a favor you aren't owed, so be extra-grateful if your friend says *yes*).

Consider carefully whether your book really *is* a match for this agent; someone who represents mostly YA (young adult) or celebrity memoirs is probably not your best target for your historical novel about the Tuskegee Airmen. Remember, in the words of my friend the writer and activist Taylor Brorby, "Agents are barraged by people wanting them to change their lives, and they're working *already* with people whose lives *they're* trying to change." Seriously: it's hard to cut through all that noise. So after you've made your manuscript truly ready, design a professional, engaging submission package that will stand out in a good way.

Identify agents you want to query and review their websites carefully to learn more about their clients and their submission guidelines: some will ask for sample pages and a letter, others for a letter only. Follow these guidelines *exactly*. Write a letter that introduces yourself and your work and gives the agent a sense of what you're like, what your book is like, and what other books in the market (comparable titles, or "comps") your book is like. It's good to give a flavor of your writerly voice, but overall your tone should be clear, authentic, and professional. It's important to polish this submission, because you only get one chance with each agent. If they decline your initial query, that's it—no do-overs, at least for that book. (Agent Anna Sproul-Latimer's Substack newsletter "How to Glow in the Dark," neonliterary.substack.com, is an excellent resource for advice.) Keep a list of who you've queried, when, and what their response is (or not).

Here—just for you, dear student readers—is an imaginary (and gently satirical) sample letter pitching an imaginary (and gently satirical) novel about my late, great orange polydactyl barn cat Pitty Sing Weldon (2000–17, named after the cat in Flannery O'Connor's "A Good Man is Hard to Find"). I wrote it to demonstrate some moves you can make: showing your familiarity with the agent's existing clients (Truman Capote and "Purrlie Purrson"), summarizing the novel's plot in present tense (second paragraph), offering some recent comparable texts and marketing points (third paragraph) to help the agent see how your novel might be pitched to editors, and providing a bio with information that helps the agent see how your life experiences shape this novel (or how you can build an "author platform"). Pitty Sing's origin story and his love of collard greens are real—so are Truman Capote, Thomas Wolfe, and some other litter-ary spoofs—but obviously I'm making some other stuff up.

Being old-school, I would put the letter in the body of an email to the agent's submission address just like this, with the headers and everything (can you tell I started submitting work in the snail-mail era?). But that's me—your email alone is fine, since the whole query and response process will happen by email anyway. Don't ask for feedback. Do be sure your email isn't something like ChildhoodNickname@yahoo.com and the photo associated with it (in Google) is professional. And although I couldn't resist bad puns here (or cat-and-writer jokes), you definitely should.

Your Address
Your City, State ZIP
Your Phone Number
Your Email Address

DATE
Ms. Tabitha Felix
The Felix Agency
6 Fifth Catvenue
New York, NY 10000

Dear Ms. Felix *OR* Dear Tabitha Felix,

Greetings, and I hope this letter finds you well. Referred by my friend Purrlie Purrson, I'm writing to ask if you'd like to read my novel *Alabama Scratch* (complete at 225 manuscript pages and 110,000 words). As an admirer of Truman Capote, whose *Breakfast at Tiffany's* put Fifth Avenue on the catwalk, I hope you might enjoy my tale of an orange tabby with six toes, nine lives, and a hundred surprises.

Pitty Sing Weldon, the protagonist of *Alabama Scratch,* dreams of writing the Great Feline Novel despite his unpromising origins. Abandoned in a hayloft at one month old, he fights to stay alive, dodging snakes, rats, and dogs. But he has a secret weapon: an extra toe on each front paw, just long enough to hold a pen. When an English graduate student, Amy, discovers him, she knows that this kitten could go fur-ther than anyone suspects. Soon, Pitty Sing is getting fat on collard greens, sleeping on

a pillow every night, and writing his first book. Yet when he moves to Chapel Hill, he must face a fearsome rival: Thomas Wolfe, whose thousand-page novel *Look Barnward, Angel* threatens to overshadow his litter-ary dreams. With the help of Ernie, a fellow polydactyl from Hemingway's Key West estate, Pitty Sing learns to banish barn-cat imposter syndrome and yowl his own story. I've attached the first thirty pages of *Alabama Scratch* for your review.

Inspired by such coming-of-age novels as Jack Purroac's *On the Rrrroad* and Charles Dickens's *David Coppurrfield, Alabama Scratch* will appeal to readers who love a good origin story, particularly a feline-specific twist on a familiar trope—the underdog. Given the popularity of cat videos and pandemic kittens, the time seems right for a playful, smart literary novel about a feline who follows his dreams, inspiring readers to do the same.

An Alabama native, I'm currently Professor of English at Luther College, where I teach creative writing, British Romanticism, and Feline Studies. My books include *The Hands-On Life: How to Wake Yourself Up and Save The World* (Cascade Books, 2018), *The Writer's Eye: Observation and Inspiration for Creative Writers* (Bloomsbury, 2018), *Eldorado, Iowa: A Novel* (Bowen Press Books, 2019), and *Advanced Fiction: A Writer's Guide and Anthology* (Bloomsbury, 2023). My fiction, essays, and reviews have appeared in *Orion, The Common, About Place, The Millions, Los Angeles Review of Books,* and many other scholarly and literary journals and anthologies. *Alabama Scratch* is shaped by my life with the real Pitty Sing Weldon and my study-away course, "Six Toes and the Truth: Cats and Their Writers in the American South." I can be reached at email@luther.edu or (###) ###-####, and more about my work, including my future projects and a photo of Pitty Sing, is available at http://amyeweldon.com.

Thank you for considering *Alabama Scratch*, and for all you do to support orange tabbies everywhere.

Sincerely,
Amy Weldon

Other sample letters can be found in resources like *Poets and Writers* and sometimes on agents' websites. Try to keep the whole letter to a single page—three or four paragraphs. Your goal is to introduce yourself and your book in a pleasant, professional way and pique the agent's interest so that they ask for more pages, not, at this stage, to provide marketing copy or hype ("*Alabama Scratch* is bound to be the bestsell-purr of the year!") Don't lie or exaggerate connections (is Purrlie Purrson *really* your friend? And have you asked Purrlie if it's okay to use her name in writing to her agent?) Let the details (and your manuscript) speak for you. *Don't* ask for feedback. Personally, I'm not a fan of "I look forward to hearing from you," in any context, since it feels demanding; instead, I write a closing sentence that, basically, thanks the agent for caring enough about books to read hundreds of submissions from people like me every week. Given the *very* wide range of self-promotional strategies that cross agents' desks every day, rife with anxiety, arrogance, naiveté, and straight-up rudeness, professionalism and kindness are a good choice.

The agent's webpage will say what happens next. If intrigued by your letter and writing sample, they'll write back to request a full manuscript. If you don't hear from them after a certain period of time, you can assume they aren't interested. (Unfortunately, silence may be the only answer you ever get from some agents; many don't even send rejection notifications anymore due to the volume of queries they get.) If they read your manuscript and would like to discuss representation, they will arrange a conversation by phone (or Zoom). They may suggest edits to your manuscript and ask to see another version before offering you representation. They may offer you representation directly in the conversation. A reputable agent will acknowledge your right to ask questions and clarify your understanding of the process before moving forward and will *not* ask you for a fee to read or represent your work beyond the 15 percent they earn for selling it. This is also a time to reach out to fellow writers for advice and "go with your gut" before accepting an offer of representation.

If you do sign on as an agent's client, they will then begin submitting your book to editors on your behalf—*after* they have worked with you to satisfy themselves that your book is as good as it can be. An agent has to really feel connected to a book, believing in it *absolutely*, to muster the strategic thinking and financial data and general moxie to approach multiple editors at publishing houses on your behalf—and *then* to negotiate with those editors for what can be very, very large amounts of money (of which they get 15 percent if they can make that deal for you). This is why you may hear in rejections from agents, "I really admired the writing but I just couldn't connect with the character," or "I just didn't feel as passionate about this project as I need to feel to take it on." To writers, this is heartbreaking and dismissive. But to agents, it's a sign they're trusting what they need to do their job: their own instincts, which lead them to fall in love with a book and work like hell to birth it into the world.

How Books Get Born

If an editor likes your book and wants to acquire it for their publishing house, and you and your agent agree to that, then the editor will negotiate a contract with you and your agent that includes a direct payment to you, called an *advance*. As the name suggests, this is an "advance" against the money the publisher expects your book to earn, and it's yours to keep. But unless your book *earns out its advance* (makes back that initial amount of money, then more, on which you'll then receive a royalty percentage of everything the book earns in its lifetime), that advance might be all the money you ever earn from your book.

Advances can range from $0 to $1,500 from a small press to $500,000 or more from a major house (these numbers are sometimes revealed on #PublishingPaidMe or in Publishers Weekly).[13] Your agent gets paid by taking 15 percent of everything they earn for you (including advances, foreign sales rights, movie rights, translation rights, magazine excerpts, and permissions fees to reprint your work in anthologies like this); that may seem like a lot of money, yet without an agent, most writers can't access those opportunities to begin with. Even a large advance may not actually put that much money in your pocket right away. Samantha Irby cautions:

> I still had a job when a publisher bought *We Are Never Meeting in Real Life* for $75,000. So my agent gets 15 percent of that. You get one-third when you sell it, the next third, when you turn in the fully edited, copyedited manuscript. So like a year later, two years later, however long it takes you. And then you get the final installment on publication. These things can be like a year apart. So divide an advance into thirds, and off the top of each third, take 15 percent that my agent gets for doing his job of selling it. Then, depending on your taxes, you take like 30 percent for the government. So what you have left, if you don't have another job, that's what you have to live on until your next installment.[14]

Remember how I said earlier that a legitimate agent doesn't ask you for money to read your work? The same is true for publishing houses: if *you* are paying *them* to publish your work, you are technically *self-publishing,* which can be OK if you just want a print book in your hands but can penalize you professionally, as many agents and editors (and academic tenure review committees) don't consider self-published work to be truly "published."

Just as a novel develops over time, it also takes time for a finished manuscript to make its way into print.[15] Colson Whitehead started *Harlem Shuffle* in notes around the spring of 2017, found himself compelled to write what became *The Nickel Boys,* then returned to *Harlem Shuffle* in 2019.[16] After a "year of eight-page weeks" (Chapter 7), he finished *Harlem Shuffle* in June 2020 and handed it to his publisher in July 2020.[17] At the end of October and beginning of November 2020, he went through his first page proofs (the book's text as formatted in the publisher's software) and made copy edits. Meanwhile, his publisher, Doubleday, scheduled the book's release date (September 2021) and set up the pre-release process. Oliver Munday, the cover artist for *The Underground Railroad* and *The Nickel Boys,* designed *Harlem Shuffle's* cover art.[18] Galleys (aka paperbound advance reviewers' copies, or ARCs) went out to reviewers and booksellers in January 2021, so they could schedule reviews in venues like the *New York Times* and plan pre-orders for their stores' upcoming seasons (just like fashion retailers do). An excerpt from *Harlem Shuffle* appeared as a self-contained story, "The Theresa Job," in *The New Yorker's* July 26, 2021, issue; this is common for highly anticipated novels. And my copy—preordered!—arrived in my local independent bookstore on September 14, 2021.

Control What You Can: Or, Riding the Emotional Rollercoaster

Whew! Having walked through all the steps of writing and revision, here you are, trying to get your words onto the page and into the world. So, how can you handle the inevitable emotional rollercoaster—from exhilaration to endurance to exhaustion to exasperation, and more?

- Invest in your life and relationships. Everybody—including writers—needs sources of purpose and health and joy that aren't bound up with words on a screen.

- Control what you can. Get an honest friend to read your manuscript and your cover letter. Get an honest friend to randomly spring on you the question, "Is there anything about this book you'd change?" If the gut-level answer that keeps coming out is "No," then your book might really be ready to send out. At the very least, this helps *you* maintain your belief in your book—and that's priceless.

- Identify a community—especially other writers, online or off—who share your struggle and will let you vent and help you celebrate.

- Admit your emotions. You have a right to feel what you feel. Including the desire to stop writing. Including the desire to keep writing. Including grief. Including anger. Including frustration. Including the happiness of finding your way forward to the page even when you're the only one who seems to care. You have a right to that happiness too.

- "Any amount is good." Move forward in a positive direction, any amount.

- Accept that, no matter how unfair and horrible (and it *can* be unfair and horrible), much of this publishing process is just beyond your control. You can't control what else is going on in the life of the agent or editor reading your manuscript—what else she's just read, what other tasks she's got, what she's feeling or thinking about—You can only control what *you* do, say, write, and submit.

- Consider how you and your community can move the needle of "what sells" and, thus, the needle of what books get sold. Novelist Wayetu Moore, speaking about her novel *She Would Be King* at a reading I attended in September 2018,[19] said that she'd started trying to sell the novel in 2015, but at that time, some publishers didn't know what to make of this sort of magical-realistic work by a Black woman. "But then," she said, to audience laughter, "[the 2018 film] *Black Panther* came out." Around this time, the work of N. K. Jemisin, Tomi Adeyemi, and Marlon James was also selling, and suddenly, to an awful lot of industry decision-makers, the audience for sci-fi / magical-realistic, Black work became visible, even though, of course, it was always there (just ask fans of Samuel Delaney, Octavia Butler, and Toni Morrison). A *New York Times* profile of Pantheon and Schocken Books publisher Lisa Lucas observes that "the future of book publishing will be determined not only by its recent hires but also by how it answers this question: Instead of fighting over slices of a shrinking pie, can publishers work to make the readership bigger for everyone?"[20]

- Consider: Are you buying and reading books like those you're trying to write? Or asking your library to buy them? Sales figures are tracked in many ways, and those numbers materially affect writers' chances of selling their next books. For at least as long as I've been paying attention, it's been true that men submit manuscripts at a greater rate than women but buy books (especially fiction) at a much smaller rate. "Step up to the fucking plate, men out there, and start buying some fiction—I mean literary fiction—because otherwise we're all just going to keep that in mind when you're trying to get published," exhorts literary agent Julie Barer. "If you're a writer and you want to be published, go out and buy a hardcover debut novel and short-story collection tomorrow. And next month, do it again. Buy one every freaking month. Because if you want to be published and you want people to buy your books, and you are not out there supporting fiction and debut authors, you are the biggest hypocrite in the world and I don't know who you think you are. I mean, *come on*, people!"[21] While humorous, Barer's point is nonetheless true. Our own reading behavior matters. For instance, people under thirty-five tend to buy (and to check out from libraries, and to read) fewer books than GenXers or Boomers. Yeah, money's a thing. But without an industry, who'll buy *your* books?

- Remember: you needn't have an MFA or publish your writing for it to still be a valuable presence and practice in your life.

And last, but most important: if you dream of finishing and publishing your book, don't give up. Colson Whitehead was "dumped" by his first agent: "I sent [the first book] out to about twenty-five publishers," he said. "No one really liked it. After six months I got a call from my agent, and she's like, 'Later for you.' [...] I had to keep doing it, though no one cared except me." Then, Whitehead said, "I sent it to this new agent" on a friend's recommendation, "and she liked it, and from then on it was a different story."[22] That new agent is Nicole Aragi, who's represented him ever since.

Writer Ayad Akhtar tells a similar tale:

As late as 2010, really just months before *American Dervish* finally sold, I remember getting an email from an agent who rejected the book. It was a very loving email about how much he liked it; he just didn't see a market for it. I was in my late thirties at that point, insolvent, divorced, struggling, and I remember getting this email and just feeling every nerve in my body tingling from pain and thinking, "This must be what it feels like to be in hell." But I remember having another thought at that moment, which was, "I'm not going to give up. I'm going to keep going, because this is why I'm here."[23]

Now, Akhtar is the award-winning author of four plays, including *Disgraced* (2013), and two novels, *American Dervish* (2012) and *Homeland Elegies* (2020). He did not give up.

Neither did British writer Mick Herron, whose novel *Slow Horses* (2010), about a misfit bunch of spies, sparked a multi-novel series and a TV show. "My original UK publisher took exception to [*Slow Horses*]," Herron writes:

He thought its plot-strand concerning the resurgence of the far-right ridiculously unlikely, and that references to, for example, Britain leaving the European Union revealed how out of touch I was with contemporary politics. I, on the other hand, thought I'd found my own voice at last; not entirely different from the one I'd developed in the earlier books, but more confident, more individual. Being dropped by that publisher shortly after *Slow Horses* appeared wasn't the most auspicious of starts, but I felt at last that I was ready to begin.[24]

So—looking at where things stand in 2022 and beyond—we might deduce that Herron was right (alas) about Brexit and demagogues, and that he was right to persist in finding a voice that fit the stories he wanted to tell. So was Mary Shelley—whose classic novel *Frankenstein* (1818) was rejected by John Murray, publisher of her friend Lord Byron.

Even though the writing process can be painful, it is also about pleasure and desire, at a very deep level—including the desire to do the thing that makes your life feel worthwhile to you. "The ideal development of the artist is libidinal, I think," says novelist Garth Greenwell, "spurred not by the demands of the academy or the world of professional publishing, but by the imperatives of desire, by seeking out complicated pleasures."[25] I'm inspired by the reminder that making art *is* pleasure, and it's discovery—no matter how far along your creative path you get. The great jazz bassist Ron Carter, interviewed in 2022 at age eighty-five, still asks himself, "Can I find a better order of notes that I didn't find last week?"[26] That "better order of notes"—or words—is out there, waiting for you to find it, as only you can.

Believe in yourself, trust yourself, and—even when it hurts—keep moving ahead, seeking those "complicated pleasures" of expressing truth, beauty, and aliveness on the page in the way that only you can. This is why you're here. I wish you luck, and joy.

DR. WELDON'S FICTION PRESCRIPTIONS

Question: I'm bored with my writing—it just feels blah.
Try: Allan Gurganus, "It Had Wings"; Karen Russell, "The Gondoliers"; Angela Carter, *The Bloody Chamber*; George Saunders, *Lincoln in the Bardo*; Paul Beatty, *The Sellout*; Douglas Stuart, "The Englishman."

Question: I'm excited about historical fiction—where do I start?
Try: Hilary Mantel, *The Giant, O'Brien*, and *Wolf Hall* trilogy; Toni Morrison, *Beloved*; Ethan Rutherford, "The Peripatetic Coffin"; Megan Mayhew Bergman, "The Autobiography of Allegra Byron"; Emma Donoghue, *The Woman Who Gave Birth to Rabbits*; Lauren Groff, "Delicate Edible Birds" and *Matrix*; Jim Shepard, *Love and Hydrogen: New and Selected Stories*.

Question: I'm writing an unlikeable character or narrator; Chapters 4 and 5 helped, but I need more.
Try: Valerie Martin, *Property*; Vladimir Nabokov, *Lolita*; William Trevor, *Felicia's Journey*; Jim Shepard, "Boys Town"; Stanley Elkin, "A Poetics for Bullies"; Patricia Highsmith, *The Talented Mr. Ripley*; Joe Wilkins, "Notes from the Bulls: The Unedited Journals of Verl Newman"; Eudora Welty, "Where is the Voice Coming From?"; Elizabeth von Arnim, *Vera*.

Question: I like reading things that make me wonder, "How'd the writer pull that off?"
Try: Barry Hannah, "Knowing He Was Not My Kind, Yet I Followed"; *Mumbo Jumbo* by Ishmael Reed; *Erasure* by Percival Everett; Mary Gaitskill, "A Bestial Noise"; Alice Randall, *The Wind Done Gone*; Wells Tower, "Everything Ravaged, Everything Burned"; Patricia Highsmith, "Ming's Biggest Prey"; Julio Cortazar, *Hopscotch*; Virginia Woolf, *Orlando*. And the Weird Books on p. 287.

Question: I'd like to try blurring the line between fiction and nonfiction—what does that look like?
Try: Elizabeth Hardwick, *Sleepless Nights*; Barry Lopez, "The Raven"; Truman Capóte, "The Thanksgiving Visitor" and *In Cold Blood*; Renata Adler, *Speedboat*; John Edgar Wideman, "George Floyd Story."

Question: I love pop culture: How can I get that into my fiction?
Try: Nick Hornby, *High Fidelity*; Colson Whitehead, *Sag Harbor*; Andrew O'Hagan, *Mayflies*; Michael Chabon, *The Amazing Adventures of Kavalier and Clay*; John Lanchester, "Reality"; George Saunders, "In Persuasion Nation" and "Jon"; Jennifer Egan, *A Visit from the Goon Squad*.

Question: How can I build a convincing alternate world?
Try: Gary Shteyngart, *Super Sad True Love Story*; Robert Harris, *Fatherland*; Aimee Bender, "End of the Line"; Susannah Clarke, *Jonathan Strange and Mr. Norrell*.

Question: How can I write about political and social issues in fiction without being preachy?
Try: Benjamin Percy, "Refresh, Refresh"; Ben Fountain, *Billy Lynn's Long Halftime Walk*; Flannery O'Connor, "Everything That Rises Must Converge"; Danielle Evans, *The Office of Historical Corrections*; Jesmyn Ward, *Salvage the Bones*; William Gardner Smith, *The Stone Face*.

Question: How can I write believably from a child's point of view?
Try: Edward P. Jones, "The First Day"; Ernest Gaines, "The Sky Is Gray"; Elizabeth Bowen, "The Jungle"; Charles Baxter, "Gryphon"; Charles Dickens, *Great Expectations*; Henry James, *What Maisie Knew*.

Question: How weird and dark is *too* weird and dark?
Try: Sam Lipsyte, "Cremains"; Franz Kafka, *The Metamorphosis*; Flannery O'Connor, *Wise Blood*; Carmen Maria Machado, *Her Body and Other Parties*; Denis Johnson, "Emergency"; Colson Whitehead, *Zone One*.

Question: How do I write about illness and death without being sappy?
Try: Andre Dubus, "Killings"; Amy Bloom, "Silver Water" and *In Love*; Alice Munro, "The Bear Went Over the Mountain"; Andrew O'Hagan, *Mayflies*; Amy Hempel, "In the Cemetery Where Al Jolson Is Buried".

Question: How do you handle multiple points of view in a single story or novel?
Try: William Faulkner, *As I Lay Dying* and *The Sound and the Fury*; Edward P. Jones, *The Known World*; Colum McCann, *Let the Great World Spin*; Alice Munro, "Lichen."

Why do we write? Because we aren't content with small lives. We're always trying to make our small lives bigger—even if the enlargement takes place primarily inside.

ANTHOLOGY SECTION

Louis Jensen
"Square Stories"
Translated from the Danish by Lise Kildegaard
From Louis Jensen's 11-volume 1001 Square Story Project
(Gyldendal, Copenhagen).
1–100: *Hundrede Historier* (A Hundred Stories), 1992
301–400: *Hundrede Firkantede Historier* (A Hundred Square Stories); 2002
439: *Hundrede Meget Firkantede Historier* (A Hundred Very Square Stories); 2005

Once upon a time there was a cheerful baker who made a special kind of cookie. Just imagine, they could walk all by themselves over to the place where they would be eaten. The baker told them to go down to Western Avenue, Number 14. And so they walked a long way down to Western Avenue (and they were singing the whole way) and rang the bell. And when the woman in the house opened the door, they told her they had come from the cheerful baker, to be eaten at coffee time.

A sixth time there was a tree and a little bird. They were good friends and they often talked together. The little bird would fly up high above the treetop and look all around. Then it would fly down again and sit with the tree and report everything it had seen. And then the tree would tell the bird all the strange things its roots could see down deep in the earth. In this way they both grew wise. And one time in a hundred, they were so filled with wonder, they both fell silent for a long while.

A ninth time there was a town that bought a pretty big truck, and when the night came, the whole town drove off in the truck, because it was tired of being walked on all the time. And in the morning, when the people in the town woke up and looked out their windows, they saw that the town was gone.

A twenty-third time there was a short-legged duck, who sold a horse, who was disguised as a car, but since the horse had not learned to say *beep* and *honk* like a real car, the whole thing was called off, and the duck was put in jail, even though he wept sincerely and with real tears.

A three hundred and fourth time there was a young man. The first night, he slept like a cat, and when he woke up in the morning, he had a cat tail on his bottom. The next night he slept like a dog, and when he woke up, he had a dog head. The third night he slept like a prince, and when he woke up, he got married to a princess, and there was a big wedding at the castle, and all the dogs and cats in town were invited and they sat at the table.

> A three hundred and fourteenth time there was a snail. He grew tired of his slow snail pace and bought a little wagon with wheels and a cheerful little flag. Now he moved quickly through the grass: hooray! But the other snails shook their heads in their snailhouses: how stupid to ride on wheels! For the best thing in the whole world is to go at a snail's pace.

A three hundred and sixteenth time, there was a boy who sat on the bottom of the sea. Winter came. Ice covered the sea. But the boy hunched his back and pressed his shoulder against the ice, until it cracked. He stood up in the hole and looked around, while a thin layer of water froze into ice on his body. He was as white as a star. Arms outstretched. Shining.

A three hundred and twenty-second time, there was an alphabet-rider. In the morning, he rode out of the stable and right into the rising sun on a big letter A. At noon, he traded the A for a shining black H and galloped away, shouting wildly. In the evening, he rode back home on a big Z. He wept, for that's what alphabet-riders do, when the night comes.

A three hundred and twenty-fourth time there was a bird. It was so light in its bird heart, for it was so beautiful to glide through the clouds. And down beneath lay the land, and its eyes could see everything: insects, and a boy with a red cap who was running over the green meadow. And at once the bird knew, that's how it was in its heart: two legs running.

A three hundred and thirty-seventh time, there was a king, whose heart was ice cold. It was so cold, a wreath of icicles grew out of his breast. And his eyes were ice. And his toes. And when he spoke, a cloud of cold stood around his words. Terrible! Frightful! But then came a princess made entirely of fire. She was steadfast. She yelled with fire out of her mouth. She was in love with the ice king. I don't know any more, but every night before I sleep, I pray to God that it all comes out all right.

A three hundred and forty-second time, there was a boy with a red cap. He was so easy in his boy heart, for the world was full of light, and high up in the heavens soared a bird. And at once the boy knew, that's how it was in the airy space of his heart: bird wings.

A three hundred and sixty-eighth time there was a duck with lots of wrinkles on his forehead. And because he never said anything, but only wrinkled his forehead, all the other ducks thought that he was walking around thinking deep thoughts about life and death. But he wasn't. He was thinking about feet—duck feet—which was entirely natural.

A three hundred and seventy-second time there was a man who wasn't particularly fast, but on the other hand he was unusually slow. When, for example, he ate a piece of bread with marmalade, the marmalade was as dry and stiff as a board by the time he slowly, slowly lifted the bread to his mouth. And when he sang, he sang so slowly that he couldn't manage more than the first note before everyone else had sung all 8 verses. But unluckiest of all was that he had such a long name. He could never tell people his name before they had all long since gone home.

A three hundred and seventy-third time the lemons dressed themselves up in green shirts and big sunhats. There should be a party! Dancing! Shouting! And singing and soda pop drinking and music playing, but under each cheerful note lay the terrible, sorrowful secret of the lemons, which no lemon dared to speak aloud.

A three hundred and ninety-second time in the night, God stood inside all the people's bodies, and while they were sleeping, sang.

A four hundred and thirty-ninth time there was a man who was always rushing about. He rushed so much, he caught on fire. On the other hand, his wife dawdled just as much as he rushed. That's why roots grew out of her feet and down into the earth. They had a very good television set, but what difference did it make, for the man burned up and the woman put down roots out in the garden. Currants! It was currants she bore. Small, round, and black.

Text by Sofia Samatar * Drawing by Del Samatar
"The Early Ones"
From *Monster Portraits* (2018)

Like all monsters, we don't belong, but our problem is time and not space. We got here too early. We have always had this sense of wrongful, unseemly arrival. We arrived before community, before there was language to describe us, before the "Other" box on the census, before the war.

We are the hiss in the woodshed, the curious stench. But to see us run on the great plain at dawn is to see the landscape returned to itself, beyond plastic and smog, returned to its archaic splendor, the panoply of acacia shadows, the thousand and one varieties of blue. We run. Sometimes we are fleeing and sometimes dancing. Once my brother was shot in the leg. We spent the night shivering in the branches of a tree. The next day, I remember, there was a festival in the town, everyone hanging their family names like lighted wreaths.

My brother leaned on me heavily, limping down the empty street. Sweet desolation of the hour when the lights come on. We peered into all the houses where, deep in the wintry windows, our reflections glimmered, crowned with electric candles.

Aimee Bender
"The Woman Was Born With Snakes for Hair"
From *McSweeney's* 12 (2003)

The woman was born with snakes for hair. But unlike Medusa, or any of her predecessors, these snakes were harmless. If you looked directly at them, you did not turn into stone, or butter, or salt. And these snakes were not evil raiders, or slithering boa constrictors, but instead simple garter snakes, evenly dirt colored, and often quiet. If you happened upon her when they were all sleeping, it just seemed like she had shiny and very thick locks, and only when they awoke, each raising a snake head and flicking out a tiny yellow tongue, did anything seem out of the ordinary.

As an old woman, the snakes changed too. They shed their brown skins for gray skins, so that she would fit in with the other old women, though three of the snakes had died by then, unable to keep up with the stubbornness of the rest of her body, and they hung down, dead weight. Soon, they would snap off and there would be a hole in her scalp line, something for her hairdresser, whom she paid very well, to contend with.

The snakes themselves were not a problem. The problem was the people. Lovers, waking up, suddenly acutely aware of what was on her head, found themselves amazed at their ability to move. But I should be stone! they all cried. No, she said, my snakes have no such powers. But the sight of those little reptilian heads raising up from her ears caused blood to freeze in some kind of fear, regardless. Only one man went the other direction and tried to employ the snakes in their sex life as a way to kink it all up but she refused that, too. They're separate from me, she said. It just wouldn't be right.

It's all power of suggestion. And she was a flexible sort. So when a Greek ambassador asked that she take a flight over, wearing a hat, and show up in front of their enemies in exchange for a cottage on an island, she agreed. She was middle-aged by then, and had seen her fair share of ups and downs. The hat she got had air-holes in it and was dramatically large so everyone on flight assumed she was crazy, or else into rock music. She flew first class and let the snakes out in the bathroom, where they gulped the air and scraggled their bodies as much as they could, weaving around each other, forming quick braids, then unraveling. They could curl up tight in ringlets or hang stick-straight. They were much more obedient than any gel or mousse. She could hear their hissing protests when she put the hat back on.

In Greece, she was escorted from the plane and taken to a large building, and from a huge picture window, the ambassador pointed at the approaching armies. We want you to do a standoff, he said. We will protect you. He dressed her in bulletproof clothing, and then over that placed the garb of old gods and warriors, so that she looked of an ancient time. She had to remove her watch, and Band-Aid, as they undermined the total appearance, but she left her hat on.

They're under there? he asked.

Yes, she said. They're ready to roll.

Fine, fine, he said. Now go climb up the hill. And wait there. And when you see the first soldier, remove your hat.

Where's my cottage again? she asked.

On the island over there, said the ambassador, pointing. You'll be able to walk to the beach and you'll be right next to an olive grove.

She shrugged her shoulders. This was worth the risk, considering her last lover had said the snakes were watching him as he made love to her and the pressure was killing him and she refused to wear a blanket or towel on her head during sex. Her parents had died. Her one sibling had always felt jealous and lived across the country and was a hairdresser for normal hair. She had an open field of time ahead of her, and facing off some warriors did not seem like such a terrible way to begin the next phase.

And are they bad people? she said.

No, the ambassador said. Not so bad. But we do not wish to fight them in this manner.

She climbed the hill and the Greek sun was warm and the water blue and the buildings white and the flowers yellow. The snakes were ready to jump right out of that hat. And so she stood on the hillside and when she saw the glinting foot of the first soldier, she removed her hat, and the snakes, delighted, relieved to be free, stretched their bodies out as far as they could, and recoiled back, and curled and straightened so that her entire head was a moving ball of lines and curves. Of springs and muscles. It was quite a sight to see. From his picture window, far away, even the ambassador felt his skin shiver up.

The armies believed in everything, and so they froze. They saw Medusa high on the hill and felt their skin harden into stone. They heard their hearts thudding deeply, and stopped cold in their tracks. The ambassador rode up on a mule and waved to them. I will free you! he yelled. If you promise to go home and stop this invasion! I will free you from the grasp of the return of Medusa!

With that the snakes stretched out again, towards his voice, so that her whole head had the look of an electrocution.

Someone dropped his gun, and the rest of them turned to look, and in that, they all realized they were not stone at all, not a bit, and they charged up again, toward the ambassador who dashed away on his mule. The woman with snakes for hair ran toward the nearest vineyard, and spent the night in between rows of grapes, listening to her snake hair quietly eating the spoiled ones, nearly raisins, baked from the sun.

The armies took over the ambassador's house and looked out from the picture windows. The woman wandered off to the ocean's edge and gave her hands and feet a good washing. People left her alone. The snakes did not like salt water, so she had to stay out of going too deep or they would gently bite her ear in protest. She had received an offer once, from an animal trainer. He had believed that with very careful cutting, he could remove the snakes from her head and they would mostly live. It seems that only their tails are wedged into your skull, he said, examining her closely with firm fingers on her scalp while the snakes hissed around his wrist. I could keep the snakes here, at the zoo, he said. You could visit whenever you wanted, I'll leave you a key.

The snakes untied his watch band. She thought about it all up until the point when he returned with a small scalpel and some local anaesthetic. No, she said. I can't even imagine it. No way. No. He looked vastly disappointed, as he had really been interested in getting that careful angle right, and was already writing the placard in his mind. Can

I do one? he asked. No, she said. It's time for me to be going. On her drive home, the snakes organized themselves into an elegant top-knot. She dressed in an evening gown while she made herself a small, modest dinner. They rumbled down on their own in curls and wisps while she got ready for bed, where she fell asleep to the gentle ssshing of their many voices.

January 29, 2002, 9:11–9:31 a.m., Los Angeles, CA

Kevin Brockmeier
"The Sandbox Initiative"
From *The Ghost Variations: One Hundred Stories* (2021)

Eventually, when the planet began to cool again, thousands upon thousands of square miles of sand were returned to the seashores. Only in the most remote technical sense of the word could they be called beaches. They had, it was true, been abandoned to the land by the ocean, but no one wanted to visit, much less live on them, and so, littered with kelp pods and baby clam shells, they slowly dried up and seeded out, growing stiff little punk haircuts of grass. So rank and gray were these brine-soaked wastelands that even the gulls avoided them. What might have been valuable seaside real estate was instead a wilderness of sand, with no sea in sight. The question arose what to do with it all. In due course the president, at the encouragement of the secretary of the interior, signed Executive Order 58716, popularly known as the Sandbox Initiative. Until such time as the supply was depleted, it declared, every American family would be entitled to thirty-six complimentary cubic feet of ocean play sand, cleansed of bacteria and other impurities, with all its shells, bones, wrack, and pebbles carefully sifted out and discarded. A fleet of excavators was hired by the federal government to dredge the beaches, factories were built to dye and process the sand, and a vessel system of trains and flatbeds began distributing it to homes far and wide. Though the plan met with the usual hostility from the opposition party and was scoffed at by its pet editorialists, the property developers who were the real engine of the nation's economy greeted it warmly, offering the only ovation they had ever needed: a great huzzah of money. Industrialists and entrepreneurs purchased long sections of shorefront along the Atlantic and the Pacific, and piece by piece, as the sand disappeared, the land was graded, paved, and fertilized. By the time a year had passed, the coasts were blossoming with street malls and condominiums. The oceans were still receding, but they had been cleansed of the worst of their beaches, and, as a result, millions of sandbox squares had been placed in backyards across the nation. Most of the children who played in them, making their hills and moats, had never owned a sandbox before. If invisible fish occasionally muscled past them as they burrowed their fingers in the sand, or if they sometimes felt the ghostly prickles of crab legs tipping across their skin, well, they supposed, that was simply what sandboxes did. They were too young to guess—and the situation too novel for their parents to have taught them—that the sand had retained its memories of the ocean. And so they grew up as they imagined children always had, haunted by the tang of salt air and the blood sound of waves, which hushed, rose up, came to life, and hushed again.

Namwali Serpell
"Account"
From *Enkare Review* (2016)

4567808823241517000067000067340000000000004

Payment Due Date:	02/14/16
New Balance:	$8543.26
Minimum Payment:	$85.00

P.O. BOX 15123
DAPHNE, AL
36526

Account number: 4567808823241517

ARTEMISIA GENTILESCHI
1611 CROSS DR
ROME, NY 30166

$_____._____ Amount Enclosed
Make your check payable to: Scape Card Services

CARDMEMBER SERVICE
P.O. BOX 87101
LIMBO IL 60094-4014

500016028 8362018910009990002249

EMERALD®

✉ Manage your account online: www.scape.com	📞 Customer Service: 1-800-510-5777	📱 Mobile: Visit scape.com on your mobile browser

ACCOUNT ACTIVITY

Date of Transaction	Merchant Name or Transaction Description	$ Amount
PURCHASES		
04/01	HARVARD COLLEGE FUND - ANNUAL DONATION	50.00
04/02	PARTIAL FOODS GROCER & HEALTH	173.54
04/02	SLENDEROSA FITNESS TRIAL MEMBERSHIP	50.00
04/03	SIMPLY THREADFUL FASHIONS	114.23
04/03	FRISKY BIZNESS LINGERIE	92.34
04/04	SCISSORS PALACE HAIR AND BEAUTY	75.00
04/04	YOU'VE GOT NAIL BEAUTY PARLOR	45.00
04/05	OOBER TECHNOLOGIES OOBER.COM CA	13.46
04/05	FONDUE YOUR THANG! FROMAGERIE	33.42
04/05	OLIVE OR TWIST COCKTAIL BAR	33.00
04/05	FLYTRAP NIGHTCLUB AND BAR LADEEZ NITE	26.00
04/06	OOBER TECHNOLOGIES OOBER.COM CA	14.42
04/06	WOK THIS WAY - DELIVERY	18.28
04/06	SLENDEROSA FITNESS MEMBERSHIP CANCELLATION	-50.00
04/07	SIMPLY THREADFUL FASHIONS RETURN	-114.23
04/08	TEQUILA MOCKINGBIRD LIQUORS	31.78
04/08	PHO BITTEN PLEASURES - DELIVERY	16.44
04/08	VIDEOSYNCRASY.COM - RENTAL ROMCOM 23:44PM	2.99
04/09	MEH CHERUB.COM A-LIST SUBSCRIPTION	19.95
04/09	FLAME.COM ONE MONTH SUBSCRIPTION	41.99
04/09	EMELODY.COM SUBSCRIPTION	59.95
04/10	SMOOTHIE MOVES JUICE & ELIXIR TRUCK	11.12
04/10	LETTUCE ENTERTAIN YOU SALAD BAR	8.29
04/10	WHAT'S UP DOG? YOGA DROP-IN SPECIAL	15.00

SCAPE ⬤
EMERALD®

📄 Manage your account online: 📞 Customer Service: 📱 Mobile: Visit scape.com
www.scape.com   1-800-510-5777   on your mobile browser

ACCOUNT ACTIVITY

Date of Transaction	Merchant Name or Transaction Description	$ Amount
PURCHASES		
04/11	FLAME.COM EXTRABOOST CUPID ARROW MESSAGING	4.99
04/11	SIMPLY THREADFUL FASHIONS	114.23
04/12	YOU'VE GOT NAIL BEAUTY PARLOR	45.00
04/12	OOBER TECHNOLOGIES OOBER.COM CA	14.56
04/12	CINESTAR THEATER - 2 ADULTS	27.00
04/12	WHEN IN ROME ENOTECA ET VOMITORIUM	85.71
04/12	BLITZ BAR	44.00
04/13	YELLOW CAB COMPANY	18.27
04/13	ST. AGNES MEDICAL ER23 CPT99285 SOEC KIT CO-PAY	130.00
04/14	UNPLANNED PARENTHOOD PrEP CO-PAY	45.00
04/14	BLOODBATH & BEYOND LABWORKS	54.36
04/15	GREEN ACRES DISPENSARY - DELIVERY	45.00
04/16	PHO GIVE & PHO GET VIETNAMESE - DELIVERY	29.53
04/18	THERE, THERE COUNSELING & RAINN CENTER	150.00
04/18	DWAYNE REED PHARMACY - RX 789654	30.00
04/19	FREUDIAN SIPS TEAS & COFFEES	5.84
04/19	HEALING HANDS BOOKS & CRYSTALS	49.98
04/19	URBAN HERBAL CLEANSES	55.00
04/19	WE KNEAD YOU MASSAGE THERAPY	75.00
04/20	FRAMED ARTS & CRAFTS SUPPLIES	243.56
04/21	ANYWHO: WHITE PAGES PEOPLE FINDER	14.99
04/22	MIGHTIER THAN THE PEN SWORDS & KNIVES	55.98
04/22	DEFENSE MECHANISMS MARTIAL ARTS	20.00
04/23	LORD OF THE WINGZ BBQ	9.23
04/24	SWEET TOOTH CHOCOLATERIA	73.30
04/24	BONE NARROW ARCHERY SUPPLIES	148.98
04/24	TEQUILA MOCKINGBIRD LIQUORS	31.78
04/24	LICK-UR-CHOPSTICKS ASIAN FUSION	19.23
04/26	PEW PEW PEW GUNS & AMMO	714.94
04/27	BULLSEYE GUN CLUB	65.00
04/28	CREPES OF WRATH	8.27
04/28	MUCHO MAAS USED CARS	1320.00
04/28	TAKE YOUR PICK HOME & GARDEN	208.98
04/28	MOM-N-POP-N-LOCK LOCKSMITH	50.00
04/29	VICE-CREAM DESSERT EMPORIUM	5.34
04/30	DETAILS DETAILS CAR WASH	39.99
04/30	BURGERTORY: A BISTRO	14.78
04/30	CURL UP & DYE	12.29
04/30	NAILED DELUXE MANI-PEDI	45.00
04/30	TOOT N' COME IN PETROL	54.23
04/30	CASH ADVANCE - ATM 666	3580.00
05/01	TOLL - STYXX BRIDGE	1.00

Cynan Jones
"Sound"
From Stillicide (2019)

The calf gave a confused hiss, and lowing, then dipped slightly as if it would bury into the water.

When the second harpoon hit, thumping its flank a second later, it seemed to groan somewhere deep within itself. A contained sound of suffering such that it was impossible not to believe the thing understood. That it was young and had a sense of the freedom and scale before it, and that this was now done.

The men in the small boats some twenty metres away braced because they knew the harpoon could put such sudden energy into the calf that it could fly at them, and that men were killed that way. Either from the direct strike or by being upturned. All they had between them and the freezing water was the five metres of Hypalon-coated polyester.

There were three men in each boat.

After the initial cowering, barely noticeable in normal time, the men recovered. All of this happened in a matter of moments. They drove the boats away, the twisted-steel harpoon lines, awkward and heavy, playing out behind.

The water was so flat it felt thick, and they—the only disturbance in it—seemed more to plough than to float through its surface. They went slowly.

The sound of the motors snapped in the air as if some communication took place between the boats.

They used modified old D-class RIBs, with big fifty-horsepower outboards. The outboards were disproportionate on the back of the inflatables but balanced by the heavy harpoon gun in the prow, and to an extent the weight of the wire lines.

At the hundred-metre knot the Lead Man called a stop.

There was still a chance the calf could blast at them and they had to suppress their instinct to put distance down quickly. But the most dangerous thing was done.

Each of the crew tried to divine what state the calf was in, watching it as if they could ascertain intention.

The boats wallowed.

The tock of their idling motors beat out into the open space. Somehow, the noise seemed to confirm the potential for profound quiet here. This sat too in the men, beneath the thoughts they were having, their estimations of remuneration. The fact one of them was madly hungry.

"Ready the anchor," the Lead Man said.

"Four hundred," the harpooner said, and the Lead Man nodded. He looked to the other boat. A hand went up in answer.

The red coats they wore were extremely bright with the sun so clear.

The Lead Man held his thumb and finger in the air before him in a backward C, as if he could squeeze the calf and lift it from the water.

He calculated its size, pushed his thumb into his nose, a thing he did, and nodded again. Should it spin on them, they were clear.

"Just to the left. Hit it there."

The thermal anchor hissed away, turning the air into a stream of steam, hitting the calved ice with a crack that made all the men momentarily sick.

They could not see it, but they pictured the anchor thumping a few lengths into the berg then dropping into its body; a strange conflict of heat, it melting and sinking into the ice, but battled, with the deep cold closing round it, refreezing, setting it inside solidly.

The berg gave a distraught boom, a strangled sound of grief that echoed over the water.

"She's a beauty," said the harpooner. "A beauty. All the way blue."

They attached the tow lines to the tugs and the RIBs were winched up in the davits, throwing a shadow on the flat water as they hung like things caught in the talons of a bird.

The main line went to the stronger boat that would take the berg eventually all the way to the dock.

For the first stage of the journey, the two smaller tugs would flank the main tug, adjusting as necessary to keep the iceberg stable as it melted somewhat with manoeuvre and the friction of saltwater.

As they secured the tow lines, the men looked up to the wheelhouse of the main tug; and when they were all aboard the main tug to eat before setting south, they looked at the wheelhouse.

Eventually, the captain came out. He'd checked the sonograph, and made calculations, and by now brokered the ice.

"She's one hundred and ten. That's six hundred and thirty-four barrels. Good leading edge, so there won't be overmuch friction; she shouldn't waist too much. She's a funny shape, but she'll hold."

"Like your wife," one of the men muttered, to muffled delight.

"We had two bids. The gallon price was higher south of Dogger. But we'll lose more in the water and she'll likely end up fetching the same. So we're best going short. We also had an offer to park it. How do you feel about that?"

The crew heckled, with mixed accents, unanimously, at the idea. Blunt in their opinions about letting the thing melt to keep prices up.

"Then we'll take her into Redcar. With the melt, means you'll only have to go as far as Sumburgh maybe. This'll take her from there. We're promised a calm sea."

The thick smell of oil and grease came up from the dismantled outboards that lay in pieces about the deck.

The pieces lay like artefacts; the crew's care of them akin to the careful homage of archaeologists.

They scraped away corrosion and the salt, with affection close to love.

Treated the motors as things that were amongst the last of their kind.

"There's no bomb big enough to blow a berg that big," said the big Icelander.

"They blow themselves easy enough," to laughter.

"Like someone I know . . ." retort.

"Well. Why would you want to, really?" asked the strange Moroccan.

"To blow up the city!" They were used to the harpooner making statements like this now.

"You wouldn't blow the city up. You'd just shower it in snow," the Lead Man said.

"The city is a mewling infant."

"The city, the city." The Moroccan's clipped-sharp sing-song sound.

"Take, take, take. Imagine how much there'd be to go around. If the cities were just . . . pwff. If they were all just popped, like the bladders on seaweed."

"He has a point." "He has an illness."

The Icelander said, "Pass me more bread."

Behind the boat, the calved berg waited to be towed away, a passive shadow thrown before it on the water.

There was a sense of unrealness to it. Perhaps because it was hard to believe the ice, that looked so fresh and newly formed, was a thousand years old.

"Check the specimen drags," the captain said, and the two men on rota went to it.

"There's never anything," the Moroccan complained, he and the other hauling the heavy seine, hand over hand. The light plankton net already lifted, draped there by their feet.

But when the net came up there was a fish as thick and long as a man's arm.

A pale subdued gold, the colour of early-morning light on soft flat water. A surprising whisker on its chin.

The fish was inert in the net, placid, and, they assumed, dead. Heavy and arched as if in a hammock.

But as they went to lift it, it flapped. They screamed like girls. A sudden life was in its eyes; some internal energy switched on; and at once it became like a pennant snapping and curling in the wind. Chewing at the air.

When they got it on the deck it stilled again, but for its mouth, small rhythmic gasps, as if it counted down silently the last moments of its life. It thudded once, with a sound on the deck like the thwack of wet rope. Then its counting seemed to slow.

It was the first large fish they'd caught.

"Shall we enter it into the record?" the crewman asked. "Fetch a knife," the captain said.

The guts slid from the incision as if in surprise; blood that was almost black leaching over the deck. The men now were like children as they watched.

It did not seem possible the guts had been contained within the fish. They came out in handfuls of alien shapes and colours that seemed to bear no relation to the lithe thing lain there split now at their feet.

They did not know, the captain nor the men, to keep the milts, nor liver. The insides hit the water like a jellyfish.

"Do we leave the head on?" someone asked. The captain said they did.

The head now seemed disproportionate. Like the outboards on the RIBs.

They could cut the fish up and fry it in the small pans they had. But this did not feel right.

One or two of the crew, seeing the fish already diminished, felt privately sad, and the notion of further dismemberment seemed undignified.

They looked at the captain for he was Captain. Rightly, the fish should be cooked intact.

Then came a moment of small genius.

They wrapped the fish in a foil survival blanket from the boat's First Aid supplies. Then slid it into the barrel of the thermal harpoon gun.

All this was done with a degree of melancholy ceremony, as if they aimed to fire the fish beshrouded out to sea in funeral.

But they set the barrel heat to one hundred and sixty and stood back.

I suppose we give it forty minutes, the captain guessed. "Give it forty minutes."

When people imagine being out here, they imagine silence, quiet.

But there's the engines. The constant struggle, noise of the engine, pulling.

Never been able to zone it out. Then again, you listen. It's like you see with your ears, not your eyes. The sea ahead, if it's still, doesn't change much to the eye. But you can hear the current thicken, in the engine sound; you can hear a drop in pressure coming, with the sound changing in the air. Even the pull of the wind, the way the sounds are taken.

When the soft tugs are clear we idle a while, exchange banter. Shouting from deck to deck. Watch the counterweights take the tow lines down under the water; the spin of the winches as they wind back in. Their pitch getting higher the less line. Then they change to the lighter solar engines, and head away. The smell of diesel drops from the air. I hear them for far longer than I see them.

When they're out of earshot I cut the motor. I know this should not be done. It's when you can lose a berg, without the movement through the water keeping it stable.

But I do it just to hear the silence. Just a little while.

It's something that if you've never heard you will not understand.

The sound of silence on the Northern water; and the sound of ice. A berg calving away from some great body.

Like something falling from the face of the Earth.

He thinks again of heading away, to somewhere without such constant sound.

The long trips have given him time to make all the calculations. How many tins of food he could amass and store in the hold of the boat, and how long they would feed him. The drums of fuel.

Ironically, the problem would be water. But it could be done.

How far could he get burning the fuel it would take to tow enough ice to keep him; and where would he go? For silence.

He imagines understanding the world with his eyes again. Having to account contours, and colours, and the solidity of a surface.

A picture of himself, in silence, on a flat sea, a raft of birds beside the boat, and the only sound the knock of his spoon against the edge of a tin of food.

But he knows, as he nears the sea defences, sees the panels moulded from the shredded blades of old wind turbines. He would never do that to the men.

Not with the chance he's been offered, now, to steer the giant city berg.

It will be historic, he knows. I am the best man for the job. And it will make us rich.

The lights of the dock in the falling light. But the silence, he thinks. The silence.

Nuala O'Connor
"Menagerie"
From *birdie: a collection of sixteen historical flash fictions* (2020)

Now that the cage is open, the wild animals are gone; now that the wild animals are gone, the garden is silent; now that the garden is silent, the trees take up their whisper; now that the trees take up their whisper, the birds listen; now that the birds listen, the cat moves away; now that the cat has moved away, the mouse is brazen; now that the mouse is brazen, the girl is frightened; now that the girl is frightened, she can't sleep alone; now that the girl can't sleep alone, the parents are frustrated; now that the parents are frustrated, the fights begin; now that the fights begin, the parents are wild; now that the parents are wild, the girl sleeps in the cage. Now that the girl sleeps in the cage, the cage is closed. Now that the cage is closed, the wild animals return.

Tommy Orange
From *There There: A Novel* (2018)

Before you were born, you were a head and a tail in a milky pool—a swimmer. You were a race, a dying off, a breaking through, an arrival. Before you were born, you were an egg in your mom, who was an egg in her mom. Before you were born, you were a nested Russian doll of possibility in your mom's ovaries. You were two halves of a million different possibilities, a billion heads or tails, flip-shine on spun coin. Before you were born, you were the idea to make it to California for gold or bust. You were white, you were brown, you were red, you were dust. You were hiding, you were seeking. Before you were born, you were chased, beaten, broken, trapped in Oklahoma. Before you were born, you were an idea your mom got into her head in the seventies, to hitchhike across the country and become a dancer in New York. You were on your way when she did not make it across the country but sputtered and spiralled and landed in Taos, New Mexico, at a peyote commune called Morning Star. Before you were born, you were your dad's decision to move away from Oklahoma, to northern New Mexico to learn about a Pueblo guy's fireplace. You were the light in the wet of your parents' eyes as they met across that fireplace in ceremony. Before you were born, your halves inside them moved to Oakland. Before you were born, before your body was much more than heart, spine, bone, skin, blood, and vein, when you'd just started to build muscle, before you showed, bulged in her belly, as her belly, before your dad's pride could belly-swell at the sight of you, your parents were in a room listening to the sound your heart made. You had an arrhythmic heartbeat. The doctor said it was normal. Your arrhythmic heart was not abnormal.

"Maybe he's a drummer," your dad said.

"He doesn't even know what a drum is," your mom said.

"Heart," your dad said.

"The man said arrhythmic. That means no rhythm."

"Maybe it just means he knows the rhythm so good he doesn't always hit it when you expect him to."

"Rhythm of what?" she said.

But, once you got big enough to make your mom feel you, she couldn't deny it. You swam to the beat. When your dad brought out the kettledrum, you'd kick her in time with it, or in time with her heartbeat, or with one of the oldies mixtapes she'd made from records she loved and played endlessly in your Aerostar minivan.

Once you were out in the world, running and jumping and climbing, you tapped your toes and fingers everywhere, all the time. On tabletops, desktops. You tapped every surface you found in front of you, listened for the sound things made back at you when you hit them. The timbre of taps, the din of dings, silverware clangs in kitchens, door knocks, knuckle cracks, head scratches. You were finding out that everything made a sound. Everything can be drumming whether rhythm is kept or strays. Even gunshots and backfire, the howl of trains at night, the wind against your windows. The world is made of sound. But inside every kind of sound lurked a sadness. In the quiet between your parents, after a fight they'd both managed to lose. You and your sisters listening through the walls for tones, listening for early signs of a fight. For late signs of a fight reignited. The sound of the worship service, that building drone and wail of evangelical Christian worship, your mom speaking in tongues on the crest of that weekly Sunday wave, sadness because you couldn't feel any of it in there and wanted to, felt you needed it, that it could protect you from the dreams you had almost every night about the end of the world and the possibility of hell forever—you living there, still a boy, unable to die or leave or do anything but burn in a lake of fire. Sadness came when you had to wake up your snoring dad in church, even as members of the congregation, members of your family, were being slain by the Holy Ghost in the aisles right next to him. Sadness came when the days got shorter at the end of summer. When the street got quiet without kids out anymore. In the color of that fleeting sky, sadness lurked. Sadness pounced, slid in between everything, anything it could find its way into, through sound, through you.

You didn't think of any of the tapping or the knocking as drumming until you actually started drumming many years later. It would have been good to know that you'd always done something naturally. But there was too much going on with everyone else in your family for anyone to notice that you should probably have done something else with your fingers and toes than tap, with your mind and time than knock at all the surfaces in your life like you were looking for a way in.

*   *   *

You're headed to a powwow. You were invited to drum at the Big Oakland Powwow even though you quit drum classes. You weren't gonna go. You didn't wanna see anyone from work since you got fired. Especially anyone from the powwow committee. But there's never been anything like it for you—the way that big drum fills your body until there's only the drum, the sound, the song.

The name of your drum group is Southern Moon. You joined it a year after you started working at the Indian Center as a janitor. You're supposed to say *custodian* now, or *maintenance person*, but you've always thought of yourself as a janitor. When you were sixteen you went on a trip to Washington, D.C., to visit your uncle—your mom's brother. He took you to the Smithsonian American Art Museum, where you discovered James Hampton. He was an artist, a Christian, a mystic, a janitor. James Hampton ended up meaning everything to you. Anyway, being a janitor was just a job. It paid the rent, and you could have your earphones in all day. No one wants to talk to the guy cleaning up. The earphones are an additional service. People don't have to pretend to be interested in you because they feel bad that you're taking their trash out from under their desk and giving them a fresh bag.

Drum group was Tuesday nights. All were welcome. Not women, though. They had their own drum group, Thursday nights. They were Northern Moon. You first heard the big drum by accident one night after work. You'd come back because you'd forgotten your earphones. You were just about to get on the bus when you realized they weren't in your ears when you most wanted them, for that long ride home. The drum group played on the first floor—in the community center. You walked into the room and, just as you did, they started singing. High-voiced wailing and howled harmonies that screamed through the boom of that big drum. Old songs that sang to the old sadness you always kept as close as skin without meaning to. The word *triumph* blipped in your head then. What was it doing there? You never used that word. But that was what it sounded like to make it through these hundreds of American years, to sing through them. That was the sound of pain forgetting itself in song.

You went back every Tuesday for the next year. Keeping time wasn't hard for you. The hard part was singing. You'd never been a talker. You'd certainly never sung before. Not even alone. But Bobby made you do it. Bobby was big, maybe six-four, three-fifty. He said that it was because he came from eight different tribes. He had to fit all of them in there, he said, pointing at his belly. He had the best voice in the group, hands down. He could go high or low. And he was the one who invited you in. If it were up to Bobby, the drum group would be bigger, would include everyone. He'd have the whole world on a drum if he could. Bobby Big Medicine—sometimes a name fit just right.

Your voice is low, like your dad's.

"You can't even hear it when I sing," you'd told Bobby after group one day.

"So what? Adds body. Bass harmony is underappreciated," Bobby told you, then handed you a cup of coffee.

"The big drum's all you need for bass," you said.

"Voice bass is different from drum bass," Bobby said. "Drum bass is closed. Voice bass opens."

"I don't know," you said.

"Voice can take a long time to come all the way out, brother," Bobby said. "Be patient."

*   *   *

You walk outside your studio apartment to a hot Oakland summer day, an Oakland you remember as gray, always gray. Oakland summer days from your childhood. Mornings so gray they filled the whole day with gloom and cool even when the blue broke through. This heat's too much. You sweat easily. Sweat from walking. Sweat at the thought of sweating. Sweat through clothes to where it shows. You take off your hat and squint up at the sun. At this point, you should probably accept the reality of global warming, of climate change. The ozone thinning again like they said in the nineties when your sisters used to bomb their hair with Aqua Net and you'd gag and spit in the sink extra loud to let them know you hated it and to remind them about the ozone, how hair spray was the reason the world might burn like it said in Revelation, the next end, the second end after the flood, a flood of fire from the sky this time, maybe from the lack of ozone protection, maybe because of their abuse of Aqua Net—and why did they need their hair three inches in the air, curled over like a breaking wave, because what? You never knew. Except that all the other girls did it, too. And haven't you also heard or read that the world tilts on its axis ever so slightly every year so that the angle makes the earth like a piece of metal when the sun hits it just right and it becomes just as bright as the sun itself? Haven't you heard that it's getting hotter because of this tilt, this ever increasing tilt of the earth, which was inevitable and not humanity's fault, not our cars or our emissions or Aqua Net but plain and simple entropy, or was it atrophy, or was it apathy?

*   *   *

You're near downtown, headed for the Nineteenth Street BART station. You walk with a slightly dropped, sunken right shoulder. Just like your dad's. The limp, too, right side. You know that this limp could be mistaken for some kind of affect, some lame attempt at gangsta lean, but on some level that you maybe don't even acknowledge, you know that walking the way you walk is a way of subverting the straight-postured upright citizenly way of moving one's arms and feet just so, to express obedience, to pledge allegiance to a way of life and to a nation and its laws. Left, right, left, and so on. But have you really cultivated this lean, this drop-shouldered walk, this way of swaying slightly to the right in opposition? Is it really some Native-specific countercultural thing you're going for? Some vaguely anti-American movement? Or do you walk the way your dad walked simply because genes and pain and styles of walking and talking get passed down without anyone even trying? The limp *is* something you've cultivated to look more like a statement of your individual style and less like an old basketball injury. To get injured and not recover is a sign of weakness. Your limp is practiced. An articulate limp, which says something about the way you've learned to roll with the punches, all the times you've been fucked over, knocked down, what you've recovered from or haven't, what you've walked or limped away from, with or without style—that's on you.

* * *

You pass a coffee shop you hate because it's always hot and flies constantly swarm the front of the shop, where a big patch of sunlight seethes with some invisible shit the flies love and where there's always just that one seat left in the heat with the flies, which is why you hate it, on top of the fact that the place doesn't open until ten in the morning and closes at six in the evening, to cater to all the hipsters and artists who hover and buzz around Oakland like flies, America's white suburban vanilla youth, searching for some invisible thing Oakland can give them, street cred or inner-city inspiration.

Before getting to the Nineteenth Street station you pass a group of white teen-agers who size you up. You're almost afraid of them. Not because you think they'll do anything. It's how out of place they are, all the while looking like they own the place. You want to run them down. Scream something at them. Scare them back to wherever they came from. Scare them out of Oakland. Scare the Oakland they've made their own out of them. You could do it, too. You're one of these big, lumbering Indians. Six feet, two-thirty, chip on your shoulder so heavy it makes you lean, makes everyone see you, your weight, what you carry.

Your dad is one thousand percent Indian. An overachiever. A recovering alcoholic medicine man from the rez for whom English is his second language. He loves to gamble and smoke American Spirit cigarettes, has false teeth and prays for twenty minutes before every meal, asks for help from the Creator for everyone, beginning with the orphan children and ending with the servicemen and servicewomen out there, your one-thousand-per-cent-Indian dad who cries only in ceremony and has bad knees, which took a turn for the worse when he laid concrete in your back yard for a basketball court when you were ten.

You know your dad could once play ball, knew the rhythm of the bounce, the head-fake and eye-swivel, pivot shit you learned how to do by putting in time. Sure, he leaned heavily on shots off the glass, but that was the way it used to be done. Your dad told you he hadn't been allowed to play ball in college because he was Indian in Oklahoma. Back in 1963, that was all it took. No Indians or dogs allowed on courts or in bars or off the reservation. Your dad hardly ever talked about any of that, being Indian or growing up on the rez, or even what he felt like now that he's a certifiable Urban Indian. Except sometimes. When he felt like it. Out of nowhere.

You'd be riding in your dad's red Ford truck to Blockbuster to rent a movie. You'd be listening to his peyote tapes. The tape-staticky gourd rattle and kettle-drum boom. He liked to play it loud. You couldn't stand how noticeable the sound was. How noticeably Indian your dad was. You'd ask if you could turn it off. You'd put on 106 KMEL—rap or R. & B. But then he'd try to dance to that. He'd stick his big Indian lips out to embarrass you, stick one flat hand out and stab at the air in rhythm to the beat just to mess with you. That was when you'd turn the music off altogether. And that was when you might hear a story from your dad about his childhood. About how he used to pick cotton with his grandparents for a dime a day or the time an owl threw rocks at him and his friends from a tree or the time his great-grandma split a tornado in two with a prayer.

The chip you carry has to do with being born and raised in Oakland. A concrete chip, a slab, really, heavy on one side, the half side, the side not white. As for your mom's side, as for your whiteness, there's too much and not enough there to know what to do with. You're from a people who took and took and took and took. And from a people taken. You're both and neither. When you took baths, you'd stare at your brown arms against your white legs in the water and wonder what they were doing together on the same body, in the same bathtub.

*   *   *

How you ended up getting fired was related to your drinking, which was related to your skin problems, which was related to your father, which was related to history. The one story you were sure to hear from your dad, the one thing you knew for certain about what it means to be Indian, was that your people, Cheyenne people, on November 29, 1864, were massacred at Sand Creek. He told you and your sisters that story more than any other story he could muster.

Your dad was the kind of drunk who disappears weekends, lands himself in jail. He was the kind of drunk who had to stop completely. Who couldn't have a drop. So you had it coming in a way. That need that won't quit. That years-deep pit you were bound to dig, crawl into, struggle to get out of. Your parents maybe burned a too-wide God hole through you. The hole was unfillable.

Coming out of your twenties you started to drink every night. There were many reasons for this. But you did it without a thought. Most addictions aren't premeditated. You slept better. Drinking felt good. But mostly, if there was any real reason you could pinpoint, it was because of your skin. You'd always had skin problems. Since you can remember. Your dad used to rub peyote gravy on your rashes. That worked for a while.

Until he wasn't around anymore. The doctors wanted to call it eczema. They wanted you hooked on steroid creams. The scratching was bad because it only led to more scratching, which led to more bleeding. You'd wake up with blood under your fingernails—a sharp sting wherever the wound moved, because it moved everywhere, all over your body—and blood ended up on your sheets, and you'd wake up feeling like you'd dreamed something as important and devastating as it was forgotten. But there was no dream. There was only the open, living wound, and it itched somewhere on your body at all times. Patches and circles and fields of red and pink, sometimes yellow, bumpy, pus-y, weeping, disgusting—the surface of you.

If you drank enough, you didn't scratch at night. You could deaden your body that way. You found your way in and out of a bottle. Found your limits. Lost track of them. Along the way you figured out that there was a certain amount of alcohol you could drink that could—the next day—produce a certain state of mind, which you over time began to refer to privately as *the State*. The State was a place you could get to where everything felt exactly, precisely in place, where and when it belonged, you belonged, completely O.K. in it—almost like your dad used to say, "In'it, like, Isn't that right? Isn't that true?"

But each and every bottle you bought was a medicine or a poison depending on whether you managed to keep them full enough. The method was unstable. Unsustainable. To drink enough but not too much for a drunk was like asking the evangelical not to say the name Jesus. And so playing drums and singing in those classes had given you something else. A way to get there without having to drink and wait and see if the next day the State might emerge from the ashes.

The State was based on something you read about James Hampton, years after your trip to D.C. James had given himself a title: Director of Special Projects for the State of Eternity. James was a Christian. You are not. But he was just crazy enough to make sense to you. This is what made sense: he spent fourteen years building an enormous piece of art work out of junk he collected in and around the garage he rented, which was about a mile from the White House. The piece was called *The Throne of the Third Heaven of the Nations' Millennium General Assembly*. James made the throne for Jesus' second coming. What you get about James Hampton is his almost desperate devotion to God. To the waiting for his God to come. He made a golden throne from junk. The throne *you* were building was made of moments, made of experiences in the State after excess drinking, made of leftover, unused drunkenness, kept overnight, dreamed, moon-soaked fumes you breathed into throne form, into a place where you could sit. In the State, you were just unhinged enough to not get in the way. The problem came from having to drink at all.

The night before you got fired, drum class was cancelled. It was the end of December. The approach of the new year. This kind of drinking was not about reaching the State. This kind of drinking was careless, pointless—one of the risks, the consequences of being the kind of drunk you are. That you'll always be, no matter how well you learn to manage it. By night's end, you'd finished a fifth of Jim Beam. A fifth is a lot if you don't work your way up to it. It can take years to drink this way, alone, on random Tuesday nights. It takes a lot from you. Drinking this way. Your liver. The one doing the most living for you, detoxifying all the shit you put into your body.

When you got to work the next day you were fine. A little dizzy, still drunk, but the day felt normal enough. You went into the conference room. The powwow committee meeting was happening. You ate what they called breakfast enchiladas when they offered them. You met a new member of the committee. Then your supervisor, Jim, called you into his office, called on the two-way you kept on your belt.

When you got to his office, he was on the phone. He covered it with one hand.

"There's a bat," he said and pointed out to the hallway. "Get it out. We can't have bats. This is a medical facility." He said it like you'd brought the bat in yourself.

Out in the hallway, you looked up and around you. You saw the thing on the ceiling in the corner near the conference room at the end of the hall. You went and got a plastic bag and a broom. You approached the bat carefully, slowly, but when you got close it flew into the conference room. Everyone, the whole powwow committee, heads spinning, watched as you went in there and chased it out.

When you were back out in the hallway, the bat circled around you. It was behind you, and then it was on the back of your neck. It had its teeth or claws dug in. You freaked out and reached back and got the bat by a wing and instead of doing what you should have done—put it in the trash bag you were carrying with you—you brought your hands together and with all your strength, everything you had in you, you squeezed. You crushed the bat in your hands. Blood and thin bones and teeth in a pile in your hands. You threw it down. You would mop it up quick. Wipe clean the whole day. Start over again. But no. The whole powwow committee was there. They'd come out to watch you catch the bat after you'd chased the thing into their meeting. Every one of them looked at you with disgust. You felt it, too. It was on your hands. On the floor. That creature.

*   *   *

Back in your supervisor's office after you'd cleaned up the mess, Jim gestured for you to sit down.

"I don't know what that was," he said. Both hands were on top of his head. "But it's not something we can tolerate in a medical facility."

"The thing fucking . . . Sorry, but the thing fucking bit me. I was reacting—"

"And that would have been O.K., Thomas. Only co-workers saw. But you smell like alcohol. And coming to work drunk, I'm sorry, but that's a fireable offense. You know we have a zero-tolerance policy here." He didn't look mad anymore. He looked disappointed. You almost told him that it was just from the night before, but that maybe wouldn't have made a difference, because you could have still blown an over-the-limit blood alcohol level. The alcohol was still in you, in your blood.

"I did not drink this morning," you said. You almost crossed your heart. You'd never even done that when you were a kid. It was something about Jim. He was like a big kid. He didn't want to have to punish you. Crossing your heart seemed like a reasonable way to convince Jim that you were telling the truth.

"I'm sorry," Jim said.

"So that's it? I'm being fired?"

"There's nothing I can do for you," Jim said. He stood up and walked out of his own office. "Go home, Thomas," he said.

*   *   *

You get down to the train platform and enjoy the cool wind or breeze or whatever you call the rush of air the train brings before it arrives, before you even see it or its lights, when you hear it and feel that cool rush of air you especially appreciate because of how much it cools your sweaty head.

You find a seat at the front of the train. The robot voice announces the next stop, by saying or not saying, exactly, but whatever it's called when robots speak, *Next stop Twelfth Street Station.* You remember your first powwow. Your dad took you and your sisters—after the divorce—to a Berkeley high-school gym, where your old family friend Paul danced over the basketball lines with that crazy-light step, that grace, even though Paul was pretty big, and you'd never thought of him as graceful before. But that day you saw what a powwow was and you saw that Paul was perfectly capable of grace and even some kind of Indian-specific cool, with footwork not unlike break dancing, and the effortlessness that cool requires.

The train moves and you think of your dad and how he took you to that powwow after the divorce, how he had never taken you before when you were younger, and you wonder if it was your mom and Christianity, the reason you didn't go to powwows and do more Indian things.

The train emerges, rises out of the underground tube in the Fruitvale district, over by that Burger King and the terrible pho place, where East Twelfth and International almost merge, where the graffitied apartment walls and abandoned houses, warehouses, and auto-body shops appear, loom in the train window, stubbornly resist like deadweight all of Oakland's new development. Just before the Fruitvale station, you see the old brick church you always notice because of how run-down and abandoned it looks.

You feel a rush of sadness for your mom and her failed Christianity, for your failed family. How everyone lives in different states now. How you never see them. How you spend so much time alone. You want to cry and feel you might but know that you can't, that you shouldn't. Crying ruins you. You gave it up long ago. But the thoughts keep coming, about your mom and your family at a certain time when the magical over- and underworld of your Oakland-spun Christian evangelical end-of-the-world spirituality seemed to come to life to take you, all of you. You remember it so clearly, that time. It never moved far from you no matter how much time had carried you away from it. Before anyone was awake, your mom was crying into her prayer book. You knew this because teardrops stain, and you remember tearstains in her prayer book. You looked into that book more than once because you wanted to know what questions, what private conversations, she might have had with God, she who spoke that mad-angel language of tongues in church, she who fell to her knees, she who fell in love with your dad in Indian ceremonies she ended up calling demonic.

Your train leaves the Fruitvale station, which makes you think of the Dimond district, which makes you think of Vista Street. That's where it all happened, where your family lived and died. Your older sister, DeLonna, was heavily into PCP, angel dust. That was when you found out that you don't need religion to be slain, for the demons to come out with their tongues. One day after school DeLonna smoked too much PCP. She came home and it was clear to you that she was out of her mind. You could see it in her eyes—DeLonna without DeLonna behind them. And then there was her voice, that low, deep, guttural sound. She yelled at your dad and he yelled back and she told him to shut up and he did shut up because of that voice. She told him that he didn't even know which God he was worshipping, and soon after that DeLonna was on the floor of your sister Christine's room, foaming at the mouth. Your mom called an emergency prayer circle and they prayed over her and she foamed and writhed and eventually stopped when that part of the high wore off, the drug dimmed, her eyes closed, the thing was done with her. When she woke up they gave her a glass of milk, and when she was back with her normal voice and her eyes, she didn't remember any of it.

Later you remember your mom saying to take drugs was like sneaking into the kingdom of heaven under the gates. It seemed to you more like the kingdom of hell, but maybe the kingdom is bigger and more terrifying than we could ever know. Maybe we've all been speaking the broken tongue of angels and demons for too long to know that that's what we are, who we are, what we're speaking. Maybe we don't ever die but change, always in the State without ever even knowing that we're in it.

*   *   *

When you get off at the Coliseum Station, you walk over the pedestrian bridge with butterflies in your stomach. You do and don't want to be there. You want to drum but also to be heard drumming. Not as yourself but just as the drum. The big drum sound made to make the dancers dance. You don't want to be seen by anyone from work. The shame of your drinking and showing up to work with the smell still on you was too much. Getting attacked by the bat and crushing it in front of them was part of it, too.

You go through the metal detector at the front and your belt gets you another go-through. You get the beep the second time because of change in your pocket. The security guard is an older black guy who doesn't seem to care much about anything but avoiding the beeping of the detector.

"Take it out, anything, anything in your pockets, take it out," he says.

"That's all I got," you say. But when you walk through it beeps again.

"You ever have surgery?" the guy asks you.

"What?"

"I don't know, maybe you have a metal plate in your head or—"

"Nah, man, I got nothing metal on me."

"Well, I gotta pat you down now," the guy says, like it's your fault.

"All right," you say and put your arms up.

After he pats you down, he gestures for you to walk through again. This time when it beeps he just waves you on. About ten feet away, you're looking down as you walk and you realize what it was. Your boots. Steel toe. You started wearing them when you got the job. Jim recommended it. You almost go back to tell the guy, but it doesn't matter anymore.

*   *   *

You find Bobby Big Medicine under a canopy. He nods up then tilts his head toward an open seat around the drum. There's no small talk.

"Grand Entry song," Bobby says to you, because he knows everyone else knows. You pick up your drumstick and wait for the others. You hear the sound but not the words that the powwow emcee is saying, and you watch for Bobby's stick to go up. When it does, your heart feels like it stops. You wait for the first hit. You pray a prayer in your head to no one in particular about nothing in particular. You clear a way for a prayer by thinking nothing. Your prayer will be the hit and the song and the keeping of time. Your prayer will begin and end with the song. Your heart starts to hurt from lack of breath when you see his drumstick go up and you know they're coming, the dancers, and it's time.

Rick Bass
"Fish Story"
From *The Atlantic* (2009)

In the early 1960s my parents ran a service station about sixty miles west of Fort Worth. The gas station was in the middle of the country, along a reddish, gravelly, rutted road, on the way to nowhere. You could see someone coming from a long way off. Pumping gas was a hard way to make a living, and my father was never shy about reminding me about this. Always waiting.

When I was ten years old one of my father's customers had caught a big catfish on a weekend trip to the Colorado River. It weighed eighty-six pounds, a swollen, gasping, grotesque netherworld creature pulled writhing and fighting up into the bright, hot, dusty world above.

The man had brought the fish, wrapped in wet burlap in the back of his car, all the way out to my father's service station. We were to have a big barbecue that weekend, and I was given the job of keeping the fish watered and alive until the time came to kill and cook it.

All day long that Friday—in late August, school had not yet started—I knelt beside the gasping fish and kept it hosed down with a trickle of cool water, giving the fish life one silver gasp at a time, keeping its gills and its slick gray skin wet; the steady trickling of that hose, and nothing else, helping it stay alive. We had no tub large enough to hold the fish, and so I squatted beside it in the dust, resting on my heels, and studied it as I moved the silver stream of water up and down its back.

The fish, in turn, studied me with its round, obsidian eyes, which had a gold lining to their perimeter, like pyrite. The fish panted and watched me while the heat built all around us, rising steadily through the day from the fields, giving birth in the summer-blue sky to towering white cumulus clouds. I grew dizzy in the heat, and from the strange combination of the unblinking monotony and utter fascination of my task, until the trickling from my hose seemed to be inflating those clouds—I seemed to be watering those clouds as one would water a garden. Do you ever think that those days were different—that we had more time for such thoughts, that time had not yet been corrupted? I am speaking less of childhood than of the general nature of the world we are living in. If you are the age I am now—mid-50s—then maybe you know what I mean.

The water pooled and spread across the gravel parking lot before running in wandering rivulets out into the field beyond, where bright butterflies swarmed and fluttered, dabbing at the mud I was making.

Throughout the afternoon, some of the adults who were showing up wandered over to examine the monstrosity. Among them was an older boy, Jack, a fifteen-year-old who had been kicked out of school the year before for fighting. Jack waited until no adults were around and then came by and said that he wanted the fish, that it was his father's—that his father had been the one who had caught it—and that he would give me five dollars if I would let him have it.

"No," I said, "my father told me to take care of it."

Jack had me figured straightaway for a Goody Two-Shoes. "They're just going to kill it," he said. "It's mine. Give it to me and I'll let it go. I swear I will," he said. "Give it to me or I'll beat you up."

As if intuiting or otherwise discerning trouble—though trouble followed Jack, and realizing that did not require much prescience—my father appeared from around the corner, and asked us how everything was going. Jack, scowling but saying nothing, tipped his cap at the fish but not at my father or me, and walked away.

"What did he want?" my father asked.

"Nothing," I said. "He was just looking at the fish." I knew that if I told on Jack and he got in trouble, I would get pummeled.

"Did he say it was his fish?" my father asked. "Was he trying to claim it?"

"I think he said his father caught it."

"His father owes us sixty-seven dollars," my father said. "He gave me the fish instead. Don't let Jack take that fish back."

"I won't," I said.

I can't remember if I've mentioned that, while not poor, we were right on the edge of poor.

*   *   *

The dusty orange sky faded to the cool purple-blue of dusk. Stars appeared and fireflies emerged from the grass. I watched them, and listened to the drum and groan of the bullfrogs in the stock tank in the field below, and to the bellowing of the cattle. I kept watering the fish, and the fish kept watching me, with its gasps coming harder. From time to time I saw Jack loitering, but he didn't come back over to where I was.

Later in the evening, before dark, but only barely, a woman I thought was probably Jack's mother—I had seen her talking to him—came walking over and crouched beside me. She was dressed as if for a party of far greater celebration than ours, with sequins on her dress, and flat leather sandals. Her toenails were painted bright red, but her pale feet were speckled with dust, as if she had been walking a long time. I could smell the whiskey on her breath, and on her clothes, I thought, and I hoped she would not try to engage me in conversation, though such was not to be my fortune.

"Thass a big fish," she said.

"Yes, ma'am," I said, quietly. I dreaded that she was going to ask for the fish back.

"My boy and my old man caught that fish," she said. "You'll see. Gonna have their pictures in the newspaper." She paused, descending into some distant, nether reverie, and stared at the fish as if in labored communication with it. "That fish is prolly worth a lot of money, you know?" she said.

I didn't say anything. Her diction and odor were such that I would not take my first sip of alcohol until I was twenty-two.

Out in the field, my father was busy lighting the bonfire. A distant *whoosh*, a pyre of light, went up. The drunk woman turned her head slowly, studied the sight with incomprehension, then said, slowly, "Wooo!" Then she turned her attention back to what she clearly thought was still her fish. She reached out an unsteady hand and touched the fish on its broad back, partly as if to reestablish ownership, and partly to keep from pitching over into the mud.

She had no guile about her; the liquor had opened her mind. I could see she was thinking about gripping the fish's toothy jaw and dragging it away, though to where, I could not imagine. As if, given a second chance at wealth and power, she would not squander it. As if this fish was the greatest luck that had happened to them in ages.

"You don't talk much, do you?" she asked. Wobbling even in her sandals, hunkered there.

"No, ma'am."

"You know my boy?"

"Yes, ma'am."

"Do you think your father was right to take this fish from us? Do you think this fish is worth any piddling sixty-seven dollars?"

I didn't say anything. I knew that anything I said would ignite her, would send her off on some tangent of rage and pity.

"I'm gonna go get my boy," she said, turning and staring in the direction of the fire. Dusk was gone, the fire was bright in the night. She rose, stumbled, fell in the mud, cursed, and labored to her feet, then wandered off into the dark, away from the fish, and away from the fire. As if she lived in the darkness, had some secret sanctuary there.

I kept watering the fish. The gasps were coming slower and I felt that perhaps a fire was going out in the fish's eyes. Lanterns were lit, and moths rose from the fields and swarmed those lanterns. Men came over and began to place the lanterns on the ground all around the fish, like candelabra at a dinner setting. I hoped that the fish would die before they began skinning it.

Moths cartwheeled off the lantern glass, wing-singed, sometimes aflame—like poor, crude, awkward imitations of the fireflies—and landed fuzz-busted on the catfish's glistening back, where they stuck to its skin like feathers, their wings still trembling.

A man's voice came from behind me, saying, "Hey, you're wasting water," and turned the hose off. Almost immediately, a fine wrinkling appeared on the previously taut gunmetal skin of the fish—a desiccation, like watching a time-lapse motion picture of a man's or woman's skin wrinkling as he or she ages, regardless of the man's or woman's wishes to the contrary.

The heat from the lanterns seemed to be sucking the moisture from the skin. The fish's eyes seemed to search for mine.

The man who had turned off the water was Jack's father, and he was holding a Bowie knife. My heart stopped, and I tried to tell him to take the fish, but found myself speechless. Jack's father's eyes were red-drunk also, and he wavered in such a manner as to seem in danger of falling over onto the dagger he gripped.

He beheld the fish for long moments. "Clarabelle wants me to take the fish home," he said, and seemed to be studying the logistics of such a command. "Shit," he said, "I ain't takin' no fish home. Fuck *her*," he said. "I pay my debts."

He crouched beside the fish and made his first cut lightly around the fish's wide neck with the long blade as if opening an envelope. He slid the knife in lengthwise beneath the skin and then ran a straight incision down the spine all the way to the tail, four feet distant. The fish stopped gasping for a moment, opened its giant mouth in shock and outrage, then began to gasp louder.

In watering the fish all day, and into the evening, I had not noticed how many men and women had been gathering. Now when I straightened up to stretch, I saw that several of them had left the fire and come over to view the fish—could the fish, like a small whale, feed them all?—and that most of them were drinking.

"Someone put that fish out of its misery," a woman said, and a man stepped from out of the crowd with a pistol, aimed it at the fish's broad head, and fired.

My father came hurrying from the fire, shouted, "Stop shooting, damn it," and the man grumbled an apology and retreated into the crowd.

The bullet had made a dark hole in the fish's head. The wound didn't bleed, and the fish, like some mythic monster, did not seem affected by it. It kept on breathing, and I wanted very much to begin watering it again.

Jack's father had paused only slightly during the shooting, and now kept cutting.

When he had all the cuts made, two other men helped him lift the fish. They ran a rope through its mouth and out its gills and hoisted it into a tree, where roosting night birds rustled in alarm, then flew into the night.

The fish writhed, sucked for air, and, finding none, was somehow from far within able to find, summon, and deliver enough power to flap its tail once, slapping one of the men in the ribs with a *thwack*! The fish was making guttural sounds now—that deep croaking sound they make when they are in distress—and Jack's father said, "Well, I guess we need to cook him." He had a pair of pliers in his pocket—evidently part of the debt reduction required that he also do the cleaning and cooking—and he gripped the skin with the pliers up behind the fish's neck and then peeled the skin back, skinning the fish alive, as if pulling the husk or wrapper from a thing to reveal what had been hidden within.

The fish flapped and struggled and twisted, swinging wildly on the rope and croaking, but no relief was to be found. The croaking was loud and bothersome, and so the men lowered the fish, carried it over to the picnic table beside the fire, and began sawing the head off. When they had that done, the two pieces—head and torso—were still moving, but with less vigor. The fish's body writhed slowly on the table, and the mouth of the fish's head opened and closed just as slowly: still the fish kept croaking, though more quietly now, as if perhaps it had gotten something it had been asking for, and was now appeased.

The teeth of the saw were flecked with bone and fish muscle, gummed with cartilage and gray brain. "Here," Jack's father said, handing me the saw, "go down and wash that off." I looked at my father, who nodded. Jack's father pointed at the gasping head, with the rope still passed through the fish's mouth and gills, and said, "Take the head down there, too, and feed it to the turtles—make it stop that noise." He handed me the rope, the heavy croaking head still attached, and I took it down into the darkness toward the shining round pond.

The full moon was reflected in the pond, and as I approached, the bullfrogs stopped their drumming. Only a dull croaking—almost a purr, now—was coming from the package I carried at the end of the rope. I could hear the sounds of the party up on the hill, but down by the pond, with the moon's gold eye cold upon it, I heard only silence. I lowered the giant fish head into the warm water and watched as it sank quickly down below the moon. I was frightened—I had not seen Jack's mother, and I worried that, like a witch, she might be out there somewhere, intent upon getting me—and I was worried about Jack's whereabouts, too.

Sixty-seven dollars was a lot of money back then, and I doubted that any fish, however large, was worth it. It seemed that my father had done Jack's family a good turn of sorts, but that no good was coming of it; I guessed too that that depended upon how the party went. Still, I felt that my father should have held out for the sixty-seven dollars, and then invested it in something other than festivity.

The fish's head was still croaking, and the dry gasping made a stream of bubbles that trailed up to the surface as the head sank. For a little while, even after it was gone, I could still hear the raspy croaking—duller now, and much fainter, coming from far beneath the water. Like the child I was, I had the thought that maybe the fish was relieved now; that maybe the water felt good on its gills, and on what was left of its body.

I set about washing the saw. Bits of flesh floated off the blade and across the top of the water, and pale minnows rose and nibbled at them. After I had the blade cleaned, I sat for a while and listened for the croaking, but could hear nothing, and was relieved—though sometimes, for many years afterward, I would dream that the great fish had survived; that it had regenerated a new body to match the giant head, and that it still lurked in that pond, savage, betrayed, wounded.

I sat there quietly, and soon the crickets became accustomed to my presence and began chirping again, and then the bullfrogs began to drum again, and a peace filled back in over the pond, like a scar healing, or like grass growing bright and green across a charred landscape. Of course the world has changed—everyone's has—but why?

Back in the woods, chuck-will's-widows began calling once more, and I sat there and listened to the sounds of the party up on the hill. Someone had brought fiddles, which they were beginning to play, and the sound was sweet, in no way in accordance with the earlier events of the evening.

Fireflies floated through the woods and across the meadow. I could smell meat cooking and knew that the giant fish had been laid to rest above the coals. I sat there and rested and listened to the pleasant night-bird sounds.

The lanterns up on the hill were making a gold dome of light in the darkness—it looked like an umbrella—and after a while I turned and went back up to the light and to the noise of the party.

In gutting and cleaning the fish, before skewering it on an iron rod to roast, the partygoers had cut open its stomach to see what it had been eating, as catfish of that size were notorious for living at the bottom of the deepest lakes and rivers and eating anything that fell to the bottom. And they had found interesting things in this one's stomach, including a small gold pocket watch, fairly well preserved though with the engraving worn away so that all they could see on the inside face was the year, 1898.

The partygoers decided that, in honor of having the barbecue, my father should receive the treasure from the fish's stomach (which produced, also, a can opener, a slimy tennis shoe, some baling wire, and a good-sized soft-shelled turtle, still alive, which clambered out of its leathery entrapment and, with webbed feet, long claws, and frantically outstretched neck, scuttled its way blindly down toward the stock tank—knowing instinctively where water and safety lay, and where, I supposed, it later found the catfish's bulky head and began feasting on it).

Jack's father scowled and lodged a protest—his wife was still not in attendance—but the rest of the partygoers laughed and said no, the fish belonged to my father, and that unless the watch had belonged to Jack's father before the fish had swallowed it, he was shit out of luck. They laughed and congratulated my father, as if he had won a prize of some sort, or had even made some wise investment, rather than simply having gotten lucky.

In subsequent days my father would take the watch apart and clean it piece by piece and then spend the better part of a month, in the hot middle part of the day, reassembling it, after drying the individual pieces in the bright September light. He would get the watch working again, and would give it to my mother, who had not been in attendance at the party; and for long years, he did not tell her where it came from—this gift from the belly of some beast from far below.

That night, he merely smiled and thanked the men who'd given him the slimy watch, and slipped it into his pocket.

*   *   *

The party went on a long time. I slept for a while in the cab of our truck. When I awoke, Jack's mother had rejoined the party. She was no less drunk than before, and I watched as she went over to where the fish's skin was hanging on a dried mesquite branch meant for the fire. The skin was still wet and shiny. The woman turned her back to the bonfire and lifted that branch with the skin draped over it, and began dancing slowly with the branch, which, we saw now, had outstretched arms like a person, and which, with the fish skin wrapped around it, appeared to be a man wearing a black-silver jacket.

In that same detached and distanced state of drunkenness—drunk with sorrow, I imagined, that the big fish had slipped through their hands, and that their possible fortune had been lost—Jack's mother remained utterly absorbed in her dance. Slowly, the fiddles stopped playing, one by one, so that I could hear only the crackling of the fire, and I could see her doing her fish dance, with one arm raised over her head and dust plumes rising from her shuffling feet, and then people were edging in front of me, a wall of people, so that I could see nothing.

*   *   *

I still have that watch today. I don't use it, but keep it instead locked away in my drawer, as the fish once kept it locked away in its belly, secret, hidden. It's just a talisman, just an idea, now. But for a little while, once and then again, resurrected, it was a vital thing, functioning in the world, with flecks of memory—not its own, but that of others—

attendant to it, attaching to it like barnacles. I take it out and look at it once every few years, and sometimes wonder at the unseen and unknown and undeclared things that are always leaving us, constantly leaving us, little bit by little bit and breath by breath. Of how sometimes—not often—we wake up gasping, wondering at their going away.

Jane McClure
"The Green Heart"
From *The Sandwiches Are Waiting* (1955)

Julian sat quite still in the darkness of his mother's closet, his legs pulled up tight against his corduroy pants, his high forehead pressed upon his knee bones, large as apples in a Christmas stocking. Above him, his mother's dresses hung silently from their wooden hangers, blue silk beside black crepe, sweet-smelling as his evening bath, still, without the quick movements of her legs to rustle the taffeta or her soft breathing to break the pleated bodices. On the high shelf above his head were her hats, carefully covered with white paper, deep in their striped boxes. He liked his mother's hats: he liked the one with the flowers growing out of the straw brim.

Opening the door of the closet he found that his sister Vicky's screams had stopped. Julian was sorry; he liked to hear his sister scream, and he had not minded the sight of her bouncing down the flight of marble steps like a beach ball, her long silken curls—brushed so carefully across his mother's fingers—flopping about her head in disarray. It was quiet now except for the angry footsteps of the nurse rushing about the house. "Julian!" He heard his name, shrill against his ears, like the sound from a whistle. "Julian!"

Julian did not answer. Leaning back he inspected the row of shoes before him: galoshes caked with mud from yesterday's rain, pink slippers of rabbit fur which his mother always wore for breakfast, tennis sneakers beside alligator pumps, high evening shoes, gold, the colour of his sister's hair, low oxfords with crepe soles. He removed one of the oxfords from the rack and slowly began to unlace it. She had worn it the day she had taken him to the doctor's, and as he looked at the small leather toe, he remembered it tapping against the office rug, tapping, impatiently.

"He simply won't eat a thing, doctor," she was saying, as Julian noticed her shoes, side by side now, heel against heel, just below her chair. "Oh, we've tried everything—I can assure you—forcing, bribes, but—stand up straight, Julian," and her hand was firm against his rounded back.

"Suppose we have a look." Placing a hand under his chin the doctor lifted up his face. The doctor's hand felt smooth and smelled of soap. Looking down, Julian could see from the corner of his eyes one brown shoe, raised now as his mother crossed her legs.

"... you can see he's nothing but a scarecrow." When his mother had taken off his shirt the doctor tapped his chest and his back with a small metal disc.

"Nothing to worry about, Mrs. Evans."

"But Julian's almost five now-"

Julian wasn't listening. He was wondering what a scarecrow was. Scarecrow, he said to himself. Scarecrow.

"Julian!" His name. Louder this time. Just outside the door. Replacing the shoe in the rack, Julian stood up and moved to the corner of the closet, stretching his arms wide around the waist of his mother's chiffon dress which, at his touch, fell in a heap to the floor.

"There you are, you wicked boy," the red-faced nurse said as Julian squinted at the rush of light when the door opened. He felt her calloused fingers pinch his ear as she led him into the hall. He stood on his toes, but she only raised her arm a little higher. "How dare you touch your little sister! How dare you! She could have been killed. Why, a whole flight of steps! Now, get in there," she commanded, pushing him ahead of her into his room. "Do you know what they do to little boys like you? Do you know? They send them away from home. You—with your sullen face—they'll send you away. You're a dangerous boy." She stormed out, locking the door behind her.

Dangerous. The street with the black honking cars was dangerous. The high open window. The kitchen matches. Julian did not know how he could be dangerous. He knew he was not a car, a window, a flaming match.

In the small upstairs bedroom cluttered with bright new and mostly unused toys—the red wagon with the real siren on the side, the cobbler's bench, blocks of every description with which he could build trains and high buildings if he'd cared to—Julian circled round and around like a dog chasing its tail. He was a tall boy—indeed he knew himself to be as tall as the garden hedge which enclosed their house—and spindly, with eyes that narrowed themselves suspiciously against the glare of his world, opening to their full brown splendour only in the presence of his mother, a trim well-groomed woman in her middle thirties.

Now, standing by the window, he looked out beyond the hedge to where the road lay winding like a discarded shipping rope in the grass, half-hoping to see his mother's car rumbling through the dust as it approached the house.

It had always seemed to Julian that his mother was very far away, farther away than the pigeons that sat in the church tower and scattered when the clock chimed. Sometimes he would see her from the window on her way to work, a scarf blowing about her throat; sometimes he would listen to her at night, and rising from his bed, would creep quietly in his pyjamas to the head of the stairs where he could hear her voice coming to him from behind the closed parlour doors, high and light, like the sounds which came from his music box. There were times, Julian remembered, when she was close to him, bending to give him a goodnight kiss, so close that he could rub his cheek against her perfumed sleeve, but, even then, his mother had seemed farther away than ever; for Julian had come to know his mother had two faces, one for himself and the other for his sister Vicky, and it was the second face, the one reserved so often for her, that he sought out and only rarely compelled. Had he done something very wrong, a long time ago, he wondered, gazing down at the yellow blooming garden flowers, something which had hurt his mother, something he could never, no matter how hard he tried, undo?

"With Julian—my God!—it was dreadful," his mother had said that Sunday as she sat on the sunny terrace pouring tea from the good silver service. Julian separated the branches of the forsythia in time to catch her frown.

". . . absolutely dreadful . . . Sugar or cream, Phyllis? . . . Strange," she continued, handing the cup to the woman called Phyllis, "with Vicky, an hour and a half—I almost didn't get to the hospital in time—but with Julian-"

"Well, the first child-"

"Even so," his mother interrupted, pausing for a moment to stir the steaming tea, "thirty-six hours is a very long time. When it was over I turned my face to the wall . . . I didn't want to see the child." She shuddered as she recalled it.

". . . Such a beautiful baby."

"Vicky?" Mrs. Evans smiled a proud smile.

"She has your eyes—yes, and around the mouth too . . . the same expression."

"Perhaps," Mrs. Evans said modestly. "Julian, on the other hand, has always been just like his father . . . Another cup?"

Julian released the branches and walked away. Just like his father. Was there something wrong with that too? He thought there was. He could tell from the tone in which it was said.

The flowers of the forsythia were darker now as the sun withdrew its beams, and, glancing across the lawn, Julian could see his mother's car parked in the driveway. And he had been there all the while, waiting at the window, and had not seen her come after all.

When Julian discovered that the small connecting door into his sister's room had been left unlocked, he went in and stood for a moment beside the blackboard watching the afternoon shadows stretch themselves in string-bean shapes along the floor, pointing out the poodle upon the rocker, the clown smiling from the shelf. Taking a piece of coloured chalk, he scribbled on a slate, then, moving, made a circle on the picture of Old King Cole, a square upon the window pane, and finally drew a long wavering line which passed first over the heads of the dolls in the corner, then below the ticking clock, coming to a stop before the crib where he printed his name in large, uneven letters. Julian. Except for the N. He could never make the N.

Although the crib had been repainted and although he could see, almost as proof of possession, his sister's pale pink dress laid across the foot, freshly pressed, with a white ribbon dipping in and out of the collar, he knew that the crib belonged to him, for he had slept in it once, before Vicky had come to the house, before he had become a big boy. When he had seen the strange men painting it, he had thought they were doing it for him. For Julian. For his birthday perhaps, for a party where he would sit at the top of a long table wearing a paper hat, as he had done before, listening to his friends singing as he leaned to blow out the candles flickering above the icing. Was it not a present his mother brought with her that day, wrapped in a blanket as she approached him? But when the flaps of the cover opened, he could see that it was not a present. Small as a doll though. But red in the face. With a mouth that screamed and often dribbled. "This is your baby sister, Julian."

And yet, there had been something special about her from the first, Julian recalled, for the people had come all day long—the grown-ups—bringing wrapped gifts of toys and strange bottles, lacey bibs, a sweater, small bonnets which settled low over her ball-like head, and finally, a great new carriage, where she could sit in the mornings on her way to the park, her small fingers clenching the embroidered coverlet, gathering smiles from the passers-by while Julian walked resentfully at her side. When she took a step, his mother clapped for joy. For a word, she was hugged. Julian did not know why. She could not eat her supper without spilling. She could not dress herself and button up all the buttons. Or tie her shoes. She could not write her name in large letters.

With a feeling that he was being watched, Julian spun around, but it was only one of the dolls, the big one that could walk and talk. Placing the doll under his arm he went to the window, and bending over, dropped it down through the tree tops, watching it fall on heavy roots below. He drew in his hand suddenly. Had someone slapped it? Or had it only been the curtain, white-fluttering above the ledge?

And why didn't they come for him? Weren't they going to give him supper, he wondered, as he opened the door slightly, but his hand trembled on the knob as he remembered another day outside the study.

"I tell you, Drew," his mother had said, glancing over her shoulder to satisfy herself that it was the wind which had pushed the study door ajar, "there's something a little bit peculiar about Julian—the way he creeps about the house, following me like a shadow."

"Nonsense," said his father, filling his pipe.

"I wish it were. Why, I found him hiding behind the curtains in the living room the other day . . . I was all alone, reading, when I saw his feet sticking out below the curtain. There was no mistaking Julian's feet."

His father removed his pipe to laugh.

"I asked him what he was doing there when he had a whole roomful of toys upstairs, and do you know, Drew, he just wouldn't answer . . . Not a word . . . Just looked up at me with those large pained eyes." Through the crack in the door Julian watched her lean closer to his father. "Drew, do you suppose—" she hesitated before speaking again— "well, I don't quite know how to put this, but he's not at all like the other boys his age . . . not at all . . . Why, Phyllis'—"

"Oh, stop it, stop it. You're just mothering him too much. What that boy needs," his father announced, rising impatiently from his armchair, "is some kind of camp life . . . away in the woods."

Julian slammed the bedroom door. Away, away. Send little boys like you away. Julian looked about for help, but the clown smiled widely with unconcern, its back against the wall, its stuffed legs dangling from the shelf. Bad boy, bad boy. But the poodle lay still across the rocking chair, its woollen chin upon its paws, asleep. Wicked, wicked, wicked, wicked, chided the clock, pointing a black finger at him as he lay on the crib, his thumb pushing desperately against the roof of his mouth. Away, away. While Old King Cole roared with laughter, his hand pressed against his round belly, his ear distracted by the music of the fiddles. And how away? Julian shivered. Like the laundry? In a pillowcase with a list pinned to the cloth? Or in a cardboard box, wrapped in thick twine and stamped with a paper stamp?

There was a wet pink haze before his eyes, and as his tears withdrew he could see from where he lay that it was his sister's dress. Julian sat up quickly and rubbed his eyes. He climbed down to the dark floor and took off his shirt and corduroys. In the small dresser where the nurse kept Vicky's things he found a pair of socks almost the same colour as the dress. He sat down and pulled them on. Too short. But he left them with the heels bulging under his arches.

In another drawer he found a pair of shoes. In another, pants with a lace border. He found a soft ribbon and he clipped it to his hair just to the left of the part.

With hurried steps he returned to the bed. Raising his arms he pushed them through the puffed sleeves, and holding his breath, he pulled the dress across his chest. Too tight. He left it unbuttoned, but tied the sash once about his waist.

He put his hand to his face and wondered if it were still sullen. He did not know much about himself, but he knew that his face was sullen, that his ears were too big, and that he had shoulders that should be pulled back, and fingers that were not to be put into his mouth, and that he had feet. He glanced down, pleased that his feet appeared smaller now, cramped as they were into the black slippers.

He had to take the shoes off when he came to the stairway, and he held them in his hands by the straps. In the downstairs hall he stopped for a moment to turn his head in the direction of the kitchen where he could see his sister Vicky eating her supper, a bib about her neck, her short legs swinging below her.

When Julian entered the living room his mother's back was towards him while the smoke from her cigarette hovered above her like a summer cloud. Beside her armchair was a small table, and beside that, a standing lamp. From time to time Julian could see his mother's slender arm reach out towards the china tray to flick away the cigarette ash. Taking one step forward he found himself within the perimeter of the bright lamplight.

Suspended from the wall as if he were some huge oil canvas, Julian saw himself in the mirror, an image in pink, framed by a blond wood frame. The light flooded about him, giving a shine to the black leather slippers, accentuating the whiteness of his legs below the billowing skirt, one placed behind the other as if he were about to curtsy, and carrying the colour of the dress to his neck, to his lips, red now as if touched by a painter's wet brush, to his cheeks which flushed deeply beneath his freckles.

In his hair lay the ribbon, as lightly poised upon a curl as a butterfly upon a leaf.

He knew that in a moment everything would be all right. That in a moment he would be nestling against her, no longer a scarecrow and dangerous; instead, beautiful, sweet as Vicky was sweet. That she would take his head between her warm hands, and, glancing down at him with love in her eyes, find him formed in her own image, feature for feature. That she would kiss his closed eyelids. Sing to him. That she would perhaps take her brush to stroke his hair about her fingers or straighten the collar of his dress. In a moment. Surely.

Julian tugged at his mother's skirt, twisting his lips into a coy, almost triumphant smile.

Jennine Capó Crucet
"How to Leave Hialeah"
From *How to Leave Hialeah* (2009)

It is impossible to leave without an excuse—something must push you out, at least at first. You won't go otherwise; you are happy, the weather is bright, and you have a car. It has a sunroof (which you call a moonroof—you're so quirky) and a thunderous muffler. After fifteen years of trial and error, you have finally arranged your bedroom furniture in a way that you and your father can agree on. You have a locker you can reach at Miami High. With so much going right, it is only when you're driven out like a fly waved through a window that you'll be outside long enough to realize that, barring the occasional hurricane, you won't die.

The most reliable (and admittedly, the least empowering) way to excuse yourself from Hialeah is to date Michael Cardenas Junior. He lives two houses away from you and is very handsome and smart enough to feed himself and take you on dates. Your mother will love him because he plans to marry you in three years when you turn eighteen. He is nineteen. He also goes to Miami High, where he is very popular because he plays football and makes fun of reading. You are not so cool: you have a few friends, but all their last names start with the same letter as yours because, since first grade, your teachers have used the alphabet to assign your seats. Your friends have parents just like yours, and your moms are always hoping another mother comes along as a chaperone when you all go to the movies on Saturday nights because then they can compare their husbands' demands—*put my socks on for me before I get out of bed, I hate cold floors, or, you have to make me my lunch because only your sandwiches taste good to me*—and laugh at how much they are like babies. Michael does not like your friends, but this is normal and to be expected since your friends occasionally use polysyllabic words. Michael will repeatedly try to have sex with you because you are a virgin and somewhat Catholic and he knows if you sleep together, you'll feel too guilty to ever leave him. Sex will be tempting because your best friend Carla is dating Michael's best friend Frankie, and Michael will swear on his father's grave that they're doing it. But you must hold out—you must push him off when he surprises you on your eight-month anniversary with a room at The Executive Inn by the airport and he has sprung for an entire five hours—because only then will he break up with you. This must happen, because even though you will get back together and break up two more times, it is during those broken-up weeks that you do things like research out-of-state colleges and sign up for community college classes at night to distract you from how pissed you are. This has the side effect of boosting your GPA.

During these same break-up weeks, Michael will use his fake ID to buy beer and hang out with Frankie, who, at the advice of an ex-girlfriend he slept with twice who's now living in Tallahassee, has applied to Florida State. They will talk about college girls, who they heard have sex with you without crying for two hours afterward. Michael, because he is not in your backyard playing catch with your little brother while your mother encourages you to swoon from the kitchen window, has time to fill out an application on a whim. And lo and behold, because it is October, and because FSU has rolling admissions and various guarantees of acceptance for Florida residents who can sign their names, he is suddenly college bound.

When you get back together and he tells you he's leaving at the end of June (his admission being conditional, requiring a summer term before his freshman year), tell your mom about his impending departure, how you will miss him so much, how you wish you could make him stay just a year longer so you could go to college at the same time. A week later, sit through your mother's vague sex talk, which your father has forced her to give you. She may rent The Miracle of Life; she may not. Either way, do not let on that you know more than she does thanks to public school and health class.

—I was a virgin until my wedding night, she says.

Believe her. Ask if your dad was a virgin, too. Know exactly what she means when she says, Sort of. Try not to picture your father as a teenager, on top of some girl doing what you and Carla call a Temporary Penis Occupation. Assure yourself that TPOs are not sex, not really, because TPOs happen mostly by accident, without you wanting them to, and without any actual movement on your part. Do not ask about butt-sex, even though Michael has presented this as an option to let you keep your semi-virginity. Your mother will mention it briefly on her own, saying, For that men have prostitutes. Her words are enough to convince you never to try it.

Allow Michael to end things after attempting a long-distance relationship for three months. The distance has not been hard: you inherited his friends from last year who were juniors with you, and he drives down to Hialeah every weekend to see you and his mother and Frankie. Still, you're stubborn about the sex thing, and still, you can't think of your butt as anything other than an out-hole. Michael has no choice but to admit you're unreasonable and dump you.

Cry because you're genuinely hurt—you love him, you do—and because you did not apply early-decision to any colleges because you hadn't yet decided if you should follow him to FSU. When the misery melts to fury, send off the already-complete applications you'd torn from the glossy brochures stashed under your mattress and begin formulating arguments that will convince your parents to let you move far away from the city where every relative you have that's not in Cuba has lived since flying or floating into Miami; you will sell your car, you will eat cat food to save money, you are their American Dream. Get their blessing to go to the one school that accepts you by promising to come back and live down the street from them forever. Be sure to cross your fingers behind your back while making this promise, otherwise you risk being struck by lightning.

Once away at school, refuse to admit you are homesick. Pretend you are happy in your tiny dorm room with your roommate from Long Island. She has a Jeep Cherokee and you need groceries, and you have never seen snow and are nervous about walking a mile to the grocery store and back. Ask the RA what time the dorm closes for the night and try to play it off as a joke when she starts laughing. Do not tell anyone your father never finished high school. Admit to no one that you left Hialeah in large part to piss off a boy whose last name you will not remember in ten years.

Enroll in English classes because you want to meet white guys who wear V-neck sweaters and have never played football for fear of concussions. Sit behind them in lecture but decide early on that they're too distracting. You must do very well in your classes; emails from the school's Office of Diversity have emphasized that you are special, that you may feel like you're not cut out for this, that you should take advantage of the free tutors offered to students like you. You are important to our university community, they say. You are part of our commitment to diversity. Call your mother crying and tell her you don't fit in, and feel surprisingly better when she says, Just come home. Book a five-hundred-dollar flight to Miami for winter break.

Count down the days left until Noche Buena. Minutes after you walk off the plane, call all your old friends and tell them you're back and to get permission from their moms to stay out later than usual. Go to the beach even though it's sixty degrees and the water is freezing and full of Canadians. Laugh as your friends don their back-of-the-closet sweaters on New Year's while you're perfectly fine in a halter top. New England winters have made you tough, you think. You have earned scores of ninety or higher on every final exam. You have had sex with one and a half guys (counting TPOs) and yes, there'd been guilt, but God did not strike you dead. Ignore Michael's calls on the first of the year, and hide in your bedroom—which has not at all changed—when you see him in his Seminoles hoodie, stomping toward your house. Listen as he demands to talk to you, and your mom lies like you asked her to and says you're not home. Watch the conversation from between the blinds of the window that faces the driveway. Swallow down the wave of nausea when you catch your mother winking at him and tilting her head toward that window. Pack immediately and live out of your suitcase for the one week left in your visit.

Go play pool with Myra, one of your closest alphabetical friends, and say, *Oh man, that sucks*, when she tells you she's still working as a truck dispatcher for El Dorado Furniture. She will try to ignore you by making fun of your shoes, which you bought near campus, and which you didn't like at first but now appreciate for their comfort. Say, Seriously chica, that's a high school job—you can't work there forever.

—Shut up with this chica crap like you know me, she says.

Then she slams her pool cue down on the green felt and throws the chunk of chalk at you as she charges out. Avoid embarrassment by shaking your head No as she leaves, like you regret sending her to her room with no dinner but she left you no choice. Say to the people at the table next to yours, What the fuck, huh? One guy will look down at your hippie sandals and ask, How do you know Myra? Be confused, because you and Myra always had the same friends thanks to the alphabet, but you've never in your life seen this guy before that night.

While you drive home in your mom's car, think about what happened at the pool place. Replay the sound of the cue slapping the table in your head, the clinking balls as they rolled out of its way but didn't hide in the pockets. Decide not to talk to Myra for a while, that inviting her to come visit you up north is, for now, a bad idea. Wipe your face on your sleeve before you go inside your house, and when your mom asks you why you look so upset tell her the truth: you can't believe it—Myra is jealous.

* * *

Become an RA yourself your next year so that your parents don't worry as much about money. Attend all orientation work-shops and decide, after a sexual harassment prevention role-playing where Russel, another new RA, asked if *tit-fucking* counted as rape, that you will only do this for one year. Around Rush Week, hang up the anti-binge drinking posters the Hall Director put in your mailbox. On it is a group of eight grinning students; only one of them is white. You look at your residents and are confused: they are all white, except for the girl from Kenya and the girl from California. Do not worry when these two residents start spending hours hanging out in your room—letting them sit on your bed does not constitute sexual harassment. Laugh with them when they make fun of the poster. Such Diversity in One University! Recommend them to your Hall Director as potential RA candidates for next year.

When you call home to check in (you do this five times a week), ask how everyone is doing. Get used to your mom saying, Fine, Fine. Appreciate the lack of detail—you have limited minutes on your phone plan and besides, your family, like you, is young and indestructible. They have floated across oceans and sucker-punched sharks with their bare hands. Your father eats three pounds of beef a day and his cholesterol is fine. Each weeknight, just before crossing herself and pulling a thin sheet over her pipe-cleaner legs, your ninety-nine-year-old great-grandmother smokes a cigar while sipping a glass of whiskey and water. No one you love has ever died—just one benefit of the teenage parenthood you've magically avoided despite the family tradition. Death is far off for every Cuban—you use Castro as your example. You know everyone will still be in Hialeah when you decide to come back.

Join the Spanish Club, where you meet actual lisping Spaniards and have a hard time understanding what they say. Date the treasurer, a grad student in Spanish Literature named Marco, until he mentions your preference for being on top during sex subconsciously functions as retribution for *his* people conquering *your* people. Quit the Spanish Club and check out several Latin American history books from the library to figure out what the hell he's talking about. Do not tell your mother you broke things off; she loves Spaniards, and you are twenty and not married and you refuse to settle down.

—We are not sending you so far away to come back with nothing, she says.

At the end of that semester, look at a printout of your transcript and give yourself a high-five (to anyone watching, you're just clapping). Going home for the summer with this printout still constitutes coming back with nothing despite the good grades, so decide to spend those months working full time at the campus movie theater, flirting with sunburned patrons.

Come senior year, decide what you need is to get back to your roots. Date a brother in Iota Delta, the campus's Latino Fraternity, because one, he has a car, and two, he gives you credibility in the collegiate minority community you forgot to join because you were hiding in the library for the past three years and never saw the flyers. Tell him you've always liked Puerto Ricans (even though every racist joke your father has ever told you involved Puerto Ricans in some way). Visit his house in Cherry Hill, New Jersey, and meet his third-generation American parents who cannot speak Spanish. Do not look confused when his mother serves meatloaf and mashed potatoes and your boyfriend calls it real home cooking. You have only ever had meatloaf in the school dining hall, and only once. Avoid staring at his mother's multiple chins. Hold your laughter even as she claims that Che Guevara is actually still alive and living in a castle off the coast of Vieques. Scribble physical notes inside your copy of Clarissa (the subject of your senior thesis) detailing all the ridiculous things his mother says while you're there: taking a shower while it rains basically guarantees you'll be hit by lightning; paper cannot actually be recycled; Puerto Ricans invented the fort. Wait until you get back to campus to call your father.

* * *

After almost four years away from Hialeah, panic that you're panicking when you think about going back—you had to leave to realize you ever wanted to. You'd thank Michael for the push, but you don't know where he is. You have not spoken to Myra since the blowout by the pool table. You only know she still lives with her parents because her mom and your mom see each other every Thursday while buying groceries at Sedano's. At your Iota brother's suggestion, take a Latino Studies class with him after reasoning that it will make you remember who you were in high school and get you excited about moving back home.

Start saying things like, What does it really mean to be a minority? How do we construct identity? How is the concept of race forced upon us? Say these phrases to your parents when they ask you when they should drive up to move your stuff back to your room. Dismiss your father as a lazy thinker when he answers, What the fuck are you talking about? Break up with the Iota brother after deciding he and his organization are posers buying into the Ghetto-Fabulous-Jennifer-Lopez-Loving Latino identity put forth by the media; you earned an A—in the Latino Studies course. After a fancy graduation dinner where your mom used your hotplate to cook arroz imperial—your favorite—tell your family you can't come home, because you need to know what home means before you can go there. Just keep eating when your father throws his fork on the floor and yells, What the fuck are you talking about? Cross your fingers under the table after you tell them you're going to grad school and your mom says, But mamita, you made a promise.

* * *

Move to what you learn is nicknamed The Great White North. Tell yourself, this is America! This is the heartland! Appreciate how everyone is so nice, but claim Hialeah fiercely since it's all people ask you about anyway. They've never seen hair so curly, so dark. You have never felt more Cuban in your life, mainly because for the first time, you are consistently being identified as Mexican or something. This thrills you until the beginning-of-semester party for your grad program: you are the only person in attendance who is not white, and you're the only one under five foot seven. You stand alone by an unlit floor lamp, holding a glass of cheap red wine. You wish that Iota brother were around to protect you; he was very big; people were scared he would eat them; he had *Puro Latino* tattooed across his shoulders in Olde English Lettering. Chug the wine and decide that everyone in the world is a poser except maybe your parents. You think, *what does that even mean—poser?* Don't admit that you are somewhat drunk. Have another glass of wine and slip Spanish words into your sentences to see if anyone asks you about them. Consider yourself very charming and the most attractive female in your year, by far—you are *exotic*. Let one of the third-year students drive you home after he says he doesn't think you're okay to take a bus. Tell him, What, puta, you think I never rode no bus in Miami? Shit, I grew up on the bus. Do not tell him it was a private bus your parents paid twenty dollars a week for you to ride, along with other neighborhood kids, because they thought the public school bus was too dangerous—*they* had actually grown up on the busses you're now claiming. Your dad told you stories about bus fights, so you feel you can wing it as the third-year clicks your seatbelt on for you and says, That's fascinating—what does *puta* mean?

Spend the rest of that summer and early fall marveling at the lightning storms that you're sure are the only flashy thing about the Midwest. Take three months to figure out that the wailing sounds you sometimes hear in the air are not in your head—they are tornado sirens.

* * *

As the days grow shorter, sneak into tanning salons to maintain what you call your natural color. Justify this to yourself as healthy. You need more Vitamin D than these Viking people, you have no choice. Relax when the fake sun actually does make you brown, rather than the play-dough orange beaming off your students—you have genuine African roots! You knew it all along! Do not think about how, just like all the other salon patrons, you reek of drying paint and burnt hair every time you emerge from that ultraviolet casket.

Date the third-year because he finds you *fascinating* and asks you all sorts of questions about growing up in *el barrio*, and you like to talk anyway. More importantly, he has a car, and you need groceries, and this city is much colder than your college home—you don't plan on walking anywhere. And you are lonely. Once the weather turns brutal and your heating bill hits triple digits, start sleeping with him for warmth. When he confesses that the growth you'd felt between his legs is actually a third testicle, you'll both be silent for several seconds, then he will growl, It doesn't actually *function*. He will grimace and grind his very square teeth as if you'd just called him *Tri-Balls*, even though you only said it in your head. When he turns away from you on the bed and covers his moon-white legs, think that you could love this gloomy, deformed person; maybe he has always felt the loneliness sitting on you since you left home, except for him, it's because of an extra-heavy nut-sack. Lean toward him and tell him you don't care—say it softly, of course—say that you would have liked some warning, but that otherwise it's just another fact about him. Do not use the word *exotic* to describe his special scrotum. You've learned since moving here that that word is used to push people into some separate, freakish category.

Break up with him when, after a department happy hour, you learn from another third-year that he's recently changed his dissertation topic to something concerning the Cuban-American community in Miami. He did this a month ago—*didn't he tell you?* On the walk to the car, accuse him of using you for research purposes.

—Maybe I did, he says, But that isn't why I dated you, it was a *bonus*.

Tell him that being Cuban is no more a bonus than, say, a third nut. Turn on your heel and walk home in single-digit weather while he follows you in his car and yelps from the lowered window, Can't we talk about this? Call your mother after cursing him out in front of your apartment building for half an hour while he just stood there, observing.

—Oh please, she says, her voice far away, Like anyone would want to read about Hialeah.

Do not yell at your mother for missing the point.

Change advisors several times until you find one who does not refer to you as *the Mexican one* and does not ask you how your research applies to regular communities. Sit in biweekly off-campus meetings with your fellow Latinas, each of them made paler by the Great White North's conquest over their once-stubborn pigment. They face the same issues in their departments—the problem, you're learning, is system-wide. Write strongly worded joint letters to be sent at the end of the term. Think, *Is this really happening? I am part of this group*? Look at the dark greenish circles hanging under their eyes, the curly frizz poking out from their pulled-back hair and think, *Why did I think I had a choice*?

Call home less often. There is nothing good to report.

—Why can't you just *shut up* about being Cuban, your mother says after asking if you're still causing trouble for yourself. No one would even notice if you flat-ironed your hair and stopped talking.

Put your head down and plow through the years you have left there because you know you will graduate: the department can't wait for you to be gone. You snuck into the main office (someone had sent out an email saying there was free pizza in the staff fridge) and while your mouth worked on a cold slice of pepperoni, you heard the program coordinator yak into her phone that they couldn't wait to get rid of the troublemaker.

—I don't know, she says seconds later, Probably about spics, that's her only angle.

You sneak back out of the office and spit the pepperoni out in a hallway trashcan because you're afraid of choking—you can't stop laughing. You have not heard the word *Spic* used in the past decade. Your parents were *Spics*. *Spics* is so seventies. They would not believe someone just called you that. Crack up because even the Midwest's slurs are way behind the East Coast. Rename the computer file of your dissertation draft *Spictacular*. Make yourself laugh every time you open it.

*   *   *

Embrace your obvious masochism. Make it your personal mission to educate the middle of the country about Latinos by living there just a little longer. But you have to move—you can't work in a department that your protests helped to officially document as *Currently Inhospitable to Blacks and Latinos*, even if it is friendly to disabled people and people with three testicles.

Decide to stay in the rural Midwest partly for political reasons: you have done what no one in your family has ever done—you have voted in a state other than Florida. And you cannot stand Hialeah's politics. You monitored their poll results via the Internet. Days before the election, you received a mass email from Myra urging you to vote for the candidate whose books you turn upside down when you see them in stores. Start to worry you have communist leanings—wonder if that's really so bad. Keep this to yourself; you do not want to hear the story of your father eating grasshoppers while in a Cuban prison, not again.

Get an adjunct position at a junior college in southern Wisconsin, where you teach a class called The Sociology of Communities. You have seventy-six students and, unlike your previous overly polite ones, these have opinions. Several of them are from Chicago and recognize your accent for what it actually is—not Spanish, but Urban. Let this give you hope. Their questions about Miami are about the beach, or if you'd been there during a particular hurricane, or if you've ever been to the birthplace of a particular rapper. Smile and nod, answer them after class—keep them focused on the reading.

At home, listen to and delete the week's messages from your mother. She is miserable because you have abandoned her, she says. You could have been raped and dismembered, your appendages strewn about Wisconsin and Illinois, and she would have no way of knowing.

—You would call if you'd been dismembered, right? the recording says.

It has only been eight days since you last spoke to her.

The last message you do not delete. She is vague and says she needs to tell you something important. She is crying. You call back, forgetting about the time difference—it is eleven-thirty in Hialeah.

Ask, What's wrong?

—Can I tell her? she asks your father. He says, I don't care.

—Tell me what?

Tuck your feet under you on your couch and rub your eyes with your free hand.

—Your cousin Barbarita, she says, Barbarita has a brain tumor.

Say, What, and then, Is this a fucking joke?

Take your hand away from your eyes and stick your thumbnail in your mouth. Gnaw on it. Barbarita is eleven years older than you. She taught you how to spit and how to roller-skate. You cannot remember the last time you talked to her, but that is normal—you live far away. Then it comes to you. Eight months ago, at Noche Buena, last time you were home.

—It's really bad. They know it's cancer. We didn't want to tell you.

Sigh deeply, sincerely. You expected something about your centurial great-grandmother going in her whiskey-induced sleep. You expected your father having to cut back to one pound of beef a day because of his tired heart.

Ask, Mom, you okay? Assume her silence is due to more crying. Say, Mom?

—She's been sick since February, she says.

Now you are silent. It is late August. You did not go back for your birthday this year—you had to find a job, and the market is grueling. Your mother had said she understood. Also, you adopted a rabbit in April (you've been a little lonely in Wisconsin), and your mother knows you don't like leaving the poor thing alone for too long. Push your at-the-ready excuses out of the way and say, Why didn't you tell me before?

She does not answer your question. Instead she says, You have to come home.

Tell her you will see when you can cancel class. There is a fall break coming up, you might be able to find a rabbit-sitter and get away for a week.

—No, I'm sorry I didn't tell you before. I didn't want you to worry. You couldn't do anything from up there.

Wait until she stops crying into the phone. You feel terrible—your poor cousin. She needs to get out and see the world; she has never been further north than Orlando. When she was a teenager, she'd bragged to you that one day, she'd move to New York City and never come back. You think (but know better than to say), Maybe this is a blessing in disguise. When you see her, you will ignore the staples keeping her scalp closed over her skull. You will pretend to recognize your cousin through the disease and the bloated, hospital gown-clad monster it's created. You will call her Barbarino like you used to, and make jokes when no one else can. Just before you leave—visiting hours end, and you are just a visitor—you'll lean in close to her face, so close your nose brushes the tiny hairs still clinging to her sideburns, and say, Tomorrow. Tomorrow I'm busting you out of here.

Your mother says, She died this morning. She went fast. The service is the day after tomorrow. Everyone else will be there, please come.

You are beyond outrage—you feel your neck burning hot. You skip right past your dead cousin and think, *I cannot believe these people. They have robbed me of my final hours with my cousin. They have robbed Barbarita of her escape.*

You will think about your reaction later, on the plane, when you try but fail to rewrite a list about the windows of your parents' house in the margins of an in-flight magazine. But right now, you are still angry at being left out. Promise your mother you'll be back in Hialeah in time and say nothing else. Hang up, and book an eight-hundred-dollar flight home after emailing your students that class is canceled until further notice.

Brush your teeth, put on flannel pajamas (even after all these winters, you are still always cold), tuck yourself in to bed. Try to make yourself cry. Pull out the ladybug-adorned to-do list pad from the milk crate you still use as a nightstand and write down everything you know about your now-dead cousin.

Here's what you remember: Barbarita loved papaya and making jokes about papaya. One time, before she even knew what it meant, she called her sister a papayona in front of everyone at a family pig roast. Her mother slapped her hard enough to lay her out on the cement patio. She did not cry, but she stormed inside to her room and did not come out until she'd said the word *papayona* out loud and into her pillow two hundred times. Then she said it another hundred times in her head. She'd told you this story when your parents dragged you to visit Barbarita's mom and her newly busted hip while you were home during one of your college breaks. Barbarita's mother, from underneath several white blankets, said, I never understood why you even like that fruit. It tastes like a fart.

Barbarita moved back in with her parents for good after her mom fractured her hip. The family scandal became Barbarita's special lady-friend, with whom she'd been living the previous eight years. You remember the lady-friend's glittered fanny pack—it always seemed full of breath mints and rubber bands—how you'd guessed it did not come off even for a shower. Barbarita took you to Marlins games and let you drink stadium beer from the plastic bottle if you gave her the change in your pockets. She kept coins in a jar on her nightstand and called it her retirement fund. She made fun of you for opening a savings account when you turned sixteen and said you'd be better off stuffing the cash in a can and burying it in the backyard. She laughed and slapped her knee and said, No lie, I probably have ninety thousand dollars under my mom's papaya tree.

Look at your list. It is too short. Whose fault is that? You want to say God; you want to say your parents. You want to blame the ladybug imprinted on the paper. You are jealous of how she adorns yet can ignore everything you've put down. Write, *My cousin is dead and I'm blaming a ladybug.* Cross out my cousin and write *Barbarita*. Throw the pad back in the crate before you write, *Am I really this selfish?*

Decide not to sleep. The airport shuttle is picking you up at 4 am anyway, and it's already 1. Get out of bed, set up the automatic food dispenser in your rabbit's cage, then flat-iron your hair so that it looks nice for the funeral. Your father has cursed your frizzy head and blamed the bad genes on your mother's side since you sprouted the first tuft. Wrap the crispy ends of your hair around Velcro rollers and microwave some water in that I-don't-do-Mondays mug that you never use (the one you stole off the grad program coordinator's desk right before shoving your keys in the drop box—you couldn't help stealing it: you're a spic). Stir in the Café Bustelo instant coffee your mother sent you a few weeks ago in a box that also contained credit card offers you'd been mailed at their address and three packs of Juicy Fruit. The spoon clinks against the mug and it sounds to you like the slightest, most insignificant noise in the world.

Sit at the window seat that convinced you to sign the lease to this place even though your closest neighbor is a six-minute drive away. Listen to the gutters around the window flood with rain. Remember the canal across from your parents' house, how the rain threatened to flood it twice a week. There is a statue of San Lázaro in their front yard and a mango tree in the back. Lázaro is wedged underneath an old bathtub your dad half buried vertically in the dirt, to protect the saint from rain. The mango tree takes care of itself. But your father made sure both the mango tree and San Lázaro were well guarded behind a five-foot-high chain-link fence. The house's windows had bars—rejas—on them to protect the rest of his valuables, the ones living inside. You never noticed the rejas (every house around for blocks had them) until you left and came back. The last night of your first winter break in Hialeah, just before you went to sleep, you wasted four pages—front and back—in a notebook scribbling all the ways the rejas were a metaphor for your childhood: *a caged bird, wings clipped, never to fly free; a zoo animal on display yet up for sale to the highest-bidding boyfriend; a rare painting trapped each night after the museum closes.* Roll your eyes—these are the ones you remember now. You didn't mean it, not even as you wrote them, but you wanted to mean it, because that made your leaving an escape and not a desertion. Strain to conjure up more of them—it's got to be easier than reconciling the pilfered mug with your meager list about your cousin. But you can't come up with anything else. All you remember is your father weeding the grass around the saint every other Saturday, even in a downpour.

Peek through the blinds and think, *It will never stop raining*. Pack light—you still have clothes that fit you in your Hialeah closet. Open the blinds all the way and watch the steam from your cup play against the reflected darkness, the flashes of rain. Watch lightning career into the flat land surrounding your tiny house, your empty, saint-less yard. Wait for the thunder. You know, from growing up where it rained every afternoon from three to five, that thunder's timing tells you how far you are from the storm. You cannot remember which cousin taught you this—only that it wasn't Barbarita. When it booms just a second later, know the lightning is too close. Lean your forehead against the windowpane and feel the glass rattle, feel the vibration pass into your skull, into your teeth. Keep your head down; see the dozens of tiny flies, capsized and drained, dead on the sill. Only the shells of their bodies are left, along with hundreds of broken legs that still manage to point at you. If you squint hard enough, the flies blend right into the dust padding their mass grave. And when your eyes water, even these dusty pillows blur into an easy, anonymous gray smear.

Your hands feel too heavy to open the window, then the storm glass, then the screen, to sweep their corpses away. You say out loud to no one, I'll do it when I get back. But your words—your breath—rustle the burial ground, sending tiny swirls of dust toward your face. It tastes like chalk and dirt. Feel it scratch the roof of your mouth, but don't cough—you don't need to. Clear your throat if you want; it won't make the taste go away any faster.

Don't guess how long it will take for the clouds to clear up; you're always wrong about weather. The lightning comes so close to your house you're sure this time you'll at least lose power. Close your eyes, cross your fingers behind your back. Swallow hard. The windowsill's grit scrapes every cell in your throat on its way down. Let this itch convince you that the lightning won't hit—it can't, not this time—because for now, you're keeping your promise. On the flight, distract yourself with window lists and SkyMall magazine all you want; no matter what you try, the plane will land. Despite the traffic you find worse than you remember, you'll get to Hialeah in time for the burial—finally back, ready to mourn everything.

Ron A. Austin
"Muscled Clean Out the Dirt"
From *Black Warrior Review* (2017)

Salesmen from Catacombs Incorporated couldn't solve every ghetto problem. They offered no solutions for gross poverty, quick death, or the weariness that congests heads and chests like a brutal cold, but they did offer one product that could restore blighted North St. Louis neighborhoods: Geb's Magic Red Bricks.

Nobody asked how those salesmen could haul wooden carts heavy with hundreds of bricks, bulky arms straining under cheap suits, halos of sweat adorning baldheads. Nobody asked why only The Finest Women could buy a brick. Nobody asked why the bricks were irregular, some of them bloated with muscle and green veins, some of them sporting coarse pubic hair, all of them pulsing with the faint heartbeat of a wounded animal. Nobody consulted apocryphal books of the Bible, divined explanations from prophetic dreams, scattered chicken bones. Nobody asked how the bricks could flex and twitch.

So The Finest Women spent the whole summer commanding their husbands, brothers, uncles, sons, and grandsons to commandeer the remains of vacant lots and condemned houses, slice machetes and hatchets through bramble and boughs of honeysuckle, bang sledge-hammers through crumbling walls and cracked foundations, cart off rubble and junk, thump shovels in hard earth, and sow Geb's Magic Red Bricks where the land had been raided, salted, turned to soot.

The most shrewd men wiped sweat from their chins and told the women *y'all done really lost your damn minds this time. You got us out here in this heat, moaning and groaning, humping and bumping—and for what? Some old hoo-doo, abra-cadabra bullshit? Call us some sad, sorry bastards—but y'all don't listen no way. God bless, and count yourselves lucky we love you.* And those same shrewd men shut the hell up and gawked when they felt the earth quake and saw brand new homes muscle clean out the dirt.

Nobody prayed for understanding or reckoned Catacombs Incorporated's proprietary alchemy, but one fact was clear: The Finest Women grew The Finest Homes. Yellow-boned Miss Bobbi with that good, long hair grew a Victorian mini-mansion complete with a pond and a waterfall in the backyard. Miss Deborah with the thick thighs and all that mess men like grew a storybook cottage flaunting stained glass windows. Miss Sasha with the sculpted arms grew a French chateau boasting high ceilings and handsome wrought-iron fences. Miss Mimi with the sweet plum lips grew a colonial farmhouse, constellations of chandeliers swaying above the grand staircase. And Miss Claudia with her fashion sense and that practiced smile that could cut you in two grew a Craftsman featuring a fireplace big enough to roast three full-grown boars, tail to snout. How folks came from miles around, knelt, and kissed Miss Claudia's steps, gray stone cooling scorched lips.

Soon bunches of colorful new houses bloomed throughout the neighborhoods like strange, fresh flowers in a garden of rot, but not everybody marveled. Brutish old bachelors, widowed men, sick and crippled women, and the plain ugly cried foul—God had favored the beautiful again.

Those lonesome, ugly folks couldn't get Catacombs Incorporated salesmen to slang them one stinking brick for all the jewels in the world. And with no grand future in front of them, these three, four, five-times cursed men and women looked behind them, scoured the past, and asked how day-to-day life got so bad in the first place—who ruined their homes? Who was to blame?

Donovan with the crooked eye blamed redlining and the petty white folks who'd rather watch you starve than call you neighbor. Wart-faced Cynthia blamed it on the Devil—she had seen him clopping through alleys, eating chow mein out of the garbage, soiling water fountains, grinding his horns against cinderblocks, scratching hexes in wet concrete. Lynn with the hand mangled in a factory accident blamed it on physical and spiritual depression. *Keep beating folks down bad enough, and they won't know what else to do* she said.

But Miss Gail didn't waste time speculating. Petty white folks, the Devil Himself, and depression conspired against her neighborhood—true—but it was those runaways she used to take in who brought ruin into her home, tracked it all through her hallways like mud.

Those badass kids used to headbutt holes in walls, rip copper wires out of fuse boxes, hide dead rats in the back of cabinets and vents, piss in any quiet place they could saturate with their scent, and pretend to never smell that sour, mournful stink lurching through the house like a dying slug. Gail would cuss them, jam spoonfuls of Borax down their throats, lick their backs and butts with belts, and that never did bunk. She wised up eventually and stopped housing thankless punks, but the damage was already done.

Poison mushrooms sprang from slimy carpet and urine-soaked corners. Fuse boxes snarled, smoked, spat sparks. Fractured support beams groaned and shifted like battered ribs. Those rats hidden in cabinets and vents dried out, mangy fur and organs atomized into fine dust—but it was worse than all that. Ruptured water pipes wept sludge. Fatty lumps bulged under linoleum like lymphoma. Distended bellies sagged from warped ceilings. Toxic malice had oozed out of those badass kids, seeped into the flesh of the house, compromised the structure with industrial necrosis.

The home Gail had paid for with her youth came closer to condemnation every day, and there was nobody to blame but those trifling, good-for-nothing, badass kids. She had sheltered them only so they could grow bold enough to leave and look back at her like she was no better than shit on a horseshoe.

No wonder their own folks had put them out, and Gail had to wonder: why did she even bother? Did maternal instinct beat out common sense? Did loneliness wrap a cord around her throat and pull? These questions were horseflies nagging at her neck, gnawing on her sense of self-worth—understand that Gail didn't enjoy playing the fool. She had acted like a chump, but she knew better.

She knew you couldn't raise up the dead, turn water into wine, squeeze blood from a stone. She knew you couldn't make nobody love you, give one damn about you, not by the strength of God, not by the strength of your back, not by the strength of whatever the hell it is you want to believe.

*   *   *

And Gail couldn't call it, not at all—what did those heifers have that made them so much better than her, so much more deserving? After cultivating callouses on her hands and heart with years of hard labor, Gail wasn't beautiful. At fifty-something she didn't gently settle into her age like other women—na'll.

Years of bitter failure stewed in her system, became acid and melted the fat off her hips, stole her softness. But while she lost softness and grace, she gained strength, hardening herself where depression would wither others. She survived by her wit, the grit in her blood, the power in her legs. She had no use for fair skin, refined airs, a thick-ass. And she wasn't fool enough to trust what everybody else called miraculous, but she had seen those brand new houses struggle out of the ground like gigantic tuber vines with her own eyes—and forget about being one of The Finest Women—she'd take her fair share of the feast and good fortune, even if she had to carve it off a man's back.

And now don't get too tough on her—she didn't want nothing fancy. No need for 4,000 square feet. She just wanted a simple house that was warm in the winter, cool in the summer, and big enough for guests, if she felt like it. She wanted a house too pretty to destroy, a comfortable home you'd be ashamed to see crumble.

* * *

None of the Catacombs Incorporated salesmen were strangers to Gail. Most of them had grown up just around the corner from her, owed her a favor or two. She stalked each man for days, memorizing his route and referencing her mental ledger of physical, mental, and spiritual debts.

Maurice's soft-ass owed her his teeth after she saved him from getting beaten to death by a mob of young roughnecks. She took a punt to the ribs snatching him from the gauntlet of fists and feet. He never said thanks. He just blew a clot of blood out of his nose, nodded and said *good lookin' out, cuz'*. And then Keenan's little mooching-butt owed her groceries after that time his refrigerator died. He ate at her house for a whole month, and the chump never did wash a dish no matter how many times she cussed him, thumped his head.

Those boys brandished hard shells of denial and pride that she'd have to crack if she wanted to get to their squishy guts—but why even bother when Big Jay owed her the most and couldn't stand humiliation? Gail knew shame worked as well as napalm on him, would burn away his skin, expose tender nerves she could twang and strum.

* * *

On a Sunday when the heat index hit infernal, Big Jay ducked into a gas station for a snack and a cold drink and left his cart of Geb's Magic Red Bricks by pump five. He came out of the gas station peeling the wrapper off of a Honey Bun and found Miss Gail perched on the back of his cart. She wore a nice lounge dress, black pumps, and her only pair of pearl earrings to come and clown on him.

"Gotcha', fat boy!" she hooted. "Now I coulda' stole your whole supply, every last pebble, but I don't believe in thievery. A damn thief should get both hands chopped off, and if that don't fix 'em—"

Big Jay shot her a weary glance, shook his head, and told her, "Hell to the na'll, Miss Gail—I ain't tryna' hear all that. C'mon and get down from there. I know what you're thinking, but I'm telling you right now—I can't use your business."

Gail leapt off the cart and shouted, "And just why the hell not?"

"Because I don't need it. And you really don't want what I got to give anyway—you just think you do, with your greedy self." Big Jay jerked the cart handle with a grunt, and trudged on, wheels squealing and rocking over cobblestone.

Gail chased him down the block and cornered him by a field overrun with knapweed, lank dandelions and wild onions. "Hold on a goddamn minute! I ain't done talking to you! I said hold up!"

Big Jay sighed, wheeled back around to face her, and asked, "Whatever could I do for you, young lady?"

"Awwww, don't you sweet talk me. I ain't got time to be playing games. Now, look—" She retrieved a leather clutch from her bra, opened it, and pulled out a few crisp twenties. She lifted her chin and told him, "—all I want is one of them bricks. My money is green. Look twice if you need to."

Big Jay yanked a handkerchief from his breast pocket and wiped his face. "I'm not one to turn down good money, but you don't understand. You can't exactly buy these bricks in stores. And to tell the truth, I don't think you could even afford it."

She closed in on Big Jay. "Boy, do I look like I'm blind, deaf, or dumb?"

"No. You seem quite lively to me."

"Then don't talk to me like I'm senseless—I seen the funny shit going on in this neighborhood, and I can't say what it is, but folks is getting rich off it, and all I want is what's mine." Gail spanked the cash on her thigh and nodded.

"I hear you, Miss Gail, I really do, but listen to me when I say—"

Gail put up a hand. "I don't want nothing from you but a pathetic lump of clay, like what you sold everybody else."

"As much as it pains me, Miss Gail, I have to say no, and before you get in my face talking all this and that, what you need to do is—"

"You don't tell me what I need to do! Now let me tell you something, you big, fat—"

"Oh, lord, here she come, Bad Mama Yuk-Mouth, 'bout to tell me what it really is."

Gail folded her arms and frowned. She'd never admit it, but she hated when folks called her Bad Mama Yuk-Mouth, The Li'l' Beastie with the Big Yap, Five Whole Feet Of Oh Fuck You—all nicknames that marked her as a crazy-ass, inner-city Baba Yaga who snatched kids off the street. She knew the tall tales men told their sons and nephews: keep acting a damn ass, and I'll send you on over to Miss Gail's house. She'll take a straw and suck the marrow out your bones. She'll lock you in her cellar, feed your guts to the rats, make shoes from your rind. They talked all that mess and got her all wrong—Gail wasn't cruel, she was pragmatic. If a man didn't move, she'd cut him—ain't that elementary? And rather than run away from a bad reputation, she leaned into it, used the weight like a cudgel.

"You damn right," she said. "Big Bad Mama Yuk-Mouth go'n dig in that ass."

"Miss Gail. Please. I'm trying to do you a favor."

"Do me a favor? You two-faced sonofabitch—do me a favor? Let me tell you 'bout doing somebody a favor."

Gail scrunched up her jaw and launched into a lengthy list of everything she had ever done for Big Jay. When silverfish infested his bed, who drove them away with cloves and dried lavender? When he had little money for a winter coat, who sewed him a jean jacket lined with wool on the cheap? When he slashed his arm open on a piece of scrap metal, who stitched him up nice with a few lengths of fishing line?

Gail knew Big Jay's laugh and cry, the smell and color of his blood. He might've been the man on the block right then, his cool fist coiled around what everybody wanted, but to Gail, he'd always be that little boy blubbering into his T-shirt, crying for her help. Try as he might, he couldn't deny their kinship.

She told him "And I didn't make you do shit for none of that, did I?"

"Na'll. You didn't ask me for a damn," he said.

"I didn't ask for a damn! Did I say, 'Fat boy, take out my trash?'"

"No."

"Did I say, 'Fat boy, clean my stove?'"

"No."

"Did I say, 'Fat boy, sweep my porch?'"

"No, no, and no. Miss Gail, you know you didn't put me to work."

"You damn right—and you mean to tell me, all I want is one single, solitary lump of clay you might find in the street, and I'm putting you out?."

"Miss Gail—let me say it one more time: I'm looking out for you."

"Ahhhh, you keep that jive for some ol' bucket-head down the block. Looking out for me? You ain't looking out for shit. Boy, all y'all bastards the same. Got the memory of a damn flea. Feed you soup one minute, and you pissing on my head the next."

Big Jay sponged sweat off his clavicle and snapped his towel in frustration. "Miss Gail, did you know you are a bitter brew?"

"And did you know if I chopped the fat off the back of your neck, I could eat for a week?"

"Alright, Mama Yuk-Mouth. I tried to tell you, but you gotta see for yourself. If you ain't busy, let's go take a look at one of them houses you say you want so, so bad. You better hurry up, before some good sense gets a hold of me."

Big Jay tugged that cart, his bison back rippling. Bricks in his cart contracted and quivered. Mosquitoes swarmed, nuzzled the clay's thick veins, drank from the flesh.

Gail trudged alongside him, her lips tightened into a thin scowl. "I am not hounding you all over this goddamn city, boy."

"Yes you will, Miss Gail. You sho'll will. I know you—you can't help yourself."

* * *

On their way Big Jay and Gail passed abandoned storefronts sagging under the sun like spoiled fruit. Soiled clothes, scattered appliance parts, and busted furniture crowded vacant lots and alleys, all that junk offered up to ancestral spirits who had been mutilated, eyes gouged and tongues cut so they couldn't warn their children. Gail remembered the owners of each storefront and recited their brief histories for Big Jay.

She pointed to an imploded plaza on the corner of Hebert and said, "You remember Miss Judy and them? They used to run a second hand shop right there. She always bought the toasters and whatnot I rustled out the trash, never haggled with me too bad. And I never known a woman smart like her. She could knock a dead TV with a wrench and make it cut on, good as new, blow on a busted blender and make it grind, sho'll could."

She nodded at the sinkhole next to the church on Palm and said, "And Mr. Isiah and his folks held down a corner store right there—right there—for 'bout three generations. Sho'll did. Way back when, they was the first black folks in this part of town to own anything, and they did it right, fed everybody. If you drained his grease traps and swept out the smoker real good, he'd hook you up with a fat burger, a bag of chips, a Vess soda, and a candy bar, too, if he could give one sorry shit about you. He didn't feel that way about many folks—but like I said—he still fed everybody."

When Gail and Big Jay passed what was left of the laundromat and drycleaners she used to own, searing pain split her chest like an axe through dry wood. The dead *thok* of sudden hurt echoed loud in the cavernous spaces behind her breastbone. Calluses on her heart didn't prove thick enough to blunt the razor edge of personal disaster. She stopped at the rubble, jabbed fists in her lean hips, spat.

Gail was never a religious woman, but at one time, she had believed in the God of Labor. She felt his presence in the hum of her washing machines, saw his jeweled eye wink in the blue pilot lights beneath gas-heated dryers, heard his cantos in the igniter clicks, smelled his musk in hot iron. The ritual of work transmuted his tears and sweat into detergent and starch. She swept and hefted and ironed and scrubbed and steamed through fourteen-hour days, believing the only good in the world comes of what you make with your own two hands. And for a time, the God of Labor rewarded her with prosperity. Gail had never been known for her smile or a kind word, but folks put faith in her forearms, the knots in her back, the steel in her spine—why did the God of Labor forsake her and Miss Judy and Isiah and so many other folks who slaved for a little bit of something? Weren't they good disciples? Didn't they preach his proverbs, praise him with toil?

After her business soured and folks chose to wear clothes rank with stains, body odor, and shame, Gail renounced her faith and believed in nothing but what was right in front of her face. For all that work and good will, she had nothing to show for it but a busted-ass house, a beat-up truck, a bony rump, and a good lead on a magic red brick.

Big Jay snapped his handkerchief, mopped his brow, and told Gail, "I remember when you was cold-blooded with a can of starch. You used to put that crease in some jeans so damn sharp, you could cut the head off a catfish. When we all said and done with this foolishness, why don't you take a crack at my suit? I sweat through it 'bout twelve times today, stomping 'round in this heat. It could use some freshening."

"Jay, I wish you would quit playing with me," Gail said. "I ain't got time for all this."

"You was the one reminiscing, and I'm serious about this suit. You know I'll pay you well."

"I don't want nothing from you but what I asked for."

"Depends on if you'll still want it, Miss Gail. Bear with me for one hot minute—can you do that? You know they say patience is a virtue and—"

"What other wisdom you got for me, boy? Good things come to those who wait? God only helps he who helps himself? I done heard all that nonsense, and every bit of it is a lie. It's the shit you tell schoolboys and chumps—now is you gon' sell me that brick or not?"

"It depends on if you're pig-headed enough to still want one. It ain't much further. Just past the water tower, we'll bust a right, a left, a right, hunker down, and take a good long look at Miss Claudia's house. Then I want you to tell me what it really is."

*　*　*

Big Jay and Gail peeked at Miss Claudia's house from behind the corner of a defunct church across the street. And from where Gail stood, Miss Claudia's house was handsome as ever.

The stone stacked porch squatted tough, brawny columns supported a neat gable, ornamental grilles framed double hung windows, smoke chugged from a fire pit in the front yard, and Gail didn't see the problem. Damn whatever Big Jay had to say about it. She told him, "Man, you need to quit playing with me—that house looks like a million bucks."

Big Jay pinched her shoulder lightly, like a child at the movies getting hyped before the big scene, and told her, "Hold up and be easy for a minute—you'll see."

Gail swatted his hand and watched the smoke build and roll out that fire pit. A stiff wind slapped a whiff of smoke her way, and her nose curdled at the stench. That putrid smoke didn't smell like dead leaves or wood or coal—na'll. It stank like charred fat and goat hide. Bad meat and burnt spam. She tucked her face in the collar of her dress and grunted. Big Jay pinched her shoulder again and said, "Look, Miss Gail. There they go."

A throng of about a dozen men wearing grimy work clothes filed out of the front door and congregated on the porch. They wore tattered t-shirts and jeans and had the crinkled faces and smoldering eyes of war veterans. Worn hatchets and machetes glinted at their sides. Gail figured Miss Claudia had hired them to renovate the house to her liking, and Gail never understood how some women possessed that power of hovering in the sky like a queen bee, hypnotizing fools into servitude with honey-dipped suggestions.

The men passed a bottle of King Cobra and a pack of cigarettes among themselves. They smoked and drank for a spell without saying a word and then bowed their heads in brief prayer. After that, they snapped on rubber gloves and medical masks, donned trash bag ponchos, and split into two groups. A man with a beard like bramble led one group back inside, and a man with a sledge-hammer at his side stationed his men at various points outside the house. The fire snapped and popped. On Sledge-hammer's silent command, the men attacked.

They raised their blades and hammers, slashed and beat the sides of the house, yielding great spurts of blood, the dull crunch of bone, and the monotonous thud of hard work—Thok! Thok! Thok! With every blow, the house shuddered and groaned like a beast of burden enduring ritual slaughter, but the men kept right on chopping and bashing, no passion in their strokes. Vinyl siding peeled off like dead skin, revealing a throbbing mess of muscle and fat, cartilage and tendon, a tight matrix of veins.

Now somebody could have told Gail. Somebody could have told her before she got to fussing with Big Jay and stepping all over his hustle. They could have told her about how unnatural flaws manifested in those houses grown from Geb's Magic Red Bricks.

Miss Deborah's stained glass windows scabbed over and peeled. Miss Sasha's high ceilings developed a bad case of razor burn, meat bumps swelling heavy and low. Half-formed femurs jutted from Miss Mimi's chandeliers. Miss Bobbi's waterfall bloated with dead frogs and teratomas big as depth charges. And a fat, anaconda-sized tongue unfurled from Miss Claudia's fireplace, flailed and thrashed furniture, flung slobber all over walls.

And somebody could've told her about how The Finest Women fell apart bad as their brand new houses. Red blotches broke across fair skin. Long hair fell out in ragged clumps. Rumpled bags darkened under eyes. Robust bosoms and bottoms deflated and sagged, and those fine women couldn't scrub away the stink of hot tar rising from their armpits.

Wart-faced Cynthia hooted *see! I told y'all—I done told y'all The Devil is at work, and he a damn lie!* Donovan shook his head and said *now don't go falling for the smoke screen. Keep in mind who's behind it all.* Lynn clucked and told everybody *my, my, my—I guess what they say is true: all that glitters ain't gold. My, my, my.* Uglier than all that, The Finest Women kept their brand new homes despite the monstrous flaws and toll on their lives. They pasted themselves in concealer, donned wigs and sunglasses, strapped bosoms and bottoms in uplifting hosiery, doused themselves in sharp, sweet perfume, and commanded their husbands, brothers, uncles, sons, and grandsons to roll that rogue tongue back inside Miss Claudia's fireplace, shave scabs off Miss Deborah's windows, slather Miss Sasha's high ceilings with antibiotic ointment, saw bones off Miss Mimi's chandeliers, and dredge Miss Bobbi's pond for hunks of flesh.

But the men raised their fists and hollered *Hell to the na'll! Y'all on a whole other level with this one, chasing nonsense. Keep carrying on like this and there won't be nothing left of you but some scraps of dog meat and rags on the floor. Now c'mon back home—y'all knew this was too good to be true—what are four walls worth if they crash on your head?* And after The Finest Women refused, their men took up tools and got busy.

Brambly Beard and his men reemerged from the house carrying that giant tongue rolled up in a raggedy, old curtain. The pink tongue tip lapped out of the end of the curtain, twitching and dripping saliva. They tossed the whole mess into that fire. Grease sputtered, and that stench flared something awful.

Gail stroked her jaw as if she'd been punched, but before she could holler, Big Jay raised his hands defensively and said, "Now you see what's up, don't you Miss Gail? I ain't been jiving you. Nobody coulda' seen this bullshit coming. Me personally, I thought it was a miracle just like the next fool—until I seen what these houses amounted to, but by then, it was too late." He took out his handkerchief, daubed beads of sweat jumping out his brow. "I paid for them bricks with my soul like everybody else, and now I got a damn quota to fill. But you don't have to get involved. That's all I been saying.

"Not everybody here sees you the way I do, Miss Gail—we can both agree on that— but you're looking at one man who appreciates what you done for him. Most folks would rather let you die of thirst than spit in a thimble, but not you. Nobody said you was sweet—sho'll didn't say that—but you 'bout the only one I know who plays fair enough. And if I can help it, I'm not trying to see you suffer for nothing."

Thok! Thok! Thok! Brambly Beard hit an artery by the front door, and a stream of blood shot out and splattered the sidewalk, but Gail didn't recoil in disgust—na'll. She watched the men work with keen interest and cocked her ear, listened to the new canto the God of Labor sang beneath the clang of metal on bone and the unsettling groans. She understood there was praise in destroying as well as building—how could she forget?

She knew rubble could feed new life, be the bed for seed and strong root. She figured that might've been her problem, how she catalogued and idolized what was no more and would never be again, how she failed to balance all that mess and lay foundation for something new.

Big Jay opened his mouth again, but Gail cut him off and said, "Jay-Jay, I see you care, I really do. But you don't know me. Not at all. Not like you think you do. I ain't seen nothing like this before—sho'll ain't—but I done had my world flipped upside down more times than I can count, and it ain't nothing new," she nodded, "And I ain't never had nobody tell me what I can or can't do. I'm not about to start now. And I been telling you I'm not the sort of woman that wilts. Boy, I don't break. What happens to this man or the next is they problem. And I couldn't give less of a good goddamn. I promise you."

*   *   *

Gail and Big Jay circled back to the rubble that used to be Gail's laundromat. She flapped her money at him and said, "Now how much is it? And don't be on no bullshit."

Big Jay pocketed his handkerchief and fixed his face in a somber half-moon. He pulled a bright knife from his back pocket. "Like I said, Miss Gail, I can't use your money."

He jerked that bright knife across Gail's scalp and palms too fast for her to fight back. Her price for one of Geb's Magic Red Bricks was her blood and a lock of her hair—and what else? She didn't know, and she didn't ask—she was too pissed. She bit back stinging pain, clenched a fist and tried swinging on him, but he disappeared—that's right— goddamn disappeared in a blink, fat ass, cart, and all. Insults flew out of Gail's mouth like shaggy bats. She cussed and raged until her tongue bloated and stuck to the roof of her mouth. Once she was spent, she opened her fists and found a pancreas-shaped brick pulsing in her palm.

That thing had a faint heartbeat. It gave off clammy warmth, seethed spittle, and stank like sweat and hard-worked hands. And you know Gail wasn't stupid—she knew that damn thing might have contained the crushed bones of pharaohs, stones from the Lake of Fire, the atomized ovaries of a high priestess, the petrified spunk of a false god, the third gonad of Beelzebub himself. But she really didn't give a good goddamn.

What withered others and became their doom was something else entirely to Gail. For her, Geb's Magic Red Brick was an opportunity, not a curse. She knelt and cleared the rubble, scraped her hands on jagged concrete and bent metal, anointed the ground with her blood and sweat, overturned a layer of rich black soil, took up a stone smooth enough for digging, and punched the dirt—*Thok! Thok! Thok! Thok! Thok!*

NOTES

Chapter 1

1   Parul Sehgal, "'Pessoa' is the Definitive and Sublime Life of a Genius and His Many Alternate Selves," *New York Times*, July 13, 2021, https://www.nytimes.com/2021/07/13/books/review-pessoa-biography-richard-zenith.html.

2   Sonya Chung, "What We Teach When We Teach Writers: On the Quantifiable and the Uncertain," *The Millions* Online, October 29, 2010, https://themillions.com/2010/10/what-we-teach-when-we-teach-writers-on-the-quantifiable-and-the-uncertain.html.

3   Frantz Fanon, *The Wretched of the Earth* (1961) (New York: Grove Press, 2004), 131.

4   Adam Mars-Jones, "Muffled Barks, Muted Yelps," *London Review of Books* 42, no. 6 (March 19, 2020), https://www.lrb.co.uk/the-paper/v42/n06/adam-mars-jones/muffled-barks-muted-yelps.

5   Matthew Salesses, *Craft in the Real World: Rethinking Fiction Writing and Workshopping* (New York: Catapult, 2021), xix.

6   Jennine Capó Crucet, "A Prognosis," in *My Time Among the Whites: Notes from an Unfinished Education* (New York: Picador, 2019), 175–96 (191).

7   Eudora Welty, "Is Phoenix Jackson's Grandson Really Dead?," *Critical Inquiry* 1, no. 1 (September 1974): 219–21.

8   See Parul Sehgal, "The Case Against The Trauma Plot," *The New Yorker* (January 3 and 10, 2022), https://www.newyorker.com/magazine/2022/01/03/the-case-against-the-trauma-plot. "Trauma has become synonymous with backstory," Sehgal writes, "but the tyranny of backstory is itself a relatively recent phenomenon—one that, like any successful convention, has a way of skirting our notice."

9   In *New York Review of Books* email newsletter, interviewed by Maya Chung and Daniel Drake: August 7, 2021.

10 From Simone Weil, *The Iliad: A Poem of Force*: I reencountered this in a notebook, offered in class w/ John Elder at Bread Loaf/Orion Environmental Writers Conference, 2017.

11 Interview in *New York Review of Books* email newsletter, August 7, 2021.

12 C. J. Hribal, "Comic and Cosmic Distance," in *A Kite in the Wind: Fiction Writers on their Craft*, ed. Andrea Barrett and Peter Turchi (San Antonio: Trinity University Press, 2011), 73.

13 https://apublicspace.org/academy/anne-elliott-friction-and-resistance.

14 Claire Messud, "Why I Write," From *LitHub* Online, August 2015; reprinted in *Kant's Little Prussian Head and Other Reasons Why I Write: An Autobiography In Essays* (New York: W. W. Norton, 2020).

Chapter 2

1 I've written about this in my previous books *The Hands-On Life: How to Wake Yourself Up and Save the World* (Cascade Books, 2018) and *The Writer's Eye: Observation and Inspiration for Creative Writers* (Bloomsbury Academic, 2018).

2 "But doesn't the Internet help writers get published and make money from their work?" Um—no. When was the last time you paid for written "content" online? See William Deresiewicz, *The Death of the Artist: How Creators Are Struggling to Survive in the Era of Billionaires and Big Tech* (Henry Holt, 2020).

3 Philosopher L. A. Paul compares becoming a citizen of social media to becoming a vampire—the person evaluating the results of the choice you've made by joining social media is so changed by the results of that choice that you lose access to the person you were before, who made the choice in the first place. See "Do You Want to Become A Vampire?" on the podcast *Your Undivided Attention*, August 12, 2021, https://www.humanetech.com/podcast/39-do-you-want-to-become-a-vampire.

4 For more about Perec, including some writing exercises he inspires, see my book *The Writer's Eye*.

5 For three short videos that explain this reality simply and well, see Jaron Lanier, "Jaron Lanier Fixes the Internet," *New York Times*, September 23, 2019, https://www.nytimes.com/interactive/2019/09/23/opinion/data-privacy-jaron-lanier.html.

6 Charlotte Chandler, *I, Fellini* (New York: Cooper Square Press, 2001), 148.

7 Fiona Pitt-Kethley, *The Autobiography of Fiona Pitt-Kethley, Volume One: My Schooling* (Hastings, East Sussex: Tamworth Press, 2000), 51.

8 Kristen Roupenian, "The Author, The Work, and the No. 1 Fan," *The New Yorker*, August 5, 2021, https://www.newyorker.com/culture/personal-history/the-author-the-work-and-the -no-1-fan.

9 August 7, 2017, https://lithub.com/writers-protect-your-inner-life.

10 See my book *The Hands-On Life*. Sam Lipsyte sketches a subtle, alarming connection in his *Harper's* essay "Ghosting the Machine: Humans, Robots, and the New Sexual Frontier" (May 2022): in Las Vegas, he explores the philosophy of "sexbots" and visits a casino, where slot machines are engineered to activate similar systems of neurological reward.

11 Craig Morgan Teicher, "Poetry Is Doing Great: An Interview with Kaveh Akbar," August 18, 2021, https://www.theparisreview.org/blog/2021/08/18/poetry-is-doing-great-an-interview -with-kaveh-akbar/#more-154082.

12 See Taylor Lorenz, "For Creators, Everything Is For Sale," *New York Times*, March 11, 2021, https://www.nytimes.com/2021/03/10/style/creators-selling-selves.html.

13 See Lanier, "Jaron Lanier Fixes the Internet."

14 Students and I heard Groff describe this process at Minnesota Public Radio's "Talking Volumes" event on September 14, 2021 in St. Paul, MN.

15 What writer Kristen Iskandrian describes as a passing mood about Twitter is my more-or-less permanent mood: "I go on Twitter and think: *Who cares?* It feels suddenly like a room of people who can't dance, trying to bust some sick move." (See "What I Deserve," *Poets & Writers,* May/June 2022: 31.)

16 In March 2022, a student surveyed thirty random fellow students in our campus's student union about the amount of time they spent per day on TikTok, as logged by the app: two hours a day was the average response.

Chapter 3

1   Jim Shepard, "Generating History from Fiction and/or Fact," in *The Writer's Notebook* (Portland: Tin House Books, 2009), 241–53.

2   In an interview with Garth Greenwell, "The Art of Poetry No. 105," *The Paris Review* 229 (Summer 2019), https://www.theparisreview.org/interviews/7424/the-art-of-poetry-no-105 -frank-bidart.

3   Lisa Cohen, "Hilton Als: The Art of the Essay No. 3," *The Paris Review* 225 (Summer 2018), https://www.theparisreview.org/interviews/7178/the-art-of-the-essay-no-3-hilton-als.

4   The writer Benjamin Percy, also a former student of Hannah's, borrowed this phrase for his excellent book on fiction writing, *Thrill Me* (Minneapolis: Graywolf Press, 2016).

5   In contributors' section of *Lapham's Quarterly* XII, no. 3 (Summer 2020): 9.

6   Shout-out here to weird books: Johanna Sinisalo's *Not Before Sundown (Troll)* (2000; English translation 2003), which I learned about from my colleague Andy Hageman, Marian Engel's *Bear* (1976), and Alan Garner's *Red Shift* (1973). Also a really great list at https://bookriot .com/i-got-your-weird-right-here-100-wonderful-strange-and-unusual-novels/, which doesn't feature any of the three, although it *does* feature Colson Whitehead's *The Intuitionist* (Chapters 4 and 8)!

7   Lise Kildegaard has a great video introduction to the Square Stories, via the Museum of Danish America (https://www.youtube.com/watch?v=UUgoX9EadRw). See also her conversation with Daniel A. Rabuzzi, "Keep Danish Weird: Lise Kildegaard Talks About Translating Louis Jensen's *firkantede historier* ('Square Stories')," *Hopscotch Translation*, May 8, 2022, https://hopscotchtranslation.com/2022/05/08/keep-danish-weird/.

8   https://enkare.org/2016/11/09/inside-fiction-account-namwali-serpell/.

9   https://www.printmag.com/post/the-morbid-roadside-ad-poetry-of-burma-shave.

10 Even better: "Within this vale / of toil / and sin / your head grows bald / but not your chin- use / Burma-Shave."

11 Quoted in Colum McCann, "His Life Was Too Boring For A Memoir, So He Wrote Ireland's," *New York Times*, March 15, 2022, https://www.nytimes.com/2022/03/15/books/ review/fintan-otoole-we-dont know ourselves-ireland.html.

12 Nicholas Triolo, "Five Questions for Megan Mayhew Bergman, Author of *How Strange A Season*," *Orion*, March 29, 2022, https://orionmagazine.org/2022/03/megan-mayhew -bergman-book-interview-how-strange-a-season.

13 Victor Shklovsky, "Art as Technique," in *Russian Formalist Criticism: Four Essays*, trans. and intro. by Lee T. Lemon and Marion J. Reis, 2nd ed. (Lincoln and London: University of Nebraska Press, 2012), 12.

14 See Megan Marz, "The Novel According to Bezos," *The Baffler*, October 21, 2021, https:// thebaffler.com/latest/the-novel-according-to-bezos-marz.

15 Patricia Lockwood, *No One Is Talking About This* (New York: Riverhead Books, 2021), 42.

16 Zoe Lescaze, "How Should Art Reckon with Climate Change?" *New York Times*, March 25, 2022, https://www.nytimes.com/2022/03/25/t-magazine/art-climate-change.html.

17 Everett's novel *The Trees* (2021) speaks to the America of George Floyd's murder with deliberate surrealism: at every murder site is found the body of Emmett Till.

18 https://www.newyorker.com/magazine/2010/02/01/fjord-of-killary. See also David S. Wallace, "Can We Find A New Way To Tell The Story of Climate Change?" *The New Yorker*, September 15, 2021.

19 James Baldwin, "The Creative Process," in *The Price of the Ticket: Collected Nonfiction 1948–1985* (New York: St. Martin's, 1985), 315.

20 See Anton Troianovski, "Russia Takes Censorship to New Extremes, Stifling War Coverage," *New York Times*, March 4, 2022, https://www.nytimes.com/2022/03/04/world/europe/russia -censorship-media-crackdown.html. Journalist John Sweeney's *Killer in the Kremlin* (New York: Bantam Press, 2022), developed from the reporting detailed in his podcast *Taking on Putin*, describes in harrowing detail the fates of journalists, dissidents, and others who have publicly opposed Putin, in Russia and elsewhere.

21 Altan was released from prison in April 2021.

22 See the compilation interview "Looking Back at Salman Rushdie's *Satanic Verses*," *The Guardian*, September 14, 2012, https://www.theguardian.com/books/2012/sep/14/looking -at-salman-rushdies-satanic-verses. As this book goes to press, Rushdie has been shockingly attacked on stage; see https://www.nytimes.com/2022/08/13/nyregion/rushdie-video -stabbed-ny.html.

23 See open letter to Boris Johnson signed by and published in *The Economist*, "Why Britain Must Shelter Afghan Journalists," August 4, 2021, https://www.economist.com/asia/2021/08 /04/why-britain-must-shelter-afghan-journalists.

24 *James Baldwin: The FBI File*, edited and with an introduction and notes by William J. Maxwell (New York: Arcade Publishing, 2017), 7.

25 See interview with reporter Craig Timberg on NPR's "Fresh Air," "Leaks Reveal Spyware Meant To Track Criminals Tracked Activists Instead," July 29, 2021, https://www.npr.org /programs/fresh-air/2021/07/29/1022255677/fresh-air-for-july-29-2021-reporter-craig -timberg-on-spyware?showDate=2021-07-29.

26 "Twenty Questions With Kevin Barry," *The Times Literary Supplement*, https://www.the-tls .co.uk/articles/twenty-questions-kevin-barry/.

27 Cohen, "Hilton Als: The Art of the Essay No. 3."

28 Patricia Lockwood, "Pull Off My Head," *London Review of Books* 43, no. 16 (August 12, 2021), https://lrb.co.uk/the-paper/v43/n16/patricia-lockwood/pull-off-my-head.

29 From Robin Hemley, *Turning Life into Fiction* (Minneapolis: Graywolf Press, 2006), 6.

30 "As a student in 2008," writes Helena Betya Rubenstein, "I participated in the workshop of a story about a Black man's murder by white plainclothes police. The writer was the only Black person in what poets Juliana Spahr and Stephanie Young have called the creative writing industry's 'mainly white room.' Per convention, he was silent as we debated whether the story was 'too familiar' or 'unbelievable,' the obviousness of the racism it portrayed resulting in a kind of cliché. When we were finished, the writer blurted, 'But it actually happened!' He'd been rewriting the 2006 murder of Sean Bell." https://lithub.com/toward-changing-the -language-of-creative-writing-classrooms.

31 Vivian Gornick, *The Situation and the Story: The Art of Personal Narrative* (New York: Farrar Straus Giroux, 2001), 91.

32 "No One Thinks In Esperanto," *New York Review of Books*, August 19, 2021, https://www .nybooks.com/articles/2021/08/19/wislawa-szymborska-advice-column/.

33 For a recent public controversy around this issue, see Robert Kolker, "Who Is The Bad Art Friend?" *New York Times*, October 7, 2021.

34 In *Fly Boy in the Buttermilk: Essays on Contemporary America* (New York: Simon & Schuster, 1992). See also Colm Toibin, "Snail Slow" (*London Review of Books*, January 27, 2022, https://www.lrb.co.uk/the-paper/v44/n02/colm-toibin/snail-slow) on how the Irish novelist John McGahern wrestled childhood abuse into novels that caused his family and hometown to disown him. "Images of old horror started to come at me without warning and with horrible violence, atmospheres of evil," McGahern wrote. "For weeks I lived in a state of pure panic. They'd always come suddenly. And the only time I was free of them was strangely when I was working with them."

35 In *A Radiant Life: The Selected Journalism of Nuala O'Faolain* (New York: Harry Abrams, 2011).

36 Qtd. in Edwidge Danticat, *The Art of Death: Writing the Final Story* (Minneapolis: Graywolf Press, 2017), 7.

37 Saul Bellow, *Humboldt's Gift* (New York: The Viking Press, 1975), 262.

38 Andrew O'Hagan (*Mayflies*) in LRB Podcast, September 16, 2020.

39 See Lisa Appignanesi, *Mad, Bad, and Sad: Women and the Mind Doctors* (New York: W. W. Norton, 2008) and Elinor Cleghorn, *Unwell Women: Misdiagnosis and Myth in a Man-Made World* (New York: Dutton, 2021).

40 Gilman, "Why I Wrote the Yellow Wallpaper?" https://www.nlm.nih.gov/exhibition/the literatureofprescription/education/materials/WhyIWroteYellowWallPaper.pdf. See also Denise D. Knight, "'All the Facts of the Case': Gilman's Lost Letter to Dr. S. Weir Mitchell," *American Literary Realism* 37, no. 3 (Spring 2005): 259–77 (19 pages). Available via JSTOR.

41 Ibid.

42 Ibid.

Chapter 4

1 After I drafted this chapter, I learned about the blog "Writing with Color," https://writingwithcolor.tumblr.com/, which I cite later. I use "Writing In," my original wording, rather than "Writing With" to avoid plagiarism and to maintain my mental image of "color" as the mindset and medium, like ink, with which words are created. My mental picture is *color*, flowing like ink from the barrel of a pen, although I also appreciate the valences of meaning that "with" brings.

2 From the Preface to her *Collected Stories* (New York: Harcourt Brace, 1980), xi.

3 Catherine Halley, "Queering Jack Sheppard," *JSTOR Daily*, June 26, 2018, https://daily.jstor .org/queering-jack-sheppard/.

4 Minrose Gwin, *Remembering Medgar Evers: Writing the Long Civil Rights Movement* (Athens: University of Georgia Press, 2013), 33.

5 Michele Filgate, "The Infinite World," *Poets & Writers*, May/June 2018: 31–7.

6 https://writingwithcolor.tumblr.com/post/95853987919/do-you-have-suggestions-for-good -sites-for-researching#notes.

7 Rosemarie Garland-Thomson, "Building a World That Includes Disability." Phi Beta Kappa Lecture at Luther College, Decorah, Iowa, April 13, 2022.

8 Bernadine Evaristo, *Manifesto: On Never Giving Up* (New York: Grove Press, 2021), 212–13.

Notes

9   "Sarah Sentilles on writing about people you know." *LitHub*'s "The Craft of Writing" email newsletter, June 1, 2022.

10 Found this in Sojourners "voice of the day" email October 9, 2020.

11 Stephen Kuusisto, "The AWP and Disability Inclusion," https://academeblog.org/2017/02/13/the-awp-and-disability-inclusion/, referred to in the article "Outsiders on the Inside" by Michele Sharpe, *Poets & Writers,* September/October 2018: 54–61 (60).

12 Nisi Shawl, "Transracial Writing for the Sincere," *Science Fiction and Fantasy Writers of America* Website, December 4, 2009, http://www.sfwa.org/2009/12/transracial-writing-for-the-sincere/.

13 John Enger, "A Church Organ's Stop With Symbolism Centuries Deep." Minnesota Public Radio News, June 20, 2018, https://www.mprnews.org/story/2018/06/20/a-church-organs-stop-with-symbolism-centuries-deep.

14 Thea Lim, "Because the Story Was Mine," *The Paris Review* Blog, September 4, 2018, https://www.theparisreview.org/blog/2018/09/04/because-the-story-was-mine/.

15 James Baldwin and Clayton Riley, "James Baldwin on Langston Hughes," *The Langston Hughes Review* 15, no. 2 (Winter 1997): 125–37 (126). Thanks to Romaney MuGoodwin for this article.

16 Nisi Shawl and Cynthia Ward, *Writing The Other: A Practical Approach* (Seattle: Aqueduct Press, 2005), 11.

17 Jan Grue, *I Live a Life Like Yours: A Memoir,* translated from the Norwegian by B. L. Crook (New York: Farrar Straus Giroux, 2021), 202. See also the short documentary by and about Samuel Habib, a twenty-one-year-old college student with cerebral palsy, at https://www.nytimes.com/2022/05/17/opinion/my-disability-roadmap-adulthood.html.

18 Quoted in Stewart, Sophia, "Imperfect Voices," *The Baffler,* April 20, 2022, https://thebaffler.com/latest/imperfect-voices-stewart.

19 Quoted in *The Common,* issue 23, Fall 2022.

20 Morgan Parker's book of poems *Magical Negro*, as she's said in an NPR interview, attempts to restore some inner life to these stock characters. https://www.npr.org/2019/02/11/693587521/magical-negro-carries-the-weight-of-history. See also Sesali Bowen, "What the Hell Is 'Big Little Lies' Doing to Bonnie's Mom?" July 16, 2019, https://nylon.com/big-little-lies-elizabeth-trope. This is also described in tvtropes.org.

21 https://www.theonion.com/ask-an-elderly-black-woman-as-depicted-by-a-sophomore-c-1819584785.

22 I'm indebted to Sea Orme for this point.

23 Milan Kundera, *The Unbearable Lightness of Being* (1984; New York: HarperCollins, 2004), 251.

24 James Baldwin, "Everybody's Protest Novel," in *Collected Essays* (Library of America, 1998), 12.

25 See the title essay of Leslie Jamison's *The Empathy Exams* (Minneapolis: Graywolf Press, 2014) and Namwali Serpell, "The Banality of Empathy," https://www.nybooks.com/daily/2019/03/02/the-banality-of-empathy/.

26 Grue, *I Live a Life Like Yours*, 48.

27 Avishai Margalit, "Human Dignity Between Kitsch and Deification," *The Hedgehog Review,* Fall 2007, https://hedgehogreview.com/issues/human-dignity-and-justice/articles/human-dignity-between-kitsch-and-deification.

28   https://livingwithamplitude.com/article/cyborg-jillian-weise/; see also Weise's essay "Going Cyborg," *New York Times*, January 8, 2010, https://www.nytimes.com/2010/01/10/magazine /10lives-t.html?_r=0. In *I Live a Life Like Yours,* Jan Grue writes, "I myself have become a cybernetic organism, a cyborg […] from the time I got my first wheelchair. Between my organic body and the machine in which I maneuver myself every day there is a blurry line, my pulse quickens whenever something or someone bumps into the wheelchair, it is an instinctive reaction" (51).

29   Andrew Ross Sorkin, "Paul Volcker, at 91, Sees 'a Hell of a Mess in Every Direction,'" *New York Times*, October 23, 2018, https://www.nytimes.com/2018/10/23/business/dealbook/ paul-volcker-federal-reserve.html.

30   https://findingblake.org.uk/tygers-of-wrath-lesson-in-dissent/.

31   Thanks to Levi Bird for suggesting "the gay best friend" as a stereotype to discuss here.

32   From Magogodi Makhene's website, http://www.magogodimakhene.com/news/2017/5/24/ city-press.

33   Kathryn Shattuck, "Benedict Cumberbatch Has Heard Your Confusion About 'The Power of the Dog,'" *New York Times,* February 8, 2022, https://www.nytimes.com/2022/02/08/movies/ benedict-cumberbatch-power-of-the-dog-oscar.html.

34   Rebecca Makkai, "How To Write Across Difference," *LitHub.com,* June 19, 2018, https:// lithub.com/how-to-write-across-difference/.

35   Joan Didion, "The Women's Movement," *New York Times*, July 30, 1972, https://www .nytimes.com/1972/07/30/archives/the-womens-movement-women.html.

36   Cohen, "Hilton Als: The Art of the Essay No. 3."

37   Joumana Khatib, "'I Just Had to Do My Emotional Homework': How A 30-Year-Old Wrote A Family Saga," *New York Times,* June 21, 2019, https://www.nytimes.com/2019/06/21/ books/claire-lombardo-most-fun-we-ever-had.html.

38   Makkai, "How to Write Across Difference."

39   Makkai, "How to Write Across Difference."

40   Shawl, "Transracial Writing for the Sincere."

41   "Writing the Other Roundtable: How to Stay in Your Lane," August 31, 2016, http:// writingtheother.com/roundtable-stay-lane/.

42   Zakiya Dalila Harris, *The Other Black Girl* (New York: Atria Books, 2021), 19.

43   Rumaan Alaam, "Mirror Writing," *The New Yorker*, August 16, 2021: 36.

44   https://writingwithcolor.tumblr.com/search/why+we+always+gotta+be+slaves. Edward P. Jones's historical novel *The Known World* (2003) examines Black Americans as slaves and slaveowners.

45   If you've wondered this, check out the story of John Blanke, trumpeter in Henry VIII's court, Miranda Kaufman's *Black Tudors* (2017), and David Olusoga's *Black and British: A Forgotten History* (2017).

46   https://writingwithcolor.tumblr.com/search/why+we+always+gotta+be+slaves.

47   Reactions to *Bridgerton*'s casting have varied. Critic Kristen Warner writes, "[*Bridgerton*] has positioned itself as a kind of representational Switzerland—neither shying away from the fact that its characters of color are visibly different from their white counterparts, nor bringing to bear the ways in which their racial difference has historical implications. It's a neutral-neutral racial positioning in an era of 'representation matters,' in which feeling seen is only connected with aesthetics. Can you see your body type, skin tone, or hair texture on

the screen? Good, our work here is done." (https://www.thecut.com/2022/04/bridgertons -season-two-has-a-diversity-problem.html) One commenter on this article points out that showrunner Shonda Rhimes is Black; another writes, "Can we not just enjoy the fantasy of TV anymore? I am a Black woman and this is a refreshing show that doesn't need to teach Race 101. We have enough poorly executed shows that display 'wokeness' and this show is a great escape from the BS. Let's just enjoy it for what it is."

48   David Treuer, *The Heartbeat of Wounded Knee: Native America from 1890 to the Present* (New York: Riverhead Books, 2019), 453.

49   Laura Da', "Q&A: David Treuer of Pantheon," *Poets & Writers,* March/April 2022, https:// www.pw.org/content/qa_david_treuer_of_pantheon.

50   See https://www.the-tls.co.uk/articles/private/alice-clarke-fiction-kindness/.

51   https://www.youtube.com/watch?v=XTZKYEimq2Y. in a podcast from the London Review Bookshop (June 18, 2019).

52   Sarah Hughes, "Edna O'Brien On Turning 90," *The Guardian*, December 13, 2020, https://www .theguardian.com/books/2020/dec/13/edna-obrien-90-ireland-greatest-writer-final-novel.

53   Sean O'Hagan, "Edna O'Brien: I Want to go Out as Someone Who Spoke the Truth," *The Guardian*, August 25, 2019, https://www.theguardian.com/books/2019/aug/25/edna-obrien -interview-new-novel-girl-sean-ohagan.

54   Ibid.

55   Charles Taylor, "In Defiance of Staying in One's Lane: On Edna O'Brien's *Girl*," *Los Angeles Review of Books*, November 28, 2019, https://lareviewofbooks.org/article/in-defiance-of -staying-in-ones-lane-on-edna-obriens-girl/.

56   Alisha Gaines, *Black For A Day: White Fantasies of Race and Empathy* (Chapel Hill: UNC Press, 2017), 2.

57   Shawl, "Transracial Writing for the Sincere."

58   Makkai, "How to Write Across Difference."

59   Andre Aciman, *Call Me By Your Name* (New York: Farrar Straus Giroux, 2007), 5.

60   Hilary Mantel, *The Giant, O'Brien* (New York: Henry Holt, 1998), 14.

61   Grue, *I Live a Life Like Yours*, 74.

62   https://www.boaeditions.org/blogs/main/71654469-jillian-weise-talks-disability-labels-and -writing-with-words-apart.

63   Jesse McCarthy, "The Master's Tools," in *Who Will Pay Reparations on My Soul?: Essays* (New York: W. W. Norton, 2021), 13.

64   https://www.lrb.co.uk/podcasts-and-videos/podcasts/the-lrb-podcast/blind-spots.

65   McCarthy, "The Master's Tools," 21.

66   https://www.chicagomag.com/Chicago-Magazine/May-2020/Oral-History-ACT-UP -Chicago-AIDS/.

67   See *Times Literary Supplement,* August 13, 2021: 24.

Chapter 5

1   Frederick Reiken, "The Author-Narrator-Character Merge: Why Many First-Time Novelists Wind Up With Flat, Uninteresting Protagonists," in *A Kite in the Wind: Fiction Writers on*

their Craft, ed. Andrea Barrett and Peter Turchi (San Antonio: Trinity University Press, 2011), 3–24.

2   Rock, "The Telling That Shows," 227–40.

3   Consider the long tradition of creepy first-person narrators, from Robert Browning's "My Last Duchess" (1842), Gilman's "The Yellow Wallpaper" (see Chapter 3 Craft Studio), Eudora Welty's "Where Is the Voice Coming From?" (1963), Stanley Elkin's "A Poetics for Bullies" (1965), and Jim Shepard's "Boys Town" (2010), to Vladimir Nabokov's *Lolita* (1955), John Lanchester's *The Debt to Pleasure* (1996), and Valerie Martin's *Property* (2003), with Ralph Ellison's *Invisible Man* (1952) and Claire Messud's *The Woman Upstairs* (2013) as special cases.

4   *LitHub*'s "The Craft of Writing" newsletter, August 11, 2021, https://link.lithub.com/view /602eabbd180f243d654b8ae4epj1i.27jv/c38f7f3a.

5   In the fall of 2019, student Juhl Kuhlemeier became the first in my career to submit a third-person story from the point of view of a nonbinary character who used the pronoun "they." I'll include that as a third-person pronoun here.

6   Catherine Steindler, "Deborah Eisenberg, The Art of Fiction No. 218," *The Paris Review* 204 (Spring 2013), https://www.theparisreview.org/interviews/6203/the-art-of-fiction-no-218 -deborah-eisenberg.

7   Seriously, you really should. I heard about *Vera* for the first time on the *Slightly Foxed* book podcast in April 2022, catching only a reference to it as "the possible inspiration for Daphne DuMaurier's *Rebecca*." Knowing no more than that, I looked up the text on Project Gutenberg and devoured the whole thing that night. The experience of reading it *without* knowing exactly what's coming is genuinely startling—addictive and unforgettable. Until then, I'd known Elizabeth Von Arnim only as the author of the novel on which the film *Enchanted April* is based. Boy, was I wrong. Twice married to aristocrats, lover of H. G. Wells, she's one of those Badass Relatively Little-Known Female Authors of the Past on a list that also includes Margaret Cavendish, Aphra Behn, Charlotte Dacre, and Mary Elizabeth Braddon. Look them up!

8   Deborah Triesman, "Tommy Orange on Native Representation," *The New Yorker*, March 19, 2018, https://www.newyorker.com/books/this-week-in-fiction/fiction-this-week-tommy -orange-2018-03-26.

9   "Tommy Orange Reads 'The State,'" *The Writer's Voice (New Yorker Podcast)*, https://www .newyorker.com/podcast/the-authors-voice/tommy-orange-reads-the-state.

10 Jennine Capó Crucet, "How First-Generation College Students Do Thanksgiving Break," *New York Times*, November 18, 2017, https://www.nytimes.com/2017/11/18/opinion/sunday /college-thanksgiving-alone.html.

11 Melissa Scholes Young, "How to Leave and Why You Stay: An Interview with Jennine Capó Crucet," *Fiction Writers Review*, August 11, 2011, https://fictionwritersreview.com/interview /how-to-leave-and-why-you-stay-an-interview-with-jennine-Capó-crucet/.

12 The YouTube clip is called "Close Talker," from Episodes 18 and 19, "The Raincoats" of *Seinfeld*, Season 5, aired April 28, 1994, https://www.youtube.com/watch?v =nWw15UgPubY.

13 Howard Mittelmark and Sandra Newman, *How Not to Write a Novel: 200 Classic Mistakes and How to Avoid Them—A Misstep-by-Misstep Guide* (New York: Collins, 2008), 68.

14 Rock, "The Telling That Shows," 227–40.

15 https://www.writerstudio.com/wp-content/uploads/2018/01/Shepard_rln.pdf.

16   Aimee Liu, "On Being a Student Again," https://www.goddard.edu/goddard-mfa-writing/on-being-a-student-again/.

17   From Elizabeth Eslami's website, https://elizabetheslami.com/2013/07/the-story-and-the-question/.

18   Stephen Kearse, "The Essential Octavia Butler," *New York Times*, January 15, 2021, https://www.nytimes.com/2021/01/15/books/review/the-essential-octavia-butler.html.

19   *Art of Subtext*, 129.

Chapter 6

1   Drew Johnson, "Reality Is Not Conventional: An Interview with Deborah Eisenberg," *LitHub.com,* September 25, 2018, https://lithub.com/reality-is-not-conventional-an-interview-with-deborah-eisenberg/.

2   Liana Finck, "Liana Finck on How to Write Like a Cartoonist," *LitHub*'s "The Craft of Writing" email newsletter, April 13, 2022, https://link.lithub.com/view/602eabbd180f243d654b8ae4gaalq.270u/bf06612d.

3   *How Not To Write a Novel*, 28.

4   From Kate Bowler's *Everything Happens* podcast, https://katebowler.com/episode-7-alan-alda-full-transcript/.

5   Christopher Flavelle, "Scorched, Parched, and Now Uninsurable: Climate Change Hits Wine Country," *New York Times,* July 18, 2021, https://www.nytimes.com/2021/07/18/climate/napa-wine-heat-hot-weather.html.

6   Benjamin Percy, "Making the Extraordinary Ordinary," in *Thrill Me: Essays on Fiction* (Minneapolis: Graywolf Press, 2016), 65–75.

7   Jill Lepore, "Are Robots Competing For Your Job?" *The New Yorker,* February 25, 2019, https://www.newyorker.com/magazine/2019/03/04/are-robots-competing-for-your-job.

8   Reem Abu-Baker, "43.2 Feature: An Interview with Ron A. Austin," https://bwr.ua.edu/43-2-feature-an-interview-with-ron-a-austin/.

9   Ibid.

10 From Woolf's journal: "30 August 1923—I have no time to describe my plans. I should say a good deal about *The Hours* [which became *Mrs. Dalloway*], and my discovery: how I dig out beautiful caves behind my characters: I think that gives exactly what I want; humanity, humor, depth. The idea is that the caves shall connect and each come to daylight at the present moment."

11 Quoted in Susan Bell's marvelous book *The Artful Edit* (NewYork: WW Norton, 2007), 52, to which I'm indebted for my knowledge of this anecdote.

12 Ibid., 54.

13 Described in her appearance at MPR's "Talking Volumes" at the Fitzgerald Theatre in St. Paul, MN, on September 14, 2021, which students and I attended.

14 Sharon Marcus, "The Places Where Things Blur: Namwali Serpell on *The Old Drift*," April 10, 2020, https://www.publicbooks.org/the-places-where-things-blur-namwali-serpell-on-the-old-drift/.

15 I began using this term with encouragement of my then-colleague, visiting assistant professor of religion (now attorney) Dr. Alyssa Henning, who invited me to lead a workshop for her students called "Reading the Bible Like the Rabbis: An Introduction to Midrash" (Religion 239, January 6, 2017, Luther College).

16 Found in the Wikipedia entry for *midrash*.

17 Also see the anthologies *My Mother She Killed Me, My Father He Ate Me* (New York: Penguin, 2010) and *XO Orpheus* (NewYork: Penguin 2013).

18 David Kluft, "10 Copyright Cases Every Fan Fiction Writer Should Know About," *Trademark and Copyright Law,* October 18, 2016, https://www.trademarkandcopyrig htlawblog.com/2016/10/10-copyright-cases-every-fan-fiction-writer-should-know-about/.

19 See Rachel Barenblat, "Fan Fiction and Midrash: Making Meaning," https://journal .transformativeworks.org/index.php/twc/article/view/596/462.

20 "Maggie Shipstead on dealing with mistakes in writing," *LitHub*'s "The Craft of Writing" email newsletter, May 25, 2022.

21 May also be appropriate in the genre of "hard science fiction": see Daniel LoPilato, "In Praise of the Info-Dump," *LitHub.com,* August 11, 2021, https://lithub.com/in-praise-of-the-info -dump-a-literary-case-for-hard-science-fiction/.

22 I learned about this concept from Nell Irvin Painter's *Old in Art School* (New York: Counterpoint, 2018).

23 Mark Binelli, "'Hamilton' Creator Lin-Manuel Miranda: The Rolling Stone Interview," *Rolling Stone,* June 1, 2016, https://www.rollingstone.com/culture/culture-news/hamilton -creator-lin-manuel-miranda-the-rolling-stone-interview-42607/.

24 "'The Light in the Piazza: From Page to Stage," online event on July 14, 2021, hosted by the Library of America for the publication of *Elizabeth Spencer: Novels & Stories* (New York: Library of America, 2021), https://www.youtube.com/watch?v=GCU7GjO0xKM.

25 Shepard, "Generating History from Fiction and/or Fact," 241–53.

26 In *The Story Behind the Story*, ed. Andrea Barrett and Peter Turchi (New York: W. W. Norton, 2004).

27 From Bonnie Friedman, *Writing Past Dark* (2020), via *LitHub*'s "The Craft of Writing," e-newsletter, August 25, 2021.

28 John Lanchester, "Maigret's Room," *London Review of Books* 42, no. 11 (June 4, 2020), https://www.lrb.co.uk/the-paper/v42/n11/john-lanchester/maigret-s-room.

29 Danticat, *The Art of Death*, 14.

30 See https://www.the-tls.co.uk/articles/public/twenty-questions-jesmyn-ward/ and https:// www.theparisreview.org/blog/2011/08/30/jesmyn-ward-on-salvage-the-bones/.

31 Benjamin Percy, "There Will Be Blood: Writing Violence," in *Thrill Me: Essays on Fiction* (Minneapolis: Graywolf Press, 2016), 51–64.

32 Ethan Rutherford, "Impossible Rooms," *Trop,* 2014, https://tropmag.com/2014/impossible -rooms/.

33 Jennifer Schuessler, "Colson Whitehead on Slavery, Success, and Writing the Novel That Really Scared Him," *New York Times,* August 2, 2016, https://www.nytimes.com/2016/08/04/books/ colson-whitehead-on-slavery-success-and-writing-the-novel-that-really-scared-him.html.

34 Alex Preston, "I'm a Cupcake: I Certainly Couldn't Be a Leg-Breaker: An Interview with Don Winslow," *The Guardian,* April 16, 2022, https://www.theguardian.com/books/2022/apr /16/don-winslow-im-a-cupcake-i-certainly-couldnt-be-a-leg-breaker.

35   See Sophie Hannah, "A Prize for Thrillers with No Violence against Women? That's Not Progressive," *The Guardian*, January 31, 2018, https://www.theguardian.com/books/2018/jan /31/staunch-prize-thrillers-no-violence-against-women-sophie-hannah.

36   Flannery O'Connor, "The Fiction Writer and His Country," in *Mystery and Manners*, ed. Sally and Robert Fitzgerald (New York: Farrar Straus Giroux, 1961), 34.

37   See Niela Orr, "The Women Who Knew Too Much: Horror Cinema Punishes Its Inquisitive Black Female Characters," *The Baffler*, no. 46 (July 2019), https://thebaffler.com/salvos/the -women-who-knew-too-much-orr; Orr also mentions the "magical negro" or "sacrificial negro" tropes we saw in Chapter 4. "Woman stalked / imprisoned by serial killer" stories are also getting old, in my humble opinion.

38   Ibid.

39   I used this line in my essay about Carter, "Belle Dame Sans Merci: On Angela Carter," at the *Los Angeles Review of Books*, https://lareviewofbooks.org/article/belle-dame-sans-merci-on -angela-carter.

40   Marina Warner, "Afterword," in *Angela Carter's Book of Fairy Tales* (London: Virago, 1992), 449.

41   Sarah Shun-lien Bynum, "Destroying What You Love: An Exercise in Setting," in *Naming the World and Other Exercises for the Creative Writer,* ed. Bret Anthony Johnston (New York: Random House, 2007), 266–8. Doing this exercise with my students yielded an image of destruction that appears in the prologue of my novel *Creature: A Novel of Mary Shelley*.

Chapter 7

1   DiDonato's MasterClass video, recorded at Carnegie Hall in January 2016 and featuring soprano Amalia Avilán Castillo with pianist Adam Nielsen on Puccini's "Donde lieta usci" from *La Boheme*, is https://www.youtube.com/watch?v=kIZZ_rw1SYs&list=RDkIZZ _rw1SYs&index=1, min. 22:29-23:00.

2   Rick Bass, "Danger: An Essay," *Narrative,* Fall 2011, https://www.narrativemagazine.com/ issues/fall-2011/nonfiction/danger-rick-bass.

3   Quoted on her website.

4   Bell, *The Artful Edit*, 2.

5   https://elizabetheslami.com/2013/07/the-story-and-the-question/.

6   Gornick, *The Situation and the Story.*

7   John Cheever's "Reunion" does this too. Shout-out to Armando Iannucci's 2019 film version of *David Copperfield*, which dramatizes this POV in visual terms, and to Ralph Fiennes' performance as Dickens in *The Invisible Woman* (2013), based on Claire Tomalin's biography of Ellen Ternan.

8   "Find out who you are and do it on purpose," Parton advised in a tweet (April 8, 2015: https://twitter.com/dollyparton/status/585890099583397888).

9   "Literary Culture Clash," an interview with Nicole Aragi, July 1, 2013, https://www .guernicamag.com/literary-culture-clash/.

10   In "Do Less," an episode of *Hidden Brain* podcast: https://hiddenbrain.org/podcast/do-less/.

11 Kerri Arsenault, "Interview with a Gatekeeper: Matt Weiland, Lover of Soccer and Talking Rabbits," *Lithub.com,* September 29, 2016, https://lithub.com/interview-with-a-gatekeeper -matt-weiland-lover-of-soccer-and-talking-rabbits/.

12 Rock, "The Telling That Shows: Some Provocations From Inside The Story."

13 Bass, "Danger."

14 Matt Bell, *Refuse to Be Done: How to Write and Rewrite a Novel in Three Drafts* (Soho, 2022), 130.

15 Ibid., 135.

16 Ibid.

17 Danticat, *The Art of Death,* 64.

18 Gerald Clarke, "P.G. Wodehouse, The Art of Fiction No. 60," *Paris Review* 64 (Winter 1975), https://www.theparisreview.org/interviews/3773/the-art-of-fiction-no-60-p-g-wodehouse.

19 "Jonathan Lee on hooking a reader with the first line," *LitHub*'s "The Craft of Writing" email newsletter, May 18, 2022.

20 Heartbreakingly, as Greg Tate writes, "We know from her secretary that Billie Holiday first wore gardenias to mask a bald spot made by an overzealous hot comb." https://www .villagevoice.com/2019/04/02/hiphop-nation-its-like-this-yall/.

21 From *Virginia Woolf and Vita Sackville-West: Love Letters,* ed. Alison Bechdel (Vintage, 2021).

22 Becca Rothfeld, "Principled to a Fault," *The Hedgehog Review,* Summer 2021, https:// hedgehogreview.com/issues/distinctions-that-define-and-divide/articles/principled-to-a -fault.

23 Andrew O'Hagan, "At the Hunterian: Joan Eardley Gets Her Due," *London Review of Books,* November 4, 2021, https://www.lrb.co.uk/the-paper/v43/n21/andrew-o-hagan/at-the -hunterian.

24 Margo Jefferson in conversation with Doreen St. Felix at a New York Public Library Zoom event on April 18, 2022, for her book *Constructing a Nervous System* (Penguin Random House, 2022).

25 George Garrett, *Death of the Fox* (1971) (New York: Harcourt Brace, 1991), 151.

26 M. P. Eve, "The Historical Imaginary of Nineteenth-Century Style in David Mitchell's *Cloud Atlas,*" *C21 Literature: Journal of 21st-Century Writings* 6, no. 3 (2018): 1–22. doi: https://doi .org/10.16995/c21.46.

27 Like another seventeenth-century verb, "cleave."

28 Parul Sehgal, "'Three Women' Takes A Long, Close Look at Sex Lives," *New York Times,* June 28, 2019, https://www.nytimes.com/2019/06/28/books/review-three-women-lisa-taddeo .html.

29 Bell, *The Artful Edit,* 147.

30 In "Talking Volumes" interview at Fitzgerald Theatre, September 14, 2021.

31 *New York Review of Books* email newsletter July 8, 2021.

32 "Aimee Bender on writing without a plan." *LitHub*'s "The Craft of Writing" email newsletter, March 30, 2022.

33 I'm reconstructing this from memory.

34 Bell, *The Artful Edit,* 50.

35 Mittelmark and Newman, *How Not to Write a Novel,* 73.

36 Image from Renata Adler's *Speedboat* (NYRB Classics, 2013).

37 Bell, *The Artful Edit,* 119.

38 Ibid., 141.

39 Anna Sproul-Latimer, "Some Easy Ways to Tell When Your Book (Probably) Isn't Ready for Submission" at "How to Glow in the Dark," https://neonliterary.substack.com/p/some-easy -ways-to-tell-when-your.

40 "Hilton Als: The Art of the Essay No. 3," *The Paris Review* 225 (Summer 2018).

41 Alexander Chee, "The Autobiography of My Novel," in *How to Write an Autobiographical Novel: Essays* (New York: Mariner Books, 2018), 197–220.

42 "But Hilary Mantel's *Wolf Hall* trilogy!" you say. I love it too. *Wolf Hall* (2009) was Mantel's tenth novel (and eleventh book) in a career securely established *before* the internet. Its well-deserved Booker Prize further cemented her publishers' willingness to take a risk. Could a young, unknown writer sell such a big book of adult literary historical fiction to a major publishing house in the ever-more-internet-decimated attention-span-scape of 2023 and beyond? Discuss. Want to tip this scale? Buy (or get your library to buy) big books, and read them.

43 In online event for the publication of *Elizabeth Spencer: Novels & Stories* (Library of America, 2021), https://www.youtube.com/watch?v=GCU7GjO0xKM.

44 Charles McGrath, "Lorrie Moore's New Book Is a Reminder and a Departure," *New York Times,* February 17, 2014, https://www.nytimes.com/2014/02/18/books/lorrie-moores-new -book-is-a-reminder-and-a-departure.html.

45 https://www.youtube.com/watch?v=NNcWq327qzY.

Chapter 8

1 Cohen, "Hilton Als: The Art of the Essay No. 3."

2 You can see my review (from *Orion*'s Summer 2018 issue) on my webpage, amyeweldon.com.

3 There are lots of conversations in higher ed about this, with general consensus being that for women in general and women of color in particular, using an honorific and last name can be a marker of necessary respect. See https://www.chronicle.com/article/do-you-make-them -call-you-professor/, https://www.insidehighered.com/advice/2015/03/11/advice-young -black-woman-academe-about-not-being-called-doctor, https://www.nytimes.com/2014/11 /02/opinion/sunday/they-call-me-doctor-berry.html, https://www.thelily.com/a-white-city -official-refused-to-address-this-black-professor-as-doctor-he-got-fired/. Colleagues, please read the discussion of names in https://www.chronicle.com/article/academe-has-a-lot-to -learn-about-how-inclusive-teaching-affects-instructors.

4 December 11, 2020 in Zoom meeting.

5 Sorry, y'all, the data is in. See Jonathan Haidt and Jean Twenge, "This Is Our Chance to Pull Teenagers Out of the Smartphone Trap," *New York Times,* July 31, 2021 (https://www .nytimes.com/2021/07/31/opinion/smartphone-iphone-social-media-isolation.html). Haidt and Twenge quote a college student who wrote to them: "Gen Z are an incredibly isolated group of people. We have shallow friendships and superfluous romantic relationships that are mediated and governed to a large degree by social media. There is hardly a sense of

community on campus and it's not hard to see why. Often I'll arrive early to a lecture to find a room of 30+ students sitting together in complete silence, absorbed in their smartphones, afraid to speak and be heard by their peers. This leads to further isolation and a weakening of self-identity and confidence, something I know because I've experienced it." For this reason and many others, I ask students to silence and stash their smartphones as soon as they walk into my classroom—even before I arrive and class begins.

6   See William Deresiewicz, *The Death of the Artist: How Creators Are Struggling to Survive in the Age of Billionaires and Big Tech* (2020).

7   Lanier, "Jaron Lanier Fixes the Internet."

8   Richard Mirabella, "On Writing (With A Day Job)," *Don't Write Alone,* July 19, 2021, https:// catapult.co/dont-write-alone/stories/on-writing-with-a-day-job-how-to-write-working-9-to -5-richard-mirabella.

9   Jennifer Wilson, "Raven Leilani Needs To Know How Her Characters Pay Rent," *Lux* 2 (August 2021), https://lux-magazine.com/article/raven-leilani-needs-to-know-how-her -characters-pay-rent/#site-header.

10 "Writing Probably Won't Pay the Bills," *The Cut,* July 21, 2020, https://www.thecut.com/amp/ article/how-writers-make-money.html.

11 Andrew Chan, "Kaveh Akbar Finds Meaning in Misunderstanding," *The New Yorker*, August 2, 2021, https://www.newyorker.com/magazine/2021/08/09/kaveh-akbar-finds-meaning-in -misunderstanding.

12 See https://www.publishersweekly.com/pw/by-topic/industry-news/publisher-news/article /88162-grading-publishing-graduate-programs-for-2021.html, and a cautionary tale: https:// www.wsj.com/articles/financially-hobbled-for-life-the-elite-masters-degrees-that-dont-pay -off-11625752773. An article titled "Passion Over Money: Careers with a Publishing Masters Degree," featured in "Publishers Lunch," the Publisher's Weekly email newsletter from March 7, 2022, begins: "Last year, the WSJ reported that graduates from top universities don't earn enough to pay off loans for their master's degrees in a number of disciplines. According to the article, 'At New York University, graduates with a master's degree in publishing borrowed a median $116,000 and had an annual median income of $42,000 two years after the program, the data on recent borrowers show.' Still, many alumni tell PL that they wouldn't have a job in publishing at all without their master's program. Graduates report that, even after internships and interviews, getting a master's—with the networking opportunities that come along with it—was their only way into the business, especially without personal connections or a bachelor's from a brand-name college. Meanwhile, publishers are eschewing degree requirements and don't pay more to employees who went to graduate school."

13 I strongly recommend Rob Spillman's classic take on big advances and literary longevity— which don't always coincide—in "Lena Dunham's Absurd Advance," *Salon*, October 9, 2012, https://www.salon.com/2012/10/09/can_lena_dunham_be_a_bossypants/.

14 See "How Writers Make Money". Among the many resources on literary agent Anna Sproul-Latimer's Substack newsletter, "How to Glow in the Dark" (neonliterary.substack.com) is a post called "Money, money, money: a primer on book deal finances and what to expect from them" (https://neonliterary.substack.com/p/money-money-money-a-primer-on-book) that describes this in more detail.

15 See a fascinating view of the book-production process—from page-printing to jacket-printing to binding—at https://www.nytimes.com/interactive/2022/02/19/books/how-a -book-is-made.html.

16 See Deborah Triesman, "Colson Whitehead on Historical Heists," *The New Yorker,* July 19, 2021, https://www.newyorker.com/books/this-week-in-fiction/colson-whitehead-07 -26-21, and Hillel Italie, "An Eventful Year for Pulitzer Prizewinner Colson Whitehead," June 30, 2020, https://apnews.com/article/virus-outbreak-colson-whitehead-new-york -entertainment-fiction-7f65a25a04d1bc092fbcb586c37db8b3.

17 November 17, 2020, talk by Whitehead online: https://www.youtube.com/watch?v =NNcWq327qzY.

18 Lucy Feldman, "'The World Always Outwits Human Ingenuity'. How the Energetic Cover of Colson Whitehead's Upcoming Novel *Harlem Shuffle* Hints at the Heist Within," *Time*, February 2, 2021, https://time.com/5935152/harlem-shuffle-colson-whitehead-cover/; see Munday's work at https://www.olivermunday.com/covers.

19 Graywolf Literary Salon, Minneapolis, September 6, 2018.

20 Marcela Valdes, "Inside the Push to Diversify the Book Business," *New York Times,* June 22, 2022, https://www.nytimes.com/2022/06/22/magazine/inside-the-push-to-diversify-the -book-business.html.

21 Jofie Ferrarri-Adler, "Agents and Editors: A Q&A With Four Young Literary Agents," *Poets & Writers,* January/February 2009, https://www.pw.org/content/agents_amp_editors_qampa _four_young_literary_agents.

22 In *Conversations with Colson Whitehead,* ed. Derek C. Maus (Jackson: University Press of Mississippi, 2019), 8–9.

23 Amy Gall, "Truth: A Q&A with Ayad Ahktar," *Poets & Writers*, September/October 2020.

24 Mick Herron, "Preface," in *Slow Horses: Deluxe Tenth Anniversary Edition* (New York: Soho Press, 2020), xii.

25 Ilya Kaminsky, "Promiscuity Is a Virtue: An Interview with Garth Greenwell," *The Paris Review* Blog, January 14, 2020, https://www.theparisreview.org/blog/2020/01/14/ promiscuity-is-a-virtue-an-interview-with-garth-greenwell/.

26 Marcus J. Moore, "At 85, Ron Carter Still Seeks 'A Better Order of Notes,'" *New York Times,* May 9, 2022, https://www.nytimes.com/2022/05/09/arts/music/ron-carter.html.

INDEX

Index

Index

Index

Index